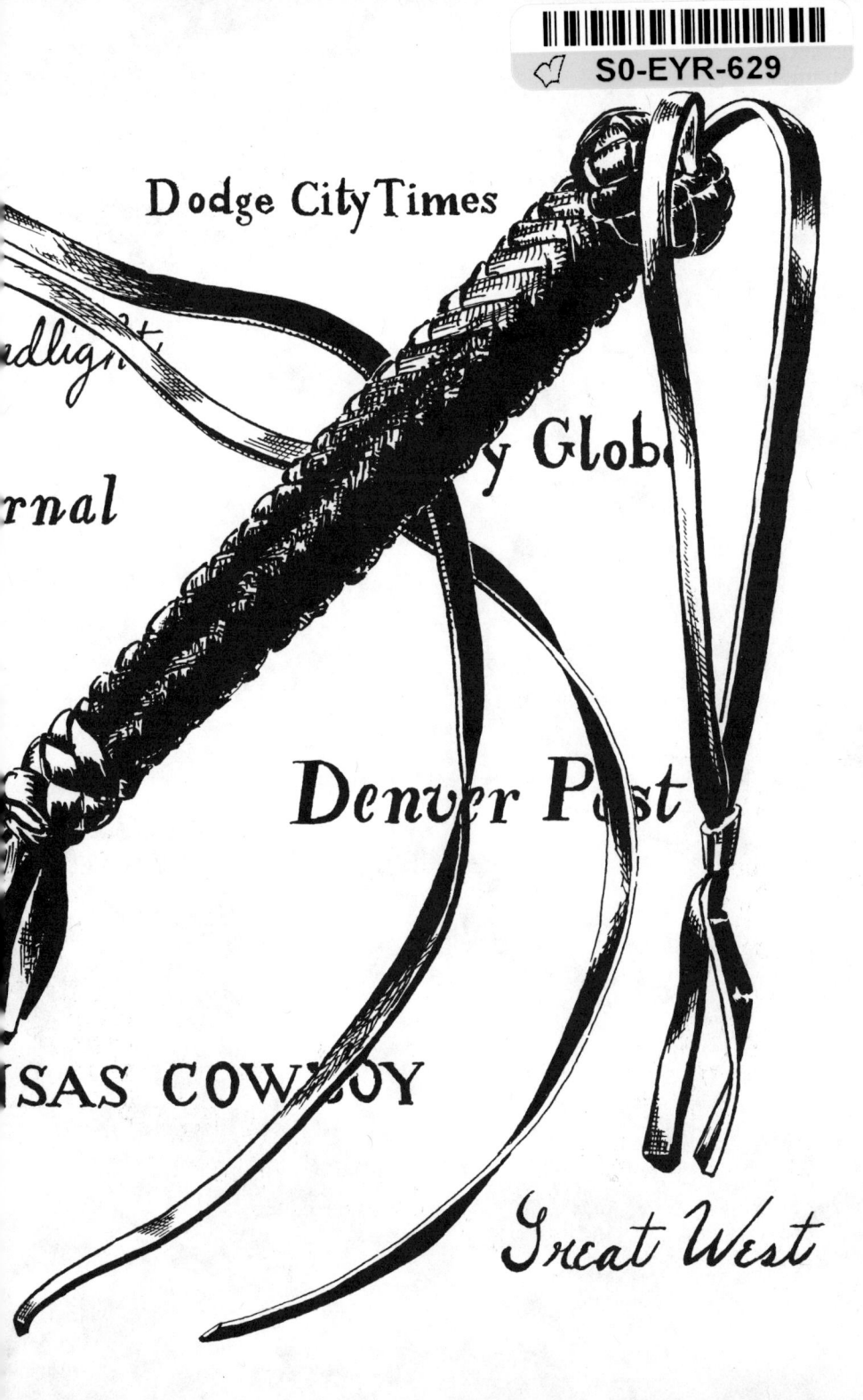

TRAILING THE COWBOY

Trailing the Cowboy

His Life and Lore as Told by Frontier Journalists

COMPILED AND EDITED

BY

CLIFFORD P. WESTERMEIER

GREENWOOD PRESS, PUBLISHERS
WESTPORT, CONNECTICUT

0814205
69072

Library of Congress Cataloging in Publication Data

Westermeier, Clifford Peter, 1910-   ed.
Trailing the cowboy.

Reprint of the ed. published by Caxton Printers,
Caldwell, Idaho.
Bibliography: p.
Includes index.
1. Cowboys--The West. 2. The West--History.
I. Title.
[F596.W5 1977]   978   77-13831
ISBN 0-8371-9866-6

Copyright 1955 by The Caxton Printers, Ltd., Caldwell, Idaho

Reprinted with the permission of The Caxton Printers, Ltd.

Reprinted in 1978 by Greenwood Press, Inc., 51 Riverside Avenue, Westport, CT. 06880

Printed in the United States of America

To Thérèse, my wife, who made the trails easier to follow.

Preface

The range cattle industry, which developed after the Civil War, reached its peak in 1885-86 and fostered, during its phenomenal growth, the vocation of the cowboy. In those days it was not unusual for one man to control thousands of acres of open range on which roamed several hundred thousands of cattle. To control these vast, nebulous empires; to carry on the work of tending the herds, to round them up, brand, and select those for market; to drive them up the long trails to the distant cow towns; and, finally, to load them on the cattle cars, warranted a large number of men. Thus, the cowboy is the central figure in the story of the American range cattle industry. He emerges as an unknown factor in frontier life and becomes, in a short span of years, a vital, dominant, and certainly the most romantic and enduring figure in Western American history; his spirit is American and particularly Western; his life story unfolds in a colorful epic embracing the greatest pastoral movement in the history of the world. In the three decades following the dawn of this great industry the cowboy left an indelible mark upon American culture, and upon the West, from which he cannot be separated.

While migration was essentially from east to west—explorers, missionaries, hunters, traders, gold seekers, and homesteaders—the herds and their cowboy drivers came from the South and bisected, in their northward drive, the westward march of American civilization. More than any other movement, these trail drives imprinted on the West its character. From this dramatic convergence finally developed the cattle industry and, with it, the cowboy who played the leading role.

Sentimentalists mourn the passing of the Old West. They lament the passing of the men on horseback, those titans clad in buckskin, large-brimmed hats, and boots; in their grief they chant a dirge for the trail of these horsemen who have passed through the sunset. However, the Old West did not die, or did it disappear; it is still here as a vital part of the New West—a sturdier West in new clothing, with a mature vocabulary and expanded interests.

In the course of years volumes have been published which tell the story of the cowboy. This impressive list includes the old-time range riders such as Andy Adams, Will James, Frank King, Ross Santee, and Charles Siringo; the cowboy "classics" of Emerson Hough and Philip A. Rollins; and more recently the specialized studies or writings of Coolidge, Dale, Dobie, Lomax, Mora, Osgood, and Rollinson. Other special studies about the cattle industry, cattle wars, bad men, vigilantes, rustlers, desperadoes, Indian fighters, two-gun sheriffs, buffalo hunters, the authors of which are too numerous to mention, also include a character study of the cowboy, his equipment, and his work. These chroniclers wove an incredibly rich tapestry of truth and fiction about the cowboy, his sturdy capable horse, his dexterity in roping the gaunt, wild longhorn, his skill in riding the fierce, unmanageable bronco, his boisterous, earthy humor, his constant faithfulness, and his rowdy, disastrous appearance in town. The facts of all these phases have been told and retold, each telling more delusive and enchanting than the previous one, until the old-time range cowboy is removed from the realm of reality and becomes essentially a creature of legend.

In addition there are innumerable autobiographical and reminiscent accounts of old-time cattlemen and cowboys who, preserving their memoirs, have made vital contributions to the character of the cowboy. Of these old-time cowboys few are left who were in their prime in the years between 1865 and 1900. Also, one must not neglect that vast collection of cowboy literature—fiction and nonfiction—the dime novels and the Western "thrillers" which are classed as subliterary.

With the exception of the latter two—the dime novel and the Western "thriller"—which appeared shortly after the Civil War, the preponderance of cowboy literature, historical, autobiographical, and fictional, is the product of the last four decades. The great majority of these authors relied upon the "old-timer" tales, which with the passing of time had been warmed by the glow of the fireplace, softened by the comfort of the armchair, sweetened by the flowing cup, and dimmed by the fading memory.

However, in this amazing collection of "cowboyana" there are few, if any, references to the timely accounts in the newspapers and periodicals—a vast journalistic literature which portrays the cowboy in the eyes of his contemporaries. These men witnessed the dramatic expansion of the cattle industry, they approved and disapproved of the actions of the leading character—the cowboy. Here are stories of truth and fiction concerning the youth, recklessness, and lonely, loveless life of the man, his hazardous occupation, sleepless vigilance, and twenty-four-hour tireless activity on the range. The tales of drinking, carousing, deviltry, dancing, and bawdy women of the cow towns contrast sharply with those of the cowboy's loyalty and steadfastness to the outfit, his respect for women and children, his faithful horse, his peculiar equipment, gear, and costume, his gay, rollicking songs and melancholy ballads, the early cowboy sports and tournaments of rival cow camps. These writers endowed the cowboy with an aura of romance and sentimentality; he has been cast in a mould of courage, violence, and sudden death, of staunchness and nobility, of blind devotion and even dark deeds, but neverthless he remained the guardian of the West. His story is one of struggle.

This book is an attempt to enrich, by means of such contemporary observations, the story of the cowboy. An examination of newspapers, periodicals, and books—most of which were published before the turn of the century—and available letters and diaries has resulted in a wealth of material which may "fill the gaps" in cowboy lore and throw new light on certain phases of the cowboy, his characteristics, and his life.

In order to share with my readers not only "fact and fiction," as seen through the eyes of the contemporary writers, but also the tangy, full-flavored journalistic style of the frontier newspapermen, I have chosen typical examples of their observations. Herein, too, we are aware of the versatility of the frontier journalist. His references to the Bible, classical literature, and mythology, his adept use of foreign phrases, and his choice of words, all coupled with a keen eye and ear and seasoned with an ancedotal style, result in a colorful, flowing account of day-by-day happenings. Interspersed, for contrast and also as a source for many of the fictional aspects which surround the cowboy, are items from the pens of enthusiastic, ambitious, and, oftentimes, highly critical observers.

I am well aware of the strong journalistic prejudices for and against the cowboy, of the misconceptions and inaccuracies found in these observations, of the personal interpretations, as well as of editorial opinions sustained by environmental interests. No attempt has been made to question, explain, or correct these impressions or opinions, for, essentially, they are balanced by innumerable sound and reliable observations. For the benefit of the reader the introductions to the chapters, and to the divisions within them, are italicized to differentiate my own comments from those of the original observers.

Lest the color and flavor of the original text be weakened, very little editing occurs therein. The additions in brackets are principally, for the sake of clarity, in reference to grammatical constructions and orthography. There are many archaic and obsolete forms; the lack or superfluity of punctuation, particularly in the use of the apostrophe, comma, and hyphen, was in most cases, let us say, due to a harried pen or a hurried press. The strange new events which the journalists witnessed in this vast country constantly demanded new vocabulary; hence the variations, "broncho" and "bronco," "cinch" and "sinch," "cow-boy," "cow boy," and "cowboy," et cetera. The frontier press was, at best, a makeshift affair—in the words of one old Western editor, "a shirt tail full of type"—and news coverage meant hours in the saddle and miles on the trail. Therefore, in tribute to these bards who sang the epic story of the knight in leather armor, I present their records of the deed as they saw and heard them.

CLIFFORD P. WESTERMEIER

University of Arkansas
Fayetteville, Arkansas
March 4, 1955

Contents

		Page
PREFACE		7
ONE	THE MAN ON HORSEBACK	17
	The Westerner	19
	The Cowboy: Who is he?	22
	The Cowboy: What's he like?	26
	Types—North and South	36
	Jargon	43
	Knight or Knave?	46
TWO	ALL IN THE DAY'S WORK	61
	Roundup Days	63
	Breakin' Broncs	84
	Workaday Dangers	94
THREE	LAW AND DISORDER	109
	Six-shooters	111
	Strikes	123
	Cattle Companies	131
	Rustlers	135
	Lawlessness	140
	Gambling	143
	Brutality	145
FOUR	FOES ON THE FRONTIER	153
	Cowboy vs. Cowboy	155
	Red Man	165
	White Man	175
	Black Man	178
	Beef vs. Mutton	179
	"Greaser"	183
FIVE	GOIN' TO TOWN	189
	The Town	191
	Innocent Fun	197
	"Red-Eye" Trouble	201
	Paintin' 'er Red	207
	Primrose Trail	208
	Taken for a Ride	213
	Murder!	223
SIX	THE "SWEET BYE AND BYE"	231
	The Text	233
	The Golden Rule	234

CONTENTS

		Page
	Meeting on the Heavenly Shore	236
	Cowboy Devotion	242
	The Last Roundup	247
SEVEN	BUCKAROO RHYMES	257
	Cowboy Life	259
	Rollicking Rhymes	270
	Fun and Frolic	274
EIGHT	TALES—TALL AND TANGY	283
	The Good Heart	285
	Playing with Danger	291
	The Tallest Tales	294
	The Jokester	299
	Escapades	304
NINE	IT'S A GREAT LIFE	313
	Boots and Belles	314
	Ladies' Choice	319
	Petticoats on Ponies	323
	Go West!	327
	I Wanna Be A Cowboy!	335
TEN	SPORTS ON THE RANGE	341
	Early Cowboy Sports	343
	Exhibitions	349
	Roping *vs.* Time	352
	The Race	355
	Contests and Tournaments	359
	Praise and Protest	373
ELEVEN	SUNSET TRAIL	381
	Farewell Cowboy!	383
EPILOGUE		393
BIBLIOGRAPHY		399
INDEX		405

TRAILING THE COWBOY

The Man on Horseback

ONE

During the peak of the range cattle industry, in the middle of the eighties, the cattlemen's frontier embraced an area of some 13,500,000 square miles and totaled almost 44 per cent of the United States.[1] This area, in which were located the western and northwestern ranges and the ranch cattle districts of the United States, comprised the main part of the Indian country—the western portions of the Dakotas, Nebraska, and Kansas, and the territories of Montana, Idaho, Wyoming, Utah, Arizona, and New Mexico. Also included were the states of Nevada and Colorado, and portions of Oregon, California, and Washington. It was a vast region extending from Texas to the Canadian border, almost one thousand miles long, about two hundred miles in width, and enclosing an area of approximately 130,000,000 acres. The greater part of this land was used chiefly for cattle raising and was known as "the Plains."[2]

Over these boundless plains the Texas cattlemen, moving northward on the trails, met and associated with the northern ranchers. Here was a blending of rich heritages —South and Southwest with North and East as well as with the older, cultural contributions of the adventurer from across the seas. From this intercourse emerged the spirit of the West. The Western cattleman and cowboy are its offspring and, regardless of background and choice of native hearths, they were united by a common bond.

The earliest cowboys came from pioneer Texas settlements and from ranches and farms on the frontier. Later, their forces were swelled by their sons and by men from farms, towns, and cities of the United States and the United Kingdom. Rich men and poor men—men of every walk of life and profession—and their sons were lured to the cattle country. These men came for many reasons—a change of occupation, the recovery of a lost fortune, the love of adventure, parental disapproval, ill-health, moral improvement, the transgression of the law, profiteering, and, in the case of the ordinary cowboy, to seek the means of a livelihood.

The cowboy's character is best revealed by his courage, independence, cheerfulness, and ready acceptance of danger and hardship. While he was suspicious of, and reserved toward, strangers, he was quick to welcome, in his limited circumstances, the honest person. His reserve was bred by the desire for survival. Respect for women transcends all his other virtues; his conversation reached the lowest level of slang, profanity, and improvisation. His perversions of the Spanish and Indian tongues, as well as the technical terms of the range, are classic.

Since there was no typical cowboy, the men following

the business in the various parts of the cattle country were distinguishable only by specific characteristics rather than by any notable contrasting differences. Environment and personal preference undoubtedly brought about a variety in the cut of the chap, the crease in the hat, the type of saddle, or the length of the spur. The Northwest was considered the home of the best bronco busters, while the Southwesterner was supreme with the rope, but, as a whole, the cowboy of the West was a horseman who "rode" for the best men and business in the world.

The cowboy suffered severely from bad publicity which was the outcome of overenthusiastic, ill-informed, and, sometimes, vicious interpreters of his life and work. The rough, crude, brutal aspects of the industry, the reckless, happy-go-lucky, indulgent visits to town, the careless, indiscriminate use of the six-shooter, the drinking, fighting, practical jokes, the gambling and profanity—all were subjects for the writer who painted, in the most lurid colors, slanderous accounts for avid Eastern readers. But the West protected its own. The adverse publicity was countered by a deluge of Western journalism which, without condoning the weaknesses of the cowboy, dignified him as the guardian of the West, the knight errant, perhaps, but, in his true light, as the man on horseback.

THE WESTERNER

The Westerner has always been looked upon as a peculiar breed of man, regardless of his antecedents or the various professions in which he might be engaged. Living in the West carries the connotation of being different, and an analysis of what comprises a Westerner has long been a subject of discussion.

There is a certain universality in the type of the Western man, and a certain freedom and electicism in his social life, which enable them [him] to reflect a partial likeness of the better traits and qualities, peculiar to either section of the country, however much these sections may differ in their standard of morals and manners.

The extreme Southerner, the Virginian, the Yankee, recognize each his own image in the many-sided man of the West. They feel they have certain affinities for him, though they have none for each other; and he in return spontaneously fraternizes with them because he possesses a genial, catholic, though, perhaps, less cultural nature. Climate, institutions and other causes have moulded them into uniformity, and have given them rigidity and angularity of character, but the plastic nature of the Western people which the inflowing of new blood in a thousand rills promises to preserve, forbids any irreconcilable antagonism, and results in boundless variety and unity. The elements which enter into the composition of character in this region are countless, and have not yet formed into an insoluble concrete. The people are not recast by artificial means. The reign of formulas has not yet begun, but nature is left to her own sweet will. Greater physical activity, greater diversity of manners, and aspirations, and greater energy and boldness of character are the results.[3]

Human nature is identical every where. It is difference of circumstances that gives it its variety of light and shade in different times and countries. Western character is often spoken of as peculiar and essentially unlike that of other sections of the country. Bayard Taylor,[4] in his letters from Colorado in 1866, confessed himself puzzled by a style of character he found here, which seemed to him a strange mixture of ruffianism and refinement. A longer study of it would have enabled him to comprehend this type better. He would have seen that the aspect of ruffianism was put on for antagonism and defense against the ruffian class in the community, while civility and courtesy were kept in reserve for the civil and courteous. Because a man goes armed, or takes a policeman with him for protection, when he explores the haunts of the desperate and dangerous classes in New York, it does not follow that he is himself half ruffian.

Lawless men delight in the freedom of a new country, before law and order are established; and the presence of this class as a large element in the front ranks of civilization in its westward march is a matter of course. But it is not long tolerated, and the extra legal means taken to hasten its departure—the vigilance committees and summary executions—which are greeted elsewhere as evidence of western barbarism, are really demonstrations of a capacity for self-government. Where law and its officers do not exist, or are powerless, the people are not only justified in taking the administration of justice into their own hands, but it is the essential first step towards the establishment of law and order. The history of California, of Nevada, and of this Territory furnish striking evidences of this; and when the history of the West is intelligently and fairly written, it will be quoted in proof of the virtue and self-control of the people that they arrested the reign of lawlessness and ruffianism by the only means that could have been effectual. And even personal resistence to injury and insult, for which less can be said, had at least the good effect to make men more regardful of the rights and feelings of others.

Eastern people mistake, too, in supposing that ruffianism is still dominant in the Far West. Lawlessness and violence made their last appearance in the vagrant towns along the Pacific railroads. In the West generally law, order and tranquility are as well established as in the East. Eastern visitors who think that after crossing the Mississippi they must lay aside the polished courtesy and gentlemanly decorum of the East, and put on some degree of coarseness and ruffianism, in deference to the barbarians with whom they are to associate, commit a great mistake, and are in danger of making themselves ridiculous as well as uncomfortable. They will find that western freedom does not mean license nor barbarism. It does mean a somewhat less regard for the conventionalities which have no better reason than fashion or custom. It does imply more frankness and directness of speech, and less use of empty compliment; but it does not require an extraordinary infusion of profanity and slang. Nor does western liberality mean the free spending of other people's money, as some seem to think. In fact, in these items and several others, our eastern friends who come here with exaggerated notions of western freedom, are apt to overdo the thing and astonish the older settlers. What the Free West aspires to, and is growing up to, is a larger degree of personal freedom, and a more manly and self-reliant style of virtue than is often to be found in old communities, where manners and morals are regulated by custom and public opinion. Certainly we have the opportunity for a high and noble style of character, and it will be our fault if we do not attain it.[5]

THE COWBOY: Who is he?

The cowboy is a product of a particular industry in a specific environment. All walks of life contributed men to this profession, bound together by a common interest of occupation.

Events were happening whose results powerfully affected the cow country. The passions of men in the Eastern States were being goaded to their highest excitement. The agitation against slavery finally culminated in war, and the nation for a while forgot its virgin lands and the men who inhabited them. Up to 1865, elbow room was abundant for the cowman, but the death knell of slavery was sounded, and its tones echoed the beginning of the end in cow-land; with the disbanding of the armies, began the rush. Thousands turned their attention thither, and "Westward Ho!" began to echo throughout the East.[6]

The creation of cities was a correlative interest of the big beef industry and fortunes in many cases awaited the investors in town lots. But the true "cow-man" had no thought for such humble occupation or inglorious rewards. Others might crawl on the ground, making money in some ignoble pursuit. For his own part, the way to wealth was plain and broad enough; and he rode it in lordly style, with a word of pity for those who trudged footsore along the trail.

This conviction of their superior calling took quick hold of the minds of the young men from the East. They fell in easily with the freedom of the new life, and soon

learned to despise the old. Unconsciously they were affected by the cowboy's disdain for anything beyond his environment; and they showed it in a hundred tricks of dress and attitude and even speech. Next to New Yorkers, there is no one in this country so well satisfied as the cowboy of the inferiority of all persons and things outside of his own immediate vision of the United States; and even this feeling had its bearing on the complacency with which the more sophisticated ranchmen regarded their chosen pursuit.[7]

The American cowman was a peculiar character. He was evolved from circumstances and environments that were born of different kinds of civilization. It was a case where the Anglo-Saxon and the Aztec met and mingled.

For years untold, the Mexican had ranged his stock over a territory so vast that he did not realize its extent. His methods were crude, yet suited to the people who used them.

The rope and the branding iron were his means of capturing and identifying his wild stock. Fences there were not, and a cow could range at her own sweet will through the chapparal. She was branded in calfhood, and turned loose to live or die of old age far distant from her owner's corral. The Mexican cowman led a simple life. His hat, heavy with silver; his spurs, bridle, saddle and boots and his mount, were the pride of his life. Cash was an article not in great demand; food was abundant; women were plentiful, and what more could one ask. The priest could insure his eternal welfare and his faith in the Virgin and the Saints was supreme.

The American came, saw and took to the life immensely. Its halfwild freedom, its danger and excitement, appealed to his Saxon blood. He modified the Mexican customs to suit himself.[8]

"And here are the drovers, the identical chaps I first saw at Fair Oaks, and last saw at Gettysburg. Every man of them unquestionably was in the Rebel army. Some of them have not yet worn out all of their distinctive gray clothing—keen-looking men, full of reserved force, shaggy with hair, undoubtedly terrible in a fight, yet peaceably great at cattle-driving, and not demonstrative in their style of wearing six-shooters."[9]

In engaging in the work, one comes into competition with bright, energetic men; graduates of the best institutions of learning in America and Europe, some of whom engage in the work temporarily while others do so for the purpose of getting a practical knowledge of the business, with a view to embarking in the occupation of cattle-raising for themselves. The person who joins forces with such men, simply prompted by a spirit of adventure and a desire to have a "high old time" beyond the pale of civilization is doomed to disappointment and he will be very apt to wish himself a thousand miles away from the cattle range before he has been in the saddle a day.[10]

The American cattle trade is exciting so much interest in England, where two of our most pressing needs just now are cheaper meat and outlets for our boys, that any authentic information about it is of value. We are glad, therefore, to be able to print the following... from the last letters received from the son of a contributor. We may state that eighteen months since he "hired" with a Colorado cattle king, Goodnight by name, to go down to Texas, and drive up a herd, and at the end of the drive he and his companion, a young Scotchman, were taken into partnership. Towards the end of last year the rumor of an unoccupied cañon on the borders of Texas tempted them south, and they struck it in November.[11]

There is a peculiar fascination in this wild life of the cow-boys which tempts many young men of culture and refinement, reared in the enjoyment of every luxury in the East, but of adventurous dispositions, to come and live with these rude spirits on the frontier. Often for thirty-six hours continuously in the saddle, the hardships of their lot are apparent, cold black coffee, without sugar, drunk whenever the opportunity offers, is the sole luxury of the cow-boy. With a piece of bread in one hand and some jerked beef in the other, he will ride around a stampeded herd, eating as he goes, and as happy as a king on his throne.[12]

I have met among these stockmen highly educated men, as herders, whose essays on literature would throw into the deepening shade some of the sentimental so-called aesthetic sickly nonsense which society calls poetry.

If you wish to do so, you can find as highly educated and refined gentlemen among the "old settlers" and "cowpunchers" of the many years ago, on these arid plains, as they were formerly called, as you can in those who come now in their Pullman cars, with Oscar Wilde aesthetic manners, accompanied with Patchouli,[13] Essence de Millefleurs or seal skin sacques.

Let me travel among these plains, and call at their cabins, the dugouts or tents of these stockmen or "cowpunchers" as they familiarly style themselves, and I find them, as a class, the soul of honor, punctiliously so, and you cannot insult them more than by an offer to pay for a meal or a bed. Go to the east, and they charge you five cents for a glass of milk. Whiskey I never met in a western "cowpunchers" camp in more than one case in twenty.[14]

[The cowboy] was a product of conditions in the East. He was lured westward by the hazards which the country offered him. It seems to be the case always that when industry needs a large body of men for some such special duty as this, civilization has just brought about conditions which supply the recruits. The hard times in the North, the ravaged farm lands in the South, the tameness of the Mississippi Valley whose elder generation of pioneers had transmitted fighting spirit to their sons—these things brought restlessness. Also there was common then a certain well-known spirit, hard to describe, which makes boys rowdies when they stay at home and men of action when they go away. The West called and the East stood ready with a few thousand lean, hard-boned young men, endowed, above all other things, with that fine quality of moral courage known as "sand." They straggled to the cattle ranges, some with shoulders damp from the tears of fond good-byes, others hard-eyed with memories of what had driven them from home. . . .

Finally the time came for the progress of the two main bodies—the farmers who would overwhelm the wide land and subjugate it with their plows; the hosts of toilers who would use its products to build cities. To prepare the way for these the cowboys, in a line that stretched from Canada to Mexico, swept on ahead. And where they rode the wilderness became a cattle range. They made the country pastoral. . . . The story of that conquest is the story of the West as it has been, the wild, free West of yesterday. The work is done; the cowboy is a vanished type. We boast of him in stories and we draw his picture to remind ourselves of a splendid past. In the halo of the picturesque his economic value has been lost sight of. Like many other men who have found life's keenest pleasures close to death, he was a constructive soldier. Probably he was the finest that the world has known.[15]

THE COWBOY: What's he like?

Those who have known the cowboy have commented extensively on, and are, on the whole, in agreement concerning, his various characteristics and traits. He has been painted by journalists as both a sinner and a saint, and too rarely as just a hard-working man, engaged in a hazardous occupation under most adverse conditions.[16]

[The cowboy] of the plains and gigantic rolling meadows of the west is as much a part of the occident as is the setting sun of the ponderous Rockies. He has an individuality as has the sailor on the seas or the dude on the avenues of New York. There is a variety of opinion regarding him. To the eastern juvenile reader of dime novels he is the *ne plus ultra* of bravery, ferocity, cunning and western skill. To the ignorant he is a bad man and the embodiment of whiskey, blood and murder. To those who know him and have dwelt with him under his tent—the sky—the cowboy is a good-natured, rollicking, whole-souled fellow, quick to do a kindness and as quick to resent an insult.[17]

The herder is a character. He is begotten of a necessity, as was the army bummer. He is sent to fulfill a mission and that that mission is "herdin' steers," no one who has ever seen him can for a moment doubt. His pedigree is as much a matter of doubt as that of his steers. His relationship to the gentle cowherd of the story-books and the pastoral poet is very remote. The cowherd of the books is depicted as a mild-mannered young man with melancholy air, lolling about in the shade, reading his Testament or the *Sorrows of Werther*.... The Texas herder, provided he can read at all, takes along a stray copy of the Police Gazette or "Beadles No. 353"[18] with which to fill up the intervals between poker and three card monte....

As I have said we know nothing of his antecedents. As to where or when he was born, or whether like Topsy, he "just growed" are unsolved problems. He may have had a babyhood and boyhood, but we have no proof of those facts. Our first acquaintance with him is in the prime of manhood, when he presents himself to us as a fullfledged herder. He is usually tall, muscular, and but for the shockingly bowed legs, from his constant seat in the saddle, well built; hair long and unkept and sun faded; in dress generally indifferent as to color and texture; a pair of jean pantaloons thrust into high-topped boots; a woolen shirt, a belt containing a small arsenal of pistols and cutlery; a slouch felt hat of great width of brim, often a genuine Mexican sombrero. A part of himself might be reckoned his horse, from which he is almost inseparable. In morals the herder is not a model young man for the Sunday school books. He possesses all the vices that his limited education permits and if he omits any it is not his fault. As a profane swearer he has few equals; as a reckless gambler he is not surpassed, and as a consumer of mean whiskey he is without a peer. Prodigal of his money, heedless of the future, he lives for the day only, and his brief life is usually brought up with a sharp turn by a pistol-shot in a drunken brawl. His vices are counterbalanced by some virtues. Generous and openhearted, he will spend his last dollar on his friends, or risk his life in defense of a comrade in danger. Living his whole life without the pale of civilized society, associated with vile men and viler women it is only a wonder that he is no worse than he is.[19]

Cowboys as a class are brimful and running over with wit, merriment, good humor. They are always ready for a bit of innocent fun, but are not perpetually spoiling for a fight, as has so often been said of them. They are at peace with all men, and would not be otherwise from choice. As a rule, if a man quarrels with one of them, he forces the war, and is himself to blame. Their love of fun often leads to trouble, though generally because the victim of it does not know how or is not willing to either "chip in" or excuse himself. They are fond of "piping off" anything that is particularly conspicuous, or vice versa, no matter to whom it belongs, and they dislike to see snobbish airs assumed in their country, though such might pass current in any Eastern city.[20]

A genuine cowboy is worth describing. In many respects he is a wonderful creature. He endures hardships that would take the lives of most men, and is, therefore, a perfect type of physical manhood. He is the finest horseman in the world, and excels in all the rude sports of the field. He aims to be a dead shot, and universally is. Constantly during the herding season he rides twenty miles a day, and most of the year sleeps in the open air. His life in the saddle makes him worship his horse, and it, with a rifle and a six-shooter, completes his happiness. Of vice in the ordinary sense he knows nothing. He is a rough, uncouth, brave and generous creature, who never lies or cheats. It is a mistake to imagine that they are a dangerous set. Any one is as safe with them as with any people in the world, unless he steals a horse or is hunting for a fight. In their eyes death is a mild punishment for horse stealing. Indeed it is the highest crime known to the unwritten law of the ranch. Their life, habits, education, and necessities breed this feeling in them. But with all this disregard of human life there are less murderers and cutthroats graduated from the cowboys than from among the better educated classes of the east who come out here for venture or gain. They delight in appearing rougher than they are. To a tenderfoot, as they call an eastern man, they love to tell bloodcurdling stories, and impress him with the dangers on the frontier. But no man need get in a quarrel with them unless he seeks it, or get harmed unless he commits some crime. They very often own an interest in the herd they are watching, and very frequently become owners of ranches. The slang of the range they always use to perfection, in season or out of season. Unless you want to insult him, never offer a cowboy pay for any little kindness he has done or for a share of his rude meal. If the changes that are coming to stock raising should take the cowboy from the ranch, its most interesting feature will be gone.[21]

Of course you would like to hear of the society on a wild Texas cow ranch, where six-shooters are served for breakfast, bowie knives for dinner and blood and thunder for supper! Well it is simply intelligent and refined. Nowhere can you go to a regular cow ranch in the State of Texas and not be hospitably received and intelligently entertained. The best is set before you and no monetary consideration is thought of. As to the habits of the boys while on a "roundup," why of course the wild, rugged and profitable business makes bold, outspoken and liberal men. They are as a class clanish, like soldiers; their business makes them so. And, by the way, they are very much like the soldier. As a rule they are fearless. Constant out-door exercise, and working with wild and dangerous animals, inures them to danger and bodily pain. So you may say that they are as a class equal to any in Texas. Being of this bold, outspoken nature, they generally make "Rome howl!" while "doing up" a place. The refined woman is to them an angel. Of all that has been written about them, did you ever hear of one mistreating a lady? I once knew a crowd of cowboys to follow an emigrant family on the Pecos river seventy-five miles, as a protective guard. The sweet influence of a lady is like the dew of heaven upon their rough, honest natures.[22]

Modern writers have pictured ... [the cowboy] as a modest, religiously inclined young man, who wouldn't say "sheol"[23] even if a steer tried to kick the roof off his dome of thought, nor do more than gently chide the erring animal if it endeavored to impale his liver on its horns. More ancient history tells us that the cowboy is a cross between an Italian brigand and a buzz saw; that he is a walking armory and arsenal; that he spends one day in the saddle and twenty-nine in the saloons, shooting out lamps and filling up graveyards; that he is a holy terror, a howling hyena, a killer from Undertakerville, a bad man from Bitter creek, etc. The truth of the matter is that the cowboy is neither one nor the other. He may respect churches but because of his mode of life, he seldom becomes "mashed" on them. He is just as apt to swear as any other man. He carries no gun, and never seeks a quarrel. He is a good rider, and long experience has made him acquainted with all the wonderful evolutions and ramifications of a bucking bronco. He can throw a lasso with unerring aim, is in the saddle twelve hours a day and as much of a gentleman as any other man, considering the lack of opportunity to acquire what the world calls "polish"—and no more so. He is neither saint nor sinner; a jovial, lighthearted, hardworking young fellow, who minds his own business, but who will not be imposed upon.[24]

The genuine cowboy of today is a faithful employee, who serves the interest of his principal with a fidelity that puts to blush the espionage and the spotting systems of centers of population. It is an error to suppose that the cowboys are wrecks that, drifting with the tide of Western emigration, find lodgment upon a ranch, from which they sally at times to paint the nearest town red. The business of a cowboy has to be learned as any other. It involves patience, endurance, skill, and prompt decision. The cowboys for a ranch are carefully chosen. A certain sort of grit—the Western phrase is sand—is demanded. It shows itself in experience, in a steady gaze from a clear eye, in strength and quickness of movement, and certain lines about the mouth and chin that tell in and out of haunts of men. As a rule the cowboys are quiet. The streets of this town are as free from disturbance as those of New Haven. The men stand together in knots, talking about their business. There are perhaps a hundred cowboys and others in the back room of a saloon next door, and a glance at them shows as quiet and earnest a company as is to be found about the faro or roulette tables of the gambling house at Saratoga. They wear sombreros and big spurs and leather overalls, but this is as decorous a dress as the silk hat and patent leathers and kerseymeres of the resort of fashion.

The sombrero is the cheapest and most comfortable hat. It is a shade to the eyes and protection to the skin, and although it costs from $7 to $15 to begin with, it lasts from four to six years, and can be cleaned like any other cloth garment. The flannel shirts are both warm and cool. There is no laundry for linen about the ranch. The corduroy trousers are most serviceable for riding horseback, as the English fox hunters long ago decided, and it is economy to wear the leather leggings in the mesquite underbrush, where cloth is but a poor armor. There is no affection about the dress, considering all things. In fact, there is more real affection to be detected on Broadway. The spurs are no longer than are useful in prompt control of the cow ponies and the chains which hold them are only used because they don't break like leather.

Those who remember the high-heeled and square-toed boots of other days would be interested to know why the fashion found its home in Texas. The mud here outsticks a brother. There seems to be glue in the soil, and Peter Cooper's best, at that. The high-heeled boots are easier cleaned of the mud by kicking than low-heeled boots, and the angles made by the square toes facilitate the kicking off of the mud. The cowboy needs a pistol for a catamount or a chance panther, and when he is heeled, as his phrase goes, he carries the weapon in a belt, usually a cartridge belt, for comfort.[25]

A picturesque, hardy lot of fellows, these wild "cowboys" as they sit on the ground by the fire, each man with his can of coffee, his fragrant slice of fried bacon on the point of his knife-blade, or sandwiched in between two great hunks of bread, rapidly disappearing before the onslaughts of appetites made keen by the pure, invigorating breezes on these high plains. See that brawny fellow with the crisp, tight-curling yellow hair growing low down on the nape of his massive neck rising straight and supple from the low collar of his loose flannel shirt, his sun-browned face with the piercing gray eyes looking out from under the broad brim of his hat. ...[26]

The showy, barbaric costumes of the cowboys, the exquisite feats of horsemanship, the excitement of the horses warming to their work, the occasional dexterous use of the lasso in subduing some animal at bay, all the rush and tumult, the roar and shouting, the grace of muscular men and animals in swift motion, make up a spectacle so stirring and picturesque that all other exhibitions of equestrian skill seem tame in comparison.[27]

Right then was the day of the cowman in all his glory. He was king of the West, clad in his green shirt, red handkerchief, wide-brimmed sombrero, and arsenal of weapons, his chaps, spurs, saddle and gloves ornamented as the fancy and pocketbook of their owner detailed—he was a picturesque character. At home, in his saddle, on the windswept ranges, he was a creature lean, swarthy, sinewy and taciturn.[28]

It is the rule for the men of the plains, and particularly for the cowboys to speak most contemptuously of Eastern fashions and Eastern "dudes." But in fact, they themselves are as much the slaves of fashion as anyone. No man, who can by any possibility avoid it, engages in any part of the business of cattle raising, however, subordinate, without first procuring a white felt hat with an immensely broad brim, and a band consisting either of a leather strap and buckle, or a silk twist like a whip lash. These are expensive, like a fine Panama, frequently costing from fifty to seventy-five dollars. A cowboy must also have a pair of fancy chapareros, or overalls, made out of calf skin, or stamped leather. Boots with high French heels are indispensable.[29]

"Cowboy—One who herds cattle." "Cowman—One who owns cattle and employs cowboys." These are definitions not found in Webster, but they are definitions of the plains. In times past the two characters were frequently united in one person, and many among our wealthiest cowmen obtained their start in life while punching cows for some one else. . . .

The typical cowboy, according to the free press correspondents of Eastern papers, is a cross between a bear and a wild cat, a short [sort] of man-eating son-of-a-sea cook, who isn't comfortable until he has been permitted to chew somebody's ear off and established his reputation as a wild horse from Texas. There may have been cowboys of that character away back, but the breed has run out. One of the festive youths so frequently described for the benefit of Eastern Sunday schools would have a queer time in a modern camp and would speedily arrive at the conclusion that times had changed for the worse when a fellow couldn't kill a man without someone getting mad about it.

Last winter I had occasion to visit a cow camp, the headquarters of one of our heaviest cattle companies. . . . I was taken into a large room. . . . A dozen cleanly built, muscular men, with intelligent faces and gentlemanly manners, were seated about the room. As I looked about me I wondered if they were all cowboys. They were, every one of them. Nobody knew who I was and nobody cared, but all could talk and talk well, and moreover had something to talk about. . . .

For several months after this I had intimate relations with the same men and many others on the range, and in all candor, I have never met with a class of men more worthy of confidence and respect.

A peculiarity of the class is its independence. They recognize no superior except the foreman of an outfit, or the ranch superintendent, and then only when on duty of the range. Promptness in responding to a call for duty is a *sine qua non* on the range. . . . Coupled with this independence is a hospitality of somewhat remarkable character. Nobody waits for an invitation to dinner, but if he wants something to eat goes to the nearest camp. If the occupants are at home he sits down with them; if not he takes what he finds and cooks for himself. This custom is the outcome of necessity, and that mutual interdependence inseparable from a life on the plains. . . .

Thrown together so far away from civilization it follows as a matter of course that mutual confidence is a necessity. As a result the code of honor is exceptionally rigid, and the tone of society with respect to the sacredness of obligation, etc., peculiarly high. A lie is not glossed over as in fashionable society. . . . Theft nothing can condone.

All men eating and sleeping as well as working together, are quick to perceive each other's idiosyncracies or peculiarities of the face, form or expression, hence the nicknames so common in all purely male aggregations of humanity. There is a certain wild expressiveness about the choice of appellations by the cowboy that is curious if not attractive, notably so, in some cases from the total want of connection between the name and its subject. One of the handsomest youths at a well-known ranch is "Snake-head," another whose features are not in the slightest degree swinish is known as "Pig-head." . . .

The cowboy is a character developed by circumstance, and his development is a credit to himself no less than to the industry which brought him into existence. . . . and [he] is, taken all in all, a manly industrious, energetic fellow, a credit . . . to the country. . . . The cowboy on his native heath is a gentleman.[30]

Perhaps some thumb-nail sketches of typical figures among these wild horsemen and the nomads of the plain will give a better idea of their characteristics than a more general description. It is needless to say that they are all hardy, bronzed by the sun to a deep red unless nature has given a darker pigment to their skin, keen-eyed, and of the free and reckless carriage natural to their manner of life, long-haired flaphatted, and dressed in the rough-and-ready garments of the frontier. Not infrequently there is a border-dandy among them, who is as punctilious in regard to his dress and accoutrements as a fashionable exquisite, and quite conscious of the elements of picturesqueness in his appearance. Such a one will show a set of white teeth through his moustache, and will very probably carry a toothbrush in his bootleg, while his locks are carefully oiled and his slouched hat is set on at an accurate angle.[31]

The cowboy may be classed as an amphibious animal, as he can live in water—diluted with whisky—or out of it. ...

The great majority of cowboys are strictly honest and have hearts in them like red steers, but there is a small class of them who, when outfits are driving up, prowl around and steal quirts, misplaced spurs—they have a fancy for—and inadvertently exchange their old saddle blankets for better ones. Under favorable circumstances, this kind of cowboy develops into an expert cow thief, accumulates cattle upon a thousand hills, becomes wealthy and is greatly respected. He finally gets religion on his death bed, and dying goes straight to Abraham's bosom, thus cheating the devil out of his dues to the sincere regret of all who knew him (the boy, not the devil) in his early days. ...

It has been said that the cowboy is lazy—that he is constitutionally opposed to exerting himself physically on a farm or garden. This is slander which my natural love for truth compels me to refute. Those who think the cowboy is disinclined to indulge in manual labor on the farm or garden have never seen a gang of them loose in a nester's potato patch. ...[32]

Certain characteristics run through the whole tribe ... their taciturnity, their surface gravity, their keen sense of humor, their courage, their kindness, their freedom, their lawlessness, their foulness of mouth, and their supreme skill in the handling of horses and cattle. ...

If one thinks down doggedly to the last analysis, he will find that the basic reason for the difference between a cowboy and other men rests finally on an individual liberty, a freedom from restraint either of society or convention, a lawlessness, and accepting of his own standard alone.[33]

The cowboy! How shall I pay a proper tribute to his courage, fortitude and his kindness? He has defied the torrid heats of summer and the frigid blasts of winter, without shelter and at times almost without food or clothing. He has braved the fury of savage beasts and still more savage men. He has turned his back upon the comforts of home and the love of his kindred to sweep across the trackless desert in the face of dangers, seen and unseen, to pave the way for advancing civilization. He has endured every hardship, scorned every danger, and surmounted every obstacle that rude and untamed nature could throw in his pathway. Civilization owes him a debt of gratitude greater than is conceivable and one that will never be either fully realized or repaid.[34]

TYPES—NORTH AND SOUTH

Since there is no typical cowboy, those differences which do appear are a result of individual peculiarities and of the occupation as dependent upon climatic conditions. The range cattle industry in the Southwest differed from that in Wyoming, Montana, and the Dakotas and produced variations in the cowboy, yet he remains essentially a man on horseback.

Your cowboy is a species variously subdivided. If you happen to be travelled as to the wild countries, you will be able to recognize whence your chance acquaintance hails by the kind of saddle he rides, and the rigging of it, by the kind of rope he throws, and the method of the throwing; by the shape of hat he wears; by his twist of speech; even by the very manner of his riding. Your California "vaquero" from the Coast Ranges is as unlike as possible to your Texas cowman, and both differ from the Wyoming or South Dakota article. I should be puzzled to define exactly the habitat of the "typical" cowboy. No matter where you go, you will find your individual acquaintance varying from the type in respect to some of the minor details.[35]

Cowboys can be divided into two classes: those hailing from the Lone Star State, Texas, the other recruited either from Eastern States, chiefly Missouri, or from the Pacific slopes; Oregon contributing no mean number of Webfoots, so called from the long winter rains in that colony. The Texans are, as far as true cowboyship goes, unrivalled; the best riders, hardy, and born to the business; the only drawback being their wild reputation. The others are less able but more orderly men. The bad name of Texans arises mostly from their excitable tempers, and the fact that they are mostly "on the shoot,"—that is, very free in the use of their revolvers.[36]

The "Cowboys" of Texas are a peculiar breed. They are distinct in their habits and characteristics from the remainder of even the Texas population as if they belonged to another race. The Lipan and the Comanche are not more unlike the civilized white man than is the nomadic herdsman to the Texan who dwells in the city or cultivates the plains. The Texan rangers who galloped after Hays and McCullough [McCulloch] were wild and daring men, and a life of adventure stamped them with strange peculiarities. But the "ranger" had not been bred to his occupation—he took it up from choice. . . .[37]

The original cowboy of this country was essentially a creature of circumstance, and mainly a product of western and southwestern Texas. Armed to the teeth, booted and spurred, long-haired, and covered with the broad-brimmed sombrero—the distinctive badge of his calling—his personal appearance proclaimed the sort of man he was.

The Texas cowboys were frontiersmen, accustomed from their earliest childhood to the alarms and the struggles incident to forays of Indians of the most ferocious and warlike nature. The section of the state in which they lived was also for many years exposed to incursions of bandits from Mexico, who came with predatory intent upon the herds and the homes of the people of Texas. The carrying of firearms and other deadly weapons was consequently a prevalent custom among them. And being scattered over vast areas, and beyond the efficient protection and restraints of civil law, they of necessity became a law unto themselves.[38]

There is no better place than Fort Worth, Texas, to observe the cowboy, that peculiar product of wild frontier life. He comes here from his home on the plains to spend his money at the saloons, swagger in the streets, buy himself a new sombrero with silver cord and binding of bright colored braid, and make merry with the painted sirens of the variety theater. Full of strange oaths, free with his cash and his revolver, boisterous, lawless, but not hardhearted, the cowboy is a character *sui generis*. He is apt to make himself obnoxious in a crowded town, but seen on his native heath, cantering over the plains on his swift mustang, swinging his lariat and shouting his whoop and hallo to the fleeing steers, he is a picturesque spectacle. He lives in a hut or a tent; sleeps in summer rolled in his blanket in the open air, is in the saddle from morning to night, settles his quarrels with his six-shooter, looks upon killing as a venial offense, and on cattle stealing as a capital crime, and is altogether the most free and independent fellow to be found in this peculiarly free and independent country.[39]

But the peculiar characteristics of the Texas cow-boys qualified them for more important public service. By virtue of their courage and recklessness of danger, their excellent horsemanship, and skill in the use of firearms, and by virtue also of the influence which they have exerted upon their gentler brethren of the northern ranges, they have been an efficient instrumentality in preventing Indian outbreaks, and in protecting the frontier settlements of the entire range and ranch cattle area against predatory incursions and massacres by Indians. This has been a natural result of the fact that the cow-boys constitute throughout that region a corps of mounted scouts, armed and equipped, twenty thousand strong. They traverse vast ranges, ford rivers, and search for cattle amid mountain fastness and in lurking places of the river bottoms. No hostile movement could for a day escape their notice. It is certain that they have done much toward subduing a vast area to the arts of peace, and that an unarmed man may now travel alone throughout Wyoming, Dakota, Montana, and Idaho, and even in

Texas, as safely as in the New England or the Middle States. As a pioneer of civilization the American cow-boy has therefore performed a public service which as fully entitles him to recognition as do the commerical results of his labors.

The cow-boy of to-day, especially on the northern ranges, is of an entirely different type from the original cow-boy of Texas. New conditions have produced the change. The range cattle business of Kansas, Nebraska, Colorado, Wyoming, Montana, and Dakota is, as already stated a new business. Those engaged in it as proprietors are chiefly from the States situated west of the Missouri River and north of the Indian Territory. Among them are also many Englishmen, Scotchmen, Frenchmen, and Germans of large means, embracing titled men who have embarked in the business quite extensively.... Some of this class have, from the force of romantic temperament and the exhilaration of range life, themselves participated actively in the duties of the cow-boy.

Organization, discipline, and order characterize the new undertakings on the northern ranges. In a word, the cattle business of that section is now and has from the beginning been carried on upon strictly business principles. Under such proprietorships, and guided by such methods, a new class of cow-boys has been introduced and developed. Some have come from Texas, and have brought with them a knowledge of the arts of their calling, but the number from the other States and the Territories constitute a large majority of the whole. Some are graduates of American colleges, and others of collegiate institutions in Europe....

Throughout the northern ranges sobriety, self-restraint, decent behavior, and faithfulness to duty are enjoined upon the cow-boys. A great improvement is also observable in the cow-boys of Texas. Deeds of violence among them are now few. The *morale* of the entire range and ranch cattle business of the United States now compares favorably with that of other large enterprises.[40]

The Colorado cowboy has been misrepresented by speakers and writers who know nothing about him but vaulted over facts to the false conclusion that because he lived in a wild and unsettled country infested by savages, buffaloes and wild beasts whom he frequently found it necessary to meet and mingle with on terms of relentless hostility, that he was a sort of reckless freebooter, pulling his gun in whatever cause afforded the best pay and most liberal license. The early cowboys on the Colorado plains were mostly young men. They were the pioneers engaged in the work of protecting the homes of their employers, their wives and children against marauding savages. They were bold and adventurous men carving their fortunes in a new country....[41]

So much has been written of the cowboy of the far west, that one would suppose at the first glance that there was nothing left to be said.... Sensational correspondents for the city journals thirsting for something marvelous, and calculated to make a noise in the world, have written this knight of the mountains and plains up in glorious colors. That is to say they have made him a perfect desperado—so much so that mention of the name "cowboy" strikes terror to the heart of men, women, and children everywhere, except among the people where he reigns. He is anything else but a desperado, and is regarded in every other light.... But instead of being the outlaw that he has been pictured, he is a good citizen, and has long been the only sure safeguard of our frontier homes. Our stockmen have pioneered every valley; to the presence of the cowboys, rather than the military, which has always been inadequate and insufficient, is due the security Montana has enjoyed for her homes and property.[42]

It would delight the heart of the average Texas cowboy to be hired by a Montana cowman, and there shown the horses from which he was to select his mount—great big tallowy horses as sleek as livery horses, and very few of them but what are gentle as a dog. And I may add that when a Montana cowboy gets back from a season's roundup, that his horses are still fat. In the first place he has plenty of them and these men do not allow their hands to dash those horses around just for the fun of the thing. And the cattle here are too different from what they are in Texas, that there is really very little hard riding to do. Boys who have worked on both ranges say that while the average Texas cow pony cannot compare with his Montana brother as to looks, yet when it comes to doing hard work and a heap of it, he is far superior to the latter. He is quicker and harder, and better adapted to just such work.... Live! Why, these cowboys live higher than anybody. They have every thing to eat that money can buy, and a cook with a paper cap on to prepare it. The cook is so neat and polite that you could eat him if you were right hungry.... Cowboys get about the same wages here that they do in Texas, but one dollar in Texas will buy as much as three in Montana, and the boys only get work three or four months in the year.[43]

Every now and then there appear in papers published outside of Texas slighting references to the class known, the world over, as "Texas Cowboys."... We don't believe for a moment that the writers of the articles referred to have any unkind feelings towards the subjects of this notice, nor that they wish or intend to misrepresent them. On the other hand, we are satisfied that they really believe all they write, and actually look upon the average cowboy as a rough, rollicking, swearing, pugnacious, fearless daredevil, who is never half so happy as when he is engaged in blood-letting....

The average cowboy is not a bad man in any sense of the term. True, there are exceptions to this rule, and such exceptions as are very marked....

The men who are really honest types of this class are distinguished for many excellent traits of character. In the first place they are almost universally men of intelligence. It is a rare thing to find a cowboy that is a fool, or even a near approach to a fool. The life he is compelled to lead calls for the constant exercise of good judgment, and if a fool starts in as a "cow-puncher," he is soon made to understand that he has mistaken his calling....

In the next place, he is emphatically an enterprising "cuss," and is ever on the alert for opportunities to put into exercise enterprising schemes. He will figure on futures in beef steers as if he was a *millionaire*.... The cattle kings of Texas today were, most of them, Texas cowboys a few years since, and the men now working for them at $25.00 to $30.00 per month, may be worth as much as they in five or ten years time.

We deem it hardly necessary to say in the next place that the cowboy is a fearless animal. A man wanting in courage would be as much out of place in a cow-camp, as a fish would be on dry land. Indeed the life he is daily compelled to lead calls for the existence of the highest degree of cool calculating courage. As a natural consequence of this courage, he is not quarrelsome or a bully.... Before the six-shooter law was enforced in Western Texas, the cow-boy paradise, every cow-puncher went armed to the teeth, nominally to protect himself against Indians, but really because it was the fashion. When fighting was engaged in, it was fighting in earnest, and it would be hard to estimate the number of good men who in the past twenty years have died in cow-camps with their boots on....

As another necessary consequent to possessing true manly courage, the cowboy is as chivalrous as the famed knights of old. Rough he may be, and it may be that he is not a master in ball room etiquette, but no set of men have loftier reverence for women and no set of men would risk more in the defense of their person or their honor.

As the frontier of Texas has been gradually forced further and further west, the old time tramping ground of these knights of the lasso have, per force, been more thrown in control with the fair sex than in former years, and the effect has been to soften down their rugged natures, and to smooth the ragged edges of character otherwise admirable. Hence it is that a non-resident, visiting for the first time the Texas frontier town, is surprised to find in the cowboy, whom he almost expects to see with horns growing out of his forehead, a man of more than ordinary culture and refinement....

Another and most notable of his characteristics is his entire devotion to the interests of his employer. We are certain no more faithful employe ever breathed than he;

and when we assert that he is, *par excellence,* a model in this respect, we know that we will be sustained by every man who has had experience in this matter.

The man who is faithful to the interests of his employer, is naturally faithful in his friendships; and if the inner history of the cow business of Texas could be written, it would show up hundreds of friendships among rough, and perhaps, untutored cowboys, quite as unselfish and romantic as that of Damon and Pythias.[44]

JARGON

It is unlikely that the old-time cowboy can take credit for introducing new and exceptional, or vulgar and obscene, examples of profanity. However, he has long been recognized as an author of breath-taking and weird combinations of cuss words which were intimately associated with his work and companions. Probably his greatest contribution in this area was the humorous and oftentimes appropriate adaptation of language to his immediate means of accurate expression. Unfortunately, the frontier press was no less inhibited than is the press of today in recording "the richer" Anglo-Saxonisms of the West.

Late in February, 188-, I found myself in the sordid, reeking saloon of a small prairie settlement, surrounded by a motley crew of bull-whackers, mule-skinners, grangers, drummers, gamblers, and cowboys, the latter easily distinguishable by their devil-may-care airs and fantastic getup.... I sat gloomily in a quiet corner of the saloon, yet could not but be keenly interested in all that went on around me.... I was a fish out of water, *voilà tout.* Never before had I heard such blasphemous meaningless oaths and mighty anathemas as were continually on the lips of the sorely-tried cowboys.... Our cowboy is shockingly cruel, hasty in temper, and unbridled in tongue. In the branding pen and with a half-broken, tired or unwilling horse, he is a perfect fiend; his contempt for life too often leads to needless bloodshed; and he is untiring as an Indian in pursuit of revenge.

With him it is frequently not a word and a blow but a word and a bullet.... The somewhat primitive code of honor I have described is not, however, without its good effects, and I am bound to say that, rough as the boys are, their voluble flow of bad language is limited to their animals, but rarely addressed to their fellows;... Of their stoic indifference to pain I could relate many instances....[45]

Among the cowboy's redeeming features there is one, however, that must not be overlooked. It is his hatred for empty show and affectation. As the devil hates holy matter, even so is the cowboy stuck on those who are "stuck up" or who "put on dog" as he calls it. He makes use of enough of the English language to make himself well and forcibly understood, but he is not given to making consignments of it in large bulks. No matter how much in earnest he may get, he seldom hurls what you would term jawbreakers at any one. While it can not be denied, perhaps, that he indulges in a pardonable ambition to keep up with the latest styles in cuss words and slang terms, yet it cannot be said that the use of "big words" is a specialty of his.[46]

He is absolutely self-poised and sufficient; and that self-poise and that sufficiency he takes pains to assure first of all. After their assurance he is willing to enter into human relations. His attitude toward everything in life is, not suspicious, but watchful. He is "gathered together," his elbows at his side.

This evidences itself most strikingly in his terseness of speech. A man dependent on himself naturally does not give himself away to the first comer. He is more interested in finding out what the other fellow is than in exploiting his own importance. A man who does much promiscuous talking he is likely to despise, arguing that man incautious, hence weak.

Yet when he does talk, he talks to the point and with a vivid and direct picturesqueness of phrase which is as refreshing as it is unexpected....

This vividness manifests itself quite as often in the

selection of the apt word as in the construction of elaborate phrases with a half-humorous intention.

But to observe the riot of imagination turned loose with the bridle off, you must assist at a burst of anger on the part of one of these men. It is most unprintable, but you will get an entirely new idea of what profanity means. Also you will come to the conclusion that you, with your trifling *damns,* and the like, have been a very good boy indeed. The remotest, most obscure and unheard-of conceptions are dragged forth from earth, heaven, and hell, and linked together in a sequence so original, so gaudy, and so utterly blasphemous that you gasp and are stricken with the most devoted admiration. It is genius.

Of course I can give you no idea here of what these truly magnificent oaths are like. It is a pity, for it would liberalize your education. Occasionally, like a trickle of clear water into an alkali torrent, a straight English sentence will drop into the flood. It is refreshing by contrast, but weak.[47]

A cow puncher writing to the *Northwestern Live Stock Journal* from Tacoma, Nevada, says: "We have no general round-ups, but instead of round-ups they are called 'Rot Hear'; and what are called 'mavericks' in Wyoming are called 'oreannas'; and what we call a 'pody' in Wyoming is called a 'lepie.' Everything goes by a different name out here from what it does in any other country."[48]

Among the cowboy literature of the Eastern press appears the following:

"The cowboys of the far West have a language of their own which no 'tenderfoot' may attain until he has served his novitiate. They call a horse herder a 'horse wrangler,' and a horse breaker a 'bronco buster.' Their steed is often a 'cayuse,' and to dress well is to 'rag proper.' When a cowboy goes out on the prairie he 'hits the flat.' Whiskey is 'family disturbance,' and to eat is to 'chew.' His hat is a 'cady,' his whip a 'quirt,' his rubber coat a 'slicker,' his leather overalls are 'chaps' or 'chapperals,' and his revolver is a '45.' Bacon is 'overland trout' and unbranded cattle are 'mavericks.' "[49]

The jokes and pleasantries of the American "puncher" are so close to nature often, and so generously veneered with heart-rending profanity, as to exclude their becoming classic. The cowmen are good friends and virulent haters, and, if justified in their own minds, would shoot a man instantly, and regret the necessity, but not the shooting, afterwards.[50]

In the use of the lasso and profane language the cowboy has no equal. He can rope a steer, throwing the noose on either foot of the animal as it runs at full speed, at the same time showing a choice in the matter of selecting appropriate anathemas, which he can deliver equally well, either in Mexican or United States language, long primer type that is perfectly amazing, considering his limited acquaintance with the drama and the refined influences of civilized life.[51]

KNIGHT OR KNAVE?

The frontier journalist took strong stands concerning the cowboy. He was painted black or white—there were no intermediate shades. All misdeeds were perpetrated by the cowboy! He was just a reckless, carefree boy, good as gold, but inclined to get into trouble. The Western journalists banded together in defense of the cowboy only when he was maligned by the Eastern press.

"Seems to be a disposition back East," said the old cowboy, voicing the sentiment of the West in general, "to blame the Western man for all the troubles between him and the Indians. They forgot that the Westerner has only been doing for the last thirty years what the Easterner did long before...."[52]

Out in the Territories there are only two classes—the "cowboys" and the "tenderfeet." Such of the "cowboys" as are not professional thieves, murderers and miscellaneous blacklegs who fled to the frontier for reasons that require no explanations, are men who totally disregard all the amenities of Eastern civilization, brook no restraint, and—fearing neither God, nor man nor the devil—yielding allegiance to no law save their own untamed passions. The "tenderfoot" is their meat. They know no higher pleasure than to use him for a target on the slightest pretext, while their sense of humor finds no greater gratification than to perforate with bullets that "tenderfoot" who inadvertently refuses to "nominate his pisen" when invited to do so. He is the best man who can draw the quickest and kill the surest. A "cowboy" who has not killed his man—or to put it more correctly his score of "tenderfeet"—is without character, standing, or respect. The "tenderfoot" who goes among them should first double his life insurance and then be sure that he is "well-heeled."[53]

It is possible that there is not a wilder or more lawless set of men in any country that pretends to be civilized than the gangs of semi-nomads that live in some of our frontier States and Territories and are referred to in our dispatches as "the cow boys." Many of them have emigrated from our States in order to escape the penalty of their crimes, and it is extremely doubtful whether there is one in their number who is not guilty of a penitentiary offense, while most of them merit the gallows. They are supposed to be herdsmen employed to watch vast herds of cattle, but they might more properly be known under any name that means desperate criminal. They roam about in sparsely settled villages with revolvers, pistols and knives in their belts, attacking every peaceable citizen met with. Now and then they take part in a dance, the sound of the music frequently being deadened by the crack of their pistols, and the hoe-down only being interrupted long enough to drag out the dead and wounded. A report came the other day that one of them marched through a village forcing all he met to insert the muzzle of a loaded pistol in their mouths. If they complied he said "you are a brave man" and moved on. The next morning this particular "cowboy" was found on the outskirts of a village, his body pierced with bullets. Another report described how a railroad official fell into the hands of a crowd of these ruffians who told him he must dance or die. At first he refused to obey, but on seeing a score of revolvers pointed at his head he set up a jig. After dancing till overcome with fatigue, they gave him a few moments rest, then renewed their threats. The poor man kept dancing till he could hardly move. They relieved him of his valuables and set him adrift. Dispatches from Tucson, Arizona, of last Thursday, announced that about 70 cowboys, well armed and equined were marauding the country, raiding the small towns and scattering consternation in their path, with the avowed purpose of avenging the death of 4 of their comrades. The dispatch expressed the general fear that there would be "bloody work, as they are the most reckless gang of desperadoes ever banded together." What these 70 cut-throats have done is not yet known, but they and their gang will soon, without a doubt, meet their just deserts. Arizona is being settled, the territory is being cut up by railroads, and the U.S. troops will give the honest settlers assistance necessary to put down these lawless vagabonds, who are more of a disgrace to this country than the worst bandits were to Spain or Italy.[54]

The Texas *Stockman* doesn't mince matters any, and comes to the front in this shape about the wild and woolly cowboys in its section: "There is a style of cowboy very rare, let it be said to the credit of the guild, who think it smart to "shoot up" a town, though of late several of these Smart Alecks have had their cowardly carcasses punctured with cold lead, and this amusement is not so popular with them as of yore. Of late, terrorizing passenger trains is a favorite pastime with them, and there it is, among women, children and unarmed men, that their peculiar style of bravery (?) finds full scope. There they can insult ladies, frighten children, terrorize train men to their hearts' content, and who is there to make them afraid. Some time they will make one of these plays in the presence of a sure-enough cowboy, one of the sort that attends to his own business, takes off his hat to ladies even in a smoking car, and if he wants a row, hunts up some one in the same humor, and then these bad men from away up high on Bitter Creek will receive a deposit of more lead where it will do the most good, and a jury of decent citizens will say, 'Amen.' "[55]

There are cow punchers and cow punchers, and as gentlemen we are ready to compare the "men" and "boys" of the Panhandle with any set of men in any business anywhere. We are led to this remark because we have lately had opportunities for comparing our boys with those from other ranges.

One outfit from the northern part of the state proper came upon a quarter section of land that was being fenced and broken, and of course concluded that there was some man trying to make arrangements to feed his children, and of course under such circumstances it would be the height of fun and wit to harass him by needlessly cutting his fence, and would be a matter of glory, and withal mirth-provoking, to recount afterward. And the brave noblemen from the lower country sneaked up, cut the fence and ran away....

Another outfit from the great, indefinite "down below" passed with a herd a few days since, and a number of the boys came in to create an impression upon the simple villagers, and did. They posed upon and spurred their poor, little, overworked, altogether miserable and unhappy ponies to make them prance of bronco agony. They swaggered along the walls with the voices and general coarseness of jackasses. They went in to dinner at the hotel with the same swagger and loudness and sat down to the table with their hats on, and all the time with a flow of wit that might edify an idiot, and betrayed an awful but futile attempt to appear wild and woolly by silly boys just emancipated from the cotton patch....

The old, sure enough cowboy, worthy the name of gentleman, is the sort we are used to here, and the invasion of weaklings with assumed coarseness shows the contrast vividly. Cheap boys cannot fool this community.[56]

The recent train robbery, according to the dispatches was the act of seven "cowboys." Now these robbers were masked, and, so far as we have been able to learn, it is not known who they were. The term "cowboy" is getting too common. It is used on occasions when it is not at all applicable. We do not believe "seven cowboys" wrecked the train. It has none of the characteristics of the cowboy. It may have been done by men who claimed to be cowboys, but there must be some evidence of the fact before we take any stock in it.[57]

As you mingle with these cowboys, you find in them a strange mixture of good nature and recklessness. You are as safe with them on the plains as with any class of men, so long as you do not impose upon them. They will even deny themselves for your comfort, and imperil their lives for your safety. But impose upon them, or arouse their ire, and your life is of no more value in their esteem than that of a coyote.

Morally, as a class, they are foulmouthed, blasphemous, drunken, lecherous, utterly corrupt. Usually harmless on the plains when sober, they are dreaded in towns, for then liquor has the ascendency over them. They are also as improvident as the veriest "Jack" of the sea....

They never own any interest in the stock they tend. This dark picture of the cowboys ought to be lightened by the statement that there is occasionally a white sheep among the black. True and devoted Christians are found in such company—men who will kneel down regularly and offer their prayers in the midst of their bawdy and cursing associates. They are like Lot in Sodom.[58]

The Palo Pinto county *News* makes a defense of the cowboys and intimates a dereliction of duty on the part of the *Journal* in not repelling the slanders uttered against them.... There is a class of uninformed writers who make the word cowboy synonymous with all that is bad. Their day of influence, however, is passing. As eastern capital, as eastern, western and northern men come into our midst and taste the generous hospitality of the ranchman and his cowboys, so does pass away the influence of the journalistic slanderer that at one time wrote with great detriment to the live stock business.

What need has the cowboy of defense against such

men? His assistants could neither be convinced nor silenced by reply. The stale slanders will go on until they rot and die of their own corruption. In the meantime the cowboy maintains his manhood, his fearlessness, his health and grows on in wealth to become the ranchman.

The cowboy needs no defense—not even against the proclamation of President Arthur.... His manliness, generosity, fidelity and energy can never be made apparent by newspaper articles to the sweet-scented, kid-gloved fool who writes and starves on a few dollars a week while the cowboy is working his way to wealth and station.[59]

We have for a long time been aware that among the uninformed an idea has prevailed that the unenviable reputation Texas has acquired, as a land of law breakers, the home of thieves and train robbers, is all due or mainly so to the cowboy element in the state.... We would have been greatly outraged at the recklessness and unfounded assertions of an ex-senator from southern Texas, in his speech before the Stockmen's Convention at Austin last week, had we believed that any considerable portion of his auditors endorsed his utterances. The Hon. Mr. Lane, while soaring on the wings of fancy and sailing far above the common-place regions of fact, had the temerity to assert that our penitentiaries were filled with cowboys. That the teachings imbibed from range life were stepping stones to the erection of characters that delighted in outlawry. We speak advisedly when we say the facts and statistics of our prisons will show that Galveston, San Antonio, Austin, Waco, and the cities of North Texas, have furnished ten inmates for the state's prisons, to one from the range fields of the state. It is true that there have been many convictions for the theft on the frontier, and for cattle and horse stealing, but in almost every case they were hardened criminals who had been educated in crime in the hot beds of vice in our Texas towns, and who having led the life of gamblers, thieves and pimps in Texas cities, and had from frequency of crime and fear of apprehension for former deeds of violence fled to the frontier and there, seeking retiracy, enlisted as line-riders or cowboys. A few months thus passed, they would tire of honest life and soon steal a yearling, when our stockmen's association would put the cowboy on their trail, arrests and convictions would follow, and when they were safely housed at Huntsville, the distinguished senator ignorantly classes them as cowboys and charges that range life is demoralizing. Had he visited the camps and been a guest of the cowboys, he could never have so misrepresented them. They are honest, honorable and manly and never figure in the role he assigned them, save in dime novels and public speeches where the parties who write and speak are seeking sensational notoriety. His argument was unfounded in theory and false in fact.[60]

We who are thrown in daily contact with them are growing tired of these never ending slurs upon the cowboys. That they are as a rule reckless of danger and frequently fond of a fight is true, but that they are criminals as a class is a ridiculous libel.... The legitamate and genuine cowboy is brave, generous and worthy— brave, because no coward can face the dangers of his daily life, generous, because the brave are always so, and honest because he works hard for an honest living. That he delights occasionally in terrifying the brainless dude who maligns him is not to be wondered at, but his real faults and offenses are those of a manly nature. He never insults a woman or betrays a trust, and if his six-shooter is quick to resent an insult to himself, it is as ready to right the wrongs of the oppressed. And when he disappears after a few years of this wild, erratic life, it is not into a dishonored grave or behind the bars of a penitentiary, but only to reappear as the shrewd and prosperous owner of an honest and hardly earned herd of his own.[61]

The New York *Hour* thinks "the irrepressible cowboy bids fair to become as perplexing a factor in the problem of frontier civilization as the ubiquitous and elusive Chiricahau [Chiricahua] himself." It qualifies this by implying a doubt as to the truthfulness of the stories printed about men who herd cattle. The *Hour* is right; if all the stories which are told of the cow puncher were true, he would be a greater enemy to civilization than the dirty redskins who are making it lively for Uncle Sam's troops in New Mexico and Arizona. But they are not true. Because the cowboy is a festive fellow, when he leaves the cattle and gets among human beings, whisky and beer, the newspaper reporters of the west have seen fit to make him the hero of a thousand scrapes—most of them extremely desperate and disreputable—which the poor cow herder has never had the fun of enjoying.... He is very much like the country in which he lives. In Texas, he is as unruly as the steers he dashes madly after over the plains. This is undoubtedly the result of association. No man could herd Texas cattle and still be a Christian. There are some things that are morally impossible. It is true in New Mexico and Arizona many men in the guise of cowboys rob unsuspecting travelers and hold up stage coaches which contain passengers with fat pocketbooks. We would not like to vouch for a New Mexico cow puncher. This may be because we have, happily, been intimate with him. But for the cowboys of Colorado, Wyoming and Nebraska we would give a certificate of good character. Though they partake largely of the festive ways which are characteristic of the genus cowboy, wherever you find him, yet they are, as a rule honest, with more or less ambition to become cattle kings, and certainly not a lot of cutthroats. Many of them are men of considerable education, and now and then you will find a graduate of Yale or Harvard among them, sitting on his pony like a circus rider and galloping over the prairie like a Comanche Indian. The Colorado cowboy, as a general thing, is quiet and unobtrusive, but, like a bank clerk and tape measurer, he likes his "fun." He occasionally comes to town arrayed in his best "togs." He goes through with what money he has in a royal fashion. When he indulges in these little vacations, his fellow cow punchers refer to his delightful state as being "drunk and dressed up and don't give a damn."

This we believe, is a reasonable, accurate description

of his appearance, and conception of his responsibility. Seriously, our cowboys are much abused.[62]

The great New York capitalist, Rufus Hatch, was interviewed, after a visit West, by a commissioner of the New York *World,* and we give below the response to the query:

"Are the cowboys as bad as they are represented, and is it really dangerous to travel in that region?

"No. As for the 'boys,' " said Uncle Rufus, "they are the essence of amiability—perfect Lubin's extracts compared with some of the people you elbow against in this same city of New York, and as for revolvers, there is no more use for a six-shooter on Wall street than out West. They may be rough on the outside, but they are really as warm-hearted and hospitable a lot of people as you will find anywhere in America. One of our guides was a graduate of Heidelberg and could talk the language of every man in the party; a dead shot, too, for he shot this silver dollar off a stump seventy-five yards distant with a rifle-ball, while one of the engineers on a locomotive, where I handled the lever, could quote Latin and Greek by the yard, knew all the classical authors and made you feel as if you were in a library. Cowboys! don't make a mistake. It may be a new country, but it's full of brains."[63]

A New Yorker, returning from an extensive trip through the west, breaks the news to his home people thus:

The cowboys are a much misrepresented class of people. It is a popular impression that when one goes among them he must be prepared to shoot. But this is a false idea. I have taken part with them in the rounding up, eaten, slept, hunted and herded cattle with them, and never had any difficulty. If you choose to enter rum shops or go on King sprees with them it is as easy to get into difficulty out there as it would be in New York or any where else.... I have found them a brave and most hospitable set of men. There is no use in trying to be overbearing with them, for they won't stand the least assumption of superiority, yet there are many places in our cities where I should feel less safe than I would among the wildest cowboy of the west.[64]

We are glad to record that our eastern and northern publications are forming a more correct conception, and giving to their readers a truer portrait of the Texas and western cowboy. The *National Stockman* of Pittsburg[h], Pennsylvania, says: "The typical ranchman is no swaggering desperado or animated arsenal—but is a business man and a gentleman. If the national political conventions to be held in Chicago in the next few months show a better average of citizenship than was exhibited recently at Cheyenne, W. T., when four hundred and fifty ranchmen met in convention to deliberate on matters affecting their interests, they will reflect the highest credit on the nation they represent. A few years hence the standard of personal character and public demeanor will be as high on the plains of the trans-Mississippi country as it is in Pennsylvania. The ranch hands now employed for the work once performed wholly by the knights of the derringer are of a character which must in a few years rob the life of the herder of much of its risk and the blood-and-thunder press of its most atrocious sensations. A great many farmers' sons, raised to habits of industry and trained in the usages of good society, are filling up the vacancies which occur among herdsmen, and in many places they preponderate among the employes of the district. They take this method of learning the business from the very beginning, and are effecting a revolution in it which is as thorough as it is gratifying. We are personally acquainted with young men of character, intelligence, education, and even of moderate wealth, who are now, with the end referred to in view, voluntarily undertaking the hardships and drudgery of the herder's lot.... There can be but one outcome to all this—and the outcome to which the whole country, and especially the west, must look forward to with satisfaction." Formerly he was unjustly classed as "wild and woolly," a dare devil, and outlaw. This character was given to the class simply from the fact that a few desperadoes occasionally were found in the ranks. They were the thieves and outlaws who were among, but not really of the cowboys. They gave the unsavory reputation to the ranches, and when stock associations were organized and the ranch business systematized this class was hounded out. Now there are no truer, better or more deserving men in the west than can be found among the managers and employes of cattle ranches.[65]

NOTES TO CHAPTER ONE

1. *House Executive Documents*, 48 Cong. 2 sess., House Exec. Doc. 267 (Serial no. 2304), Joseph Nimmo, "Range and Ranch Cattle Traffic in the Western States and Territories" [Washington, D.C.: Government Printing Office, 1885], XXIX, 9.
2. *Ibid.*, p. 12.
3. "Traits of Western People," *Daily Missouri Democrat* (St. Louis, Missouri), September 8, 1858.
4. Cf. Bayard Taylor, *Colorado: A Summer Trip* (New York, 1867).
5. "False Notions of Western Character," *Rocky Mountain News* (Denver, Colorado), June 26, 1869.
6. Matthew J. Herron, "The Passing of the Cowman," *Overland Monthly*, LV (February, 1910), 197.
7. William T. Larned, "The Passing of the Cow-Puncher," *Lippincott's Magazine*, LV (August, 1895), 268
8. Herron, "Cowman," pp. 195-96.
9. *New York Daily Tribune* (New York, New York), November 6, 1867.
10. Thomas Holmes, "A Cowboy's Life," *Chautauquan*, XIX (September, 1894), 731.
11. "Cattle-Herding in the Great West," *Littell's Living Age*, XVIII (April 14, 1877), 126.
12. Louis C. Bradford, "Among the Cow-Boys," *Lippincott's Magazine*, XXVII (June, 1881), 568-69.
13. Perfume made from the oil of East Indian mint.
14. *Cheyenne Daily Leader* (Cheyenne, Wyoming), May 25, 1882.
15. Frederick Bechdolt, "The Field Agent of Settlement—The Cowboy's Contribution to American Civilization," *Collier's Weekly* XLIII (September 18, 1909), 19.
16. Cf. Clifford P. Westermeier, "The Cowboy—Sinner or Saint!" *New Mexico Historical Review*, XXV (April, 1950), 89-108.
17. "Sport Among the Cowboys," *Field and Farm* (Denver, Colorado), June 4, 1892, p. 6.
18. Lewis W. Carson, *The Specter Spy; or, The Wizard Canoe*. This item was first published on January 25, 1870, by Beadle & Company, under the banner of Frank Starr's American Novels, and afterward reprinted.

19. "The Texas Cattle Herder," *Rocky Mountain News*, April 4, 1872; *Columbus Journal* (Columbus, Kansas), April 9, 1874.
20. "The Festive Cow Puncher," *Denver Tribune-Republican* (Denver, Colorado), October 31, 1886.
21. "On a Texas Cattle Range," *Texas Live Stock Journal* (Fort Worth, Texas), July 14, 1883, p. 8.
22. "The Cowboy's Life," *El Anunciador de Trinidad* (Trinidad, Colorado), December 1, 1887.
23. Hell, the underworld.
24. "The Cowboy," *Trinidad Daily Advertiser* (Trinidad, Colorado), July 16, 1885.
25. "The Cowboy as He Is," *Democratic Leader* (Cheyenne, Wyoming), January 11, 1885.
26. Rufus S. Zogbaum, "A Day's 'Drive' with Montana Cowboys," *Harper's New Monthly Magazine*, LXXI (July, 1885), 190.
27. Alfred T. Bacon, "A Colorado 'Round-Up,'" *Lippincott's Magazine*, XXVIII (December, 1881), 622.
28. Herron, "Cowman," p. 199.
29. General George Wingate, "My Trip to the Yellowstone," *American Agriculturist*, XLV (April, 1886), 152.
30. "The Cowboy of the Day," *Trinidad Daily Advertiser*, January 31, 1885; *Kansas Cowboy* (Dodge City, Kansas), February 7, 1885.
31. Alfred M. Williams, "An Indian Cattle-Town," *Lippincott's Magazine*, XXXIII (February, 1884), 169-70.
32. "The Cowboy by Slade," *Texas Live Stock Journal*, October 21, 1882, p. 8.
33. Stewart E. White, "The Mountain, XIX—On Cowboys," *Outlook*, LXXVIII (September 3, 1904), 83.
34. "The Cowboy," *Stock Grower and Farmer* (Las Vegas, New Mexico), July 25, 1891, p. 1.
35. White, "On Cowboys," pp. 82-83.
36. William A. Baillie-Grohman, "Cattle Ranches in the Far West," *Fortnightly Review*, XXXIV (October, 1880), 447.
37. "Texas Cowboys," *Ellsworth Reporter* (Ellsworth, Kansas), August 28, 1873.
38. Joseph Nimmo, Jr., "The American Cow-Boy," *Harper's New Monthly Magazine*, LXXIII (November, 1886), 880-81.
39. "The Texas Cow-Boy," *Times* (Baxter Springs, Kansas), July 3, 1879.
40. Nimmo, "Cow-Boy," pp. 881, 883-84.
41. "The Old Time Cowboy," *Field and Farm*, January 1, 1898, p. 17.
42. "A Good Word for the Montana Cow Boy," *Kansas Cowboy*, August 2, 1884.
43. "The Montana Cowboy," *ibid.*, July 25, 1885.
44. "Texas Cowboys," *Texas Live Stock Journal*, October 21, 1882, p. 5.
45. John Baumann, "Experiences of a Cow-Boy," *Lippincott's Magazine*, XXXVIII (September, 1886), 312, 314-15.

46. "Still More About the Cow-Boy," *Texas Live Stock Journal*, November 4, 1882, p. 5.

47. White, "On Cowboys," pp. 83-84.

48. *Caldwell Standard* (Caldwell, Kansas), March 7, 1884. Rot Hear—*rothear* (cattle or horned beast—Danish *rund* or German *rind*, meaning "cattle"—obsolete or dialect English). Oreannas—Spanish *orejano* (meaning "long-eared," but used in some Western states to designate an unmarked animal). Lepie—*onlepy* (meaning "alone," "single"—English, "leap").

49. *Democratic Leader*, February 27, 1887.

50. Frederic Remington, "A Rodeo at Los Ojos," *Harper's New Monthly Magazine*, LXXXVIII (March, 1894), 524

51. "The Cowboy," *Texas Live Stock Journal*, October 14, 1882, p. 6.

52. M. J. Reynolds, "The Texas Trail," *Munsey's Magazine*, XXIX (June, 1903), 578.

53. "An Eastern Cowboy," *Rio Grande Republican* (Las Cruces, New Mexico), December 13, 1884.

54. "Cut Throat Cow Boys," *Las Vegas Daily Optic* (Las Vegas, New Mexico), June 28, 1881.

55. *Laramie Weekly Sentinel* (Laramie, Wyoming), March 20, 1886.

56. "Cow-Punchers," *Texas Live Stock Journal*, July 5, 1884, p. 3.

57. *Trinidad Daily Advertiser*, November 30, 1883.

58. "The Cow-Boys of the Western Plains and Their Horses," *Cheyenne Daily Leader*, October 3, 1882.

59. "Cowboys and Their Slanderers," *Las Animas Leader* (Las Animas, Colorado), June 30, 1882.

60. "Cowboy Life," *Texas Live Stock Journal*, January 10, 1884, p. 2.

61. "Cowboys," *Kansas Cowboy*, October 3, 1885.

62. "The Festive Cowboy," *Las Vegas Daily Optic*, October 16, 1883.

63. "Rufus Hatch's Estimate of the Cowboy," *Texas Live Stock Journal*, October 20, 1883, p. 6.

64. "The Real Cow Boy," *Kansas Cowboy*, November 1, 1884.

65. "Cowboys in the West," *Texas Live Stock Journal*, May 10, 1884, p. 2.

All in the Day's Work

TWO

The work of the cowboy was his very life. From the moment he awakened, stiff and sore, in the still, chilled, pure air of the plains, until he surrendered to his blankets at night, worn and tired from the strenuous work of a long day, he had participated in violent, dangerous, hazardous tasks. In the struggle of man against beast and nature, the latter two were constantly in combat with him who strove to be master. This is the plot of the daily drama of the cow country, for an immense, tempestuous, crude West produced immense, tempestuous, crude situations and men. The forge which shaped the rugged environment and the brutes also created these Herculean men who were determined to rule the domain. In order to survive, the cowboy had to equal and surpass, both in knowledge and understanding, the Indian, the hunter, and the plainsman. The great plains, which rested on the broad bosom of the West, as a cradle of vastness, rocked by storm and strife or protected by the strength of hill and mountain, nurtured only the strong. Survival meant work to live—the elemental law of nature.

Thus, to understand the cowboy we must understand the environment—the pristine, basic, disordered, brutal forces bearing down upon him, for he is but a reflection of his surroundings. Since the cowboy is a part of the West —and to understand one necessarily means understanding the other—they are inseparable.

The erect, virile, lithe man on horseback who rode jauntily as guardian of the trail herds was being tested in the crucible of the range. He who pressed with brawny hands, hour after hour, the glowing branding iron into the quivering hide of the helpless calf at his feet, stood as some merciless god, with head clouded in the malodorous incense from burning hair and seared flesh. The boy, riding line day after day, subjected to a pitiless, brassy sun or to the silver shroud of sleet and snow, was crucified on days of homesickness, monotony, and loneliness. The man who rode at night through gully and ravine in torrential rains, amid the mighty, dreadful roars of wind, thunder, and the rumbling din of thousands of rushing hoofs, while the awesome spectacle of great jagged streaks and balls of flame poured forth from the black, cavernous heavens—this man, good or evil in his heart, rode with death. In breaking broncos, he endured the violent joltings of the stiff-legged brutes and accepted philosophically the falls, the broken legs and arms, the bloody mucus from strained lungs. Heat, cold, dust, flies, stench, brackish water, river crossings—all were a part of the life of the cowboy.

A cowboy, returning to camp at the close of the day's work, did not joke and play as he might have been inclined to do earlier in the day. With clothes soiled and stained by the dirt and filth of his labors, stiff and rancid from his own sweat and from that of his charges, he was too weary to perform anything but the last daily task of his profession—removing the saddle from his wearier companion of the long day. After the evening meal, a smoke, and a bit of quiet conversation, he made his bed under the stars.

ROUNDUP DAYS

During the spring and fall roundups the cowboy practiced his specialized skills—riding, roping, and branding. The frontier journalist created, for the newspaper reader, a gigantic panorama—vast herds of cattle and horses; chuck wagons in the vanguard; numerous cowboy outfits, representing their owners' brands; dust, noise, and confusion—the roundup, the very heart of the range cattle industry.

The genuine cowboy is not always beautiful, but he is conversant with his business, knows every brand in his district at least and who owns it, is brave where bravery is most needed, that is in the discharge of his duty. To stand watch all night in a blizzard and hold a band of restless, bellowing cattle from stampeding, to ride all the next day half asleep in his saddle, to fall occasionally from his pony when the latter makes a mistake and steps into a prairie dog village, or to have a collar bone broken when fifty miles from a physician, are some of the features of cowboy life which the boys who run away from school to cross the Missouri do not know.[1]

A sign of spring on the range: Green grass is appearing, the festive cowboy dons his summer sombrero, straddles his restless bronco, and puts out over the plains to the distant cow-camp to get a job for the season.[2]

The cowboys are stocking up on tobacco, poor whiskey and cartridges preparatory to work on the spring roundups.[3]

The sun is beginning to lift its broad disk above the line which marks Eastern sky and land. It is a big, red sun and will become smaller and hotter as it climbs the dome of day. It is sunrise in the Cherokee strip and the first long slanting rays light up a rolling prairie, illimitable in expanse and stretching away until its irregular, wavy outline is masked against the sky. Now and then, and miles away, small clumps of stunted cedars and jack oaks make a dark green polka dot in the lighter colors of the grass, while a streak of thickly growing trees which serpentines across the scene marks the rocky channel of some water course. There will be a breeze today and the long grass now cool with dew, is already seen to bend and move under its influence.

Over to the north a mile, glances the white canvass cover of a wagon. It is the "chuck wagon" of a roundup outfit, and the thin blue smoke which rises near it shows that breakfast is going forward. To the left a herd of some 2,000 cattle of all sorts and sizes, from the complaining calf to the adult, is stretching slowly to the northwest, the members whereof are feeding as they move. Three cowboys in big hats, booted, spurred, with cotton handkerchiefs knotted loosely about their sun-browned necks and waists adorned with a cartridge-laden belt and its dependent six-shooter, ride slowly about on the sides and rear of the herd, never urging, but holding and pointing the animals in the proper direction. The present purpose of this outfit is to work to the nearest pen and brand the unmarked calves it has collected.

Branding is the most important feature of ranch life. It is the purpose of a ranch owner to keep his cattle within certain limits, which limits, however, expand and grow with his herds. These limits are called his range, and, being free pasture, are occupied, not only by his, but by the cattle of perhaps twenty other owners. Each owner, to protect himself has his brands, such as 7K, LX, LIT, etc. . . . These brands are on the left or right side of the animal, and owner's rights find further exposition in certain earmarks. These are divers methods of earmarking, well known to cattlemen, and are variously called swallow-fork, under-crop, under- or over-bite [bit],

ALL IN THE DAY'S WORK

under- or over-back, crop, half-crop, etc. The purpose of an earmark is greater safety to owners, but, aside from that, it is a labor-saver to the cowboys. Brands are difficult of discernment when cattle are crowded into herds, but both ears are ever pointed forward for inspection as soon as one attracts the animals' attention. This enables a rider, as he moves through a herd searching for the cattle of a certain brand, to find his animals with ease.

Branding goes on all the year round and as often as an unbranded calf is found. Every rider carries as part of his outfit a curved iron, not overlarge or long, which he calls his "running-iron," and at any time if he discovers an unmarked calf he ties it down, builds a fire and brands it.

The latter spring and earlier summer months is the epoch for the general roundup for the purpose of branding calves. This spring roundup is engaged in by all owners on a certain range in concert. They form among themselves an association, the books of which point to the number of calves the owner brands each year, and in making up these roundup outfits and in furnishing men, the proportion of each owner is determined by the number of calves he last branded. The number of men and ergo the outfits necessary to roundup, is determined by the number of cattle and calves shown by the association books. The number of men fixed on, they are broken up into outfits, each in charge of a range boss and accompanied by a cook and chuck wagon, which serves the dual purpose of purveying the grub and packing the blankets. Generally there are from eight to twelve men in each outfit, not all representing the same brand, but all taking their orders from the range boss of that outfit. Each rider has seven horses, and as these form quite a bunch, two of the men are detailed as "hoss-hustlers," and one of the two has charge of the bunch night and day, holding it near and carrying it along with the grub wagon as the cook moves camp.

The number of men and outfits being determined and the quota to be furnished by each brand being fixed, on a certain day they all start for the south side of the range. Each outfit takes an assigned post and all together making a line along the southern border of the range, reaching from its eastern to its western limits—sometimes a distance of one hundred and fifty miles. Then the round-up begins, all moving to the north, covering the entire country, and bringing the cattle along much on the same principle that a room is swept. Every man save cook and hoss-hustler rides to the right and left of his chuck wagon, so far as to touch the work of the outfits next in hand, and the cattle as fast as found are driven into a herd—one herd with each outfit. Two or three men are then detailed to hold and bring on the cattle thus collected, while the rest of the men still scour the range for more, every hour in the day seeing fresh additions to the general herd. This is hard work on horses, and a cowboy generally saddles three of his seven ponies each day, reserving the best one for hard and unusual work during dark and stormy nights.

The object of the roundup at this time is to brand, but as it first starts out it sweeps northward with all the cattle it can find; steers, bulls, cows and calves alike. When a bunch grows so large as to handle with difficulty, a stop is made to cut out all except the cows and calves, the cattle thus eliminated being turned loose on the range again. The work then proceeds as before, and this cutting out process is resorted to as fast as the size of a herd makes it necessary.

The purpose of bringing all the cattle as far northward as possible is to keep them on the proper range. Cattle in any voluntary movement of their own never work north and but seldom and slightly to the east or west. Every storm, however, coming as storms do from the north, sends the cattle to the south and unless turned back yearly, to drift over the same range again, the cattle of the entire Western country, from the Yellowstone south, would in time pack themselves into the southern extremity of Texas between the Rio Grande and the Gulf.

An outfit from the commencement points to some corral or branding pen. On its arrival there the marking of the calves begins. A branding pen proper and constructed for the purpose is circular in form and made of twelve foot palisades stuck endwise in the ground and flaring outward towards the top like the sides of a funnel....

There is one opening through which the cattle are driven, and the center of the corral is marked by a large snubbing post two feet in diameter. A roundup outfit on coming to the pen may meet some other outfit similarly bent, in which event they join herds and forces. As many of the cows and calves as will fill the corral are forced through the entrance and locked in, and then the fires are lighted and the fun begins. Every calf is branded with the brand on its mother, the roper calling the brand to the men at the fires, as he rides up dragging the victim. As fast as a pen full is branded it is turned loose on the range and the pen is refilled from the herd. The work is continued until completed when the outfit again moves northward and resumes the further collection and branding of the cattle until the range has been completely and thoroughly combed and the work performed.

Returning to overlook the outfit discovered in the Cherokee Strip, the scene is found to have changed but little. Breakfast is over and the rolls of blankets which had before been scattered about on the ground are now in the wagon. The cook is hitching on his four mules preparatory to a journey to a bunch of timber which conceals a spring, distant about seven miles, and where it is intended the next camp shall be.

This cook, like all good roundup cooks, is a great man and his favor is much sought after. His wages are about twice as large as a cowboy's, and in his way and business he is supreme. His duties are arduous, and besides cooking for the whole outfit, extend to hitching up and driving the four mules which impel the chuck wagon. This is done twice a day, to a noon and a night camp, the selection of which camps is performed by the range boss.

All through the blistering, sunburned day, the bunch of cattle, guarded by the men mentioned, crawl slowly to the north. Occasionally, at intervals, away over to the right or left, a small herd of cattle is discerned, and presently comes panting up to join the main herd. The cowboy who brought them seizes on the chance, and after a copious drink at the water barrel in the wagon, saddles a fresh horse and rides away. So the work, hard and driving on horses and men alike, goes patiently on.

At night a gently sloping hillside is picked to bed the cattle on. The range boss, assisted by the riders, who are all come in by now, rounds up and stops the herd, the horned members of which, first standing or slowly moving about at last lie down to sleep. The nine riders are marched off into three guards of three men each—the first to ride the herd until eleven o'clock, the second going on until three o'clock and the third holding the herd until morning.

"It looks like it might be a bad night," says the range boss, "so you all better ketch up and saddle your night ponies and be ready to go on herd any minute."

Supper of bacon, biscuit and canned sweet corn is over and every man's best horse, brought up and saddled, is left to wait any necessity which may arise. By eight o'clock each tired rider not on herd is asleep in his blankets. Two hours go by and the fire has burned out and no longer shows red in the darkness. Suddenly a flash of lightning blazes in the northwest and soon a dull rumble of thunder follows. In an instant every horned idiot is on his feet and moving uneasily about.

All hands are roused out and, grumbling, cursing, and blaspheming, ride to the herd. A stampede must be avoided for with so many grazing cattle in a herd it would be doubly disastrous. The riders—some ten in all—go circling about the herd at a trot or gallop, turning in any cattle which attempt to point out or get away and accompanying their efforts with whistle, song and shout. Meanwhile the rain begins and is presently falling in torrents. The lightning grows brighter and its flashes more frequent and at last as the storm readies its climax, it seems to quiver, leap and dance on the very horns of the cattle sans intermission. The thunder itself has grown into a constant, never ending roar, and the frightened herd with head upraised and glaring eyes push about ready on the instant to stampede. This would mean serious business, this turning $100,000 worth of cattle loose in pitch darkness, to break their scampering legs and frightened necks over precipice and rock. So the boys crowd upon the herd, still circling it, riding harder and singing louder than ever.

At last morning breaks and the storm, with the coming of the sun dies away. The herd again is composed and the tired boys, leaving it to stretch out to feed, come riding up to breakfast.[4]

In a roundup party of cowboys there are all sorts of men, some careful enough in their living, though the liveliness and dash of the work may make all alike seem reckless....

As I have said, some of the boys were careful to get their creature comforts, even in a country where it was raining every day and nights were frigid cold.... One old campaigner gave me the particulars of his daily life. He never took off his rubber coat, he told me while it was raining. He wore his leathern "chaps" all day long; he wore shoes, not boots, but also wore leggings. In the evening he was dry from head to foot, even if it had rained all day. He was especially careful to keep his feet dry. His bedding was not nearly so bulky as that of some others, but he thought it ample. Some men carry with them heavy coverlets, and even make up a kind of mattress. This man, however had three woolen blankets, a rubber blanket, and a piece of tarpaulin. In making up his bed at night he spread the rubber blanket on the ground first. Next he laid his tarpaulin so that its top was even with that of the rubber blanket. Then he stretched the tarpaulin out flat, and it was perhaps twenty feet long and eight wide. Next he put a coarse woolen double blanket down over the rubber and tarpaulin, leaving the lower half of the blanket rolled up at the feet. Another was placed in the same way. On top of these he laid another blanket. Then the half of the other two blankets which had been rolled up was drawn upon the rest. In this way a bag bottom was made at the foot of the bed, protecting the feet. The lower part of the tarpaulin was then turned up over everything. It reached a foot above the sleeper's head. Last of all the sides of the tarpaulin was doubled under the bed. The man worked his way down into this sack from the head, and no cold could penetrate it. I should add that before making his bed he dug away the ground to conform to the curve of his body, and he said it made him as comfortable as if he were in a feather bed.

On the roundup there is an abundance of canned fruit served out to the boys. The rest of the food is fresh meat, bacon, dried fruit, beans, soda biscuit, tea and coffee. But little can be said to the credit of the average cook. In crossing the plains fifteen years ago, I thought the race of bad cooks then at work must surely die out in this age of progress, but some of the same school are on the roundup this summer. I spoke to the careful chap I mentioned, and asked him why it was that the fine steaks were spoiled by being cut up into little bits and fried in black grease, when they could be just as easily broiled. He said he doubted if the cooks knew what a broiled steak was, but if the steaks were broiled a cowboy might walk off with a whole steak, eat of it what he could and throw the rest away, just as, when loaves of bread are baked, he breaks off a quarter of a loaf, munches a portion of it, and flips the rest at some fellow's head. This man said he always kept a piece of wire about the wagon and cooked his own steaks on the end of it over the coals.[5]

Having spent several years as a cowboy upon ranches in Western Texas, between the Brazos and Colorado ... I have thought a brief letter detailing old-time experience in running cattle and the way of the camp and range might prove of interest to your readers and preserve from oblivion the manners and customs of ranchmen and ranch life.... No wire fence enclosures then marked out the boundary line of any range. Possession of the range, its grass and water was held simply by occupancy.... Here, under employ, were some thirty cowboys as hardy and devil-may-care a set as ever roped a beef, branded a calf or mavericked a yearling. Good ponies, black coffee, light work, and abundance of fun rendered camp life agreeable to most of the hands. Six shooters and Winchester rifles were worn by all, and seldom used except in killing buffalo, deer or turkey, or in an occasional personal difficulty brought about by some incoming outfit locating upon range already claimed. Then there was no market for cattle except by a long drive. Stock could be bought at from $5 to $7 around, and by buying brands and locations by range county, they were disposed of at much lower figures. It was soon after the memorable disasters of 1873, when heavy losses had been sustained by the handlers of trail cattle north; there was no such thing then as either close herding or line-riding. Hands were so numerous that duties were not confining, and more of them could be found at the frontier towns or groceries "bucking at monte," throwing chuck-a-luck,[6] or playing billiards, than about camp. Rounding up and cutting out time, in the spring and fall, were the only times of real hard work in the year. An occasional breeze would stir up the blood of the boys, when a gang of rustlers, Indians or Mexicans made a raid after ponies or cattle, and a pursuing party took the trail to corral them.[7]

When compared with the lot of the average farm laborer in this state, that of the cowboy is full of ease and comfort. Coming home, I see farms neatly fenced, with well-kept buildings, and with other evident signs of thrift. The women, coarsely dressed, were in some cases paddling about in the barnyards, milking the cows; the men dressed in a pair of overalls, supported, perhaps by a pair of suspenders cut from the salvage of a piece of cloth, with a cotton shirt and an old hat, were working barefooted in the muddy fields. What they do get is the result of hard and constant toil under hot suns, in the mud or dust as the case may be. The only advantage they have over the cowboy of the plains is in eating off a table in company with women, and in having dry and comfortable beds in which to sleep. As a rule the cowboy is warmly clad, rides a pony in the care of which he does not spend in a year as much time as the farmer does in a week over his horses. The ponies are seldom, if ever, curried. As a general thing each herder has four ponies, furnished sometimes by the herder himself, but usually by the owner of the cattle. The cowboy lives upon the clear, grassy plains, and can, if he will, keep himself clean and comfortable.

There I think they have an advantage over the average farmer. The cowboy works for a man who has capital, is making great profits, and is naturally liberal in the use of money. The result is that there is plenty of food and a great enough variety. Many of the cooks are skilled in their art and in spite of the fact that they have comparatively few utensils, and frequently only a fire of buffalo chips to cook by in the open air, they get meals which would shame the cookery of many a farmer's wife. I have eaten in the camp, puddings, which, to put it mildly, are seldom surpassed for excellence in our city hotels. Fresh meats of the best quality they can have at any time, and canned fruits and vegetables are found at almost every camp. Coffee, syrup, sugar and tea are among the comforts found, while of the more substantial kind of food there is no lack in either quantity or quality.[8]

... While on the range [the cowboys] are found in gangs of from six to perhaps ten men, under the guidance of a boss herder. Their outfit generally consists of two six-shooters, a Winchester repeating rifle and a knife. While herding cattle they seem to be hardened against all kinds of weather, and any one of them will throw himself down on the ground at night with only a blanket wrapped around him. A gang will generally have charge of about 5,000 cattle, which are allowed to graze on a range ten miles square. At the best point on each range an adobe hut is built, which is the headquarters for the entire party. There they stay, and at regular periods a couple start out to follow the dividing line between that and the other ranges to look for any indications of cattle having passed over. If a trail is seen one of the two follows it up as quickly as possible. This search may last for days, and then if the lost cattle are found in charge of another gang of cowboys a free fight ensues, in which somebody is pretty sure to be brought down. Then with the recaptured cattle the attacking party, if successful, returns to await the next skirmish.[9]

From the father of the family to the youngest son, each has his favorite cowhorse, a saddle and bridle of rawhide, a horse-hair lariat, a pair of bell-spurs, and a cow whip. They live on their simple jerked beef, clabber and corn bread; and one, perhaps, goes riding, to no particular benefit, since the herds are tethered with a lariat long as the wind. The others in the dewiest hours plough some weeds from the cornfield, and then sit on the cow pen, where one boy holds a frantic calf by the tail, while another practices on it with the *lazo*.[10]

"Now sling yourselves together." This was the salutation of the cowboy who acted as cook. He attended to his duty with his spurs on. The table was bare, the plates and cups were of tin, and the coffee was in a pot so black that night seemed day beside it. The meat was in a stewpan, and the milk was in a tin pail. The tomatoes were fresh from a can, and the biscuits were fresh from the oven. Delmonico never served a meal that was better relished. The boys have a way of putting sweet breads, liver, a bit of tenderloin, marrow, and some calves' brains in a dish that do honor to the Manhattan Club's *chef*. This was the nicest bit of tenderloin, too, in keeping for a guest.... The milk was certainly as sweet a draught as ever nourished a hungry man. By a smoky oil lamp, far from civilization, a Sunday night meal was enjoyed in peace.

Here were several genuine cowboys, and more came loping into camp later. They were used to rough life, and, as this was a quiet night, when there was no storm to make the cattle drift over the boundary, they ranged themselves on a bench before a cook stove, where the mesquite roots were crackling into a hot blaze, and without swagger or bluster, horse play or boisterousness, chatted quietly and good-humoredly about their rides over their ranches, and their droves of cattle, and the roundups of the cattlemen in the vicinity.[11]

A staple article of diet on the ranges of the west in summer time was variously known as jerky, *carne seco* and dried beef. It was prepared by cutting up the meat into long strips about an inch in diameter. These strips were salted or dipped into hot brine, in order to keep the flies off, and then hung on a riata stretched in the hot sun. Only a few hours exposure was necessary to thoroughly dessicate the meat, which was then carefully packed away in boxes or in bags. It was a very palatable article of diet when properly prepared, much better than salt meat in hot summer.

The method generally preferred was to hammer the jerky on a piece of iron or on a smooth stone, then cut it across in small powdery fragments by means of a sharp pocket knife. Then it was put on the fire with enough water to almost fill the frying pan, and skimmed when the water had boiled. When the water was almost gone, if the cow camp boasted of an egg or two, it was stirred in. If not, a little flour went into the mess, with abundant seasoning, embracing a red pepper if one was to be had, and the stew was ready in a minute.

As care was used to eliminate all the stringy portions when cutting up the dried meat, the result was excellent indeed, much appreciated by the hungry range rider. The best jerky was made from deer or antelope meat. Vension appeared to have a granular structure that rendered it easily powdered after being dried, and it was usually better appreciated dried than fresh.[12]

The branding finished, a heifer was killed for dinner and fires built, round which the vaqueros gathered, roasting small pieces of meat on long sharpened sticks. The rich mahogany of the swarthy faces, brightened into a coppery glow next the firelight, the fierce black eyes, the glitter of the white teeth, the free gestures and picturesque dress gave a strange foreign aspect to the scene. It required no great stretch of the imagination to fancy that we were beholding the orgies of a party of banditti, and our own faces would have done well for the terrified prisoners as we shudderingly watched several of the Mexicans tear out the small intestines from the carcass of the heifer, and, smoking as they were from the heat of the newly killed animal, throw them into the coals to roast, and greedily devour them. This dish is highly regarded among the Mexicans and is known by the relishing name of "marrow-guts."[13]

... Eating was no delicate business with these centaurs. It had the certainity and savagery of a farm threshing crew. There were no tables and no frills like cups or butter knives. Some ate standing, others sat on rolls of bedding. Every man helped himself.

They were rough, iron-sided fellows—mainly Missourians—and were mostly less than 30 years of age. They wore rough, business overalls and colored shirts—quite generally gray, with dirt and sweat. Their boots were short and very high heeled, and their wide hats and "slickers" were the only uniform articles of dress. Revolvers, bearskin leggings and cartridge belts have been discarded, as they were considered an affectation.

As night fell the men built a great bonfire, and surrounding it sang and boasted and told stiff yarns and exploded in obscenity till time to turn in. Then they packed into the tents like sardines and became quiet in sleep—they were quiet at no other time in the day.

As we were eating breakfast the next morning, everybody feeling damp and stiff in the joints, there came the dull throbbing of hoofs and down the valley the horse wrangler came, shouting "Horses." Before him the troop was rushing like a wild herd.

Others took up the cry "Horses! Get your bridles!"

The wrangler rounded the drove toward the tents, whence issued the riders, lariat in hand. The horses are all bronco grades, small, alert, flat-limbed, wild-eyed and tricky. They have to be caught with the rope each day. The men surround them, herding them into a compact squad. The riders advanced into the herd one by one, with coiled ropes ready, and noosed and pulled out their best horses, for the ride was to be hard.

One man tried three times for a wicked-looking buckskin bronco. The men jeered him, but he noosed him at last and drew him out with wild eyes rolling. The saddles went on meanwhile, the horses wincing at the cinch. At last all were secured, the riders swung into the saddle and dashed away with that singular, swift, gliding, sidewise gallop so characteristic of these men and their ponies.

They were off now for some seven hours of the hardest riding in a blinding fog and a thick falling rain. We plunged into a wide, ragged-walled canon for a five-mile ride and then came out upon a small valley. Here the boss drew up and the riders grouped themselves about him. He lifted his hand and pointed west and called off four names—the riders dashed away into the steep gulch and were out of sight in a moment. Four went to the east, six to the south and two remained with the wrangler to keep the herd of relay horses.

For a couple of hours the bunching place was silent; the rain dropped from the rim of my hat and ran down my slicker. The creek roared sleepily but sullenly below. I rode up a hill to see if I could see any of the riders, but the great curling masses of wool-like fog hid everything from me. I came suddenly upon a half dozen cattle in the mist and rain—they rushed away, snuffling like elk, and stones rattling behind them.

I returned to the valley and waited. In a short time I heard a trample and hallo and the clatter of hoofs, and over a shingly ridge came a herd of fifty or more bawling, snorting cattle. Behind them, riding like mad, were a couple of herders. They came down the bank with a rush, the horses coasting on their haunches, the shingly-stones grinding and clattering behind them, while their riders sat calm and easeful in the tumult.

One by one the other hands came in out of the gray, wild obscurity, and a herd of several hundred of excited cattle circled and fought and bellowed in a compact mass. At the west the herd began to move toward the corral and toward the camp, wading streams, plunging into gulches and rising tumultuously over ridges. The jocular, boyish voices of the herders rang out. The blur of their yellow slickers came to the eye through the rain with a glow-like dull flame. There was in the scene something big and strong and manly. At such moments these riders are completely admirable.

These hardy horses and their powerful and reckless men are a product of these hills as truly as the cattle. It is not a lonely life—it does not appear to be a very high sort of civilization. It will give way before civilization; it makes men rough and coarse, and yet it carries with it something fine and wholesome. It has retreated from the plains to the mountain valleys—from the mountain tops themselves, where grain and fruit will not grow. At an altitude twice as high as the peaks of the Alleghenies, these cattlemen have fixed their ranges. Whether the settler or the miner will dislodge him from these rigorous and rugged altitudes remains to be seen.[14]

Having obtained the lead of the herd, [the cowboy] does not attempt to stop the now frantic horde of cattle, but rides steadily in the lead, singing a hymn or a song or perhaps yelling at the highest pitch of his voice. Having attracted the attention of the leaders, he gradually veers off to right or left—the herd following—and in a short time leads the rushing herd into a circle, which he gradually contracts until all are rushing around in a compact body.

Each cowboy as he rides around the herd sings or shouts a sort of lullaby, old Methodist hymns being the most popular, although too, old fashioned negro minstrel songs have been found equally effective in soothing the breast of the wild Texas steer.[15]

One by one the herders drop away to camp as the cattle grow quiet, till but two are left riding in opposite directions about the sleeping herd, each singing vigorously, for the double purpose of warding off sleep and keeping the herd aware of their guard. The songs are continued by the successive watch till dawn, each singer pursuing his time with a glorious independence of harmony with his mate; yet in the distance, as we sit beside the campfire or in waking moments at night, it is a cheerful, vigilant sound. In the cowboys' dialect, "singing to 'em" has become a synonymous expression for night herding.[16]

The long twilight sets in, gradually melting into the shades of night; silence reigns over the prairie, broken only by the far-off yelp of the prowling coyote, or the crackling of a dry twig as some restless steer moves about in the sagebrush. The tired cowboy, the events of the day briefly discussed with the after-supper pipe by the glowing embers of the fire, spreads his bedding on the ground, rolls his blanket about him, and, his head resting in the seat of his saddle, is soon buried in the dreamless sleep of the hardy frontiersman.[17]

Get up in the morning when you are first called, or you will be apt to rise rapidly on the toe of the foreman's boot. Roll up your bed snug, tie it up tight and firm and lay it near the wagon convenient for loading. Take a good wash. It is most refreshing and prevents sore eyes and other things. If there is no pool or stream of water don't use up all the water in the water butt, remember good drinking water can't be found everywhere, and it is considerable trouble for the cook to fill that butt. Don't open your eyes under water. If it is very dry and dusty and in alkali country don't wash your face at all. It is the experience of those dusty sons of Adam, the bullwackers, that washing the eyeballs in cold water gives you cold in the eyes, makes the lids rough and harsh, induces granulated eyelids, and causes very sore eyes. If you have drawn water from the water barrel just leave the faucet open and the water dropping out and wasting, if you want to get a blessing from the cook. Leave dirty water in the wash pan if you want your brother cowpuncher to love you.

. . . Make yourself spry and useful. Such things are generally relegated to the patient, despised tenderfoot, but you'll lose nothing by such little extra attentions to the cook. Sometimes when you ride into camp hungry, tired, wet, cold and indifferent whether you are alive or dead, you'll be apt to find kept warm for your Royal Bengal Bigness some nice strong coffee and may be a little side dish like brains, or sweetbreads, kidneys, heart, liver or the luscious luxury marrow-gut. They are not regular grub, because they won't go all around, but they are cook's perquisities, and he can give them to whom he likes. . . .

Never rush for grub till you have made things up in shape. If the horses are up before breakfast, saddle up, etc., Yes, and don't throw away more than you eat. It would bust any boy in camp if he had to pay the grub

ALL IN THE DAY'S WORK

bills for the roundup outfit for one season. Don't make a habit of telling vulgar yarns at grub time. Very probably everybody will laugh at the time, but when they get off to themselves and begin to think things over they are sure to sorter lose their good opinion of a chap who seasons his grub with dirty talk. When you are done running your hash mill put your knife, fork and other grub tools on your plate and set them up on the cupboard lid, handy for the cook. If you have time help the cook wash and wipe up the dishes and kettles, and help him to load the mess wagon.

In the evening catch up your quietest, most reliable pony for a night horse. Stake him out to good grass within easy reach....

Find out what relief you are to go on, who to call and where they will sleep, so you won't be waking up everybody in camp to find the right man. It makes a cowpuncher fighting mad to wake him up from his needed sleep when not wanted. Double with some boy on the same relief as yourself and make down your boar's nest so as not to take up all the room in the tent. If there is no tent pick out a high, level spot of ground so that you will sleep dry if it rains. A tarpaulin of one solid thick piece of canvass 8 x 16 or 9 x 18 feet is indispensable. Sleep with pants on and stuffed in your socks. Never take the spurs off your boots. Put your boots down first, your chaps on top of them and your jacket over all for a pillow. It's nice to leave your boots outside in the weather and find when you try to pull them on in a hurry that they are either froze stiff as dry rawhide or full of rainwater. Put your hat on top of your blankets under the tarpaulin to keep it from blowing away. A handkerchief tied around your head is not very healthy either when the thermometer is away below zero, or away up hugging 120 close....

Have everything ready to rise up, fling on, and skin out like a flash of lightning if there is a stampede, or to get out on time when you are called to go on guard. Remember that the safety of the herd depends on good ponies and good men ready to roll the instant they are needed. If the cattle are restless and there is liability of a stampede, you'd better go to bed just as you are—hat, jacket, pants, boots, spurs, chaps; and if snowing, or raining, your slicker, too—all on. A cowpuncher can sleep anyhow....

There are times when a boy is nearly petered out, and he gets so worn out that human nature gets to be brute nature and the boy is mean and snappish as the old Devil could wish, but you want to be civil and obliging whenever you can. And when you move you want to rustle around and move quick. A slow poke is out of his element in the cattle business, sure....[18]

The rapid strides which ranch owners have made in the science of cattle growing must cause them to often feel elated at the success that has been attained by them in curtailing expenses and increasing the profits of the business. The losses from reckless handling, from drifting, from estrayed stock, from infertility of their cows, caused by impotent or scant supply of bulls, all, have been so diminished, as of themselves to render the profit side of the account larger by far than any reasonable man could have anticipated, and have served as a foil to ward off the growing tendency of the pioneer and experienced growers, to become careless and indifferent as to the expense side of the account. In the old style of ranch management, as the facilities for reaching ranch supplies were poor and the supply stores were remote from the ranch and range, the cattle owner bought as few necessaries as he could obtain. Coffee, tobacco, blankets, saddles, bacon and flour—the indispensable articles —covered about the range of his purchases. These cost him fabulous prices, as the merchant from whom he bought held the vantage ground. The credit system, that great bane of the producer's life, was freely indulged and in addition to the high prices paid for supplies, a heavy interest was added on the money value of the goods, so the articles required on the ranch actually cost the stockman one hundred per cent more than the local cash buyer had to pay. The profit on sales in great part went to pay these enormous expenses. This led into furnishing only dugouts, rough fare and the bare necessities to sustain life to their employes. The sturdy cowboy, often with only the grass for a bed and the sky for a covering, a cup of black coffee, a pone of hard bread and a slice of fat bacon for a meal, a bucking pony and many hard days' rides, passed his life, either in solitude or having an occasional glimpse at the worst phases of frontier town life. Now, by the advent of railroads, the organization of stock associations and the nearness and cheapness of all the material out of which comforts can be secured, we know that every consideration of a moral and pecuniary nature—inducement beneficial to pride and pocket—will lead cattle owners to better provide for both the mind and bodily comforts of their hands. Good, comfortable ranch houses should take the place of tents and dugouts; better beds should be ready for the cowman when he reaches the ranch after a long, hard day's ride in the rain and sleet; generous, wholesome food, properly cooked and served in neat, clean dishes should be placed before him.[19]

Frequently of late we have heard the cowboys complain that the work on the range is not what it used to be; and this reminds us that down in Texas and out in New Mexico or Arizona, the same complaint is made, and the Sidney (Tex.) *Independent*, speaking of this, says: "Cowboys don't have as soft a time as they did eight or ten years ago," remarked one of the fraternity. "I remember when we sat around the fire the winter through and didn't do a lick of work for five or six months of the year, except to chop a little wood to build a fire to keep warm by. Now we go on the general roundup, then the calf roundup, then comes haying—something that the old-time cowboy never dreamed of—then the beef roundup and the fall calf roundup, and gathering bulls and weak cows, and after all this a winter feeding hay. I tell you times have changed. You didn't hear the sound of a mowing machine in this country ten years ago. We didn't have any hay, and the man who thinks he is going to strike a soft job now in a cow camp is woefully left."[20]

PANHANDLE, March 12th, '85

TO THE COWBOY.

I see in your issue of Feb. 28th an item headed, "For the Cowboys." I am one of the boys; please let me give your readers my opinion of the matter. The main reason the boys "blow in" is because they cannot invest, as they could years ago. Ten years ago, when I first saw a cow camp, the owners encouraged us to invest our wages in cows. They were worthless then, we thought. Now if a man owns cattle the big companies won't give him work. They think a man will steal from them. That is where they miss it. When a boy has a few cattle on a range, his scatter with the rest. He will ride for his own, and of course he will get the outfit's cattle too. He will naturally take an interest in his work, for we are not all fools. We know when we have a good thing and a man can't maverick like he could some time ago. There are plenty of boys that would invest if they could. As the old saying is, a man that saves for himself, will save for the outfit. . . .

"BIG SPURS"[21]

On Tuesday of last week we had visitors. Six of the boys from Hardman's ranch descended on us like a wolf on the fold. They meant to stay, they said, until they had eaten us out. From the way they handled the dinner that day it looked as if their visit would be mighty short. As they brought sundry flasks of their western kill-at-a-hundred-yards, they were received with open arms. After dinner everybody was feeling good and the fun began. In our ranch there are only three rooms—kitchen, dining room and sleeping apartment. The walls of the dining room are covered every inch with pictures from illustrated papers. Worthies of all races and condition lend their august presence to our meals, and beauties of all styles look down upon the admiring faces of the cow punchers.

"Say, Hank," said the leader of the visitors to our cook, "that old duffer in the wig is too *snide*. Watch us bore him." Thereupon that irreverent herder pulled out his six-shooter and shot Benjamin Franklin square in the eye. That opened the ball. Our foreman was away, and

ALL IN THE DAY'S WORK 83

our boys and the visitors did just as they pleased. The whole crowd began to blaze away at the pictures on the wall.

There was a picture of Guiteau posted above the kitchen door. I believe that every fellow in the room shot into him. "That pretty girl's nose is too long," one would say, and then proceed to shave off pieces with the revolver. The ballet girls received special attention. After shooting there was mighty little left of their scant clothing. When they had paid their respects to the picture gallery, the crowd was ripe for any mischief. The ranch we live in was built last fall. Up to the severely cold weather, half of us had lived down at the old ranch, about half a mile distant, but when winter set in it was deserted. The boys feared that when spring opened the old rickety building might be fixed up and again made habitable. Now that the foreman was away they determined to spoil the chances of ever having to live in it again, and at the same time to have some fun. Accordingly, the whole crowd mounted their mustangs and ran a race down to the old building. Some of the boys wanted to burn it, but that was decided too tame a way of disposing of it. Hank Carson, our cook and the mischief-maker, proposed that it be blown up. The plan was hailed with shouts of delight. One of the boys was sent back for a bag of powder. When it was brought a train of powder was laid along the floor against each of the walls, and carried out of the door down the path. Then the whole party, with the exception of Hank, mounted their mustangs and drew up off at a safe distance. Hank touched off a light to the train, then vaulted into his saddle and dashed out of danger. That building just bumped itself in the middle and the roof sailed skywards, while the four walls went skipping about over the prairie. How that crowd did cheer and howl with delight! They all agreed that it was the biggest picnic they had had since the lynching of a horse thief in the summer. Then the parties separated and rode home. The owners of the building are now about to send a little bill of damages to each of us. On the whole the winter is not a perfectly uninteresting season out here.[22]

BREAKIN' BRONCS

Among the cowboys the man with the specialized talent for breaking broncos occupied a position of respect. Often he was not a permanent member of an outfit but moved from camp to camp and made his livelihood by breaking the cow pony. Bronco busting demanded skill, time, and patience. Although many a "buster" lacked the latter two requirements, he "cooled" the fiery-blooded wild pony with varying degrees of success.

Mark Twain, Bill Nye, the Texas Siftings, and in fact many wits of our Western experience, have paid their humorous respects to the energetic equine, known as the bucking "Bronco."

Fun has been poked at his pitchings, his lunges laughed at, and his antics under the persistent cowboy have been, by inexperienced "tenderfeet," ofttimes pronounced a fraud. This is because they who have made this charge know nothing of the nature of the "Bronco," and are not familiar with his early life and training.

The idea that the tough little horse we see trying to dislodge his rider is a trained trickster, taught to make the vices of his race a cause of laughter for thoughtless persons, has gained a foothold in the public mind, because they see him making lunges for liberty day after day in some Wild West exhibition.

Those who know the "Bronco" know why he bucks; they know that he is in this manner protesting a condition he finds himself confronted with, and against which he inaugurates active rebellion. . . .

The "Bronco" is a pioneer. In his veins flows the blood of an ancestry on the backs of which were borne the Spanish invaders, who, centuries ago, subjugated the people of the gentle Montezuma and conquered the sun-kissed valleys of the south land.

Escaping from their Castilian masters, on the broad "pampas" of Texas, in the kindly vales of New Mexico and Arizona, the ancestors of the "bronco" multiplied into limitless herds of wild horses.

From these ownerless herds the Indian made captives

ALL IN THE DAY'S WORK

and became a beggar on horseback. By the privations the wild horses endured with their savage captors, who took them into a more northerly climate, they became the hardy, compact Indian pony.

On the plains of Texas they were known as "mustangs," while under the kindly skies and fed on the nutritious grasses of the far Pacific valleys, they grew to be the bony, loose-jointed, tireless "cayuse" of the coast region.

"Bronco" is a Spanish word, and signifies rough. "Bronco caballo," rough horse.

These wild horses years ago by capture became the property of the stockman who had invaded the region where they roamed free.

These wild horses were inbred with the hardy horse on the backs of which the hunter, trapper, soldier, and stockman had been carried into their country, and the result was the bronco of today.

Until he is four or five years old he roams as free-footed and as halterless as did his wild ancestors; he is foaled on the boundless prairies; he has a colthood as unrestrained as the antelope that shares his range. Summer and winter he feeds on the sweet grasses, drinks the pure water that comes roaring and murmuring down from the eternal snows of the ice-capped peaks of the Rockies; his tough sinews strengthen and his great lungs distend like a bellows with the draughts of pure air he drinks. He has probably never seen a man on foot in his life.

But a day comes when some cowboy says, "I guess I might as well ride that fellow." Then the young bronco finds he is pursued by a band of yelling, rope-throwing cow punchers. He finds his feet inextricably entangled in rope fetters, or the cruel thongs choking him into oblivion.

When he regains his feet he finds strange trappings fastened to him; a yelling steel-heeled cowboy astride him; frantic with fright he makes the best fight for freedom he knows how. He rears, he plunges, he pitches, he runs, and he jumps stiff-legged in heroic efforts to dislodge his yelling rider. Sometimes he succeeds, but far oftener the strong hand, firm seat and the iron bit gain the victory.

But the spirited bronco fights again, and again, if he ever quits depends on his spirit, his temper and the handling he receives. As a rule no friendly glance, no soothing voice, no caressing hand, no sugar-laden palm is extended to the pony on the plains; but in battle royal, with rasping rope, tightening "sinch," cruel bit and wicked spur, his fate is unconditional surrender, or fight to the death.

Thus, in the start, every "Bronco" is a "bucker"; some fight for years, have to be broken every time they are saddled, and a few never quit, but fight on to the end.

I have known a horse that had been "bucking" for years to suddenly and without apparent cause, cease, become as decorous as a deacon, and continue on his good behavior for years, then as suddenly fall into his old tricks and inaugurate an earnest effort to dislocate some rider's backbone. But there is generally an apparent cause for a "bucker's" backsliding. A new rider, new trappings, a strange sight, or any of the hundreds of causes that have been known to stampede staid old family steeds.

The bronco and his bone-breaking pastime is not an equine picture that would inspire the brush of Bonheur, Detaille, or Schreyer. Though his efforts to dislodge his rider are indeed royal battles, they are more marked for vigorous action than for picturesque poses. Yet he demonstrates that he is a foeman worthy the steel of the athletic, fearless "cowboy" who conquers him.

When a bronco out on the ranges of the West, by bad handling becomes thoroughly vicious, has earned the name of the "Colorado Cloudburst," the "Dakota Demon," the "Montana Man-Killer," or some such reassuring title, and there is not a "bronco buster" on the range who will tackle him, and he is not worth two trade dollars to anyone, they ship him to a "Wild West" show. There he meets with a welcome and finds a good home, if he kicks about it and bucks against it, and Eastern people see this outlaw of the range and think they know all about the bronco when they have only seen his vices. He has virtues in abundance.[23]

Every season the same old problem is presented to

small cattle owners, whom shall we get to break our horses? To the man that buys horses for his hands to use, simply as he would buy hobble-rope or grub, it may not matter so much, but to the aforesaid small owner, with his little bunch of graded mares and colts, it is often a serious question. First came the cowpuncher and bronco buster, later came the "kid-gangs," and finally evolution will bring us stock hands and horse men. The fashion of pounding a bronco into a quiescent state with a club is happily less fashionable this year than last. The ancient method of "spurring and quirting between jumps" the unfortunate victim, is giving way to common sense, and let us hope next year will see the man that whoops and bawls relegated to the shades of "innocuous desuetude."

Many small ranchers cannot afford the prices that a good breaker earns, and so will often give the use of a horse for a year, to perhaps some irresponsible incompetent buster that should be fined heavily for every horse he ruins. At the end of the year the poor, misused, dumb skeleton is returned to the rancher with the usual twaddle about "he'll buck some, it can't be helped; it's their nature." Rot and nonsense! The mustang of Texas and New Mexico, the cayuse of Wyoming and Utah, and the Indian ponies of Arizona and Southern California, are all from the same hardy, intelligent and well-blooded ancestors, and a good stock hand may defy any locality to furnish him with a perfectly green horse, that cannot be broken without acquiring the habit of pitching and bucking.

If the following hints can be used by anybody they are welcome, as they are neither copyrighted nor patented. The bronco should be hauled in a corral by himself, as other horses or men serve to distract his attention from the subject in hand. Cross hobble him if he is disposed to fight or be mean. Then, with a blanket, rub and stroke him from his ears to his heels. Stroke him with the hand and voice, and remember his ignorance of you and have patience. Show him that harm cannot come to him so long as he is near you, and that the best friend he has is his trainer. While he is still hobbled put the saddle on and draw it off over his hips, up on his neck, cinch it, and flop the stirrups on to the seat and back again. Do everything easily and naturally. Don't whoop, nor holler whoa too much. After he is accustomed to your movements, take off the hobbles and flop the stirrups some more. Tie your hackamore, get into the saddle and turn him loose. Don't attempt to guide him with the bit at first, but use the hackamore entirely. Use the quirt and hit but sparingly until he learns what the punishment is for. Take plenty of time and do your work well, and it will save lots of time some day when time is money. Remember that no two horses are exactly alike, and govern your training accordingly. In short, break your horses to use, in preference to busting them for show. Many horses show no disposition to buck or pitch, but will kick, bite, or strike wickedly. With many it is simply nervousness, and fear lest they shall be hurt. Biters and strikers generally belong in this class. Where kicking degenerates into a regular thing it should be checked as speedily as possible. Kicking from nervousness may be checked by allowing the kicker to run the range a couple of days with a straw-stuffed gunny sack tied to his tail and dangling against his heels. Where a horse kicks from inate viciousness, however, the old Spanish way will be found about as effectual as any. Pass a surcingle around the horse just back of the withers. Then two stout cords to the heels up between the surcingle and body, making fast to a plain bit in the mouth. Then give him opportunities to kick, and after he has jerked his jaw a few times he will conclude that an easier method of doing his work may be found.

I have found cayenne pepper for confirmed biters, about the best cure that I can use. Strikers can be taught best by a small hand whip or quirt.

If care and patience are used in the first handling of a bronco, it will save many an unnecessary hour of after breaking. If better plans than mine can be given, by all means let us have them that our knowledge and stock may both be improved and we thus progress and not degenerate.[24]

The cowboy is the real horseman. He keeps his seat under circumstances that would result in unhorsing any one not having much nerve and constant practice. When a yearling steer held by a rope to the pommel jerks the saddle halfway round the body, the cowboy must stay on the pony or run the gauntlet of wild steer and scared pony. When the half-tamed bronco, just caught from a "cavvy" of one or two hundred horses, indulges in ten minutes' spell of bucking, the cowboy must keep his seat or have a rebellious pony always on his string. When the cowboy dashes after a running steer, and the steer turns like a billiard ball, when it hits a cushion, the cowboy must turn with the pony, who runs with the steer, and not shoot over his head. When the pony stands on his hind legs "on a tin plate," and paws the air with his fore feet, the cowboy must cling to him.[25]

Judging from what we have seen and experienced, we should think that a careful estimate would place the value of all the bronco horses in the world, at about seven dollars and a half, running measure. Their only merit is their excessive playfulness; and they have the happy faculty of using all four legs with the agility of an infant drummer. If horse meat was recommended as a passable substitute for beef, the bright idea would certainly occur to us, that contractors for Indian rations might make broncos useful. Have you ever seen the boys at work breaking broncos? If you have not, a fiendish delight is in store for you. Get out on some ranch where a half dozen of this sweet breed of equines are undergoing this process. They take to it kindly—and they will *take to you,* if you happen to get within striking distance of their fore or hind legs. They have excellent teeth, too, as a "torn, but flying," pair of pants in our groaning wardrobe, sadly attest. And then, after a bronco, is "well-broken," and you buy him and take him home, he reminds you, in a variety of delightful ways, that he has not forgotten—will never forget—his natural instincts. He is troubled periodically with the "buck-fever"—all hunters know what that is. You mount suddenly, and as suddenly discover that you are *not* mounted. You try it again, then sit down on the ground for awhile and bathe your head in arnica. While thus employed, your mind is kept active in contemplating the gyrations, the plunges, and kicks of the noble animal in which you claim a proprietary interest. You may possibly experience a feeling of relief if your favorite bronco falls suddenly upon his head, dislocating his beautiful neck, and quietly subsiding into a dead horse. It is about the only safe and peaceful position a bronco was ever known to be in.

The hide of a bronco may be worth something to hang on a fence in a sparsely settled region, as an evidence that somebody has done something for civilization in that desolate spot; but no respectable dog would be guilty of barking at it. If there was a glue factory in the region, broncos might be utilized to some extent; but until one of those savory institutions is established here, a whole herd of broncos may be accounted as of no more value than a patch of sage brush. We mean it.[26]

"How do you break broncos?" asked a *Tribune-Republican* reporter of a well-known horseman yesterday afternoon.

"Why, sometimes we use an axe and sometimes a stone-crusher," replied the horseman, who was real funny when he felt good natured. " ... when you come to that, a bronco never becomes like a well-behaved horse until he is ready to drop into his grave or the hands of rendering works probably from extreme old age.

"The first thing is to catch one. You know they run wild like other colts until we get ready to try and use 'em. Unless you use a lariat you'll find that catching a bronco in a field or even in a corral isn't a spiritualist's picnic. When you've got him you must mount him, and that ain't no coming home from the picnic by moonlight, neither.

"He will dance and kick and kick and dance like all possessed. If you are patient he will stop still time enough for you to get near enough to get on, after a little while, say about an hour. Of course he's got no idea what you want to do, for nobody ever tried that on him before.

"So as soon as you make a jump he'll jump sideways about eight or ten feet, and if you've got him by a halter or a lariat he'll jerk you about twenty feet unless you let go.

If you do let go you'll not catch him again for about a week unless you've been doing all this in a brick building. If it's any other kind of building he'll kick the side of it out and get away.

"Suppose that you get on him finally, you won't need a bridle the first time; just grab him by the hair and lay down. If you can, get your feet locked underneath him at the same time. If you were nailed onto him, he'd get you off him in a few minutes anyway, but you have to give him as much of a tussle as you can.

"The first thing he'll do is to run like lightning, and shake himself from side to side. A part of the time he'll run sideways, and a part backwards, and now and then he'll go a little ways straight ahead. If you keep on all this time he'll stop suddenly when he's going full tilt, with all four legs as stiff as iron bars. If that don't throw you off his back, it'll jerk your entrails into your mouth. I've seen a man thrown twenty or thirty feet off a bronco's back before now.

"For the first lesson all you can do is to try and keep on him as long and as often as possible. After you've done this several days you can try and get a bridle onto him and bits into his mouth. You'll have a circus getting them fixed and another one when you try a saddle, and a side show attached when you try to hitch him to a wagon, but all you've got to do is to make him know that you intend to be the boss, and in time, if you are patient enough, you'll get your bronco as near broke as it's possible to break one of the nasty little cusses."[27]

"It's all bosh, this talk about cowboys learning to enjoy the sport of riding bucking horses," said a reformed cowboy. "Riding a bucking horse is like having boils—you never get thoroughly used to it. When you hear a fellow say he would like to ride a bucking horse he is either a liar or a greenhorn. The first day I ever went out with a herd of cattle I was dumped nine times because of the presence of a cactus burr in my saddle blanket. I have seen but one man that had grit enough to sit a real bucking horse until it had bucked all it wanted to, and he was bleeding at the nose, mouth and ears when they took him off the horse at the end of a half-hour's struggle. As a general thing a cowboy will pull a horse's head up, wind the reins around the saddle horn, take a firm grip on the saddle with his hands, and then rowel the bucker until the animal becomes convined that it is better to behave than to buck."[28]

The bronco pony can not well be judged collectively. Individuals of them vary almost as much as individual men. Some of them, after awhile get perfectly gentle, not many. The genuine Spanish pony, untainted with any other strain of blood, generally requires to be broken over again every time it is ridden. When it begins to get fat its wickedness increases. It is like a great many people, who can be religious in times of adversity, but are apt to lose it when prosperity returns. At least two cow ponies out of three will pitch a man, but it may be because the cowboys actually encourage them in it. The average cowboy likes to ride a tolerably bad pony, and the pony shapes its conduct accordingly. After all the cow pony is a hard working, painstaking little animal, and often gets poorly treated for its services. Many of them never know what corn tastes like, living on grass exclusively. A good cutting pony—that is, one used for cutting out, or separating cattle from the herd—often becomes more expert in the business than its rider. A horse can see a cow dodge almost a second before a man can, and then it turns, quick as a flash to head it off. Sometimes it turns before the man can. It takes a good rider to stay on one. Sometimes a rider spurs his pony at a steer and then drops his bridle reins altogether, trusting to the pony to single the animal out. The cow pony is a great friend to stockmen, and they could not well do without it. A larger more valuable and better horse could never do its work.[29]

Around the roundup camp fires, every summer one hears curious tales of the woolly mustang and his riders. So long as ponies will buck, and men will ride them, just so long will the subject be inexhaustible in cow camps. The innocence of inexperienced riders is always mirth-provoking to the older hands and their desperate attempts to appear dignified and at ease on the backs of their gum-arabic steeds cause the solemnest to grin. Down on the Purgatoire one year, came a gentle Hebrew child, that had a few cows and calves, that he came to look after. As a clothing merchant he was assured success, but thirty years in the store had not taught him much about broncos. So it was he was inveigled onto a horse with a disreputable character. Realizing what was expected of him, the little cayuse commenced the performance amid the usual accompaniment of yells from the delighted cowboys. "Hold him down," "Stay with him," "Pull his tail," "Let me ride him," "Grab the horn," they shrieked, and then one rascal with a stentorian voice, whooped out, "Rowel him in the shoulder and jump off." Now Jacob was doing well until that last shout came but supposing his advisor knew what he advised, he grabbed the horn with both hands, threw his feet from the stirrups, and raked both spurs up and down the horse's neck, and then jumped for the ground reaching it upon his neck and shoulders. When they asked him why he got off, and he found he should have stuck on, the scamp that yelled "Rowel and jump off," came very near having a row on his hands. Another innocent, when asked if he was hurt by his fall, said, "No aw'm not hurt, but aw never was so glad of anything as aw was when aw struck the ground!" Yet another, when asked why he came down so quick replied with biting sarcasm, "Why did I come down so quick, did you see anything up there for me to hold on to?" Over in Nevada in '78 came a true born Englishman. He came, so he informed us, to break horses for a livelihood. The boys mentioned that probably these horses were different from those he was accustomed to, and might be harder to break. His reply was "Mon a 'oss is a 'oss the world hover, hand h'I've ridden 'osses after 'ounds and broke many a bad 'un. Besides, mon, these little fellers aren't big enough to 'ave much strength." Well, the days passed on and finally Tom got a 'oss to break. The boys brought him up, and blindfolded him, helped Tom put on his little pancake saddle and snaffle bit, and held the "baste" while Tom got on. The blinder was whipped off, and the 'oss stood braced and still, and then Tom wagged his legs and clucked. Four jumps and a whirl, and Tom was sailing, sailing, sailing. When he came to, and had got the dust out of his mouth he gave us an account of it all.

"Why," said he, "the dom baste was nothing like a 'oss. First 'e stood on 'is 'eels, and then 'e stood on 'is 'ead. Then 'e 'umped 'is back like 'e was sick at the stomach, and wanted to puke a bit, and then 'e came down with one of those dirty shakes, 'umped 'is back again and hoff h'I went."[30]

WORKADAY DANGERS

The work of the cowboy was filled with danger. Scarcely a day passed that he did not face death from the ever-present occupational hazards. The dangerous terrain, the violent storms of summer, the blizzards of winter, and the stampedes took their toll yearly. Of all the dangers the stampede brought fear to even the most experienced horseman and was the theme of many a cattle trail and camp story.

One of the Texas delegates to the National stock-growers' convention in Denver this week gave a good account of a cattle stampede which occurred in 1876, on the big prairie in the center of which now stands the town of McGregor. Fifteen thousand cattle and twenty-five cowboys participated. Late in the afternoon of July 4th there had been a thunder storm that made the cattle nervous. At 10 o'clock at night, however, they seemed to be sleeping all right. The stars were shining and there was no cause for the arousing of the herd. They appeared to get up all at once, with a single purpose, and the roar that was heard seemed to come from a single throat. The Wilson brothers and their cowboys, who were sleeping in their camp, rushed to their ponies, which were grazing with saddles and bridles on, and as fast as the bits could be placed in their mouths they mounted and galloped to the flanks of the disappearing mass, headed in the direction of the Brazos.

ALL IN THE DAY'S WORK

The usual course on such occasions is to get in front of the herd—a risky place to work—and start it to running a circle. This attempt was made. Some cattle can outrun others, and in this case there was a bunch of fifty fully twenty yards in advance and toward the leading group two rescuers rode. Of the leading group also some were faster than others, and this group ran in a diamond shape, with two immense steers leading all. When Mr. Wilson and his companion reached the two leading steers they began shooting their revolvers close to them, and in that way the bunch was made to oblique, and the first step in milling had been taken. By mistake a drunken cowboy passed to the front on the inside and when he reached the head of the herd he was just in time to defeat the manoeuvre.

He began shooting and the effect was to straighten the run and bring the advance toward a precipice—a wash in the prairie forming a deep ravine thirty yards wide. When Mr. Wilson and his lieutenants saw that it was impossible to save the cattle all hands commenced firing into the herd, the object being to build a breast work of carcasses and save the rear from destruction. The gully was nearly full of cattle by this time. The herd turned then because it could not do otherwise. In a short time the boys had the cattle halted, forming an incomplete letter O, and there they stood, blowing bellowing, shivering. All hands remained on watch all night, and in the morning when a count was made it was ascertained that 2,700 head were missing.[31]

One of Denver's temporary residents this winter is a typical cowboy from the sagebrush ranges of Idaho. He is a good story teller and this is one of his best efforts: "I was with what is known as the Shoesole outfit on the banks of Oyee river in Idaho in July, 1889. There were thirty-eight cowboys in the camp, and on July 23d we had just completed a roundup of beef cattle that we were to drive to Shoshone Falls to ship east. There were between 1,700 and 2,000 head of big steers in the band, and we had them all safely bunched for the night. There was a storm brewing all the afternoon and the boss cowboy,

Coon Foster, thought we had best not unsaddle our ponies at all that night. He laid his uneasiness to the weather, and most of the boys in the outfit took it for granted that that was what was troubling him, but when we crossed a creek I saw moccasin tracks as plainly as I ever saw anything and I knew better.

"I knew that Foster had seen 'em, too, and it was Indians and not weather that worried him. About six o'clock in the evening it commenced to rain, and Foster stationed six of the cowboys, myself among the number, at various parts of the camp as guards over the camp and cattle. The main body of the herd was fully half a mile from the wagons, but the guard kept going to and from them all the time. There were continuous flashes of sheet lightning, but the cattle did not mind that any, and as I looked out across the herd everyone was lying down but one or two. It was as peaceful and quiet as a graveyard.

"Everything was quiet, seemingly, but I heard several suspicious sounds, coyote barks and other noises that made me uneasy. Suddenly a big steer that stood far out on the mesa beyond the herd twisted his tail and let out a bellow that would raise the dead. In an instant the entire herd was on its feet. They came straight at me and only about fifty yards away. Foster came at me yelling like mad for the boys to saddle up and get the cattle stopped. He had just reached my side when the leaders of the herd surrounded us. Our ponies turned and ran with them. The bellowing and rearing of the cattle was frightful.

"We were managing to get the steers nearest us separated a trifle so as to get room to turn, and had a fair chance of getting out of the bunch, when Foster's horse stumbled and fell. My pony fell over him and I landed between his body and that of Foster's horse, and that is the only thing that saved my life. The whole herd tumbled and pitched and tossed over us. Foster was literally mangled to sausage meat. His horse was little better, and mine was crushed into a bloody mass. I found that I could not get up, for my leg was broken just below the thigh. I was soon cared for, however, and in six weeks was all right and on the range again. We found 341 dead cattle, two dead horses, one dead cowboy and two more with broken legs after the herd had passed. Indians had stampeded the herd."[32]

[The cowboys] who were on watch that night would circle slowly around the great army of cattle, driving them in closer and closer together and singing as they rode to put them to sleep.

This seems an absurdity to the eastern mind, but the sound of something familiar quieted and satisfied these great stupid animals that can be soothed like a child with a nursery rhyme and when frightened can not be stopped by a river. The boys rode slowly and patiently until one and then another of the herd would stumble clumsily to the ground, and others near would follow, and at last the whole great herd would lie silent and immovable in sleep. But the watchfulness of the sentries could never relax. Some chance noise—the shaking of a saddle, some cry of a wild animal, or the scent of distant water carried by a chance breeze across the prairie or nothing but sheer blind wantonness—would start one of the sleeping mass to his feet with a snort, and in an instant the whole herd would go tearing madly over the prairies, tossing their horns and bellowing and filled with a wild, unreasoning terror. And then the skill and daring of the cowboy were put to their severest test, as he saw his master's income disappearing toward a canon or a river, or to lose itself in the brush. And the cowboy who tried to head off and drive back this galloping army of frantic animals had to ride a race that meant his life if his horse made a misstep, and as the horse's feet often did slip there would be found in the morning somewhere in the trail of the stampeding cattle a horrible mass of blood and flesh and leather....[33]

Hungry prospectors . . . caused the loss of 361 head of fine cattle and the death of two cowboys near Bannock Butte [Idaho]. The prospectors, who are now under arrest, attempted to capture a stray calf which ran into the herd. The prospectors tried to cut out the calf. A stampede resulted. The cattle ran toward the brink of a cliff. Two cowboys, Jerome Wasson and Daniel Hancock, succeeded in getting in front of the herd and attempted to bring the animals to a standstill. Their horrified companions saw them swept off the cliff as the maddened animals, unable to stop, rushed over. Three hundred and sixty-one cattle were forced off the cliff and fell seventy-nine feet. The bodies of the two cowboys were found dreadfully mangled.[34]

"One of the slickest things I ever saw in my life," said a veteran army officer the other day, "was a cowboy stopping a cattle stampede. A herd of about 600 or 800 head got frightened at something and broke away pellmell with their tails in the air and the bulls at the head of the procession. But Mr. Cowboy didn't get excited at all when he saw the herd was going straight for a high bluff, where they would certainly tumble down into the canon and be killed. You know that when a herd like that gets to going it can't stop, no matter whether the cattle rush to death or not. Those in the rear crowd those ahead, and away they go. I wouldn't have given a dollar a head for the herd, but the cowboy spurred up his mustang, made a little detour, came in right in front of the herd cut across their path at a right angle and then galloped leisurely on the edge of the bluff, halted and looked around at that wild mass of beef coming right toward him. He was as cool as a cucumber, though I expected to see him killed, and was so excited I could not speak.

"Well, sir, when the leaders had got within about a quarter of a mile of him I saw them try to slack up, though they could not do it very quickly. But the whole herd wanted to stop, and when the cows and steers in the rear got about where the cowboy had cut across their path I was surprised to see them stop and commence to nibble at the grass. Then the whole herd stopped, wheeled, straggled back and went to fighting for a chance to eat where the rear guard was.

"You see, that cowboy had opened a big bag of salt he had brought out from the ranch to give the cattle, galloped across the herd's course and emptied the bag. Every critter sniffed that line of salt, and, of course, that broke up the stampede. But I tell you it was a queer sight to see that man out there on the edge of the bluff quietly rolling a cigarette, when it seemed as if he'd be lying under 200 tons of beef in about a minute and a half."[35]

Yesterday's storm was undoubtedly the worst ever experienced in this section, and must necessarily entail a heavy loss on cattlemen on the ranges of Eastern and Southern Colorado and Western Kansas....

The north bank of the Arkansas, above and below here, is lined with Platte herds, which have drifted here in the past eighteen hours and your correspondent counted over one hundred lying dead in a bunch near the river, from the effects of the last day's storm.

The experience of the past week and especially the last twenty-four hours, should teach the most obtuse and sanguine range man that the way of the transgressor is hard, and that the days for trusting large herds of cattle to the tender mercies of even an exceptional winter will not pay, and does not show good business-foresight in handling cattle on the range, now that the herds are larger and the range for each narrowed to circumscribed limits.[36]

"I can tell you of one place where the festive cowboy is somewhat subdued," observed a cattle dealer at the stockyards. "I have just got home from Montana and a sorrier lot of cow punchers than you will see out there now cannot be found in the whole country. They have had an awful winter of it on the ranges, with the snow belly-deep and the mercury often frozen in the bulb. Lots of the boys are in the hospital, and those who are on the range have a quiet air that is foreign to them. One chap that I saw out there had his fingers all off, but when I asked him to take something, he said, 'I will, pard' if you hold the bottle.' I did it, too, and I had to choke him off when his eyes began to roll. A new crop of cowboys will have to grow in Montana before you hear anything about their capturing a town or stampeding a court in that region."[37]

One of the results of the terrible blizzards which swept over Eastern Colorado and Northern New Mexico... last week reached here today from Folsom, New Mexico. Thursday night Henry Miller, the range foreman for Col. R. G. Head, with several cowboys, camped near Sierra Grande with 1,800 beef cattle which they were holding for the purpose of loading in cars. At 4 o'clock that morning a blizzard from the northwest struck the herd, driving the cattle toward Panhandle, Texas, the cowboys being unable to hold them. The snow was so blinding that it made it impossible to see 50 feet ahead. Miller called his men together and they started to follow the herd and made an attempt to keep them bunched so far as possible. The men became separated. Friday night one of them wandered into Head's home ranch, half dead with cold and hunger. He told his story and a rescuing party was sent out, and at noon the frozen bodies of Henry Miller, Joe Martin and Charlie Jolly were found on the open plains not far from Folsom. The other men succeeded in finding their way into camp before being overcome with cold....[38]

Advices from nearest points continue to tell of great loss of life among shepherds and cowboys who remained faithful to their flocks and died at their posts of duty. All the bravery was evoked by a beggarly allowance of $30 a month.... R. G. Head, manager of the Head ranch and cattle company, left Denver one morning with coffins for three of his cowboys who perished the first day of the blizzard.[39]

The outfit was on a beef roundup. Ed. Randall, the night herder, had a bay horse which he had always boasted could beat anything in the country. His claim was not disputed until a few weeks ago, when a Mexican, who had been engaged at Fetterman a few days before boasted of having a horse that could beat his without any trouble, so a race was soon made and the contestants were to run a mile for $25. The race took place in a lane about fifty yards wide. At the end of the mile stretch the lane turned sharply to the right, so that it was with difficulty that the

ALL IN THE DAY'S WORK 101

Mexican, who came out first, succeeded in turning the corner and escaping being cut by the barb wire fence, but Randall did not fare so luckily. Being unable to turn quick enough, the horse ran square into the fence. Both it and the rider fell soon after, and as neither one moved, they were thought at first to be killed. Randall, however, soon regained consciousness. His injuries were numerous and painful, his right leg being broken above the knee, his shoulder dislocated, and one of the wires cutting a rough gash through the calf of his left leg to the bone. His face and body were also badly lacerated by the barbs. The horse's throat had been cut as with a knife, and he died almost instantly.[40]

Mr. George W. Stevens, who came in Saturday last from his ranch on the Eagle River, gives the following information of the fatal attempt to swim a horse across the Grand River recently, with $490 in gold, under his belt, so to speak.... It seems that the crossing where the drowning occurred, is in common use. There is a rowboat there in which the ranchmen cross. The horses are driven in and made to swim. They have a signal in vogue for night use, in case a belated traveler finds himself on the opposite side of the river from the boat. Two weeks ago last night a cowboy whose name we did not learn, employed on Corrigan's ranch, came up to the river late in the evening and could arouse no signs of life, and no means at hand to secure the rowboat which was on the opposite side of the stream from him. He determined not to be balked but to lash his clothing and effects to the horse and together they would swim the raging torrent. No sooner did he decide upon this course than he prepared for the attempt; having $490 in gold on his person, this was lashed to the saddle with his clothing. The horse, a strong one, that had swam the river many times before, was double cinched, and thereby hangs this tale. Stripped for the fray the dauntless cow puncher started with his steed into the rapid current, but, instead of seeing his horse swim as usual, the animal sank at once from view, and that was the last that was seen of him. After a struggle the man regained the shore and found shelter.[41]

Charlie Beck brings information of the drowning of a cowboy in Beaver Creek near Jenny's stockade about two weeks ago, under the following circumstances: The unfortunate man's name was Charlie Lahr, and in company with a party of a dozen other cowboys, just off a roundup, they were returning to the ranch where they belonged, and crossing to the creek found it very much swollen. Lahr declared his intention of swimming it on his pony, and the others tried to dissuade him, but ineffectually. When they saw he was determined to go in one of them told him to unloos his flank cinch, but saying, "To h—l with the cinch!" he plunged in, horse, saddle, chaparajos, six-shooter and all, and horse and rider went out of sight. He arose once and a comrade threw him a rope, but he paid no attention to it and went down again. His hat was then seen on top of the water, but the men on shore supposing that it was not on his head, but floating, paid no attention to it. The hat was in reality tied to the man's head and if that had been known he could have been lassoed and saved. As it was, he was drowned and a short time afterward the body was taken out of the stream at a ripple below. The horse, after a long struggle, came out alive.[42]

A herder near Pueblo, named Albert Jones, a few nights ago, became sleepy and tied himself on his horse with his lariat. He was found dead, having been dragged and jumped over the prairie for a long distance.[43]

Yesterday morning a young man known as "Budd" Kimball ... met with a serious accident. He was engaged in chasing some cattle, his horse running at the usual cowboy gait, when the animal stumbled, and in falling caught his rider, pinning him to the ground by one leg. While in this position the man attempted to cut the cinch, in the hope that when relieved from the saddle the horse would make an effort to rise. In doing this he in some manner cut the horse, which was dead when the man was found an hour or two afterward. "Budd's" leg is very seriously injured, though it is not known whether it is broken or not.[44]

W. J. Davis, who has been employed on the 4J roundup, died at the Antlers hotel here [Newcastle, Wyoming,] Sunday from the effects of injuries received by being thrown from a pitching horse. Davis was thrown into a bunch of horses and trampled under their feet. He was 45 miles from where he could receive medical attention and was hauled that distance by wagon.[45]

... Not long since a herder was knocked down by a wild steer and his face disfigured for life. His nose was torn completely from his face. That he was not killed was owing to the fact that the long horns, wide apart, touched the ground on either side of the poor fellow's head as he lay prostrate.[46]

Particulars reached here yesterday of an occurrence near Ogallala which will probably result in the death of a cowboy named Andrew Walker.

Walker was in the employ of one of the numerous cattlemen of the section, and was ordered to rope a large and wild Texas steer. Riding at full speed close behind the wild Texan, Walker's horse became unmanageable, and recklessly rushing on, entangled his legs with those of the steer. Man, horse and steer at once came heavily to the earth. The horse was badly hurt, and lay motionless on the earth, pinning with the weight of his body Walker's lower limbs. The steer leaped to his feet, and with blood-shot eye and lowered horns, charged upon the defenseless and pinioned cowboy. Again and again the sharp and heavy horns cut, tore and bruised Walker's breast. Again and again the heavy hoofs crushed him to the earth. Life was fast leaving the bruised and mangled body, when a party of riders dashed up to the rescue.

The steer was at once killed where he stood with lowered front, defying all, and Walker dragged from beneath his prostrate horse. He was a fearful sight, being a mass of gaping and bloody wounds. He was conveyed to Ogallala and sent to Omaha. His recovery is very doubtful, indeed.[47]

The *Tribune* says "a man that is run into by a Texas ox may be said to be steer-o-scoped." If that ox were a different gender we presume it would be merely a cow-lesion and the man would be cow-lapsed.[48]

A cowboy named Baker, herding cattle near Bozeman, Montana, ... conceived the idea of running a race with a freight train just passing. Putting spurs to his bronco he caught up with the flying cars, and for awhile the race was an even one. While galloping along side of the train, by a sudden lurch the horse and rider were thrown against the cars with fatal results. The poor horse was instantly killed. The cowboy also.[49]

Harry Oelrichs, the millionaire cowboy, who has been leading a wild life on his cattle ranch in Dakota, is now in New York, under the care of his physician. Mr. Oelrichs' athletic training and remarkable physique have led him to believe that his constitution could stand more than that of most men; and so it can, but he put it to too severe a test. The cowboy life led by most of these young easterners is more picturesque than practical and frequently winds up with a broken limb or an invalid liver.[50]

NOTES TO CHAPTER TWO

1. "Bill Nye on Cowboys," *San Marcial Reporter* (San Marcial, New Mexico), February 18, 1888.
2. *Field and Farm* (Denver, Colorado), April 19, 1890, p. 5.
3. *Santa Fe New Mexican* (Santa Fe, New Mexico), March 26, 1898.
4. "Cowboys' Hard Work," *Georgetown Courier* (Georgetown, Colorado), August 28, 1890.
5. "A Cowboy's Life," *Trinidad Daily Advertiser* (Trinidad, Colorado), June 24, 1883; *Kansas Cowboy* (Dodge City, Kansas), January 10, 1885.
6. A game of chance played with three dice.
7. "Frontier Life," *Texas Live Stock Journal* (Fort Worth, Texas), May 17, 1884.

ALL IN THE DAY'S WORK 105

8. "The Round-Up," *Las Animas Leader* (Las Animas, Colorado), July 27, 1877.

9. "Western Cowboys," *Trinidad Daily Advertiser*, May 13, 1883.

10. Socrates Hyacinth, "On the Texan Prairies," *Overland Monthly*, II (April, 1869), 373.

11. "The Cowboy as He Is," *Democratic Leader* (Cheyenne, Wyoming), January 11, 1885.

12. "The Old Time Cowboy," *Field and Farm*, January 1, 1898, p. 17.

13. F. M. Osbourne, "Sargent's Rodeo," *Lippincott's Magazine*, XXV (January, 1880), 18.

14. Hamlin Garland, "Round-Up on the Range," *Rocky Mountain News* (Denver, Colorado), August 18, 1895. (A cattle roundup held in the high country of Colorado in the region of the Cripple Creek mining camp.)

15. *Kansas City Journal of Commerce* (Kansas City, Kansas), June 19, 1873.

16. Alfred T. Bacon, "A Colorado 'Round-Up'," *Lippincott's Magazine*, XXVIII (December, 1881), 618-19.

17. Rufus S. Zogbaum, "A Day's 'Drive' with Montana Cowboys," *Harper's New Monthly Magazine*, LXXI (July, 1885), 193.

18. "Cowpunchers!—Sensible Advice to Sensible Cowboys," *Trinidad Weekly News* (Trinidad, Colorado), July 20, 1882.

19. "Comforts for Cowboys," *ibid.*, October 2, 1883, p. 4.

20. *Breeder's Gazette* (Chicago, Illinois), October 23, 1884, p. 608.

21. "From the Panhandle," *Kansas Cowboy*, March 25, 1885.

22. "Cowboy Fun," *Trinidad Daily Advertiser*, February 26, 1885.

23. "A Friend of the Bronco," *Denver Republican* (Denver, Colorado), October 8, 1894.

24. "Breaking the Broncho," *El Anunciador de Trinidad* (Trinidad, Colorado), September 30, 1886.

25. "How Cowboys Ride," *Cheyenne Daily Leader* (Cheyenne, Wyoming), June 29, 1883.

26. "Bronchos," *Denver Daily Times* (Denver, Colorado), July 19, 1872.

27. "How to Break a Bronco," *Denver Tribune-Republican* (Denver, Colorado), January 7, 1886.

28. *Field and Farm*, March 24, 1894, p. 9.

29. "The Horse Review," *ibid.*, December 14, 1895, p. 9.

30. "A Few Mounts," *El Anunciador de Trinidad*, December 2, 1886.

31. "Frontier Sketches," *Field and Farm*, January 29, 1898, p. 6.

32. "Frontier Fancies," *ibid.*, February 16, 1895, p. 6.

33. "Reminiscences," *ibid.*, August 27, 1892, p. 6.

34. "Plunged Over a Cliff," *Denver Republican*, August 13, 1892.

35. "The Cowboy's Stratagem," *Facts* (Colorado Springs, Colorado), IV (July 8, 1899), 11.

36. "Lost in the Storm," *Rocky Mountain News*, January 10, 1886.

37. "Where Cowboys Are Subdued," *Texas Live Stock Journal*, April 2, 1887, p. 4.
38. "Cowboys Frozen," *Republic* (St. Louis, Missouri), November 7, 1889.
39. "A Great Snow Storm," *Field and Farm*, November 16, 1899, p. 8.
40. "A Cowboy and a Wire Fence," *Democratic Leader*, October 28, 1886.
41. "A Horse and a Bag of Gold," *Denver Tribune-Republican*, July 11, 1885.
42. *Democratic Leader*, August 16, 1885.
43. *Denver Daily Times*, October 7, 1872.
44. *Ibid.*, April 4, 1877.
45. "Trampled by Horses," *Denver Republican*, August 8, 1898.
46. "Cowboys and Texas Cattle in the Stock Yards," *Cheyenne Daily Leader*, August 2, 1882.
47. "An Infuriated Steer," *Democratic Leader*, September 15, 1886.
48. *Daily Colorado Miner* (Georgetown, Colorado), November 6, 1873.
49. *Cattlemen's Advertiser* (Trinidad, Colorado), December 2, 1886.
50. *Field and Farm*, December 24, 1887, p. 12.

Law and Disorder

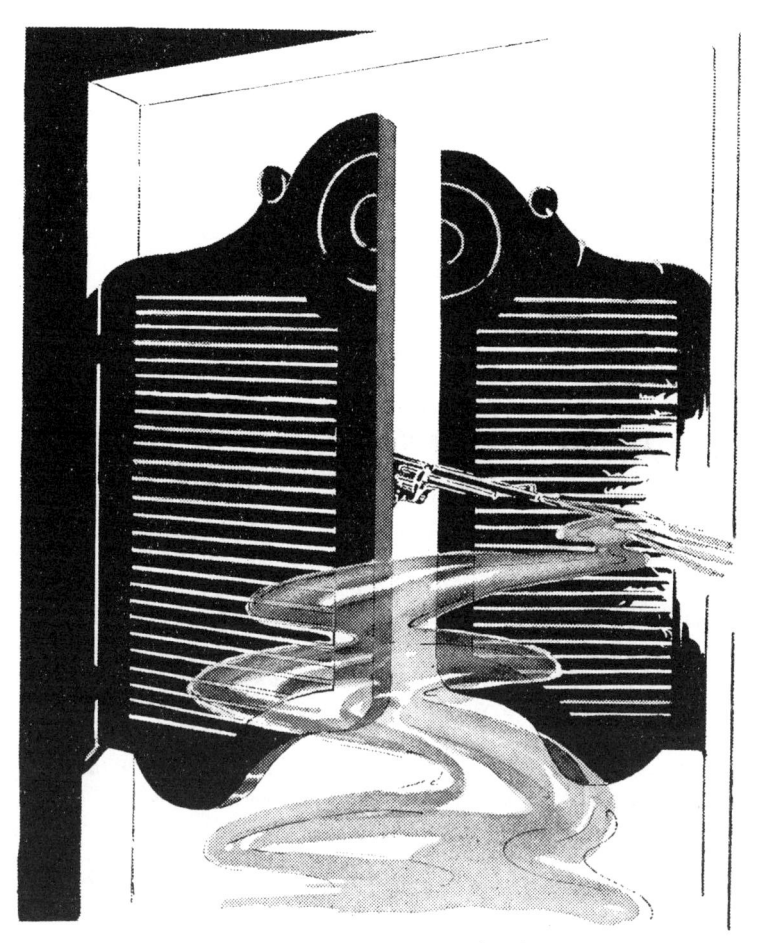

THREE

The reckless freedom with which the cowboy used his revolver, to uphold his code and as a matter of personal safety, created a serious problem in the cow country. This problem became very acute when the cattle industry assumed the aspects of regularity as a developing business and brought the bearer of arms in contact with organized society.

In the early days the cowboy did "pack guns" and

carry Winchesters; practically all shootings and killings grew out of a combination of liquor, hilarity, and quarreling, punctuated with the staccato of the six-shooter. In the late seventies sentiment against the armed cowboy was aroused to such an extent that some laws required that he lay aside his weapons when he entered town, and by 1882 the protests reached full expression in strongly worded newspaper comments. During the following years some important cattlemen made efforts to disarm their cowboys, with varying degrees of success.

Significantly, during this attempt at disarmament, two unusual activities appeared on the Southwestern range which may be considered as protests by the cowboy against the increasing power of the cattle kings, or at least as attempts to better his lot. It has been maintained that cowboy strikes were unknown, yet the rarity of demands for increased wages may mean a lack of publicity concerning them rather than a lack of protest. Only occasionally do such measures of protest on the part of the cowboy reach the newspapers.

Another interesting development which may have been an outcome of the attempt to "tame the cowboy" was the formation of cowboy cattle companies. This was an effort on the part of the cowboy or the small cowboy-cattleman to gain a foothold in the business in which he was one of the most important but, nevertheless, neglected figures. Before either of these two efforts became much more than a threat, the cattle industry underwent drastic changes which eliminated the need of action.

Efforts to subdue the "festive cowboy" were directed mainly at the man who worked as a respected and loyal employee, who tried in the best manner he knew to maintain the industry. The chief offender was the renegade who joined the nomadic cowboys to escape his pursuers. After he had eluded them, he found the work of the cowboy undesirable and forthwith abandoned it, but retained the accoutrements of the profession and in this guise continued his crimes. Thus his nefarious deeds of thievery, train robbing, rustling, and murder were designated as those of the cowboy. This unfortunate case of mistaken identity continued until the word "cowboy" struck terror in the hearts of all respectable people and resulted in a threat to use federal troops to put down the supposed "gangs of unruly cowboys."

The cowboy was severely criticized for his gambling and his brutality. Both are understandable, if not forgivable, in the light of his work and life. The lack of normal amusements and companionship, and the ever-present dangers made him careless of money and personal possessions. The savage, cruel, gross aspects of his work blunted his finer feelings and made him insensate toward animals—both human and dumb. Severe censure by his critics, who lacked an understanding of his problem, did not correct these failings, nor did it accomplish any particular results.

SIX-SHOOTERS

The six-shooter was a dangerous weapon in the hands of any man on the cattleman's frontier, and even more so in the hands of the quick-tempered, reckless, and fun-loving cowboy. The effort to disarm the cowboy brought forth a deluge of editorial comment, pro and con, from the frontier journalist.

For a long time past, the citizens of Baxter have been disturbed by reports of revolvers fired on the street. The matter has become positively alarming. Scarcely a night passes but some villain recklessly shoots up or down the streets, endangering the lives of peaceable citizens. We hoped the city authorities would take cognizance of the matter without our suggestion; but, so far, we see no signs of improvement. If our police force is insufficient, let it be increased. The cost of an ample force would not equal that of a single murder trial, nor repay the injury to the good of Baxter, even from a financial standpoint. . . .[1]

It is a deplorable fact that young men in our western cities are becoming too familiar with the use of firearms. They have a sort of desperado spirit instilled into them by constant association with those older than themselves who carry weapons. They should be taught that safety to life does not lie in the 44-cartridge but in the avoidance of melees and bad men, and in the maintenance of order. Whatever may have been the condition of this Territory when it was a veritable border it is certain that young boys of our communities should be forbidden to carry firearms.[2]

[*Texas Live Stock Journal,* with reference to the Cattlemen's Convention, Caldwell, Kansas, February, 1882] ... We hope to see the stockmen then assembled to adopt a resolution to dispense with the services of those cowboys who cannot move, eat or sleep without being armed to the teeth like a Mexican bandit. As the *Journal* says, the day for that class of cowboys is played out, and it is time stock owners were realizing the fact. They will find the new order more profitable and pleasant to themselves and the men in their employ.[3]

No man who is acquainted with the past as well as the present of cattle raising in Texas and the Southwest can fail to note, and to note with satisfaction, the vast improvement that has been accomplished in the methods and means of conducting this grand industry; nor can such a man fail to note that the improvement is not general—that a few still cling to old ways and means. It is now high time that there should be no exception to the new rule, and that stockmen of this and other portions of the Southwestern grazing fields should no longer bind themselves to the inevitable tendency of the business, and accommodate themselves to the change which they are powerless to resist and can only incur trouble and vexation by endeavoring to resist.

These men should prepare to make some changes in their employes and to exact in the future other qualifications than those which recommended "cowboys" in the past. The day of the Winchester rifle, ivory handled pistol and cartridge belt belongs to the past—it is gone never to return, and with it should go every man who cannot discharge his duties on the ranch without being thus accoutered. There was a time in Texas when the rifle and the pistol was rendered necessary by the inroads and depredations of Indians—but there are no Indians now, and no need for men who cannot drive cattle without firearms. The necessities of the past produced a cowboy who is out of place in the civilization of the present; but the remnant of that past still lingers to retard the rapid advancement of the business to its full measure of profit.

... There is nothing more disgusting to business men than to see cowboys in these times of peace and safety loaded down with guns and pistols. There is no need for this display of firearms, they do not indicate courage, but cowardice rather, and it reflects upon a business whose employes cannot go without being armed to the teeth. Such displays are revolting to civilized people and deter many good men from engaging in the business.

This wholesale arming of cowboys is a disgrace to stock raising, injurious to the business, provocative of lawlessness and crime, and should be prohibited by the laws of the State, the rules of the association and by the owners of the ranches.[4]

The time is rapidly approaching, if not already at hand, when the average cow-boy need not carry the suggestion of a walking arsenal wherever he goes. Nowadays, when a "tenderfoot" decides to try his luck on the cow-pony in the ranching regions his all-important piece of luggage is a six-shooter and ammunition enough for a seven days' siege. In fact, the widely-prevalent opinion that a cow-boy is not a cow-boy, without one or more revolvers, makes it an easy matter for the public to credit the claim of professional ruffians and horse thieves, that they are cowpunchers. A change is necessary.[5]

"The six-shooter must go," will be the sentiment expressed in a resolution that will be offered before the stockmen's convention at its March meeting by the Hon. E. M. Hewens. Mr. Hewens and James Hamilton could illustrate the wrong done by the indiscreet carrying of revolvers by cowboys in their experience with the Hunnewell case of Mills, Chastain and Carter. It cost each of these gentlemen six hundred dollars, simply because they were friends of the boys and had not urged the boys to leave off their arms to any effect. The day of the six-shooter cowboy is past, and that class should not be employed on the range. It is both dangerous to the party carrying arms, and the employers of the cowboys. It will not take long to make it so unpopular that the cowboy will be glad to conform to the new order of things and lay off his six-shooter. Peaceable citizens will gladly hail the day when this shall be accomplished.

This is the most sensible move that has been made for a long time. It is hoped that Colorado and New Mexico stock men will adopt the same idea.[6]

The *Stock Journal* is aware that there is a prejudice in favor of the revolver among an inconsiderable number of those who labor on the plains. It could not be otherwise. Indeed, at one time in the history of stock raising in Texas, the revolver and the rifle were all that made stock raising possible. But that time has gone by never to return and in its wake are rapidly going all the conditions of "the long ago." The six-shooter is a relic of barbarism, as it were, in the annals of stock raising; but, withal, so handy that some of the cowboys will cling to it with tenacity. But it must go.[7]

For years our managing editor has defended the legitimate cowboy as against the thieves and highwaymen in editorials as well as communications, and we are glad that a movement is now on foot, started by the *Texas Live Stock Journal,* which, if successfully carried out, will be the best proof that the real, live cowboy of the plains is the man whose house ever has the latch string on the outside and the person ever ready to defend the weak and supply the needy. As seen from a slip printed elsewhere, Texas wants to inaugurate the system of unarmed cowboys. We hope they will succeed, and the *Chronicle* [Red River, New Mexico,] will continue to contribute its little mite toward making the practice universal in this neighborhood. It will be the end of shocking sensitive persons in seeing walking magazines and it will be to the benefit of the stock raisers and cowboys in general in getting used to doing without arms. In fact, it will be the making of our heroes, the cowboys, who are as brave as the lion in the hour of danger, and as meek as the lamb under the scepter of Venus.[8]

The convention at Caldwell, Kansas, sounded the first note of war against the armed cowboy. In their own behalf nine-tenths of the cowboys will thank the Caldwell convention. A cowboy animated by mean whiskey and girded about with pistols and cartridges disgraces every gentleman in the business—and this the gentlemen in the business know. Cowboys are brave, generous, true men, and they are tired of being illustrated by the desperado style of cow puncher.[9]

The cattlemen in convention at Caldwell, Kan., resolved unanimously that the six-shooter is not an absolute necessity adjunct to the outfit of a cowboy working on the range of the Cherokee Strip, and that "we deprecate its use only in extreme cases of necessity while on duty in protecting the right of property against Indians and outlaws, and we deprecate the carrying of the six-shooters in all cases while visiting the towns on the border."
The *Texas Live Stock Journal* notes with pleasure the improvements which have been made in the manner of carrying on the live stock business in that State, and urges as another needed step that a higher standard of honor in the cowboys be insisted upon by stockmen; in short that "ranchmen should no longer make proficiency in handling firearms the requisite qualifications to employment—as has sometimes been the case—but honesty, industry, and experience should be the test of a man's fitness for a cowboy's duties."[10]

The stock growers of Las Animas county ... passed a resolution condemning the practice of carrying revolvers by cowboys on the range. This is well enough as far as it goes, but if they had agreed to discharge all employes who indulge in the practice they would have shown that they meant what they said. But that is probably what they did not mean.[11]

Early last Monday morning a dozen pistol shots in Sarge's saloon startled the natives. It was lucky that not many of said natives were in the saloon at the time, for it was a warm place. John Callison and Rufe Thomas, two boys, both under twenty years of age, got into a dispute about a deck of cards. Harsh words soon led to pistols, and the ball opened. Each party fired six shots, but only one took effect. Rufe Thomas was shot in the abdomen, the ball entering the right vest pocket and coming out through the left one. The wound is not thought to be a very serious one, and Thomas is said to be doing as well as could be expected. Callison was placed under bond to await the action of the grand jury, now in session. A petition is now being circulated to have the six-shooter law put into operation in this county. It is needed, and if enforced will prevent just such boyish pranks as happened....[12]

There seem to be reasons for fearing that the gentle cowboy of the plains will be compelled to put some restraint upon his exuberant spirits, and check those little exhibitions of joyousness which make the residents of border towns hunt their holes to escape perforation by the bullets which a free generosity, inspired by Jersey lightning, leads the cowboy to lavishly distribute with the aid of his revolver. The papers which erstwhile sounded the praise of the cowboy have turned from their accustomed ways, and now demand that he or his revolver must go. There are many intelligent and respectable men employed on the stock ranches of the plains, but, some way, the rest of the world seems to be falling into the belief that about the best use that can be made of these border ruffians is to lengthen their necks by aid of convenient cordage.[13]

Every few weeks we are called upon to chronicle the effects of the practice of carrying six-shooters by cowboys. Sometimes it is a murder, and other times, like this, an accident.

On Saturday morning last word was received here that a cowboy had been accidentally killed by a revolver over south of the stock yards. Upon investigation it proved to be Hugh Calvert, one of Montgomery's hands, that had met death by the accidental discharge of a revolver. From an eye witness, the only person besides Calvert at the camp at the time, we learn the following facts concerning the tragedy:

Calvert and our informant were unloading the traps from the camp wagon on the banks of a small branch about one mile south of the stock yards. Calvert was in the wagon handing the things out to him, and was nearly through the work when he picked up a blanket or something, and the revolver fell from it, the hammer striking upon a skillet and exploding the cartridge, the ball striking Mr. Calvert just above the eye and coming out at the base of the brain at the back of his head. He fell and expired in a moment. His face was black from the powder. The revolver remained in the scabbard, the ball tearing away a part of the end of it.

Calvert was an excellent gentleman and cowman, and was well liked by all with whom he came in contact; his hobby, tho', was a six-shooter, with which he was forever fooling, twirling it on his fingers and discharging it rapidly....

Just as long as six-shooter cowboys are employed on our local ranches will we have items of this class to give our readers. It is a well-known fact that five cowboys and cattlemen are killed by the accidental discharge of fire arms, and especially six-shooters, where one is killed by a murderer. The practice of carrying six-shooters on the range and leaving them around the camp and wagons should be condemned by the ranchmen, as it generally proves to be the best hand on the ranch, or the quietest men, who meet with such accidents, and not the bad man, who could so easily be spared, and who encourage the young cowboy or new beginner to load himself down with a villainous six-shooter of the biggest calibre and most deadly make.[14]

Have you in your employ a cowboy who invariably re-enacts the old role of "hell broke loose in Georgia" every time he goes into town, or gets where the concentrated, double-distilled hell-fire denominated whiskey is retailed?

If so, give him the grand bounce at once, and thus say to the world that you will not even indirectly encourage men in habits of law breaking. We remember that when within the year past certain cow men resolved at a public meeting not to give employment to men who habitually wore six-shooters, it was predicted that they would soon be hunting around for new hands. But, instead, they not only retained their old ones, that were worth keeping, but the cowboys themselves heartily endorsed the resolution and heartily acquiesced in the determination of their employers to put a stop to the six-shooter business. We say again, what we have often said before, that there is no reason for packing pistols in cow camps, on the range or in towns and cities, and the surest way for cow men to break up the custom so long in vogue in Texas, is to have no men in their employment who persist in conveying such dangerous toggery about them.[15]

The Texas stockmen are reported to be making progress towards dismantling the armaments of their cowboys. In their convention efforts have been made to recommend the passage of laws prohibiting the carrying of six-shooters by herdsmen, but the sensible and practical plan seems to have been adopted of leaving the matter for their employers to adjust to their own liking. A number of stock men some time ago announced that they would not keep men in their employ who carried arms. It was predicted that they would soon be hunting for men, but the *Stock Journal* says that they find no difficulty in keeping the ones they want, and that as soon as the plan is put in force on two or three adjoining ranges the cowboys like it well enough to become its strongest advocates. The paper advises, as a means of putting the finishing blow to cowboy riotings, that employers positively refuse to employ the class who, whatever their behavior on the range, never go into town except with arms and a consuming craze for whiskey. This would undoubtedly have a powerful civilizing influence on the necessary sportive child of the plains, and a few mischievous spirits would thereby lose the power to give a great industrial class a bad name. It would certainly be more effective than any amount of legislation on the subject.[16]

Slowly but surely our cherished institutions are melting away, and soon the wild, wild west will have taken upon itself the customs and peculiarities of "the states." The latest is a cowboy without the five chambered Gatling gun which usually hangs over the caboose pocket and bobs up and down as he dashes by on his fiery, untamed bronco. Strange as it may seem to the average eastern reader, and particularly the younger ones who have devoured any great quantity of yellow covered literature, several Wyoming ranchmen have disarmed their employes. A similar movement among Texas stockmen is now said to be making considerable headway. Several stockmen announced that they would not employ anybody who carried a deadly weapon. It was predicted that they would be compelled to rescind this order, but the *Stock Journal* says that they find no difficulty in getting and keeping employes, and that, as soon as the plan is put on trial on adjoining ranches, the cowboys will be the strongest advocates.

This new departure may tickle the stockmen, and not be objectionable to the cowboy; but it knocks the romance out of the latter individual—leaves him merely a common smoke-tanned person, rigged out in leather pants with the seat cut out, white hat and jingling spurs, who does nothing but chase steers over the plains. Once let this custom become general, and what will be the result. No more will the festive cowboy, loaded to the muzzle with tarantula juice, caper up and down the streets, yelling like a Comanche and bidding defiance to the city marshal. No more will he help out the coroner by shooting a half-dozen companions in a drunken row. No more will he ride into a gin-mill, and with his cannon pointed at the diamond stud on the barkeeper's shirt-front, order up the drinks for all hands, then shoot out the lights and three or four spectators' gizzards. Disarm him; if he indulges in any such pleasantries the police will have him in the cooler inside of three wobbles of a diseased mutton's caudal appendage, like an ordinary man.

Disarm the cowboy? Take his pop from him and bring him down to the level of a common man? Ye Gods, no! In the name of 10,000,000 eastern readers of fiction—no!

Let our young bloods wear skintight pants and Seymour coats; let fried shirts and paper collars become the rule, and not the exception; let the electric light and the telephone plant themselves right in our midst, as they have already done, but touch not the cowboy and his revolver.[17]

SAN HILANO, N.M.
Oct. 8, 1883

HIS EXCELLENCY, GOV. L. A. SHELDON:

SIR—This country is in a terrible state of affairs. Armed men in large numbers are coming down here from the northern part of New Mexico and southern Colorado on roundups for cattle; camp followers accompany them and foremen of ranches, their men and hangers on, drive everything before them. No matter who presents himself to inspect the herds of animals for animals of their brands, the lawless horde intimidate with arms in hand. Men are shot down in cold blood, women are not safe in their houses, and the whole Ute creek and Red river country is in a state of frenzy which, if not speedily remedied, will cause a terrible loss of life and property.

Could your excellency do nothing in the matter? A good deputy sheriff or two, one for the county of Mora and another for San Miguel, might help the matter along....

If we had a law forbidding cowboys to carry arms, or which would hold the owners, superintendents or foremen of ranches liable for the carrying of arms of their men, a great good would be achieved.

There is no use of talking; this matter has to be arranged speedily, or another Lincoln county war will break out in the counties of Mora, Colfax and San Miguel on account of this lawlessness.

Hoping your excellency will take this matter into consideration, I respectfully remain,

LOUIS HOMMEL[18]

Every association of range cattlemen in New Mexico has passed a resolution against the six-shooter, card playing in camp, and fast running of cattle, and they promise to carry them out. The *Tombstone Record* thinks that Arizona cattlemen would probably not quit any losses if they adopt the same code of laws, and insisted upon their enforcement.[19]

[An excerpt from a speech made by R. G. Head, accepting the managership of the Prairie Cattle Company.]

Do not deceive yourself by the delusion that if you can be connected with some six-shooter notoriety it will be a big thing for you. In the name of high heaven, nothing was ever more false. The imprint of civilization is too firmly fixed upon this country to ever take more than a momentary step backwards in the manner of lawlessness, and in no section of this broad earth and no people thereon have had a better opportunity of observing this than you and I.

I do not refer to this from any apprehension that you or any of you are so short-sighted or light headed as to think you are wild and woolly, and can't be handled, but I simply allude to such matters from the fact that you and I have been made familiar with such occurrences, and that any influence that I may bring to bear in throwing a damper on such features comes from a simple duty I owe to you, to myself and the community.

I shall insist and expect you to comply with the rules and requirements of the different live stock associations of which the company, through myself and ranch superintendents, are members. Such rules and regulations are arrived at by a full discussion of the general interests by the people at their annual meetings. It therefore becomes the duty of each member, in his individual capacity, to enforce or carry out the laws thus adopted. To me it will be a pleasant duty, to by example, advice and influence, assist you in complying with such laws. Live stock associations over almost the entire country have spoken against the pernicious and useless habit of carrying six-shooters and fire arms at roundups. It is a useless and expensive habit to say nothing about the danger of such a practice. The common laws of the country forbid the carrying of fire-arms—and sooner or later this law will be enforced just as all other laws regulating customs of society must of necessity be enforced. So I cannot too earnestly ask and advise you to begin now to free yourself of the habit when you go out to the spring roundups. If you cannot freely and finally give up your pistol, then take it off, leave it at camp or rolled up in your bedding; by doing this I am inclined to the belief that you will soon learn to appreciate the absence of such an appendage.[20]

... The cattlemen in this part of the country assume that their business may be followed in a legitimate way, and in obedience to the usages of civilized life, hence they have resolved that the six-shooter is no longer necessary and [any cowboys using one] should be discharged. This is a move in the right direction. It is absurd to strap a brace of revolvers and a belt full of cartridges about a young man and expect him to exist any great length of time outside the limits of savage life. Take off his deadly weapons, and it will be easy for him to remain a gentleman, humane in his feelings and practices, which is decidedly best for the interests of his employer, as well as for himself, individually....[21]

The cowboys are not armed with guns this year and all the outfits running in the San Miguel county association will conduct their business without the aid of the customary forty-five. This is the most sensible thing the cow men have done since rounding up became a feature of the industry and it will go a great distance towards convincing people abroad that cowboys are not barbarians.[22]

Since Pat Garrett took charge of the V.V. range the cowboys are not allowed to carry arms, and he will discharge any man in his employ who disobeys this rule. Every ranchman in the country should do likewise. The six-shooter must go.[23]

A quarrel occurred between some cowboys who were driving a herd of cattle from Texas through the eastern part of Bent county [Colorado] on the 9th instant when south of Trail City five or six miles which resulted in the killing of one of the parties. Items of this kind will continue to appear in the papers so long as "the petulent pistol" is allowed to go along with the drive.[24]

We saw a cowboy from Weld county [Colorado] this week—one of the oldtime range riders—and he told us that he felt like old Othello when he lost his favorite occupation. He says the camp outfits will go out this spring probably for the last time on a general roundup, but that the cowboys expect no end of trouble with their hated enemies, the grangers. The rodeo young man said also that he was going out this season with a "shotgun outfit" regardless of the association rules prohibiting the use of the mess-wagon as an arsenal.[25]

STRIKES

It is primarily through the Western press that labor problems of the range are revealed. Scattered newspaper reports of threatened strikes for higher wages and better working conditions appear in the early eighties. The strike, not a common method to achieve the demands of the cowboys on the range, could be used as a serious weapon against the cattleman.

Telegraph advices from the Panhandle report difficulties between cowmen and cowboys in regard to rates of pay. Particulars beyond the bare facts of the existence of the trouble have not been ascertained owing to quarantine from small-pox at Mobeetie. The boys are at Tascosa and strike for fifty dollars per month; they will have a meeting on April 1st and decide their programme. It is reported that two hundred are in the movement and the talk is of range burning, and wire-fence cutting if their demand is not granted.

Heretofore men have been paid on their merits, receiving different prices although in some instances where large numbers of hands were employed some regular scale has been established. However there is a great difference in cowboys as workmen, some being worth almost any money as faithful servants while others are not worth the horses and calves they will kill.

The sooner this business is amically settled, the better it will be for all parties interested. Cowmen and cowboys on any but good terms with each other will destroy confidence on the one side and interest on the other, making a change in temper and spirit which can be but unsatisfactory to employer and employee.

In the absence of particulars, it is useless to make further remarks, except that cowboys worthy of the name, are well worth treating with liberality, are entitled to all ranchmen can afford to pay, but when demands are actually made accompanied by threats of lawlessness, the adjustment of difficulties can only be difficult.[26]

An extensive strike among the cowboys in the Panhandle of Texas is progressing, and trouble is apprehended. They demand an advance from $30, the present wage, to $50 per month, which the stockmen refuse to pay. The cowboys threaten violence to new men, if brought into the ranges, and the cattle owners will call upon the State forces to protect them, if their own means fail. It is a very critical time for such a strike, as preparations for the season's drive are at a head, and efforts are being made to compromise matters.[27]

The strike of the cowboys in the Panhandle seems to be more serious than was first thought. The boys threaten to prevent men taking their places. It is thought a compromise will be effected. Cowboys have some knowledge of the immense profits cattle owners are making, and it should not be at all surprising if they asked fair wages for what is the hardest kind of hard work.[28]

The cowboys' strike in the Panhandle will likely prove a serious thing, coming as it does just at the beginning of the spring roundup. It would be hard to imagine any other class of employees who can more completely control the situation than the Texas cowboys. Their places cannot be well supplied, at least in a short time. It takes men who know the country, and who are trained to the ranges to be efficient in the business. The cowboy of the Panhandle, if a good one, has received a special education in training. He must know the landmarks, mesas, patches of timber, peaks and outlines of the landscape. He must likewise be familiar with the location of water holes, springs and the courses and distances of the streams. He must know how to camp in the plains with nothing but his blanket, and be well up in the general lore of the ranges. A new man is no good on earth and is more liable to wander astray himself and be forever lost on the boundless plains than to find stray cattle.

The superior cowboy, or the "pride of the Panhandle," as he is styled, is no slouch, and a stranger cannot take his place simply for the lack of the technical knowledge of the profession. It is to be hoped that the threatened strike may be averted by a compromise of the differences between the parties.[29]

The movement of Texas cattle will be impeded this year unless the owners and cowboys agree upon terms in the Panhandle country. According to information from Fort Worth, the latter have struck for a raise in salary to $50 per month. They now receive from $30 to $40. This strike assumes a serious phase, for they are armed with Winchester rifles and six-shooters and the lives of all who attempt to work for less than the amount demanded, are in great danger. The strikers number about 200, and are located in Tascosa county, near the New Mexico line. They threaten to cut fences and burn ranches if their demands are not acceded to. The novelty of the strike is that the men have struck before work has begun, and the serious feature is that it is in anticipation of the spring work, or the regular annual roundup which can not go on without them.[30]

The *Journal* cheerfully gives space to the following letter from Mr. Harris, who, in addition to being a member of the strike States, is the recognized leader of the striking cowboys near Tascosa: This is the communication:
EDITOR TEXAS LIVE STOCK JOURNAL:

SIR:—Permit me through the columns of your paper to state, in reference to the article headed "A Cow-Boy Strike," in your issue of March 24, that your informant's statement is entirely false when he says, "range burning and wire fence cutting is the intention of the strikers if their demands are not granted." Being a member of the strikers, I will say, that it is not the intention of the cowboys to resort to any violence or unlawful acts to get adequate compensation for their services, but to do so by all fair and legal means in their power.

Hoping you will do the cause of the cowboy the justice to publish this statement, I am respectfully,

T. B. HARRIS

Tascosa, April 5, 1883.

It is hoped that Mr. Harris and his followers have kept and will continue to keep the peace, and only by all fair and legal means apply for what they deem adequate compensation for their services. In following this course, whether successful in having their wages raised or not, they will at least command the respect of all who take an interest in the matter including their old employers. In regard to the article in the *Journal* of the 24th referred to in which we said "It is reported that two hundred are in the movement, and the talk is of range burning and wire-fence cutting if their demand is not granted." We must state now that we know of a certainty that men who have connected themselves with the strike have made these threats, coupled with others to shoot down cattle, to overpower ranchmen and disarm them.

The men who talk this way may not be experienced cowboys competent to do their work on the range or drive, but may be a kind of cross of the desperado, ready and willing to join any movement showing a promise of revolution and disorder, and who rejoice in a general chaos in all kinds of business. Mr. Harris and his immediate followers may be high-minded men, determined in a fair and legal way to assert their value as ranch hands and who could confine themselves to proper representations of their grievance, and club together for their mutual interest, but the report, now verified, still remains that threats have been made and openly made by some strikers.

If Mr. Harris is in earnest in his statements, and is able to control his followers and keep them from committing unlawful acts, this local strike will soon be settled much more to their satisfaction than it ever can be should they place themselves outside of the law.

Cowboys have perfect right to ask for a proper remuneration for their services, they have also the right to leave work in a body, unless satisfied; they assert their manhood in so doing. They may benefit themselves by such combined action, but directly they make threats of damage to property of others, they laid themselves open to suspicion, and the good among them, the law abiding element, are likely to suffer from the acts and words of those who do their best to bring into dispute the interests they are apparently trying to advance.[31]

The stockmen of the Texas Panhandle at their recent meeting decided to begin the spring roundup of cattle in the Canadian and Wichita Rivers and Wolfe Creek districts on May 10 and in the Salt Park and Red River districts May 20. If there be any trouble with the striking cowboys it will develop at these roundups. Lieutenant John Hoffer, with a company of frontier battalion Texas rangers, is in camp near Mobeetie, in the center of the troubled district, and will do everything possible to preserve order.[32]

The cowboys of Texas are on their muscle and nerve. They demand an increase of pay from $30 to $50 a month. Failing to get it, they propose to burn the ranches, confiscate the cattle and kill the owners in that particular part of the world called the Panhandle, which was recently sold by the state of Texas to a Chicago syndicate and transferred by them to an English company. With the country the English millionaires have bought a hard constituency, as they are in a fair way to find out. An ordinary cowboy is as explosive as a nitro-glycerine bomb, and a good deal more dangerous. We shall watch the war with interest, not caring much which side whips or gets whipped.[33]

It seems that some of the striking cowboys have been sending Billy Edwards of the *Panhandle*, illustrated communications (with skull and crossbones perhaps), judging from his comment which we give below. Billy doesn't scare worth a cent. He says:

Some weeks ago, at the inauguration of the strike of the cowboys on some of our ranches, *The Panhandle* gave them a period or two of good advice, meant only for their good. Within the past few days, Peleg Q. C. Stone has sent us from Wheeler a communication, brief and to the point but not of the sort to place before the more wellbred of our readers, admonishing us to attend to our own affairs. That's just it, Peleg: *The Panhandle* has no affairs of its own at all, and so tries to work for the best interests of the range generally. And we have tried to draw as lightly, as might be the distinction between stockmen and cowboy, regarding an honest toiler in any sphere as entitled to the respect of men. But see here, Peleg— when you raise a clamor for more while you are receiving reasonable compensation, a gob of doubt dims our sense of respect for you. Down in the state, where this scribe gained his wealth and his capacity to tote a headache at punching cows, the boys are now getting from fifteen to twenty dollars per month. Out west they get twenty-five, while you fellows who have struck are getting thirty to thirty-five, and are vastly better fed than the boys in either section named. You think, Peleg, that the old man's receipts have been raised and that yours should be also. But he is taking chances and you are not. With him it may be possible for the proceeds of long years of toil and care to go higher than an ace tomorrow. Reason with the old duffer, Peleg, but don't try to scare him, for it won't pan out, and you will only lose your place; and raising a fog with your cutter will amount to nothing but empty hulls, for it is generally the case that the old man has been long on the turf and knows how it is himself. In conclusion, Peleg, your drawing is very fair considering your advantages, but a little off in some respects. Skeletons of editors don't have such big feet nor vivacious expressions of countenance, and you show the brace of the scaffold as much heavier than the cross tie. We only make these suggestions with the strongest wishes for your advancement. We love you, Peleg, but don't be a fool.[34]

The *Republican* St. Louis has, on various occasions, said a good word for the cowboys, and has steadily maintained that as a class they were a hardworked, industrious body of men who had to endure an indefinite amount of abuse bestowed on account of the deviltries of a comparatively small portion of their number. We are willing to believe that this is a true statement of the case, but in order to settle all doubts it would be desirable to have the unvarnished facts about the strike in the Texas Panhandle. The dispatches state that several hundred cowboys have struck for an advance of 66 per cent in wages, and threaten not only to kill any new men who may offer to take their places, but also to burn the ranches and run off the stock. If the dispatches are correct, perhaps it would be well for the Tombstone rangers, organized to exterminate the Indians at San Carlos, to transfer their operations to the Panhandle and make a clean job of it.

The unvarnished facts about the strike in the Panhandle are these as nearly as it is possible to glean them from so great a distance. Instead of several hundred cowboys being on strike, the number only amounts to some forty or fifty. The leader of this movement informed a representative of the *Journal* that they would *not* destroy life or property, and this is to be hoped that he and his followers have made his words good. It is nevertheless true that some connecting themselves with the strike have made threats against life and property and should the counsel of this class of men prevail, and the strikers attempt to carry out these threats of lawlessness simply because they have demanded higher wages than stock owners are willing to pay, then the *Republican* is justified in saying that "a clean job" should be made of them, though the Tombstone rangers will hardly be called in to do the work. Lieutenant Hoffer is camped in the Panhandle with as trusty a band of rangers as ever roamed the West and the stockmen themselves are pretty good hands at protecting their own interests, and should the strikers become so lost to principle and so reckless of their own welfare as to undertake to carry out threats of murder and arson the performance will only last a brief period, and the Tombstone rangers will never be disturbed in their work of exterminating the San Carlos Indians."[35]

The Fort Collins *Express* says: "The cowboys of the northern country have struck for an increase in their pay of $5 per month. It has been refused by the employers, consequently there has been a general walk-out. Especially as not a man is left on the range. Just what the result will be cannot be foretold. The occupation of a cowboy is one gained only by long experience upon the range. It is not the acquisition of a day. The stock owners will probably accede to the demands, as now is the time competent hands are most needed."[36]

It is reported that some of the eastern railroads are now employing western cowboys to operate them in the face of strikers, with a decided success. President Lyon, of one of the roads, says: "We have seventy cowboys running cars now, and we expect fifty more tomorrow. They are ugly customers to tackle, I can tell you. Some of them hail from Texas and the Southwest, others from Colorado and the western prairies. I warned them to steer clear of the strikers when going home at night, and they all exclaimed: 'Not much. We're looking for a fight, and nothing would suit us better than to get into one.' "[37]

The throng at the Santa Fe depot yesterday afternoon was treated to an unusual sight, fifty cowboys. They came from Garden City and were on their way to Minneapolis, Minnesota, to fill places left vacant by striking street car drivers.

The picture made by the sturdy representatives from the plains was like a breeze from the flowery and fragrant sand hills of the Arkansas, refreshing and invigorating.

Mr. Jones (captain of the company) told the story to the reporter when they found out they were not being interviewed by a "tender-foot."

Mr. Jones told the story of their journeying briefly as follows: "The company is composed of fifty cowboys.

We came from Garden City and are going to Minneapolis, Minn., to run street cars left idle by the strikers. The boys want to see the city and have a little experience. The manager of the street car company offers from three to five dollars per day to those who will fill the vacant places. It is dull out west and we were all out of work and out of money. We had to have work some place and this is the first offered. It rained yesterday and the boys were, many of them, in town. I received a telegram asking for men to drive street cars. We were soon gathered together and ready to start.

"Yes, some of the boys have families who will hold down their claims while they are away. Others are single and have claims of their own which they have proved up. Some of them were brought up on the plains and some of them are old county-seat fighters."[38]

CATTLE COMPANIES

Just as the range strikes were uncommon, so also were the attempts to unionize the cowboys with initiation fees, dues, a scale of wages based on experience, and a division of labor. With this movement appears the small cattle company, a co-operative attempt to make every cowboy a cattleman.

Several of the cowboys in the vicinity of Deer Trail, Colorado, are agitating the subject starting a company to be called the Cowboys' Cattle Company. Any cowboy on the range can invest his earnings at so much per share, hard earned dollars which are now thrown away or worse, be saved to the country as a whole and the toilers of the range in particular. There can be no question that interests of a substantial nature as this would be, must make the boys better citizens in every respect and more faithful in their work for their employers. It would also, to no small extent, influence their feelings in regard to the coming and going of thieves, and there would be vastly less winking going on and less camp chuck eaten by crooks. Where cowboys regard their employers simply as a driveling[39] regards his master, it is possible that there the thief may receive his dinner or lodging and not be "given away." The scheme among the boys in Colorado is a good one, for themselves, their employers and the range interests generally.[40]

[Inquiry to the editor of *Socorro Bullion*, Socorro, New Mexico, March, 1886.]

Have you, Mr. Editor, heard anything of the rumor about the Cowboys' Cattle Company, and their 20,000 head of cattle being shipped and located about 35 miles north-west from here? A joint stock company of three punchers, with lots of loose cash, intend to go into the business that promises such heavy profits. I understand that the contract for shipping the bovines has been let to a gentlemen 15 miles west from here, who is in all respects a very reliable party. The delivery has to be made on September 1, 1886, precisely, or a heavy forfeit will be the result. In case you could state anything positive in regard to the matter, as this is a very important case which concerns stockmen out here in general, as we are all short of range, especially myself, I would most respectfully ask you to communicate to me at once, anything, everything, and all news in regard to this new enterprise. The Cowboys' Cattle Co., I also understand have for their business sign 3CCC. This is for a hint in your future investigations. In my next letter expect further developments should I be fortunate enough to make such.[41]

At a called meeting of the small cattlemen and cowboys, held at Dorsey station, Colfax county, N.M., on the 1st instant, for the purpose of forming a permanent organization, C. J. Young was made chairman, with R. L. Wayland acting secretary. The meeting proceeded to organize. It was voted to call the association by the name of "Northern New Mexico Small Cattlemen and Cowboys' Union," with a membership of eighty to begin with; its object being mutual protection of its members; to be composed of small cattle owners and cowboys, and that no cattle owners who employ more than two men be received into the union; that there shall be an initiatory fee and quarterly dues, which will be settled at their next meeting at Dorsey station, March 15, 1886.

We, the cowboys, pledge ourselves to look after the interests of small cattlemen who are members, and the small cattlemen pledge themselves to do all in their power for the interest of the cowboys. The following resolutions were adopted:

Resolved, That the interests of this organization and the Northern New Mexico Stock Growers' are each protective; their work and ours should not conflict, our interests being mutual; and whereas there has been a private circular prepared to be presented to the N.N.M.S.C. association to regulate our wages, therefore be it further

Resolved, That we are willing to work for wages, as per circular, but that the cattlemen or companies must give us work the year round, as we are willing to live and let live.

Resolved, That the working season of the average cowboy is only about five months, and we think it nothing but justice that the cowmen should give us living wages the year around. Realizing the fact that they cannot keep us all the year in idleness, we are therefore willing, when the cow work is over, to do an honest work that may be needed by our employers, that they may get value received.

Resolved, That recognizing the fact that they can import cheap labor, but after making the cow business our profession we deem it nothing but right that we should be recognized first, and get what we are worth after many years' experience. You cannot do without us, and we are dependent on you, and we expect to be treated like men by men.[42]

At the second meeting of the Northern New Mexico small cowmen and cowboys' union, ... it was voted that the executive committee draw up a schedule of wages to govern this union, and the following prices were adopted by the organization, with four classes, viz: No. 1, one year's experience; No. 2, two or more years' experience; No. 3, extra good men or outside men; No. 4, cooks. No.

1, work the year at $25 per month; No. 2, work the year at $30 per month; No. 3, work the year at $35 per month; No. 4, work the year at $40 per month; No. 1, work for six months at $35 per month; No. 2, work for six months at $40 per month; No. 3, work for six months at $45 per month; No. 4, work for six months at $50 per month.[43]

Mr. S. E. Land, of Montrose, Colorado has conceived an idea whereby he proposes to make cattle barons of every cowboy who wishes to join a mutual benefit association organized for the purpose of jointly herding its members' stock. Many of the heaviest cattle holders in the country today began in a very small way. By picking up an occasional steer and adding to the purchase whenever opportunity afforded, a goodly-sized bunch eventually grew into a herd of magnificent proportions. The plan mostly was for the cowboy to run his little band with his employer's outfit, sometimes on shares, oftentimes otherwise, especially if the owner but seldom visited his herds in person.

But in course of time the big baron rebelled at this method, and envious of his employe's gradual success he put a veto to the custom until now it is infrequently practiced. In order to give the deserving cowboys a chance to "get on in the world," Mr. Land has organized his co-operative herding scheme and proposes to go ahead and place the cowboy on his old-time footing, "as he should be, a cowman and live stock owner." A humble beginning is all a thorough cowman wants. In time he will get there, and the natural increase of his bunch will eventually make him opulent, provided, of course, his stock be rightly handled in the meantime.

Mr. Land says the cattle business is not in the hands of experienced cattlemen as it was a few years ago, but is in the hands of financiers and speculators; instead of the cattle of today being herded by experienced cow hands, who have made it their profession—which is not recognized as such nor appreciated by the eastern investors— the herds are going into the hands of the inexperienced and incompetent pilgrim, who is the cow servant of the would-be cattlemen of the west. Better for the consumer, better for the producer and better for the herder that the cattle on the western ranges be handled by the expert roper and rider; the knife and branding iron be used by experts and cattle graded up and improved by the judgment of experienced men. When this is a recognized fact, the cowman will be honored, respected and trusted.

We agree with the gentleman that there is no business in the world representing such a large amount of capital which is placed in the hands of young men, as the cattle business. Thousands, and we may say millions of dollars' worth of stock are left at times in the hands of the herder, expecting him to be cowboy, foreman, superintendent and general manager, and not be adequately paid for his ability. Is there any other class of labor more worthy of respect and yet is so little appreciated by moneyed men? The experienced labor of a cow hand is invaluable on our western ranges, and therefore we hold that he should be given an opportunity to develop his plans and realize his desires in being a high-bob among cattlemen himself.

The plan is simple: With every animal turned over to the company, or for every $25 put in, a share of stock is issued. The money is invested in female stock. The company takes care of the cattle for five years at their own expense, and five head of cattle are then turned back for every head put in. At the end of each and every five years they agree to divide up the profits or turn over stock to each and every shareholder, buy it in or further invest in cattle for him on the plan described. After the first year, if any of the shareholders desire to withdraw from the company, their stock will be bought in at market value and a reasonable interest per annum allowed them on the amount of actual cash they have invested.[44]

RUSTLERS

The story of the rustler is found everywhere throughout the West, and the frontier journalist records almost daily these depredations on the rancher. Invariably, the records include lively accounts of the cowboys' swift and terminative frontier justice.

Forty-two head of cattle were stolen from Watt's ranch, on Red River, on the night of the 25th of Dec. They were followed by Wm. Mansico, Watt's herder, accompanied by four Mexicans, who overtook the thieves at Pendregosa, seven miles below the New Mexico Woolen Factory. The pursuing party came upon the thieves at night, and after they had made their fire for the night they attacked them. In the fight one of the pursuing party (Mexican) was killed, and both the thieves were wounded. Manisco withdrew his party after having one killed which enabled the thieves to get away on their animals. They were tracked directly to the house of Louis Shroyer, where one of them was arrested.

Enough information has been obtained to satisfy the people that we have in our midst a formidable organized band of thieves operating among us. Three persons belonging to the gang have been arrested, and had an examination... before Justice Greggart at La Junta, and sent to Fort Union for safe keeping.[45]

Two men named Ketchum and Mitchell, accused of stealing stock, and who recently killed a herder named Stevens while he was trying to arrest them were... taken from the sheriff of Custer county [Nebraska] and his posse by a mob of armed men, who tied them to a tree and burned them both to death. The mob was composed of twenty-five men nearly all herders and masked.[46]

Arizona is not a good place for horse thieves to ply their nefarious vocation, for as one of the boys who so successfully followed the rustlers said, "The Arizona boys generally accomplish what they set out to do." If some of that party of horse thieves do not stretch hemp before many moons have passed over their heads the *Journal* is slightly mistaken in its conjecture.[47]

The western cowboy may suffer, forgive and forget, but there is one thing he will not condone—a horsethief and his work. An Indian horsethief was lassoed and dragged to death at Lewiston, Idaho, by white cowboys, for attempting to sell them stolen horses.[48]

Information received [states] ... that an attempt would be made by cowboys to rescue Jess Pruden, arrested for horse stealing at Miles City, Mont., and are en route for Deadwood. A posse left Spearfish to assist the officer, arriving at Stoneville, seventy-five miles north of Deadwood.... The posse was attacked by cowboys, and a man named O'Hara was killed, and Fred Willard wounded. One cowboy named Cunningham was killed, and another whose name is unknown, was wounded and captured. The cowboys then fled. A party is now organized at Spearfish to pursue the outlaws.[49]

Later information from Stoneville [South Dakota] says that it was horse thieves and not cowboys who had the fight with Deputy Willard's posse. They killed Cunningham, a bystander. The body of Jack Campbell, one of the outlaws, was found five miles from the scene of the encounter, perforated by fifteen bullets. Tuttle, the wounded outlaw, is not expected to live. Axelbee, their leader, escaped but was severely wounded. Deputy Willard and nine others are in pursuit of the outlaws. Jesse Pruden, the prisoner over whose arrest the tragedy occurred, has been safely jailed here.[50]

Meager particulars are received of another slaughter of horse thieves in the Musselshell region, 150 miles north of here, [Helena, Montana,] by cowboys. While in pursuit of stolen horses a log house was discovered in the timber on the mountain side. It was secretly watched a day or two, during which time several small parties came and went; some by day others by night, having in their possession horses evidently stolen. It becoming evident that it was a horse thieves' rendezvous, the cowboys congregated and ... crawled up close to the house and attacked it. Fourteen horse thieves were about the premises at the time. Nine were killed and five escaped. The cabin was set on fire and burned.

No particulars have yet been received of the fight of Granville Stuart's cowboys with a band of thieves at the mouth of the Musselshell. It is thought the fight must have occurred several days ago. The locality is over two hundred miles from Helena with no telegraphic communication. There never was a period in the history of this or any other Territory when so much horse thieving was going on. The citizens are determined to effectually stop it. Fully thirty thieves were hanged or shot in the past month.[51]

Frank Stewart, a well-known cowboy of San Miguel county, New Mexico, was arrested for cattle stealing. He executed a bond for appearance and after it had been accepted he went to the justice of the peace and asked to see it again. When the document was brought out Stewart snatched it from the justice, ran out to his horse, jumped into the saddle and frisked away over the range in the direction of Texas. This is a specimen of justice in the cowboy districts of New Mexico.[52]

A warrant was sworn out ... for the arrest of a man working on A. C. Fisk's ranch on the Poudre, accusing him of killing a calf belonging to Grant Parks. The Fisk outfit has been near Loveland, [Colorado] for some time gathering up their cattle and were about two miles from town when Deputy Sheriff Henry Spotts overtook them.
The accused man refused to surrender, and the outfit, numbering four men, supported him. Spotts sent to town for Marshal David Jones and secured the assistance of Will Ellenmeyer. The cowboys made a break for their ranch on the Poudre, and Spotts, who had a slow horse, sent Ellenmeyer after them on a faster one. Shots were exchanged clear to the Fisk ranch, when the officers overtook and arrested the whole gang. They were brought back to Loveland and are now held awaiting trial.[53]

While moving the crossed-S cattle through Huerfano county [Colorado] ... the cowboys were arrested for "rustling" along the road. Judging from reports the prosecuting witness was a little cranky. At all events the boys were released, and nobody suspects them of having intentionally picked up any stock not belonging to them.[54]

Jack Porter, a well-known cowboy, who has been on the range in this section for a number of years, was arrested

... and lodged in jail, charged with cattle stealing near Clayton, New Mexico. Deputy Sheriff Jones of that place came after the prisoner this evening. It is said that Porter is one of a gang that has been engaged in the cattle stealing business on rather an extensive scale, and that about 800 head of range cattle have been stolen and placed in the market. The names of several well-known men are connected by rumor with the gang, but the evidence will not warrant the publication of their names. There is considerable excitement in cattle circles over the affair, and developments will be watched for with a great deal of interest.[55]

The criminal of influence is like a mad bull in a spider's web. The laws are not ropes for him. Understanding this fact the cowboys of Mesa county [Colorado] forestalled further uneasiness when they went out in search of the Brock gang of cattle thieves and put a terrible quietus to any further operations.[56]

Advices from Billings county, west of the Missouri river, state that a fight occurred Friday between cattlemen and cattle rustlers, who had been running stock off ranges. There are no means of communication from that section except by courier to Dickinson, [North Dakota] eighty miles away. News of the fight was brought to Dickinson Sunday night by a half-breed, who said the cowboys had overtaken the rustlers and a fight ensued, in which the thieves were worsted, but they retreated into sand hills, where the cowboys did not dare follow them.

Each winter, as soon as the river freezes up, these rustlers commence to run off stock, which are driven by owners into protected ravines, where they remain until spring opens. A thorough organization has been perfected among the stockmen and the rustlers will be driven from the country. Five hundred head of cattle have been run off the Little Missouri valley in Billings county in the last six months. They are driven into the Bad Lands, where they cannot be found, and are sold off in small bunches.[57]

The fight which was reported to have taken place between the cowboys and cattle rustlers took place on the South Dakota side of the line. The stock which was run off last week is thought to be the property of Pierre, South Dakota men who have large herds grazing in the valleys of the Little Missouri and north fork of the Cannon Ball. The cowboys are still in pursuit of the rustlers, who have got in the Bad Lands where it is difficult to locate them. A hundred head of cattle, which they ran off the range Sunday, have been recovered, the rustlers being compelled to leave them in their flight.[58]

LAWLESSNESS

Unfortunately, too often the lawless elements of the West were misconstrued by many journalists, particularly those in the East who did not delineate between the hard-working range cowboy and "the bad men" who used his name and work to disguise their crimes.

President Arthur has shown one tendency which has never thoroughly characterized the Executive. He has an evident desire to consider the claims and needs of the far west. The silver states have just reason to regret the position he took with regard to silver—though there has been much exaggeration on that point—but in all other matters he has uniformly listened to the claims and complaints of this region.

Recently he sent to congress a special message inclosing a communication from Secretary Kirkwood and letters from acting Governor Gosper of Arizona, relating to the depredations of the cowboys. In his annual message the president briefly referred to this topic, suggesting that the United States military forces be permitted to assist the territorial authorities in the maintenance of order; and he now again urges that point.

The suggestion is one which will receive hearty commendation throughout the west. The depredations of the cowboys and other lawless elements are doing a grievous wrong to the west, not so much because of the actual murder and robbery committed, but because of the reputation which the west is thus receiving as a region where outlaws reign without hindrance. Even Cheyenne is, in some quarters of the globe, credited with an outlaw element, when, in truth, this city is as far advanced in safety and culture as cities of the east. Wyoming has therefore, as good reason to be gratified with the course of the president as Arizona and New Mexico.

Acting Governor Gosper, in his letters, does not mince matters in describing the evils of cowboy rule. The people of Arizona, he says, have been too busy in their money-getting to pay sufficient attention to the enforcement of laws. As a result the evil elements got the upper hand, and the criminal officers, assisted even by the newspapers, have played into the hands of the criminals.

Governor Gosper, therefore, urges that something be done, and Secretary Kirkwood suggests that, where sheriffs or other officers show cowardice in handling these elements, new officers be appointed in their place.

The suggestion is a good one, and should be followed by congress. The west has only certain places where this lawlessness exists, and the entire west suffers, as well as the parts thus troubled. Decisive action is necessary.[59]

It is more than probable that the president will send a message to congress recommending that a law regulating the use of the posse comitatus be amended so as to allow the president complete authority to supress lawlessness in a state or territory where local authorities are powerless to act. The question of the power of the president to employ a posse comitatus to supress the cowboys in Arizona is now under consideration by the attorney general and the message in question will be mainly based upon his conclusions in the premises.[60]

A message from the president to congress ... recites that great lawlessness exists in Arizona, that the governor reports that violence and lawlessness reign, that robbery and murder are common and citizens are alarmed, and that cowboys cause this trouble. To suppress this the president recommends that the army be permitted to cooperate with the civil authorities; that the soldiers be permitted to be employed in that territory as posse comitatus. It was referred to the judiciary committee.[61]

The Washington correspondent of the *Mail* and *Express* says: Senator Edmunds of the judiciary committee, to whom the president's message about the outrages of cowboys in Arizona was referred, reported ... that it was the opinion of the committee that there was no necessity for further legislation and that the executive had power to put down lawlessness in the territories, using if necessary the army as a posse comitatus. Garland made a brief address in support of the committee's finding.

Senator Call offered a resolution to the effect that murderous and other outrages by the Apaches in Arizona demand that the entire military power of the United States should be used for the punishment of the perpetrators and for the protection of our citizens.

Dawes hoped that such outrages would be stopped, but charged that it was a scandal on the administration that such outbreaks should occur yearly.

Ingalls was in favor of the general objects of the resolution, but said he was opposed to it if any reflection was intended on the executive.

Hawley took the same ground and after further debate the resolution was referred to the committee on territories.[62]

At the cabinet meeting today it was decided that the president should issue a proclamation for the lawless cowboy in Arizona to disperse, and if the order is not obeyed to use the military to enforce it.

The cabinet sustained the action of the president in his message for additional legislation on this subject and disagree with the action of the senate judiciary committee in reporting that no further legislation was necessary.[63]

The Tucson *Star* denounces the president's cowboy proclamation as uncalled for and based on malicious misrepresentations, and concludes as follows: The origin of this scandalous proclamation is simply this—a band of

LAW AND DISORDER 143

deputy United States marshals are engaged in the most wanton and criminal practices under color of their official authority. They murder innocent people and when the sheriff of the county in which their crimes were committed sought to arrest them they interposed their official position and resisted the execution of the law. These are the facts.[64]

A Tombstone special says the cowboys and their political friends held an indignation meeting last night which was a complete failure. Its action in no way represented the sentiment of the respectable portion of the community. Resolutions denouncing the president and the government were introduced, and when a vote was taken the noes stood six to one but the presiding officer declared them carried.[65]

The secretary of war has instructed Gen. Miles, in command of the department of the Missouri, to hold troops in readiness to enforce the president's recent proclamation in relation to cattlemen on the Cheyenne and Arapaho reservations. By the terms of the proclamation cattlemen will be compelled to remove their herds by Sept. 4 [1885]. The troops will be held at Fort Reno.[66]

GAMBLING

The cowboy was a notorious gambler. Although this practice proved to be a hardship on the participants, it was of no concern to the cattlemen for whom they rode. Nevertheless, gambling resulted in camp rivalries and feuds, but efforts to control it met with little success.

"Sage Brush," in the *Northwestern Live Stock Journal* talks in his fatherly fashion to the cowboys: "When will the cowboys learn the advantage of having a few spare dollars in their pockets for a rainy day? Boys, good wages and plenty of work will not always last. Hard times are coming, and then he who has spent his last dollar will look back with regret on days that have been, but are no more. Why can't we save as well as others. Surely we work hard enough for it. We have always kept up a lot of men that have not manhood enough to earn an honest dollar, but must run a saloon or gambling hall for our benefit, and we have always stood and delivered up our hard earning to these favored few. Let us stop and think just for once."[67]

Gambling in cow camps is an evil which is commencing to attract the attention of thinking stockmen, as was shown by the passage of resolutions at the ... Texas association meetings which do not permit cards in roundup parties. An intelligent cowboy correspondent of the *Northwest Live Stock Journal* writes the following letter:

"Why cannot our cattle owners do something to stop this growing vice? To say 'I pay my men and it is none of my business what they do with their money,' will not answer. It is not only the foolish cow puncher who suffers from this practice of gambling, but also his employers. Just picture to yourself what I have seen times out of number. Some shark is dealing monte, and, of course, all the boys huddle around him like ants upon a lump of sugar. A foreman comes up and says to his men, 'Go and let Sam, who is on herd, come to his dinner or supper,' and the reply will almost invariably be, 'wait until this deal is out,' or 'wait just one more deal,' and the chances are that the puncher who is on herd has been there since early morning and is hungry and impatient, for he knows full well that he should be relieved and consequently he is not in good humor. If a steer or cow takes a notion to wander, he either sits and watches it indifferently or fires it back into the herd on full run; and this is not beneficial to the stock, and of course is detrimental to the interests of the owners of the same. All from the game of monte being dealt at camp. Perhaps the owners will wonder why the foreman does not discharge those tardy monte fiends. There is just about one foreman in a hundred that has the sand to say that there shall be no gambling in his outfit. Perhaps he is in the midst of a general roundup and has his hands as full as he can well have them and at the same time one half of his men are stuck on old monte, as the boys have it. If he discharges one of them, they will leave him in the lurch; for, they will argue that if this foreman will not allow them to gamble there are plenty of outfits that do allow it. They will demand the small balance due them and declare they will go where they can gamble; or, in other words, do as they please and get paid for doing so. Now, have we not got laws in Wyoming requiring dealers of Spanish monte to pay a license for the same? Why not let a few of these sharks feel a little of the law? It would surely be good for the welfare of the cowboys at large. There are other games that are played at cow camps, but none so detrimental to the interests of all as Spanish monte, a benefit that will be felt at sometime."[68]

[R. G. Head, upon assuming mangership of Prairie Cattle Company.]
I will now call your attention to the most objectionable habit that is liable to find its way into cow camps—gambling—playing cards. This, I consider, like whiskey drinking, a business of itself, and I have never yet, in all my varied experience, known gambling and true business to jibe very readily. So if you feel like you cannot live without gambling, be man enough to say so, get what is due you and go to town, or some place, where you can gamble unmolested. You cannot play cards in camp during the working season and do your work properly at the same time. It will not be tolerated, and any employe knowingly violating this rule will be subject to discharge, and the strict attention of superintendents and foremen is called to this requirement....[69]

BRUTALITY

Cowboys drank and gambled partly because of their need for companionship and fun. The brutal side of their nature seems to have been a direct outcome of the insensitive side and the vulgarity of their life and work. Lacking even the most basic refinements and comforts of civilization, they could hardly be expected to display sensibility or compassion for their charges.

Editor Chieftain:—That most cheerful and refreshing recreation—cow hunting—is again within the reach of all. Is not this a cause of great joy; to know that every person, if ever so poor, may partake continuously and in large quantities of this bliss without wrong and deprivations to any man, is felicity indeed. The very quintessence of civil right. Go where you will, you see or hear of cow hunting. I met one the other day, he rushed upon the hill where I was standing, his horse restless and dangerous because the saddle was partly embedded in the flesh, having what is called a "cow hunter's sore back." They tell you a man is not a good cowboy unless he makes his horse's back sore, and said: "Stranger, did you see a piebald yaller brindled, yearling, half-breed Texas steer, branded on the left hip with a wagon box, on the right side with an ox yoke, left jaw branded with a mule's hoof, on the right shoulder, a rail brand, has a dewlap, is jingled bobbed in both ears, swallow fork in the right and slip in the left and lower and upper bit out of the ear." I saw he took a long breath and asked: "Are there no other marks or brands?" "Yes sir," he said, "there are if you've seen the steer you'd remember his left horn is off, his right eye is knocked out and either the left or right hock joint is stiff." I informed this gentleman I had not seen his wealth, not too soon however, as the tortured horse could not be restrained, and the saddle was almost out of sight in lacerated flesh. Now I come to questions. Is all this suffering necessary to make cattle raising safe and profitable? Here we have our miserable, poor, wild, vicious tough animal, that has lived one year and has been tormented every day since its birth. It is impossible that all the cutting and burning could have been done short of three hundred and sixty-five days. Does any sane person believe this necessary, that horses should be used to the extent of the one I saw yesterday?...[70]

"A merciful man is merciful to his beast," is a saying that is full of wisdom and humanity as it is full of age. It used to be the rule in Texas for every cowboy to be allowed about one dozen ponies every year—to ride down and otherwise ruin as a matter of course. The most practical cowmen are now recognizing the fact that one half the number of really good horses, well fed and otherwise well cared for, will do better service; and they will do well to require in the future that their boys shall handle them as if they were something better than coyotes.[71]

All men who wish well to the cattle business of America will hail with deep satisfaction the position taken by the associations in this territory, in relation to the treatment of cattle and horses by the cowboys. It seems to have been the prevailing idea with young men who are engaged in service upon cattle ranches, but the nearer the savage life they approach the more of a cowboy they become. This idea has developed such a degree of cruelty to the cattle they drive and the horses they ride that serious loss has been entailed to consequence thereof. The proprietors of the ranches have seen and felt the extent of this evil, and in their recent meetings have passed resolutions condemning the cruel practices, and pledging themselves to discharge any employe who persists therein.... These radical reforms instituted by the cattle men of New Mexico, indicate a degree of intelligence and moral force not surpassed, if indeed equaled, by those from any other section of our country.[72]

Mr. O. K. Lapham, representing the National Tanners and Hide and Leather Dealer's Association, spoke at length upon the subject of reckless branding of cattle and the consequent damage to hides. The most practical suggestion that was thrown out by Mr. Lapham was that branding on one side would answer the purpose and prove a saving of upwards a million dollars yearly.

Mr. Lapham urged that his system be adopted, and that the Association by rules backed with penalties regulate the entire matter. The advantages of small brands is urged as giving an opportunity to utilize the head, neck, legs and shoulders, thus leaving the side unimpaired. By this system all hides would have a value of $3 to $5 more than is now received. Many hides by reason of reckless branding bring but $1 and are fit only for glue. Foreign buyers are already refusing to buy branded hides. The paper went so far as to intimate that the cattlemen owe it to the public who have given them the use of the public domain to prevent this annual destruction of millions of dollars' worth of property, and the suggestion was given that unless there be reform in this matter the time will come when branding will be prohibited, and the cattlemen will be compelled to conduct their business in fenced enclosures like the cattle growers of the East. The recent action of the Humane Association on the subject of branding cattle was referred to.[73]

To my mind the most important feature adopted by the association this spring is one in reference to the manner of handling stock on the ranges and at the roundups. The habit of abusing cattle on the range at the roundups, or on the drives, is wholly unnecessary, and is calculated to destroy annually property to the extent of the salaries you receive. The time has come when more care must be taken of such property. Mark, what I tell you. Your own business interests, your future success, depends upon the manner in which you handle the business entrusted to you, or the duties you agree to perform for a liberal compensation. I ask you to think of this just one moment; take it home to yourself. Would you keep the employe in your service that you knew abused your property to the extent of the value of the honest money you are to pay him for his supposed attention to your business? No, indeed you would not. I have too much faith and confidence in your honest manhood to allow myself to think so. It is my wish to set a good example by handling stock carefully at roundups, or on the drive. Take more time. Running and abusing cattle by overheating, destroying calves unnecessary, thumping and beating animals made vicious by over-exertion is unnecessary, and must be stopped. This must apply, not only to the company's property, but to the property of our neighbors and co-workers. I want you to use your influence to bring about such improvements, among the general employes with whom you work or are associated. You are promptly paid to do your duty, and this is part of your duty. The habit of beating and abusing horses is one of the most detestable you could be guilty of. It is not only cruel, but it is cowardly in the extreme. Just think of abusing a poor dumb brute that cannot defend or protect itself. If you will only think I am sure you are too much of a man to do such an act....[74]

There is a progress even among the cowboys and stockgrowers on the plains. The rough hurrah style of handling cattle, we are told, has become unpopular. It is discovered that abuse and excitement entail loss wherever and whenever indulged in. At the annual meeting of the Lincoln County Live Stock Association, in New Mexico, President Eddy said: "Too much stress can not be placed on the importance of handling cattle quietly and carefully. Bunch the cattle in small bunches, take plenty of time; see that all work is done satisfactorily, and allow no gambling of any kind in camp." If this thing goes along in this way, the ideal cowboy will soon disappear, and we shall have to content ourselves with a knowledge of him through reading a history of the "Wild West."[75]

NOTES TO CHAPTER THREE

1. "The Reign of the Cowboys," *Baxter Springs Republican* (Baxter Springs, Kansas), July 14, 1876.
2. "Forbid Firearms," *Las Vegas Daily Optic* (Las Vegas, New Mexico), April 16, 1881.
3. *Caldwell Commerical* (Caldwell, Kansas), February 2, 1882.
4. "A Word as to Cow-Boys," *Las Animas Leader* (Las Animas, Colorado), February 24, 1882.
5. *Caldwell Post* (Caldwell, Kansas), February 23, 1882.
6. "Six-Shooters Must Go," *Trinidad Weekly News* (Trinidad, Colorado), March 2, 1882.
7. "Shoot the Six Shooter," *Caldwell Commerical*, March 2, 1882.
8. "The Cowboy and His Little Pistol," *Caldwell Post*, March 16, 1882.
9. *Caldwell Commercial*, March 16, 1882.
10. *Breeder's Gazette* (Chicago, Illinois), March 23, 1882, p. 417.
11. *Denver Daily Times* (Denver, Colorado), April 12, 1882.
12. "Six-Shooter Must Go," *Caldwell Post*, April 27, 1882.
13. *Breeder's Gazette*, May 25, 1882, p. 672.
14. "The Fatal Six-Shooter Again," *Caldwell Post*, July 20, 1882.
15. *Texas Live Stock Journal* (Fort Worth, Texas), December 16, 1882, p. 6.

16. "Stock Notes," *Las Animas Leader*, December 29, 1882.

17. "The Regenerated Cowboy," *Daily Express* (Fort Collins, Colorado), January 9, 1883.

18. *Weekly New Mexican Review* (Santa Fe, New Mexico), October 18, 1883.

19. "Reforming the Cowboys," *Sunshine and Silver* (Tucson, Arizona), May 9, 1885.

20. "R. G. Head," *Trinidad Daily Advertiser* (Trinidad, Colorado), May 27, 1885.

21. "Civilizing a Cowboy," *Kansas Cowboy* (Dodge City, Kansas), June 6, 1885.

22. "Live Stock Notes," *Fort Morgan Times* (Fort Morgan, Colorado), June 25, 1885.

23. "Northern New Mexico," *Cattlemen's Advertiser* (Trinidad, Colorado), December 3, 1885.

24. *Field and Farm* (Denver, Colorado), July 16, 1887, p. 9.

25. *Ibid.*, April 14, 1888, p. 8.

26. "A Cowboy Strike," *Texas Live Stock Journal*, March 12, 1883, p. 6.

27. "Cowboys' Cunning," *Denver Republican* (Denver, Colorado), March 27, 1883.

28. *Caldwell Commercial*, March 29, 1883.

29. "Cow Boys," *Trinidad Daily Advertiser*, March 30, 1883.

30. *Fort Collins Courier* (Fort Collins, Colorado), April 12, 1883.

31. "The Cow-Boy Strike," *Texas Live Stock Journal*, April 21, 1883, p. 6.

32. "Texas Round-Up," *Denver Republican*, April 25, 1883.

33. "The Latest News," *Trinidad Weekly Advertiser*, April 25, 1883.

34. "He Don't Scare," *Texas Live Stock Journal*, April 28, 1883, p. 8.

35. "The Striking Cowboys," *ibid.*, April 28, 1883, p. 8.

36. *Field and Farm*, May 29, 1886, p. 5. Cf. John Clay, *My Life on the Range* (Chicago, 1924), pp. 123, 125.

37. *Field and Farm*, May 15, 1886, p. 8.

38. "Cows vs. Mules," *Topeka Capital Commonwealth* (Topeka, Kansas), April 18, 1889.

39. An obsolete form of "drivel," meaning a slave or menial.

40. *White Oaks Golden Era* (White Oaks, New Mexico), April 24, 1884.

41. "Cowboys' Cattle Company," *Socorro Bullion* (Socorro, New Mexico), March 6, 1886.

42. "The Northern New Mexico Small Cattlemen and Cowboys' Union," *Cattlemen's Advertiser*, March 18, 1886.

43. *Cattlemen's Advertiser*, April 1, 1886. "The Cowboys of Wyoming are Forming a Knights of Labor Assembly"; *Fort Morgan Times*, April 16, 1886.

LAW AND DISORDER 151

44. "A Chance for Cowboys," *Field and Farm*, May 7, 1887, p. 5.
45. *Weekly New Mexican*, January 12, 1869. [Title varies.]
46. *Cheyenne Daily Leader* (Cheyenne, Wyoming), December 13, 1878.
47. *Trinidad Daily Advertiser*, September 5, 1883.
48. *Albuquerque Morning Journal* (Albuquerque, New Mexico), October 15, 1882.
49. *Democratic Leader* (Cheyenne, Wyoming), February 16, 1884.
50. *Ibid.*, February 20, 1884.
51. "Cold Days for Thieves," *Democratic Leader*, August 10, 1884.
52. *Field and Farm*, November 26, 1887, p. 9.
53. "Frisky Cowboys," *Denver Republican*, August 28, 1888.
54. *Field and Farm*, July 26, 1890, p. 9.
55. "Charged with Cattle Stealing," *Denver Republican*, August 23, 1892.
56. *Field and Farm*, August 27, 1892, p. 8.
57. "Cattle Thieves Worsted," *Denver Republican*, December 13, 1892.
58. "Chased by Cowboys," *ibid.*, December 14, 1892.
59. "After the Cowboys," *Cheyenne Daily Sun* (Cheyenne, Wyoming), February 17, 1882. Cf. Stuart N. Lake, *Wyatt Earp, Frontier Marshal* (New York, 1931).
60. *Cheyenne Daily Leader*, April 20, 1882.
61. *Ibid.*, April 28, 1882.
62. "Cowboy Outrages in Arizona," *Leadville Daily Herald* (Leadville, Colorado), May 2, 1882; *Cheyenne Daily Leader*, May 2, 1882.
63. *Cheyenne Daily Leader*, May 3, 1882.
64. "The Other Side of the Cowboy Question," *Leadville Daily Herald*, May 7, 1882.
65. *Cheyenne Daily Leader*, May 13, 1882.
66. *Democratic Leader*, August 16, 1885. Cf. Clifford P. Westermeier, "The Legal Status of the Colorado Cattleman, 1867-1887," *Colorado Magazine*, XXV (May and July, 1948), 164.
67. *Kansas Cowboy*, January 24, 1885.
68. "Cards in Cow Camps," *ibid.*, March 28, 1885.
69. "R. G. Head," *Trinidad Daily Advertiser*, May 27, 1885.
70. "Cow Hunting," *Colorado Chieftain* (Pueblo, Colorado), April 8, 1875.
71. *Texas Live Stock Journal*, October 28, 1882, p. 6.
72. "Civilizing a Cowboy," *Kansas Cowboy*, June 6, 1885.
73. "Cattle and Horse Raisers," *Denver Tribune-Republican* (Denver, Colorado), November 28, 1885.
74. "R. G. Head," *Trinidad Daily Advertiser*, May 27, 1885.
75. "State Live Stock Items," *Denver Tribune-Republican*, June 7, 1886.

Foes on the Frontier

FOUR

Probably the cowboy was his own worst enemy. By the nature of his calling, to which he was completely devoted, he had, and was guided by, a clear-cut, precise sense of morality which was based on justice as a virtue in its pure, stark, classical meaning. The key to his relationships with others, his motives and methods, crude and haphazard as they were, are found in this explanation. A strong belief in, and an intense appreciation of, the basic rights of property, ownership, and person, with a respect for these, formed the creed of the cowboy and reflected the principle upon which the American cattle industry was built. The symbol of this belief was the brand, upheld by fleet horsemen armed with revolvers and rifles.

All serious disagreements on the range among cowboy outfits grew primarily out of a disregard of this basic principle. The immediate disaffections were many and varied, but fundamentally respect for, and loyalty to, the brand was the impetus for the fierce duels and conflicts of outfit against outfit which resulted in range wars. The shootings and killings among cowboys within the same outfit bore testimony of this strict code of justice on a more intimate and personal scale, regardless of locale.

The cowboy's foes were many. The Indian he hated and feared because the red man was a clever and merciless fighter—a threat against the industry's control of the domain. This foe, in the light of the cowboy's code, was not just a thief but an avaricious one who was, at the same time, protected by law other than that of the range.

The granger and nester, as the sheepherder, came to grips with the cowboy because they were also a threat, striking at the very foundation of the range cattle industry. The division of the land into farms and the fences which cut the range and crossed the trails impeded the progress of the herds with their drivers and tolled the death knell of the industry. The cowboy also cast hostile eyes at the flocks of sheep. In his interpretation of justice, all this meant the destruction of the grass and the free range; both granger and herder, the enemies in his domain, he scorned all the more because they were on foot in this kingdom of horsemen.

Evidence of discrimination appears not necessarily because of color, creed, or politics, but because the invaders of the cattle country were from a different environment, their reasons for coming were different from those of the cattlemen, and they refused to conform to the established pattern—their way of life, activities, dress, manners, and law were alien.

The essentially generous, fun-loving, hard-working,

sincere cowboy became a man of steel when his high standard was challenged. Although his methods were rude, he became the active agent of the creed. The spirit of fair play was best expressed by him in a manly, bold, strong, and honest adherence to the code.

COWBOY *vs.* COWBOY

Cowboys fought cowboys because of loyalty to the brand, personal disagreements, quick tempers aroused by liquor, and practical jokes which went astray. Their reasons for quarreling and killing among themselves are typical of any closely knit group composed entirely of men living under harsh conditions in an inhospitable environment.

Late last evening a courier rode into town and summoned a doctor, bringing the information that a row had occurred at the Prairie Cattle company's ranch, ten miles below Madison, N. M., and that two persons had been fatally shot. The particulars of the case, as near as could be ascertained, are that a cowboy named William Wing and a tenderfoot cowboy named Harry Burner, both in the employ of the Prairie Cattle company were in a saloon ... on the company's ranch, where they had been drinking heavily. During the sport that followed, the couple adjourned to the front of the store, where they regaled themselves by firing at each other's hats as they were thrown into the air. A quarrel soon arose between them, which ended by Wing firing deliberately at Burner, hitting him just above the left nipple, the ball passing clear through the body. Before falling, Burner opened fire on his antagonist, and shot him dead. Burner is in a precarious condition, not being expected to live, and is being nursed as well as possible at the ranch. Full particulars of the affair are not obtainable at present, but it is understood that the whole difficulty was owing to bad whisky, of which the two belligerents had an over dose.[1]

H. H. Player, of our city, [Cheyenne] is in receipt of the particulars of a most cold blooded and brutal murder committed upon his ranch, at the crossing of the north fork of the Cheyenne river, at Canom, in Dakota, on the telegraph road between Cheyenne and Deadwood. On the morning of the 2nd inst., Ed Graham, a Texas cowboy, shot and killed Chas. King, an employe on the ranch. He shot him three times, twice through the bowels, because he spoke to him about abusing a horse. The murderer took one of Player's horses and another belonging to Ernest, of Running Water. Help went to Custer for a surgeon, when Graham returned and shot his victim again through the head and escaped. King was a jovial good-natured fellow, and not quarrelsome.[2]

The particulars of a strange duel between twelve cowboys have just reached here. George Howard, owner of a herd of 3,000 cattle, and John Kelly, owner of a herd of 4,000, were driving in company from Arizona east. North of Trinidad, Col., on the plains the two herds were separated, Howard to take the old Santa Fe trail to Kansas City, and Kelly to drive north to Denver. On the way an accidental exchange of cattle had been made, and Howard insisted on having his stock, but was unwilling to deliver Kelly's. It was agreed to settle the matter in a battle between six picked men of each party. Accordingly the twelve men ranged themselves on horseback, the two sides fifty feet apart, and at a signal from the employers the fight began. At the first fire four men were instantly killed. George L. Ester, of Kelly's party, was shot through the breast. One of Howard's men fell with a ball through his head, and two others of the same party were shot through the hearts. Dismayed, the Howard party, with the exception of their employer, fled to the camp. Kelly then rode up to Howard, and proposed that they fight it out. Howard declined, saying that he understood the matter to be settled according to the terms of the battle made beforehand. This settled the matter. An equal exchange of the mixed cattle was made. The dead were buried by the men of both herds, and the two drovers and those in charge separated for their different destinations. Kelly arrived here tonight enroute east, and it was from his lips the story was had.[3]

Special to the Denver *Tribune* from Santa Fe says: Information has just reached here that on the 28th instant George Withers wantonly and without provocation shot and killed George Jones (colored). Both were cowboys and employed on the Canaditas cattle ranch, in San Miguel county. The murderer fled toward Texas. He is a heavy, large man, light complexion, well-armed and rides a gray pony. The sheriffs of the border counties of New Mexico and Texas have been telegraphed to look out for him, and besides posses of cowboys are in pursuit. If captured, Judge Lynch will doubtless have a job.[4]

A Springer special dispatch to the *New Mexican Review* ... made meager announcement of the fact that a desperate shooting affray took place at Lake ranch, Mora county, some twenty miles distant, ... by which one man lost his life and two others were dangerously wounded. ...

It appears from a statement made by Thomas Johnson, and corroborated by others that the trouble originated several days ago. Thomas Johnson is foreman for the Illinois Cattle company. In the employ of the same company was a man known by the name of Rufus Ruff, alias "Windy." The latter beat the foreman over the head with a pistol. Murray Johnson interfered and took the pistol from "Windy." The latter then said if Johnson ever attempted to discharge him he would kill Johnson. The story told by Johnson is as follows: "Windy" said he would not take a word from me; that if I attempted to discharge him he would shoot me. I then concluded to get rid of him; for I knew he would be of no use in the outfit. Saw Mr. Woods and talked the matter over with him. On Sunday evening I told him to go to the bookkeeper and get his time as he was discharged. He replied: "You — —, didn't I tell you I wouldn't take a discharge from you?" He then went for his gun and I went for mine. We fired nearly together. He missed me but I hit him in the stomach. We fired again and I was struck in the leg. His third shot missed me. Think I fired three shots.

At this point in the trouble Johnson fell and "Windy" staggered, but recovered himself went into the kitchen and got a Winchester and going into another room shot Norton in the back, killing him instantly. Norton was supposed by "Windy" to be Murray Johnson, a brother of Thomas.

It is reported that about this time Murray Johnson appeared on the scene, and participated in the shooting. At all events "Windy" is shot in the mouth, arm and stomach, and probably by this time is dead.[5]

A shooting affray occurred among the cowboys engaged in the roundup that has just been made in this vicinity, which it is more than likely will result in the death of the wounded man.

... just at dusk while the party were making ready to camp at Jack Dalglish's old ranch on the head of Poverty creek, M. H. Speare of the Graham and White company and Charley Yaple of the Gila cattle company outfit quarreled over the hobbling of their horses. Whether there was anything of animosity between the men back of this or whether it was simply an outbreak of tanglefoot does not appear, but in either case there were not many words wasted in the racket. All accounts agree that Speare reached first for his revolver while warning Yaple to do the same, which request was so promptly complied with that it is hard to say which of the men shot first, and they do not pretend to say themselves. Each one emptied his revolver before resting but the twilight made the shots more of chance than of aim. One of Speare's bullets passed through Yaple's clothes and burned his flesh, and one of Yaple's shots struck Speare in the abdomen an inch below the navel passing through the bowels and making its exit on the left side near the hip, and another made a slight wound in the shoulder. After the affray a messenger was dispatched to Chloride [New Mexico] for a physician and Dr. Blinn responded. The wounded man lies at the camp where he was shot and his companions are doing all for him that they can with their limited resources. Yaple is exonerated from blame by the sufferer whom he assisted to make comfortable after the unfortunate circumstance occurred. Dr. Blinn says that the wound though a bad one is not necessarily fatal and the result of it depends more upon the inflammation which is likely to set in than anything else.—LATER: Speare died Friday night (it would be tonight if the paper had not been held for particulars) and Yaple tried to give himself into the hands of an officer but could find nobody authorized to take him. An inquest is called for and Judge Holmes will hold an inquiry over the body. The dying man and all others justify Charley Yaple in the shooting and there is no doubt that the coroner's jury will do the same.[6]

Two cowboys in Idaho, opposite Assoten, Washington Territory, tied their left hands together and fought to the death with knives. One received twelve stabs and the other seventeen.[7]

Bill West, a cowboy of Leustrom's ranch, twenty miles south of Ashland [Kansas] was sent to glory ... by the sheriff, Mike Shugnue. He is the one who created the disturbance and commenced shooting promiscuously at the Englewood dance on the night of the 4th. Mike and five deputies started for the ranch to capture him. The officers, not finding him at the ranch, started for a search and were about to give him up when he appeared from a hidden spot in the canyon and commenced firing, one load wounding Buck Vandervert in the neck, Buck exchanged five shots. West turned and ran, the officers blazed away forty shots, three of which told the tale. He was buried at Ashland the next day.[8]

Information has been received of a double killing in the Chickasaw nation on the 13 inst. Murray and Williams, partners in a cattle ranch on the Washita river, disagreed concerning the payments of their debts. Williams sent two cowboys, Dick Jones and Dick Cavitt, to bring his share of cattle from the ranch. Murray's men resisted and killed Jones and Cavitt. Further trouble is apprehended.[9]

Billy Green, who had the recent unfortunate encounter with Tom Pridemore,[10] was shot near Juan de Dios ranch by Dick de Graftenreid, a cowboy well known in the city. ... The wounded man was brought to the city by W. H. Howard and Billy McKeon. Howard, who was an eyewitness to the shooting, gave a *Gazette* reporter the following account of the affair:

"Early in the evening Billy Green, Charley Thompson and I started from our ranch to go to a dance. Billy and Thompson had revolvers, but I had none. After we had ridden about five miles we overtook Dick de Graftenreid and John Gayhart, going to the same dance. Our party was sober and hadn't drank a drop, but Dick and his partner were pretty full. Dick was very loving, and would ride alongside of us—we were all on horseback—throw his arms around our necks, and tell us he loved us better than he did his brother. We rode along for a few miles, and Dick kept firing his revolver, but he finally agreed to quit, and gave the revolver to Billy, who stuck it in his hip pocket. Along about 5 o'clock the trouble commenced. Dick rode up alongside of Billy and drew down on him with his Winchester. Billy grabbed the gun and pushed it aside. Then Billy, Thompson and I rode on ahead, and soon Dick fired at Thompson. Billy shouted back, 'Don't do that; this man is a friend of mine.' De Graftenreid then accused Billy of having $500 of his (Dick's) money, and said if he denied it he was a liar. Then Dick began shooting with his Winchester. The first shot hit Billy and passed through his hip. His horse shied, and as he leaned over in his saddle the second shot struck him. He then reached for his revolver, but got Dick's. He fired five shots and so did Thompson. One shot from Dick's Winchester broke the buckle of Billy's cartridge belt, his revolver, cartridges, and all fell to the ground. I had no revolver, and when Billy got out of ammunition it was time for us to go. So we rode off as fast as we could. De Graftenreid fired two shots after us as we rode away. We rode about four miles to Puerto de Luna, where we took supper, and I advised Billy to come to town. We started just as the moon rose and drove all night. Billy laughed and joked with us all the way as he lay in the wagon. The last we saw of de Graftenreid he was making for a Mexican's house.

"Billy Green stood his ride of ninety miles from Puerto de Luna in an open carriage remarkably well, and he was very lively and talkative when he arrived. He insisted that he was not hurt much, as he rolled down the blankets and showed his wounds to the doctor. At a late hour last night he was resting easy. During the shooting, which occurred in broad daylight none of the parties dismounted. Green's overcoat, which was behind him on the horse, had sixteen holes through it."[11]

For several days quite a number of cowboys have been "taking in" the town, and although they have been drinking quite freely, no trouble has occurred until yesterday afternoon, when a fight occurred between George Carter and Bill Woods of the J. J. division of the Prairie Cattle Company, and two Mexican cowboys, named Nestor Sandoval and Francisco Garcia. During the morning of yesterday they had some trouble, and just after dinner they met in front of the Pencel House and renewed the quarrel.

At first no weapons were used excepting rocks and their quirts, but they separated and procured revolvers, when the shooting began.

During the fight Sandoval received a ball in his back, fired by Carter, the ball passing through his heart, from which death was instantaneous.

During the row Marshal Easely got on to the racket, and was in sight when Sandoval was killed, but being unarmed he was compelled to return to his office for his revolver. In the meantime Carter and Woods made a circle out through the country and came into town by the river road, riding up through Main street at full speed, yelling. They were confronted in front of Rossa's office by the City Marshal, but they paid no attention to his drawn revolver or orders to halt. The officer drew a bead on Carter and pulled the trigger, but his revolver refused to go off and the two made their escape.

It is supposed that they made their way direct to camp, which is near Swatzell's *vega*,[12] and after procuring fresh horses probably made a break for Texas. Deputy Sheriff Taylor and Marshal Easely started in pursuit, but returned from the chase about midnight. They were in sight of the fugitives once, but their horses gave out, and as Carter and Woods had procured fresh horses at the camp they would follow no further and were compelled to return home.[13]

The usual quiet of our town was broken on Saturday night by the crack of the festive revolver. When the smoke of the battle cleared away, two dead men were left on the scene. It seems that two cowboys named Johnny Lynch and Joe Vanwinkle got into a row at the Montezuma saloon, which resulted in the shooting of Vanwinkle by Lynch. After killing Vanwinkle, Lynch attempted to escape, but was followed by a man named Brown, a companion of the murdered man, who fired at Lynch as he ran. Lynch was hit in the left leg, the bullet severing the femoral artery, which caused Lynch to bleed to death in a few minutes. A coroner's jury was empanelled and held an inquest, copies of which are enclosed. Brown, after shooting Lynch, escaped, compelling McGeehee the livery man to saddle his horse, while he held a loaded Winchester pointed at him. Justice Blake is severely censured for his failure to cause the arrest of Brown, which could at one time have been easily accomplished, as the man was pointed out to Blake and a request for his arrest made by one of our citizens.[14]

Advices from the Chickasaw nation say that . . . Mud creek [Oklahoma] was the scene of a desperate fight between a party of cowboys, who were driving cattle off the nation under the proclamation recently issued by the Chickasaw authorities. The men had been quarreling for some time, and had halted at the spring. As Ben Tabor was bending down to drink he was shot in the neck by Franklin Scales, who started to run away, when he was in turn shot at by a man named Adams. The firing then became general, the combatants dodging behind trees and bushes and reloading. The fight ended in one gang of the cowboys driving the other from the field. Tabor and

Scales were alive at last accounts, but are not expected to recover.[15]

Ben Carter, a cowboy in the employ of Johnson & Son, on Sandy Creek, [Wyoming] shot and killed a companion named James Jeffrey while lying in bed. The cause was a drunken quarrel. The culprit was brought to town and lodged in jail by two cowboys. He claims the shooting was accidental, and feels all broke up.[16]

Information has reached here from Frio Town, the seat of Frio county, of a duel which took place Friday afternoon in Zavales county, between two of the wealthiest ranchmen of Zavales county, Hiram Bennett and John Rumfield. The men for several years were close friends, and owned many cattle and sheep jointly. About a year ago they dissolved business relations, and a difficulty arose regarding the number of cattle in a certain bunch, which figured in their settlement at a valuation of $10,000. The break grew wider with time, each sending word that he meant to kill the other. On Friday afternoon the two rich ranchmen, with a few cowboys, happened to meet near the edge of the little village of Batesville. They were both on horseback and carrying Winchesters. It was agreed they should dismount and fire at the word of command from one of the cowboys. They stood about one hundred yards apart. Both were crack shots and each fired at the word. Bennett fell dead, with a bullet hole through the brain. One report says Rumfield was wounded in the thigh; another says he is uninjured. No attempt has been made thus far to arrest Rumfield, who is on his ranch, and would doubtless fight before being carried to jail. The dead man was worth about a quarter of a million dollars in cattle, sheep and lands, and leaves a family.[17]

The Red River Cattle Company's ranch, but a few miles from Springer, and owned largely by H. M. Porter, of Denver, and M. M. Chase, of New Mexico, was Thursday the scene of another bloody tragedy. A few weeks ago Ira B. Gale, the foreman, was shot by a Mexican sheep herder, and he had gone home to have his wounds nursed, leaving in charge a man named J. W. Wartenbe. Wm. Alley, who was working on the ranch, seemed to think that he was entitled to boss the affairs in Foreman Gale's absence, and he was continually stirring up trouble among the other hands, and Wednesday Wartenbe discharged him.

Alley wanted a company horse to ride, and Wartenbe refused to let him have it for fear that he would not return it. This caused words to follow from both parties, their pistols coming from the pockets of each, followed by two shots from Alley's pistol and one shot from Wartenbe's, resulting in the death of young Alley and a very bad wound for Wartenbe.

The verdict as rendered by the jury is self defense, on the part of Wartenbe, who is now at Springer with a bullet still in his breast, but he is liable to recover.[18]

Monday afternoon Johnny Davenport, a railroader, was sitting in a chair on the sidewalk at San Marcial, [New Mexico] when Al Chapman, a drunken cowboy, came along and gave him a kick. Davenport got up and shot three times at Chapman and Chapman returned the fire with two shots. Then Marshal Blunt came along and shot twice at Chapman, after which the cowboy was arrested and lodged in the cooler. Nobody was hurt. Good shots down that way.[19]

A. L. Billings was brought into town today with a bullet hole through the groin. He was shot by John Grimes at the roundup camp at the head of Bitter creek at noon yesterday. Bitter creek is 65 miles northwest of this point [Fruita, Colorado,]. Remarkable time was made by the cowboys in coming here for aid, as well as by M. Beard in reaching him. Some of the cowboys went over the road three times, a total of 195 miles in 24 hours. The shooting was the outgrowth of an old feud. Both men had made threats, but Billings was unarmed at the time of the shooting. Four shots were fired, when Oscar Turner, a 14-year old boy, who was in camp alone at the time, interfered and stopped him. Grimes stole a horse and made his escape, after concealing all the arms in camp.

The sheriff of Garfield county, in which the crime was committed, has been notified, but it is not probable that the man can be captured, as he has too much of a start and the country is wild and remote. Grimes has a record as a bad man and a killer. Billings is resting as easily as can be expected, after a 60-mile ride over rough road, but as the bullet passed upward and through the bladder his recovery can hardly be expected. Dr. Beard reports the wound as very serious, but not necessarily fatal.

Your correspondent interviewed the wounded man, but he was too exhausted to detail the causes which led up to the shooting. From other sources it was learned that they were of a trivial nature....[20]

Frank Johnson, a cowboy for the Erie Cattle Company, accompanied by his brother, rode into Bisbee, Arizona, and gave himself up for the killing of Andy Darnell. He claims self defense, and the officers believe him, as is shown by his release on his own recognizance.

Johnson's reputation is good, but Darnell is chiefly remembered for having shot at C. A. Overback at a steer-tying contest at Bisbee, Independence Day last year.[21]

Dan Sullivan, employed as a cowboy in the C. Y. outfit, states that he was shot at by two men while at work on Lower Muddy creek.... Sullivan says the two men came out of the brush and commenced shooting at him. As soon as the firing commenced Sullivan wheeled his horse and made his escape. Sullivan immediately rode to the camp of the outfit and gave up his position. He says he could not afford to risk his life for $30 a month.[22]

RED MAN

The story of the cowboy versus the Indian not only made interesting reading for the subscribers of a newspaper but also increased its circulation. The frontier journalist could always rely upon a cowboy-Indian fracas to raise his status with the editor, and sometimes to embroil the editors of rival newspapers in an argument concerning the justice of the conflict.

An Indian trail has been seen about 15 miles from this place. It was doubtless made by a party of Cheyennes who have slipped around Camp Robinson. It can't be the main band but only a portion, as the main body scattered Sunday.

Cattlemen and settlers near the trail are very uneasy. At Hat Creek [Wyoming] there is a stampede of cowboys. Finally, at 8:45 p.m. a party was organized and it started out to reconnoitre.[23]

A Little Rock special ... says: During the fight here between the cowboys and Indians on the border of the Indian territory four of the former were killed. Col. Alexander Polk, of Howard county [Arkansas] had employed some cowboys to drive a herd of 2,000 cattle to Colorado. The boys were herding the cattle in the nation en route for their destination and were ordered to remove the stock but failed or refused to do so, when the fight ensued.[24]

Last summer General Sherman made his last annual inspection of the military posts of the army, and a good story is told by one of his staff officers of his visit to one of the western frontier posts. When the general arrived there was a large crowd of Indians on hand to look at the "big chief of the whites," as they called him. After they had looked him over to their hearts' content, one of them approached and said, "Ugh, big Indian heap want present of cannon." Gen. Sherman glanced at the brave and replied: "I cannot give you cannon. What do you want them for? You mean to use them against my soldiers." Now, an Indian is not often guilty of anything approaching wit, but this one did very well, for he said, as he shook his head, "No want cannon to kill soldiers. Can kill soldiers with sticks. Want cannon to kill cowboys." The reply was a good one, but Mr. Indian didn't get his cannon all the same.[25]

Our special dispatches from the southwestern part of Colorado this morning indicate very clearly that the cowboys were the aggressors in the affair which began with the murder of six Ute Indians and ended with the murder of one white man and the serious wounding of his wife. It is claimed, apparently with truth, that the Indians in question were off their reservation when they were fired upon by the cowboys, but we fail to find any law, either human or divine, which justifies cowboys to murder Indians who are off their reservation. It is a deplorable fact that the innocent settlers, who have made their homes in the vicinity of the reservation in question, are placed in peril of their lives by the lawlessness of the cowboys, who are quite irresponsible for their acts and in no great danger of punishment for their crimes. It may have been a mistake to let the Southern Utes remain on a reservation that is at best but poorly adapted to their mode of life, but so long as it is part of the policy of the government to permit them to stay there they are entitled to fair play. It is true that they may occasionally stray from their reservation, but we would like to know how long the cowboys of Colorado would last if they were to be shot down every time they were caught on lands that did not belong to their employers.[26]

Of course the *Hyphen* [*Tribune-Republican*] knows it ignores the truth when it speaks of "the fight between the Indians and cowboys" in La Plata county [Colorado]. There was no fight at all. A party of cowboys found a batch of seven Indians, one of whom was a squaw and two were pappooses, on ground that belonged to neither the cowboys nor the Indians. Apparently without parley or provocation, the cowboys fired upon the Indians, killing six of the seven. A half-grown boy escaped and carried the tidings to other Indians, who in a fit of revenge set fire to the house of a peaceable white settler, and when he and his wife stepped out to fight the flames, fired upon them, killing the husband and inflicting a wound that will probably prove fatal upon the wife. So far as is known that is all the trouble that occurred and we would like to know where the fight came in that the *Hyphen* prates about? It was assassination on both sides and if the cause of disturbance shall prove to be as reported, we think the cowboys must be responsible for all the killing done. They had no moral or legal right to fire upon the Indians and they must have known that the effect of their murderous volley would be to provoke a raid of retaliation on the inoffensive white ranchmen, who were living on terms of peace and friendship with the Indians. There seems good ground for the suspicion that there was some sinister purpose, not yet fully made public, behind the outrage committed by the cowboys. Possibly a prospective claim of $100,000 to be presented to Congress at its next session for alleged losses inflicted upon some of the employers of these cowboys by the Utes a year ago, may have had something to do with it. We hope the facts will be thoroughly investigated. Only sympathy will be felt for the unfortunate Genthner family who were crushed between the rapacity of the white and the revenge of the redskins.[27]

Ex-delegate Ouray of Arizona, and Colonel Hughes, of the territory, called upon the commissioner of Indian affairs today to urge the disarming of the Indians of the San Carlos reservation in Arizona. They expressed the belief that this movement, if adopted, would prevent a conflict that seemed to be impending between the Indians now on the reservation and the white settlers.

Commissioner Atkins met the request with a proposition that the cowboys also be disarmed, and then proceeded to expound his view upon the Indian question at some length. He said he failed to see any reason why the cowboys should carry arms when the Indians were disarmed, and added that it was entirely improper for any person, white, black or red, to be permitted to ride around the country with a Winchester rifle and army revolver, free to shoot any one in sight.[28]

General Augur shows his good sense and fitness by quoting *The News* in his official dispatches to the War Department regarding the assassination in La Plata county. General Augur is entirely right in attributing whatever crimes may have been committed in the San

Juan between the whites and Indians last month, to the cowboys. Carlisle has a claim for mythical cattle alleged to have been killed by the Utes last summer, and Mr. James McCarthy ("Fitz Mac") is Carlisle's "attorney" for the collection of that claim from the government. "Fitz Mac" works the newspaper side of the racket while the cowboys attend to the business of assassinating the Utes.[29]

Agent Stollsteimer's report to Commissioner Atkins shows conclusively that *The News* has been right from the first in holding that the cowboys were wholly to blame for the recent trouble in the San Juan.

It proves that early on the morning of June 19 a large party of cowboys fired into a teepee containing a number of sleeping Utes, and that six of the Indians were killed by the fusilade. The only cause assigned for this massacre is that the Utes were "off their reservation."

It would be interesting to know what justification can be offered for this wanton act on the part of the cowboys. There is nothing in the laws or customs of the land to warrant anybody in killing an Indian beyond the limits of a reservation. It is said in defense of the cattlemen who employ these cowboys that a year ago they notified the Secretary of the Interior that it was their determination thenceforth to kill every Indian found off the Southern Ute reservation, but we fail to see that this action gave the cattlemen or their employes any right to commit murder. Indeed, it seems that if such a notification was actually given it was the duty of the government to take steps to prevent the cattlemen from carrying their lawless threat into execution.

The Utes may not seem to be desirable neighbors, but they are entitled to the protection of the government so long as it sees fit to leave them in possession of their present reservation, and nothing can excuse the bloodthirsty spirit which prompted the recent attack upon the family found off the reservation by the cowboys.

It must be borne in mind that the cattlemen in question are themselves unlawful trespassers on the public domain. They have no more right under the law to roam at will over the government lands than the Utes; they occupy their present ranges merely on sufferance, and they cannot be permitted to kill human beings of any color at pleasure.

Their criminal misconduct in making an attack which was calculated to provoke reprisals that might have drenched the San Juan in the blood of innocent white settlers and their families should be punished in some way. There can be no doubt that the attack made by a band of Indians on Mr. Genteur and his family on the night of June 20, was in retaliation for the massacre of June 19, and the only wonder is that Agent Stollsteimer and the military at Fort Lewis were able to check the Indian demand for vengeance so promptly.

The very fact that in the face of such strong provocation the Utes repressed their natural tendency to take the war path is excellent evidence that they are in a fair way to become civilized by fair treatment.

It is feared by some that during the roundup which is advertised to begin next Friday, the cowboys who are all heavily armed and apparently eager for a fight, will renew the hostilities begun a fortnight ago and Governor Eaton has been urged to send a few militia companies into the disturbed region for the protection of the ranchmen. We believe that the United States troops are better adapted to this work and that the militia should not be called out. It is reasonably certain that if the cowboys do not attack the Indians no further killing will take place and the cattlemen should be held to a strict accountability for the good behavior of their employes.[30]

After full investigation I consider that the killing of the Indians, June 19, was done by a band of horse thieves that have infested this county since last fall, ...

STOLLSTEIMER, AGENT[31]

Though the evidence was very strong, yet we never thoroughly believed that the killing of the six Utes, on the Dolores, two weeks ago, was the work of cowboys— at least we never believed that the killing was without provocation, if it was the work of the cowboys. Mr.

Carlisle, who has large cattle interests in La Plata county and in Eastern Utah, has, it seems, taken the trouble to go to Indian Agent Stollsteimer to know if the articles which have appeared in the *News* of Denver, charging the cowboys with the killing, represent the views of the Indian Department. The Agent thereupon requested him to telegraph to the Denver papers that he was convinced from his investigation that the Indians were slain by a band of horse thieves which infests that section of the country.

This puts a different phase upon the situation. It is a vindication of the cowboys. This will be a great blow to the *News,* for it has set out to annihilate the cowboys of the Southwest. It believes that they and not the Utes should go.[32]

From Mr. Fitzgerald who came in on the train this evening we learn that a fight between some cowboys and a band of Indians took place last night at Stein's Peak. The cowboys killed two Indians and captured one pappoose. They saw a band of about 30 Indians as the train passed today between San Simon [Arizona] and Stein's Pass [New Mexico]. The train was stopped 10 miles west of Stein's Pass by a party of cowboys to get water from the train.[33]

Companies from Fort Custer, [Montana] under Captain Jackson, are guarding Yellowstone valley, near Junction City, against depredating Indians, and have already captured and sent to the fort about forty Crows.

Pidgeons and Cheyennes are also found off their reservation. Vigilant watch is kept by the cowboys and the military. Report now comes that the Cheyennes are raiding Mispah valley, and troops will probably be sent from Fort Keogh [Montana] to return them to their agency on the Rosebud.[34]

The Ute outbreak in the western part of the state [Colorado] turns out to be, as is usually the case, a row between the cowboys and the Indians, which will probably last until one or both are exterminated. It will not be bad for the people of the state when both cowboys and Indians have disappeared and their places are taken by steady prosperous ranchmen. As a matter of justice between the Indians and cowboys, we feel safe to say that they are both aggressors. It appears to be a cardinal principle with the Indians to steal the property of the cowboys and of the latter in recovering their own to steal that of the Indians. If the row could be confined to the two parties it would not be a bad idea to let them fight it out.[35]

A little boy named Wallace Owens who was sent yesterday by his father, N. Owens, to his ranch to get some garden truck, reported that he was suddenly surrounded by Indians. Comanquack, Eney Colorow, Pant, Pear and three young bucks were in the party. Pear is the Ute's war chief. They did not harm the boy, but ate watermelons with him and told him to tell the settlers on White River to return home, as the Utes would not hurt them. "Utes not mad with ranches, mad with cowboys." The boy asked if the Utes had enough of fighting and they replied, "Maybe so; if Ute no get back ponies maybe so fight cowboy, and steal 'em hoss."

Later in the day young Owens' father tried to approach the Utes, but they galloped off. These Utes were some of the party whose trail was found in and around the battle ground.[36]

It is reported, by the way of Albuquerque, that a fight has occurred, near Fort Wingate, [New Mexico] between a number of cowboys and Navajo Indians.[37]

Although the cattlemen of the territory held title to the pasturage by virtue of contracts made with the different tribes, yet all was not peace between the Indians and cowboys. The agreements between the cattle owners and the chiefs did not always extend to the subordinates. It was no uncommon thing to have the herds stampeded by some reckless, dare-devil redskin who had been imbibing too much fire-water. There is no more villainous compound on earth than the whiskey that was sold the Indians in the territory. Arsenic and rain-water, with a dash of pepper sauce, would be comparatively mild beside it.

The savage throat craved it, however, and when about half a pint had moistened it the owner of the throat cared little for law, order, the right of property, or the agreement which his chief might have entered into with regard to the protection of cattle. Dashing into a herd with fiendish yells and swinging a blanket about his head, the crazed and infuriated buck would send the whole mass off on a fear-stricken race. There was no stopping, no halting, until wearied by their long miles of running the animals at length slowed down out of sheer inability to go farther, leaving the plain behind dotted with carcasses of the weaker ones which had been unable to keep up with the pace of the herd.

James Slocum, a cattleman running a fine bunch of cattle just on the southern border of the strip, was entirely ruined by an attack of this kind. Like many another man who essayed to make a fortune out of cattle, he was working largely on borrowed capital. He had done well, however, and in September of 1883 he had ready for market something over 400 head of the fattest four-year-old steers in the country. At the price cattle were worth then the returns from these steers would have been sufficient to pay all his debts and leave him a neat surplus. He had already begun to congratulate himself on his success in the cattle business, and was laying plans for the disposition of the surplus—plans which for a lack of reckoning with his hosts, the Indians, were destined never to be fulfilled.

One day about noon, just as the final preparations for starting over the trail to Kiowa, [Oklahoma] the nearest shipping point, were being made, and the bunch of beeves was in charge of three cowboys about two miles from the Canadian river, a band of three drunken, crazy, devilish Indians suddenly appeared, and in an instant, by their wild yells and frantic maneuvers, had stampeded the cattle. The latter headed straight north toward the Canadian. In a quarter of an hour they had reached it, their speed not yet relaxed nor their fears allayed. Into the river they rushed, only to be caught and held fast by the treacherous quicksands. Out of the herd of 400 head, 325 met their death there and Slocum's chance for freeing himself from debt was gone. The drop in prices a few months later made his creditors anxious and they squeezed him, leaving him without a cent in the world.[38]

There was a pitched battle about ten miles from this place, Coolidge, New Mexico, yesterday between cowboys and Navajos. The latter were charged with looting Bennett's sheep camp. They were overtaken by the cowboys and one of their number was taken prisoner as hostage for the return of the goods. Soon after they started with him he gave a war whoop and the other Indians began shooting, the fire being returned by the cowboys. Considerable ammunition was wasted on both sides but no corpses were found on the battlefield. The boys arrived here yesterday at 2 p.m. and sent their prisoner to Fort Wingate. It has been learned that the Indians passed Mitchell in a demoralized state. Some of them were bloody and several horses showed the cowboys' marksmanship. It has not yet been learned whether any of the Indians were seriously wounded.[39]

A band of Indians raided a cowboy camp just below the border of Old Mexico yesterday. The men in the employ of the Old and New Mexico Ranch and Cattle company and the Diamond A company established a camp two miles south of the line in Plyas valley on Tuesday. Five cowboys left the camp with the horse herd to obtain water some miles away; when they returned they found the camp in the greatest confusion, all the food supplies being stolen and everything about the place being scattered. Two new hats were slashed and new boots met a like fate. The camp chest was broken open and the marauders supposedly destroyed the contents and polluted the box. The marauders are supposedly a remnant of the Apaches under the leadership of the notorious Kid Albough, although it is possible that they belong to the Yaqui tribe.[40]

WHITE MAN

It was not uncommon for the cowboy to come in conflict with other white men—particularly the sodbuster, who was probably the greatest threat as an invader of the rangeman's domain. The story of the struggle between cowboy and homeseeker is bloody and fierce; it is a struggle of survival. In the eyes of the frontier journalist the cowboy lost face in this clash.

A dispatch from Kearney Junction, [Nebraska] says that a party of twenty Texas herders came in late last night and camped on the Platte at the bridge. During the night their horses got into a corn field of Mr. Calter's. He took up the horses, and this a.m. the herders came up town, got drunk, went back, and shot Calter four times, killing him almost instantly. Citizens organized, and are in pursuit of the Texans.[41]

An Associated Press reporter today visited Captain D. R. Payne and his Oklahoma "boomers," where they are held prisoners at the camp of Lieutenant Jackson and a detachment of the 9th Cavalry in the Cherokee nation, opposite Fort Smith [Arkansas]. Payne said: "I first went to Oklahoma five years ago, when informed by able lawyers that these lands were open to white settlement and located a colony. Since then I have been removed seven or eight times by the military.... Cattlemen and cowboys were against us and threatened to assassinate us. The cowboys tore down our flag to use for a saddle blanket, but Captain Moore recovered it.... The officers seemed to fear the cowboys would attempt to assassinate us.... I want to get our matter before the courts of the country for we believe we have the right to locate homesteads on these lands and intend to keep trying until the matter is properly adjusted.[42]

The range man has for some time past been casting tiger-eyes at the granger and the two have not dwelt in harmony together. Still we anticipate that time will wipe out the present animosities and restore good fellowship among the dwellers of the plains. This week Mr. Jacob Scherer, a heavy range man with a large herd in the eastern end of Arapahoe county, [Colorado] made the statement that he was rather well pleased with the advent of farmers in the range country. He realizes that the ranges must give way to cultivated fields, and by this change there would be vast quantities of corn and alfalfa hay grown which he could buy reasonably cheap for his herd in winter. He could pasture and graze in summer, and in winter feed the product of adjoining farms.

But down in New Mexico the granger is not welcome by the big cattle companies. At the present time settlers are being bluffed and intimidated to prevent their making locations in the eastern part of Colfax county, which has always been a cow country. One gentleman is known to have received written notice that he could not go ahead with his improvements though his claim being on government land was not disputed. The other day a Texan, accompanied by his wife and daughter, looking for a location, while camped on government land, were visited by a party of five men and told that they were encroaching upon the rights of a certain cattle company and that they had better leave. Owing to the fright of the women the man moved away.

Just as if such intimidating measures are going to keep the country from being settled upon by the farmers. A cowboy who has lately been in the employ of a cattle company out there informed a *Raton Range* reporter last week that five men were employed by the different outfits to bluff settlers. They actually traverse the country in a wagon and are working up a feeling that if continued will result in a surprise party in which the settlers will not be the ones surprised. Most of the trouble so far has been in the neighborhood of Kiowa Springs, [Colorado] a locality with an unpleasant local history of outrage and bloodshed.[43]

Kit Carson, Colorado, is on the line of the Texas cattle trail, and there are herds going through there every day now. J. R. Blocker of Texas is there with 6,000 head, bound north. Several Denver and Wyoming men have been looking at cattle, with view of purchasing. Among them were W. A. and M. D. Murphy of Wyoming. Cattle are in fine shape, but water is scarce south of Kit Carson. The fences of the new settlers delay the herds a good deal, and there is a constant howl from the cowboys about the dadgasted "grangers." Nevertheless the boys manage in some way to get their steers through and several trail herds of Texas cattle have gotten as far north as Snyder and Holyoke. They are later this year than usual. The boys say the grangers have built too many fences for them to travel very fast. Part of the Texas and Montana drives were made by rail however and all the drovers say this is the last season they shall attempt to run the Colorado gauntlet.[44]

A young fellow named Stanley, a cow puncher for the O—O Ranch, meeting the old German gardner, Merk, on a lonely road near Deming, [New Mexico] one day last week, attempted to rob him. Stanley drew his six-shooter and demanded the old man's money. The old man gave him $3—all he had. Stanley became enraged at the smallness of the amount and beat Merk over the head with the revolver. The revolver went off and blew one of Stanley's fingers away. The cowboy then permitted the gardner to depart. On reaching Deming, Merk caused Stanley's arrest, and the cow puncher languishes in the county jail awaiting the pleasure of the next grand jury.[45]

William Davis, a cowboy, formerly in the employ of Ed Skinner of this city, [Grand Junction, Colorado,] was shot through the shoulder this morning . . . by Henry Waller, a farmer. . . . Davis, in company with another young man, was driving into the city. They were followed by Waller and his brother. When Waller reached the wagon of Davis, he said, "You —- - —, have you a loaded quirt with you now?" Davis replied: "I have nothing." Waller then pulled a gun and commenced flourishing it. Davis made an effort to go toward him to disarm him if possible, and received a ball in the shoulder.

The cause of the shooting was offensive remarks by Waller regarding Davis, which Davis had refuted a week before, at the same time slashing Waller with a quirt. The wounded man was brought to this city and his wound dressed. Waller escaped.[46]

BLACK MAN

Evidence of color discrimination on the part of the cowboy is not very pronounced. Difficulties between the Negro and cowboy arose only as differences between men and were probably found more often in the Southwest, although the Negro was accepted as a member of the riding fraternity in the cattle kingdom.

A lively set-to occurred between a cowboy and a darkey named Sam Washington at Raton [New Mexico] ... in which pistols were drawn but no shooting done. Later in the evening the cowboy and Tim McAuliffe had a set-to, Tim coming out ahead.[47]

A Democratic cowboy, by the way, a few days since, said: "Well, I have always voted the straight ticket in Texas, and everywhere, that I had the chance and am proud of it, but I can't stomach quite so much 'nigger' blood as the man Joseph has this time.[48]

A colored cowboy named Lawson Fretwell, employed by the Home Land and Cattle company, a bad man from the Indian nation, was shot and killed by an officer at Trinidad on Monday night. Fretwell was in a gambling institution and got up a gun play in which he himself was killed. The cowboy seems to be keeping up his reputation this year as well as ever, and the mortuary reports are as entertaining as usual. It's generally the cowboy that gets the worst of the racket and he is not such a successful bad man as he has been pictured.[49]

A deputy sheriff has just arrived from the line of the eastern Indian lands, bringing news of a race war in progress there just on the line of the Iowa reservation. The town of Langston [Oklahoma] was founded several months ago and is inhabited solely by negroes. There are several thousand of them. These and more are arriving daily on the line of the new lands. The negroes contemplate settling in a body in the Cimarron valley as soon as the lands are opened. A gang of cowboys from the Cherokee strip also have their eyes on the locality, and say that any negro who attempts to settle there will be killed.

Yesterday the cowboys visited Langston, got into a row and attempted to shoot Eggleston, editor of the *Herald*. Last night they returned, all drunk, and fired a score of shots into a crowd of negroes on the streets. Several received slight wounds. The cowboys left, swearing they would return today and wipe out the town. The negroes have all armed themselves and if they do return many will likely be killed. A force of officers have left for the scene.[50]

BEEF vs. MUTTON

The sheepherder, like the sodbuster, threatened the cattleman's kingdom, and here, too, it was a question of survival. In his records of these bitter feuds the frontier journalist portrays the brutality of the rangeman's savage attacks on the herder who, with his flocks, invaded the grazing land.

Of the numerous feuds between the cowmen and the sheepmen, volumes might be written. Many of them were shot out on the streets of the cow towns, and many a duel took place in the brush of which nothing was ever heard.[51]

The physical and mental differences between the cowboy and the sheep herder are as great as those of their respective callings. From the very nature of his occupation the cowboy is a wild, free being.

He breaks the savage and almost untamable ponies to the saddle, and then rides them. His work is swift and vigorous, and his charges are the great, strong, free bulls and cows that have never known the touch of the human hand. He lives and endures hardships with others, of his kind, and his pleasures are as fierce as his work. His is the strenuous life.

The sheep herder, on the other hand, pursues his solitary occupation afoot, his only companion being a dog and the thousands of stupid sheep, which have no individuality, and are maddeningly, monotonously alike. The very loneliness of his occupation has made the herder either a morose and sullen brute or a poetic dreamer, with all the fight worn out of him.

In the Northwest a sheep herder is looked upon as a "scrub," even more to be despised than the farm hand by the cowboy. Occasionally sheep herders have been known to display great personal bravery in their conflicts with the cow men, but generally they are at a great disadvantage.

As a rule, cowboys are Americans, while the sheep herders are usually foreigners—Mexicans, Frenchmen, or Spaniards from the Basque country, while sometimes Indians are employed. The question of diet in this comparison is not to be despised, for, while the cowboy eats pork, beef and beans and drinks strong, black coffee, the herder subsists for months on a monotonous round of tea and mutton.

The West still rings with the stories of the conflicts between the cow men and the sheep raisers. When the flocks began to grow in the West the cow men fought the herders as individuals. Their resentment was at first merely personal.[52]

About two weeks ago a party of cowboys who were in the employ of the Prairie Cattle company, attacked the herders and killed 4,000 sheep belonging to J. M. Perea, while grazing on the range. Perea threatened to sue the Prairie Cattle company for the value of the sheep, but settlement will be effected without resort to law.[53]

Hon. Jesus Ma. Perea, of Bernalillo [New Mexico] informed a New Mexican man that the Prairie Cattle company has agreed to pay for the sheep the cowboys killed near his ranch in Colorado recently. Mr. Perea went up to Colorado when he was informed of the wholesale slaughter of his stock, and found four thousand head of dead sheep. It appears that the herd was grazing on the cattle range and that the herders were ordered to drive them off. Not obeying the order, the cowboys attacked them and drove them off, after which they slaughtered the sheep by the thousands. Mr. Perea prepared to bring suit against the Prairie Cattle company, whose men had done the mischief, but has been notified the sheep will be paid for. He owns a fine herd in Colorado, and intends to protect his interests.[54]

A shooting scrape near Tesquiquile, Colfax county, [New Mexico] ... resulted in the death of a Mexican, whose name was not learned. A herd of about 5,000 head of sheep had been driven on the range of the Dubuque Cattle company, and Jim Follis, one of the foremen, went out to the camp and ordered the Mexican off. He declared he would not go, and went into his tent and returned with a Winchester rifle, and just as he was going to raise it to his shoulder to fire, Follis fired and killed him almost instantly. Follis went to Springer ... and delivered himself to the officers. He is a son of William Follis, of the Purgatoire, and as the shooting was done in self defense, it is very probable there will be no further proceedings in the matter.[55]

Mr. Carlisle's cowboys in the Southwestern part of the state have been fighting again, this time with some sheepmen, who dared to intrude upon that portion of the public domain which Mr. Carlisle claims as his particular cattle range. But it is difficult to understand why American sheepmen have not as good a right to the free use of the public domain as the foreign cattle corporation which Mr. Carlisle manages for revenue only.[56]

Intelligence of a fearful fight between cowboys and sheepherders near Grants Station, on the Arizona line, has just reached here. It appears that the sheepmen were watering their flocks at a water-hole when four cowboys came on the scene and ordered the sheepmen away. The herders refused to leave until their flocks were watered. Hot words followed, when, the herders say, the cowboys rode a few yards away and opened fire upon them with their Winchesters. The first shot killed Myer Domeo, one of the herders. They returned the fire, wounding one cowboy, but they could not say how seriously. The cowboys then fired a second volley, wounding three more herders, and then rode off at the top of their speed toward the Arizona line. This morning another herder, Jesus Maria Chaves, died from his wound, having been shot through both hips. A strong posse has gone out after the murderers, who, not having much start, will likely be caught.[57]

From a Mr. Edwards, a sheep raiser in the mountains, it is learned that a terrible hand-to-hand conflict, in which pistols and knives were used, took place the other evening between the sheep herders from Sam Lund's ranch and cowboys supposed to work for W. B. Slaughter. The battle resulted in the killing of two and the wounding of four sheep herders. The sheriff has left for the scene with a posse heavily armed, and it is predicted that more murders will be committed.[58]

A special to the *Record* from Chadron, Neb., says:

"As a sequel to the court scene at Hot Springs, S.D., last week, in which 32 cattle men were acquitted of the charge of killing John Eckman, a sheep herder, in Fall River county, South Dakota, last August, a cavalcade composed of the exonerated cattle men rode up to the little cabin occupied by the destitute family of the dead man. The leader knocked at the door and Mrs. Eckman responded. Her face grew pale and she trembled.

"'Mrs. Eckman,' says the leader, 'We have come to make you a little Christmas present. We shot your husband, but it was in self defense. We know you are without funds. We would gladly restore you your husband, but that is impossible, so we do the next best thing—give you the means to support yourself and children. If you need more call on us,' and he handed her a bag containing

$1,000 in gold. The plainsmen raised their hats, mounted their horses and rode away."[59]

Call a cowboy a thief and he may possibly reply in kind; call him a liar and, unless time is hanging heavily on his hands so that he is pining for excitement, you may ride away in safety—though no guarantee goes with this statement; curse him and he is likely to express his admiration of your command of invective; but call him a sheep herder and your blood or his will flow.

It may be said incidentally that if you called him a shepherd he would probably fail to gather your meaning.

In his world there are two classes of human beings—white men and sheep men. In this connection white has nothing to do with color.

So it has been ever since the first wool bearer made the grazing range cows snort with its aggravating "ba-a!" The lion and the lamb may lie down together, but the steer and the lamb's progenitors never.

There is nothing theoretical or academic about this war of beef and mutton raisers. It is a real fight, with shootings, slaughterings, burnings, raids and reprisals. Within the past ten years, along the border of Colorado alone, a score of men have been killed, five times as many wounded, and six hundred thousand sheep slaughtered and their carcasses left to the buzzards; and that section is only one department of the field of operations. Take the full theater of war, and the loss inflicted upon the sheep raisers by the cattle men's raids must amount to fully five million dollars in the decade.[60]

"GREASER"

The Mexican suffered no more at the hands of the cowboy than any other "outsider" who came into the sphere of the range cattle industry and threatened the status quo. As a "foreigner" he was subjected to the same cruelties as were the Indian, the sodbuster, and the sheepherder.

A dispatch from Tucson, Arizona says: Advices from Santa Cruz say that cowboys have been running off stock belonging to the people of Santa Cruz, four miles south of La Noria. Some have lost all of their stock. Great indignation is manifested against the United States authorities for permitting a band of villains, who are worse than the Apaches, to commit such frequent and damaging incursions on them. Word from other ranches on the line say the cowboys are growing more numerous daily, and their raids more frequent.[61]

A dispatch from Tucson says: About three weeks ago four Americans were killed near Frintares, Chihuahua, three of whom are supposed to have been cowboys. For the week past cowboys have been concentrating near Galeyville, with the avowed purpose of avenging their comrades. They threated to take Frintares last week. Word was sent to the Mexican consul at this place, who sent warning to the people at Frintares, and also notified the Mexican federal troops, of which there are 200 stationed on San Bernardino ranch. On Tuesday morning the cowboys, 70 in number and well equipped, left Wilcox [Arizona] for the purpose of carrying out their threats, and it is believed there will be bloody work, as they were probably the most reckless gang of desperadoes ever banded together. The Mexicans will either have to leave the place or make a hard fight. Frintares is about forty miles from Wilcox.[62]

The *Republican's* Trinidad special says: A fight between three Mexicans and two cowboys, on a ranch near here, resulted in Duchy Brown receiving a fatal wound, W. B. Cartright two slight wounds, and one Mexican two shots in the breast. The Mexicans escaped.[63]

Reliable information has been received from San Pedro river, below the Sonora line, that the San Simeon cowboys are depredating fearfully upon the Mexican stockraisers in Sonora. J. N. Elias, whose lands extend for eighty miles along the line, is the greatest sufferer. The people are in terror. There are about two hundred of these cattle thieves, mostly from Texas, who are scattered along the border, in bands of from ten to twenty, and all co-operative. Mexicans are arming themselves and say that if the United States authorities will not interest themselves in punishing these invaders, they will not allow an American to cross the line along the localities of these ranches, as they are unable to distinguish between good and bad Americans.

They claim that the depredations of the Apaches was not half so destructive as the work of the cowboys. A prominent Mexican rancher who arrived in this city today, with a view of purchasing twenty stand of arms to defend his property, stated that if something was not done by the American government to prevent these American marauders from invading their homes, that serious complications must arise. It appears that these cattle thieves are largely made up of the same bands who gave so much trouble on the Rio Grande for years past. The cattlemen of southeastern Arizona are also losing much stock from the same source.[64]

News was received here tonight of a fight between cowboys and Mexican smugglers last Monday a few miles from Presidio [Texas]. The Mexicans were driving off about 500 cattle from the ranch of Michael Medonez, when they were attacked by twenty-five cowboys, who opened fire on the thieves with their Winchesters. The smugglers returned the fire.

The battle lasted thirty minutes, when the Mexicans retreated across the Rio Grande. Carlos Thomas, superintendent of the ranch, and Juan Pelasco, a cowboy, were killed, while the smugglers lost three men. The cattle were stampeded by the firing and many of them crossed into Mexico.[65]

NOTES TO CHAPTER FOUR

1. "The Sportive Cowboy," *Trinidad Weekly News* (Trinidad, Colorado), October 20, 1881.
2. "Cold Blooded Murder," *ibid.*, January 5, 1882.
3. "A Strange Duel," *Las Animas Leader* (Las Animas, Colorado), September 29, 1882.
4. "The Latest News," *Trinidad Weekly Advertiser* (Trinidad, Colorado), June 2, 1883.

5. *Santa Fe New Mexican Review* (Santa Fe, New Mexico), June 30, 1883.
6. "Death by the Bullet," *Black Range* (Chloride, New Mexico), June 6, 1884.
7. "Telegraphic Brevities," *Fort Morgan Times* (Fort Morgan, Colorado), December 18, 1884.
8. *Kansas Cowboy* (Dodge City, Kansas), August 1, 1885.
9. "Two Cowboys Killed," *Democratic Leader* (Cheyenne, Wyoming), August 16, 1885.
10. Cf. *Field and Farm* (Denver, Colorado), January 30, 1886, p. 8.
11. "A Duel on Horseback," *Denver Tribune-Republican* (Denver, Colorado), July 13, 1886.
12. A flat lowland.
13. "A Cowboy Fight at Trinidad," *Denver Tribune-Republican*, July 13, 1886.
14. *Soccoro Chieftain* (Socorro, New Mexico), August 17, 1886.
15. "Cowboys Have a Battle," *El Anunciador de Trinidad*, (Trinidad, Colorado), August 26, 1886.
16. *Democratic Leader*, October 6, 1886.
17. "Wealthy Ranchmen Fight a Duel," *El Anunciador de Trinidad*, November 11, 1886.
18. "Another Tragedy," *ibid.*, December 9, 1886.
19. *Cerrillos Rustler* (Cerrillos, New Mexico), July 10, 1891.
20. "Shooting at Cowboy Camp," *Denver Republican* (Denver, Colorado), August 22, 1895.
21. "Killed by a Cowboy," *ibid.*, July 7, 1898.
22. "Fired on a Cowboy," *ibid.*, September 11, 1898.
23. *Cheyenne Daily Leader* (Cheyenne, Wyoming), October 9, 1878.
24. *Ibid.*, June 21, 1882.
25. "Indian Remedy for Cowboys," *Las Vegas Daily Optic*, December 17, 1883.
26. [Editorial] *Rocky Mountain News* (Denver, Colorado), June 25, 1885.
27. *Ibid.*, June 26, 1885.
28. "Opposed to Cowboys," *Rocky Mountain News*, July 4, 1885.
29. *Rocky Mountain News*, July 4, 1885.
30. "The Southern Utes," *ibid.*, July 6, 1885.
31. "Not the Cowboys," *ibid.*, July 9, 1885.
32. " 'Twas Not the Cowboys," *Denver Tribune-Republican*, July 9, 1885.
33. "Cowboys Make a Capture," *Beef and Bullion* (Tucson, Arizona), July 6, 1885.
34. "The Military and the Cowboys," *Rocky Mountain News*, October 7, 1885.
35. *Field and Farm*, August 20, 1887, p. 5.
36. "In the Watermelons," *Denver Republican*, September 6, 1887.

FOES ON THE FRONTIER

37. "Deeds of Violence," *Las Vegas Daily Optic*, August 13, 1891.

38. "Indians and Whiskey," *Field and Farm*, July 22, 1893, p. 6.

39. "Cowboys and Navajos," *Stock Grower and Farmer* (Las Vegas, New Mexico), August 19, 1893.

40. "Indians Raid Cowboys' Camp," *Denver Republican*, September 6, 1900.

41. "Twenty Texas Herders Corralled for Murder," *Las Animas Leader*, September 24, 1875.

42. "Payne's 'Boomers,'" *Democratic Leader*, August 28, 1884.

43. "The Grange and the Cowman," *Field and Farm*, December 24, 1887, p. 8.

44. *Field and Farm*, June 30, 1888, p. 9.

45. "A Naughty Cowboy," *Southwest Sentinel* (Silver City, New Mexico), October 7, 1890.

46. "Shooting at Grand Junction," *Denver Republican*, September 28, 1892.

47. *Trinidad Weekly News*, October 6, 1881.

48. *San Miguel County Republican* (Las Vegas, New Mexico), October 23, 1886.

49. *Field and Farm*, July 23, 1887, p. 8.

50. "Cowboys vs. Negroes," *Rocky Mountain News*, September 18, 1891.

51. Matthew J. Herron, "The Passing of the Cowman," *Overland Monthly*, LV (February, 1910), 199.

52. "War between the Cattle and Sheep Men of the West," *Denver Republican*, December 9, 1900.

53. *Cheyenne Daily Leader*, February 22, 1882.

54. *Denver Daily Times* (Denver, Colorado), February 24, 1882.

55. "The Bullet," *Trinidad Daily Advertiser* (Trinidad, Colorado), December 21, 1883.

56. *Rocky Mountain News*, January 31, 1886.

57. "A Fight with Cowboys," *El Anunciador de Trinidad*, April 7, 1887.

58. "New Mexico Fun," *Republic* (St. Louis, Missouri), January 8, 1889.

59. "Generous Cowboys," *Denver Republican*, December 28, 1898.

60. Charles Michelson, "The War for the Range," *Munsey's Magazine*, XXVIII (December, 1902), 380.

61. "Cowboys Running Off Stock," *Cheyenne Daily Leader*, March 11, 1881.

62. "The Cowboys Want Revenge," *ibid.*, June 21, 1881.

63. "A Cowboys' Jamboree," *ibid.*, December 3, 1881.

64. "Depredations of Texas Cowboys," *ibid.*, February 17, 1881.

65. "Cowboys and Smugglers Fight," *Denver Republican*, September 15, 1892.

Goin' to Town

FIVE

Both in fiction and nonfiction the cowboys invariably ride into town on a cloud of dust and, with six-shooters blazing, rush to the saloon. Some dismount and tie their horses to the ever-present hitching rail; others ride through the swinging doors and cause much consternation among the customers who scatter tables, chips, gold, and chairs in all directions in their frenzied efforts to escape the wild hoofs of the excited horses and the bullets of the hilarious visitors.

Thus the cowboy goes to town! Such a notorious description occurs so frequently that it has practically been accepted as a standard. It appears at least once in every Western picture—whether a "quickie" or a "super-special colossal"—produced by one of the major studios.

Occasionally the theme is varied. A lone cowboy rides into town; he approaches the bank with intent to rob it; he arrives at the sheriff's office with a problem; he goes to the local saloon for a drink; he seeks a little vine-covered house on the edge of town to visit his mother, girl friend, or an old-time crony—the prospects are endless, but the theme is not. It has invariably been associated with the cowboy ever since he has appeared in story.

The constant repetition of these hackneyed themes allows two conclusions—either the cowboy was a very dull individual without imagination, or the whole truth has not been told of his excursions into town. The cowboy lived a life of isolation. It seems stupid and unimaginative for him to try to "take over the town" or "shoot it up" when the purpose of his visit was to do and to see things. The easiest way to curtail these opportunities was to try to "take over." In the rowdiest, law-forsaken towns there were just as many law-abiding citizens who were determined to prevent this action as there were cowboys who attempted to carry it out. Most often the townsmen had the advantage.

This leads one to the other conclusion—that all was not told about the cowboy visiting town. A careful check of the local news items, personal columns, and the marshal or constabulary reports of the newspapers between 1870 and 1890 gives a more accurate account of the cowboy in town. Many of these items deal with the arrival of one, two, or several cowboys on a merrymaking lark, fully intent upon painting the town red, but some other items relate events which are just as interesting as, or even more interesting than, the legendary theme of "cutting high jinks and capers."

The cowboy did not always plan a wild afternoon or night; however, the combination of the man and his horse amid the many attractions of the town usually resulted in a commotion. Not unlike the college student, free from academic restrictions, the cowboy, free from responsibilities, wholeheartedly joined in the amusements of the city. The spirit created a series of atomic actions and reactions, involving noise, fighting, destruction, injuries, shooting, liquor, women, and, finally, the law with its resulting consequences. Sometimes the most innocent visit to town involved a cowboy in more trouble than he encountered when he actually planned an excursion of hell-raising; whereas, an organized "town painting" visit often resulted in nothing more than a "boys will be boys" account in the papers on the following day.

An important factor is that the cowboy attracted attention. His mode of life, dress, actions, manners, and work were news items; a story—anything which might involve him in the life of the community—was worth at least two or three paragraphs, and often a half or full column in the local newspapers.

His reputation preceded him, and, when he came into town from the cattle trails or from the ranch, a fairly well preconceived idea of what to expect of him paved his way and conditioned his reception and position in the community. Many times this reputation was not justified. His crudeness and roughness were not only intensified by the lack of normal affection and friendship during the months of isolation but they were also inflamed by his contact with liquor and the temptations of the town. On the whole the cowboy was civil, obliging, hospitable, and generous, but his inquisitive, daring, reckless, and fun-loving nature often led him into difficulties which became disastrous because he was not a member of the community.[1]

THE TOWN

The cow town or, in fact, any town which became the destination of the cowboys, was bound to have certain unique features and attractions for the men. Wide open, rugged, and earthy, these centers of civilization offered every kind of amusement and pleasure for the fun-loving friendship-starved cowboy. Abilene, Dodge City, Oga-

llala, Cheyenne, and Denver—all could not be "Queen Cities," but they made a king of every cowboy who visited them.

Cut loose from all the refining influences and enjoyments of life, these herdsmen toil for tedious months behind their slow herds, seeing scarcely a house, garden, woman or child for near 1000 miles, and like a cargo of sea worn sailors coming into port, they must have—when released—some kind of entertainment. In the absence of something better, they at once fall into liquor and gambling saloons at hand.[2]

The prairies on the State Line are now covered with immense herds of Texas cattle, and our city [Baxter Springs, Kansas,] once more begins to feel the healthy influence of a brisk trade. At least twenty thousand cattle are now on the line. The shipments for the past two weeks have been very heavy and still they come. Our streets are crowded with cowboys and mustangs; our hotels are jammed to overflowing with stock dealers and landseekers. Merchants, artisans, professional men, all begin to feel that a new era has dawned upon us.[3]

Dodge City is bracing herself up for the cattle trade. Places of refreshment are being gorgeously arrayed in new coats of paint and other ornaments to beguile the festive cowboy. Materson & Springer's place can scarcely be recognized since the bar has been moved and operated upon by Mr. Weaver's brush. The graining is finely executed. Charley Lawson's orchestra are mounted on a platform enclosed by and tastefully ornamented with bunting.[4]

The grass is remarkably fine, the water plenty, drinks two for a quarter and no grangers. The facts make Dodge City *the* cattle point.[5]

In common with all other human beings, the cowboy requires and must have amusement of some kind, and his isolated condition depriving him of the privileges of theaters, parties, billiards and other varieties of amusements that young men in the States usually indulge in it is natural that his exuberance of spirits should cause him to find sport of other kinds. His only source of amusement on the ranch are his rifle, revolver, bronco, lariat and cards, and in course of time he tires of these and seeks a change.

He goes to town, and meets there some of his comrades or acquaintances, and they indulge in some wild pranks which to Eastern people, and especially those who happen to fall victims to their practical jokes, appear ruffianly. Their love of excitement and adventure sometimes gets the better of their judgment, and they carry their fun to excess. . . . [6]

We are very sorry that some of the cowboys who come in here allow whisky to get the better of them; because when sober, they are as are the majority of them, as nice fellows as ever lived. We expect them to have all the fun they can get, but they must acknowledge that the citizens of our town [Caldwell, Kansas,] have a right to insist upon a strict compliance with the city's laws. Visitors had better bear that in mind, and also the fact that we have a police force determined to do their duty.[7]

A small army of cowboys filed into town yesterday afternoon. They were direct from Texas, having come up with Driskell's herd. Later in the evening they left for Sturgis [South Dakota,] where they were paid. About $4,000 were distributed among them.[8]

Here ride a couple of cowboys up the streets on their ponies, which are thin and worn with the long trail, but hardy and vigorous. The riders are likewise somewhat subdued, although not fatigued, by the journey, ride in a business-like way, with their thoughts on the herd and the camp. Their minds are not yet relieved of the sense of responsibility as they will be when the herd is delivered at the shipping-point. Then they will "turn themselves loose" with their fellows in one grand and prolonged spree, in which they will very likely "take the town," and turn its streets into a pandemonium, charging to and fro on horseback, shouting, yelling, and pistol-firing, until they have worked off the enthusiasm of the "hurrah," or the forty-rod whiskey has laid them out senseless on the ground. A cattle-town on one of these occasions is a very lively place, in which those who are not protected by the divinity that hedges drunken men would do well to keep within doors. For the present these cowboys are under the burden of responsibility, and, having renewed their supply of tobacco at the stores, are on the way to camp, where, after supper, they will take their turns as sentinels of the herd, which will be "rounded up" at sunset.[9]

Most of the Texas through drovers are in the city and a jolly set of whole-souled fellows they are; always ready to make a cow trade. That is their business, and all else is laid aside when a cattle trade is mentioned. They are all well pleased with their drive. Cattle came through in good condition and a little earlier than usual, with no particular loss on the trail. They look for a good advance over last year's price, and from the present indication will get it. They don't appear to be in a hurry to sell, and say as long as cattle are going up in prices all over the country they are perfectly content to hold them, and as long as grass grows and water runs freely as it does on the plains of Kansas, they will have a corresponding advance in their stock cattle, or they will hold them over and become, not only cattle drovers to Kansas, but cattle raisers of Kansas. They feel as though the price of stock cattle was always too low and that their Northern neighbors had made more money out of their cattle so driven, in buying and holding them, than they had made in raising and driving them.[10]

It is a wild, rough set of men that camp around the herds after they have been driven through the Nation and are resting on the grassy plains of Kansas. Clad in the soiled and dusty jeans of the trail, for weeks in succession no water has touched their hands or faces, and, unshaven and unshorn, they give free rein to their exuberant spirits, taking some quiet Kansas village by storm, setting the tame local laws at defiance and compelling the authorities to acknowledge the sovereignty of their native state.[11]

The dullness which had so weighed upon us through the long, uneventful afternoon was but a lull, we soon learned, and not a stagnation. With the first approach of darkness, the lethargic town rubbed its eyes, so to speak, and leaped to its feet—and in a twinkling, it seemed (like an incantation, Eastman said), Grand avenue was a carnival of light, and motion, and music. The broad board sidewalks were crowded with promenaders; smiling groups passed in and out of the drinking saloons and gambling places; in every quarter glasses clinked and dice rattled (and is there another sound in the world like that of shaken dice?) [;] violins, flutes, and cornets sent out eager, inviting strains of waltz and polka from a score or more establishments, and a brass band was playing patriotic airs in front of the theater, where, oddly enough, the crude morality of "Ten Nights in a Bar-Room" was about to be presented, "with the full strength of the company in the cast." Everywhere the cowboys made themselves manifest, clad now in the soiled and dingy jeans of the trail, then in a suit of many buttoned corduroy, and again in the affluence of broadcloth, silk hat, gloves, cane and sometimes a clerical white necktie. And everywhere, also, starred and shone the Lone Star of Texas—for the cowboy, wherever he may wander, and however he may change, never spends his money or lends his presence to a concern that does not in some way recognize the emblem of his native State; so you will see in towns like New Sharon a general pandering to this sentiment, and lone stars abound of all sizes and hues, from the big disfiguring white one painted on the hotel front down to the little pink one stitched in silk on the cowboy's shilling handkerchief. Barring these numerous stars, the rich lights, and the music, we missed sight of any special efforts to engulf or entrap passers by—perhaps because we were not looking for them: nor was there for some hours a sound to reveal the spirit of coiled and utter vileness which the cheerful outside so well belied. It was in the main much the kind of scene one would be apt to conjecture for an Oriental holiday. But, as the night sped on, the festivities deepened, and the jovial aspect of the picture began to be touched and tainted with a subtle, rebuking something, which gradually disclosed the passion, the crime, the depravity, that really vivified and swayed it all, and made it infernal. The saloons became clamorous with profanity and ribald songs and laughter. There were no longer any promenaders on the sidewalks, save once in a while a single bleared and staggering fellow, with a difficulty in his clumsy lips over some such thing as "The Girl I Left Behind Me." An inflamed and quivering fierceness crept into the busy music. The lights paled, flickered, and here and there went out. Doors were stealthily closed, window shutters slammed to with angry creaks. And at length, as we looked and listened, the sharp, significant report of a pistol, with a shriek behind it, was borne toward us from a turbulent dancing hall to certify its tale of combat and probably homicide, and to be succeeded by a close but brief hold in the noisy quadrille—presumable for the removal of the victim.[12]

Sheriff T. S. Harper of Elbert county [Colorado] was in the city yesterday on official business. Kiowa is the county seat, but Sheriff Harper spends most of his time just now at Hugo. The Texas cattlemen are coming in and that town is quite lively. It is the usual custom of the Sheriff and his deputies at Hugo to request the cowboys to lay aside their guns during their stay in town, in the interest of peace and harmony. These requests are generally complied with, so that in case of overexuberance the boys are comparatively harmless. If they demur the guns are taken by force and safely stored until the owners are ready to leave town.

Saturday afternoon a gang of five Texans, just in from the trail, undertook to fresco the town crimson. They had, as they announced, stopped at Trail City, Grenada and Wallace and had filled those towns full of holes. They intended to wind up at Hugo with a circus that would cap the climax. They were flourishing their guns around in the most reckless and indiscriminate manner when Sheriff Harper walked into the saloon where they were and ordered them to put up their weapons. The Texans promptly disclaimed their intention to do anything of the kind. The sheriff quietly went to his room, took down his trusty Sharps rifle and opened fire on the gang. He shot one fellow in the shoulder and he dropped. The balance promptly threw up their hands and allowed themselves to be disarmed. The wounded cowboy was cared for, but no arrests were made, as the sheriff did not wish to put the county to any expense. The war was all over in half an hour and the cowboys have raised Sheriff Harper fifty per cent in their estimation.[13]

INNOCENT FUN

The cowboy, out for fun, found pleasure in the simple amusements of the city. As a spectator, full of suspicion and curiosity, he entered into the spirit of the occasion and then, because of his natural boyish enthusiasm and tendency for merrymaking, became an active participant, with no other intention than uninhibited enjoyment.

Last evening Blake street was somewhat surprised by the sudden irruption of between fifty and sixty cowboys, who came into town for a "time." A roundup occurs four or five miles up Cherry Creek today, and being so near, the boys could not resist the temptation to round up Denver. They first struck the Theatre Comique. One of their number is an amateur burnt-cork artist, and him they blacked up and put on the stage, applauding his performance with all the vigor of foot and hand. After they had taken this they circulated about town until nearly morning, but were comparatively orderly, and all left town at an early hour to commence the labors of the day.[14]

[Cheyenne, Wyoming, July, 1884.]
Yesterday afternoon a cowboy named Bill Smith created not a little amusement and considerable commotion by riding, or trying to ride a bucking pony through some of the streets in the western portion of the city. The pony was bound to throw the rider off and that

individual was equally determined to stay on. In the meantime the pony had condescended to make his way for a little distance north of Thomas street, and attracted by the outcry that was made and the yelling of the little boys, a very large crowd had gathered around, thinking that there was a fight in progress or would be one soon. Finally a small boy fired a Roman candle into the crowd and close to the pony. This had three effects: It started the pony, partly dispersed the crowd and so alarmed some of the residents of the neighborhood that they imagined a shooting affair was in progress. Constable Nolan soon appeared upon the scene and set things right, but for a few minutes there was about as much excitement over the affair as there would have been had the city been on fire. No arrests were made.[15]

[Cheyenne, Wyoming, February, 1885.]
They had some fun at the west side skating rink last Tuesday evening. When the rink opened for the evening session a cowboy chartered a pair of skates. It looked easy to skate and he " 'lowed as how he tackel um once fur luck."

The rollers were accordingly strapped to his feet, or "sinched blamed tight" as he expressed it. Then he was turned loose on the floor. His gyrations and eccentric evolutions were erratic and astonished him as much as they amused the spectators. He eventually broke one of the skates, gave up the attempt to skate and left the rink.

About two hours afterwards he returned on his cow pony, and about half drunk.

Riding to the door he spurred his horse into the anteroom and forced the animal partially through the door of the main entrance. The glare of the electric lights and the roar of the skates frightened the pony and it refused to enter. While the cowboy was using his spurs and endeavoring to force the animal into the hall, an attendant came forward and suggested that he turn the horse around and back into the hall. The suggestion was made with the purpose of getting him to back the horse out of the door when it would be closed and his entrance prevented. The proposition was not favorably received, however, and just as the pony was about to enter, another attendant seized it by the bit and backed it out into the street, kicked it on the ribs, and told the cowboy if he returned the coroner would have a professional call. The cowboy looked the man over, concluded it would not pay to return and expressed his sentiments by riding down the street at a breakneck speed and yelling at the top of his voice. They have an extra large dynamite cartridge at the rink now and ready for the next cowboy who yearns to turn himself loose in that neighborhood.[16]

[Cheyenne, Wyoming, April, 1884.]
On yesterday two cowboys rounded up to a jack somewhere in the city and brought him up in front of the Simmons House where they proceeded to have considerable fun with the animal, riding him around in front of the hotel and also up and down the street for a short distance to the great amusement of a large number of bystanders—mostly cowboys. Attracted thither by the fun there came two small colored children, a little boy and a girl. It occurred to some of those present that these little ones would like to take a ride on the back of the frisky little jack. They were consequently, with their own consent, placed on the back of the animal, while one of the bystanders led the mule around, which for a time seemed agreeable to all parties interested. Finally, however, the children were suddenly thrown to the ground by a quick movement of the jack and the little boy's arm was broken by the fall.[17]

Minnie Maddern, who makes her initial appearance . . . at the Tabor Grand Opera House next Monday evening, was the heroine of quite a thrilling adventure during her Texas tour. It was in an interior town, where the festive cowboy flourished even as a green bay tree and has an occasional panic when it strikes his erratic fancy, that Miss Maddern, held forth to a crowded house as *Chip*, in "Fogg's Ferry." The play progressed without especial interest . . . until the steamboat scene in the third act when *Chip* is discovered at an old mill on the banks of a river.

She has overheard the villain's plot to blow up the steamer on which her benefactor is bearing the papers to a place of safety, by placing a torpedo in the channel directly in the way of the coming vessel. *Chip* is armed with a pistol, and nerving herself, aims at the infernal machine, hoping by a well-directed shot to explode it. The whistle of the approaching steamer betokens its rapid coming, and soon the sound of escaping steam and the splash of the revolving wheels break on the listening ear. Nearer and nearer the ominous sounds ring out on the night, and soon the bow of the boat greets the expectant gaze of the audience. *Chip* nerves herself for the telling shot, but alas, on this particular occasion the cartridge failed to explode. A moment more and all would be lost, for there, plain to be seen, bobbing up on the turbid waters, was the torpedo. Miss Maddern, though a little surprised at the missfire of her weapon, was cooling it for another shot, when, suddenly a cowboy jumped to his feet in the audience and, flourishing a navy six, shouted, "Stand just a little to one side, gal, and I'll bust it for you. Blame my eyes but them chaps ain't going to dish up that boat that way." The ominous click of a 44 calibre was distinctly heard, and as he pointed his pistol Miss Maddern, with great presence of mind, without moving from her position, for the second time pulled trigger, fortunately with better success. The torpedo duly exploded, and the steamer glided majestically on in safety. The audience felt relieved, and nobody more so than Miss Maddern, who did not care to be a party to a cowboy's marksmanship.

As Miss Maddern was leaving the theater that evening, she was accosted at the stage door by the identical cowboy, who, *sans ceremonie,* said: "Say, little gal, little more'n there'd been the devil to pay, an' all a owin' to that little popgun of your'n. You can't depend on 'em. You want somethin' that when you get the drop on a fellow you know you've got him right then. I was agoin' to help you out this evening without asking you and blow the blamed thing up myself, only you was right in the road and I couldn't draw a bead on it. Don't never let it happen again, and I'm going to heel you so you'll be in proper shape." Suiting the action to the word he produced a Navy Colt and bashfully handed it to her with the remark: "It's your'n, little gal, an' it's a daisy. I hate to part with it, but then, what's a fellow to do when he's hit as bad as I am. Maybe I'll get the laugh for this, but none of 'em's game enough to show their teeth to me, you bet! Good-bye!" He strode away, leaving the little lady, Colt in hand.[18]

"RED-EYE" TROUBLE

"Texas lightning" and "bug juice" always brought out the boisterous, hilarious, and, sometimes, dangerous side of the cowboy and accounted for many of his difficulties on a visit to town. The frisky, whiskey-loaded cowboy provided a choice theme for the frontier journalist. The "morning after" found the local calaboose filled with cowboys nursing the scars inflicted by "the spotted snake."

"A cowboy is drunk twenty minutes after he strikes town. We used to 'shoot up' the towns, but now they disarm us. Was I ever in a fuss? Well, little ones, once in a while."[19]

I struck up an acquaintance with one of these insouciant and sprightly cowboys. He was drunk, but he showed a rare degree of moderation in his drunkenness. He was not only drunk, but indignant. Quoth he: "There is a good deal of exaggeration about us cowboys. We're not near so bad as we're painted. We like to get up a little racket now and then, but it's all in play. Of course, sometimes we fall out amongst ourselves and then there is a corpse."[20]

In the cow town on his annual vacation he was a different man. Ordinarily, quiet and well behaved, when filled with Texas tanglefoot or "Missouri lightning rod," he became dangerous in the extreme. His proclivities were strange and his impulses took queer turns. Shooting up a town or a saloon were but exuberant follies prompted by the same spirit that led him to open his purse at the call of distress. To spend a year's wage over the gambling table in a single night was common. One fellow was known to have received a handsome legacy from relatives in the East, and he blew it all in in less than a week, and was found one morning dead drunk on a manure pile back of a saloon in Reno.[21]

[Cheyenne, Wyoming, July, 1878.]
About seven o'clock yesterday evening a drunken "cow-puncher," whose name we are unable to learn, rode his horse over a little boy seven years of age, the son of Mrs. Mary O'Donald, who lives in a little room, in the rear of Copeland's paint shop, adjoining Terry & Hunter's livery stable. The boy when run over, was pushing a baby carriage on the sidewalk by the corner of the paint shop and this fellow came up Sixteenth street on his horse at full speed. Turning on the side walk, his horse knocked the boy down and stepped upon his right arm, breaking it just above the elbow. Aside from bruising the boy in several places no other injuries were inflicted. . . .

The "cow-puncher" was immediately taken from his horse and Officer Martin lodged him in the calaboose, where he will await his trial today. We were informed that this party had been up around Terry & Hunter's stable prior to this time, and was ordered away, but soon came back with the result as above.[22]

For several days past a large number of cowboys have been collecting at Ogalalla [Ogallala] from Texas, who have been engaged in driving cattle from the state to Nebraska. It seems to have been an old custom with the boys on arriving at Ogalalla after the long drives beneath the scorching sun, to pitch in and have a good time. In fact a great many liberties have been granted them by the authorities, and many of their harmless drunken freaks overlooked in the past. But this time it seems that they jumped over all bounds and the sheriff was forced to step in and call a halt.

From the information at hand it appears that a party of four or five were upon the streets of that place on Tuesday, who amused themselves shooting at an old colored man, just to see how near they could come to him without inflicting a wound. This kind of sport was kept up until one of the shots entered the railroad station and came very near striking the wife of the station agent. But their work of riot and revel did not end there, nor with that day.

On Wednesday this same party commenced similar demonstrations to those of the day previous, and people endangered their lives to even go upon the streets. Night came with these fellows still on the war path, howling, cursing, and vowing vengeance and death upon any one who should attempt to restrain them or question their right to do as they pleased. They entered a saloon on one of the principal streets where they remained until nearly 12 o'clock at night, and at each drink they became more troublesome and determined to have blood before the night was over.

The sheriff, making up his mind that they had abused their liberties long enough, summoned a posse of twelve men, who after arming themselves, proceeded to the saloon where the mob of drunken cowboys were assembled, and ordered them all to throw up their hands. Instead of complying with the officer's command they went for their pistols. Sheriff Hughes then fired his revolver at one of them, Wm. Shook, the ball entering his neck. This did not stop his warlike movements and the sheriff discharged one barrel of his shot gun at him, the contents taking effect in the left side of Shooks, killing him instantly. The rest of the mob ran out of the saloon at another entrance and made for their homes. The sheriff and posse followed and ordered a halt, which was not heeded, and the sheriff discharged the second barrel of his shot gun at Henry Parker, killing the horse which he was about to mount, and severely wounding him in the abdomen. The rest of the party escaped with a few parting shots from the sheriff's posse, and have not been seen since. The wound of Parker is fatal, but our latest telegraphic advices state that he is still alive, though reported dead by some of our citizens who left that place yesterday morning. His death, however, is momentarily expected.[23]

Ten or twelve cowboys came to town Saturday night, and, as they had not seen one another of late, decided to have a jolly time by "rounding up" the town. They first purchased enough cartridges for thirty or forty shots each, so they could make good use of their six-shooters. They first "rounded up" Hellers, conducting him to Doc Middleton's bar and made him "set 'em up" to the crowd, which was done willingly. Then they repeated the process with McCarty and several others. After the firewater began to make the boys feel exceedingly happy they pulled their revolvers and for many minutes the atmosphere truly rang with the reports and the roof of Middleton's saloon presented the appearance of a sieve on very short notice. The boys, however, treated the citizens with the best of respect. No one was injured in the least, and everything ended in the very best of cheer.[24]

Nine cowboys visited the town of Burlington, Texas, and after becoming crazed with liquor, succeeded in terrorizing the populace during the entire night. Deputy Sheriff Coole, with a posse, succeeded about daylight in driving the ruffians from the town, killing four of their number and five horses in a running fight. The killed are Luke Jackson, Bill Wimms, Ed Tremble and one Hartley.[25]

A decided sensation was caused by Charley Maurice, a cowboy tough, today. He saddled his horse, filled his hide with whisky and started out to take in the town. He rode into three saloons and up to the bar and ordered drinks at the point of a revolver. He attempted to ride up to the general delivery window in the post office but was headed off by the police, who jerked him from his horse and threw him into jail. This is the second time he has figured in this frontier business.[26]

A cowboy named Taylor who has been drinking considerable lately, was shot and killed at Winslow, Arizona. Taylor rode into a saloon and announced to the occupants that he intended cleaning out the house. He was heavily armed, but before he carried his threat into execution he was shot by an unknown man, his head nearly severed from his body. There is much excitement among the cowboys over Taylor's death, and fears are entertained that trouble will ensue.[27]

[Denver, Colorado, December, 1887.]
Before Judge Cherry this morning W. J. Landow, a bold cowboy, will be arraigned on the charge of assault to kill. On Monday evening Landow entered car no. 26 of the Larimer street line at Fortieth street. He was so drunk that the driver, Frank Gillenstein, kindly assisted him in, paying his fare by opening his envelope containing the change. In receiving the money Landow dropped a nickel on the floor. He was unable to locate the missing coin. This angered him and he became abusive so much so that at Twenty-sixth street the driver put him off the car. As Landow reached the street he ran to the front of the car and drew a pistol just as the driver had reached the reins. He fired point-blank at Gillenstein who, fortunately, dodged in time to escape injury, the missile imbedding itself in the car after crashing through the lamp. After shooting, Landow ran down Larimer street and was captured by Officer Burnett near Twentieth street.[28]

[Denver, Colorado, August, 1896.]
Luck, pure and simple, in a negative form, was all that saved disaster, and, possibly, a loss of life at the crossing of Seventeenth and Pearl streets yesterday afternoon. As it was a damaged cable car, an injured horse and a badly scared gripman were the only sufferers.

Two drunken cowpunchers from Middle Park came racing along Pearl street, their broncos on a dead run, and reaching the center of the Seventeenth street crossing simultaneously with a cable car, smashed three of the roof supports, splintering the seats and breaking down the grip guard. One rider went hurtling through the car like a human cannon ball, and landed on all fours in the street on the other side. His horse was mixed up with the car seats and wreckage. His companion struck the side of the car and bounced back into the roadway. Marvelous to relate, neither was hurt. The gripman, too, escaped scot free, and as there were no passengers on the grip car no one was injured.

Detectives Ingersoll and Taylor happened to be in a car following, and before the man who struck the grip guard and rebounded could collect his wits they placed him under arrest. His companion had gathered himself together, however, jumped on the least injured of the horses and escaped.

The prisoner proved to be Frank Lockhardt. He was too drunk to give an intelligent account of himself or his companion, and he was locked up. His horse was injured about the shoulders, but it will recover. Lockhardt will have to answer charges of drunkeness, disturbance of the peace and reckless riding, and the cable car company will be likely to make things interesting for him.[29]

[Denver, Colorado, October, 1900.]

Charles Woodward and Arthur Maus came to the city from Middle Park a few days ago with a bunch of horses. Yesterday morning they set out in cowboy wise to "tear up the town." They had only one pistol between them and as they could not agree which should have the honor of "shooting up the town," the weapon was not used. Besides, bad men on the rampage merely put out barroom lights with bullets, and it was too early by several hours for the appearance of their targets. They decided that they would ride up the steps of the principal barrooms and call for a drink. They started for the nearest saloon which happened to be Burke & Murphy's at Santa Fe and West Fourteenth avenues. On the way they met Henry Morris, who lives at West Fourteenth avenue and South Eleventh street. Mr. Morris has lately returned from the Philippines and labored under the impression that he was entitled to a share of the sidewalks. The cowboys rode him down, pushing him against a fence, bruising him slightly. They rode to the saloon door and bellowed for drinks, but their amusement was stopped. The barkeeper was not at all frightened; the retainers did not cheer the bad men and there was not even a crowd of small boys at the door. They accordingly rode toward the center of the city.

Stories of the cowboys' behavior had been telephoned into Police Headquarters. Captain Martyn detailed Policemen Askew and Barhausen to arrest them. The policemen came up with the bad men at West Fourteenth avenue and south Tenth street and ordered them off their horses. The bad men refused and the policemen swung their clubs. Then the bad men were taken to the police surgeon for repairs after which they were locked up. Maus was released on bail but Woodward spent the night in jail.[30]

"PAINTIN' 'ER RED"

It is a prevalent conception that cowboys visit a town with the purpose of "taking it over." However, innumerable newspaper accounts of these "paintings" reveal that the visitations were of a very short duration, and often the culprits were much besmeared with the crimson hue of their own blood.

A shooting affray occurred here [Dodge City] last night between saloon keepers and cowboys in which one man was shot in the back, which is believed will prove fatal, another man came out with three fingers shot off, and the third man—a soldier—was rewarded for participating in the trouble by receiving a 36-calibre in the leg.[31]

A dispatch from Trinidad dated June 29th says: A lively encounter between a sheriff's posse and a party of four cowboys from the Texas Pan-Handle ... took place in Cimarron, N.M., last Saturday. The Texans were en route to Morrison's ranch, somewhere in the San Juan country, and had camped near Cimarron for the night. Friday evening they all went into town, and soon began a carouse such as only a Pan-Handle cowboy knows how to inaugurate. After a few glasses of Taos lightning were had, the inevitable pistol was pulled from belt and a firing at lamps, mirrors, etc., begun. When fully satisfied with firing at bar-fixture ornaments, the gang betook themselves to a disreputable house, where the desperadoes continued their orgies until a late hour when they mounted their ponies and rode off to their camp....[32]

A party of cowboys set out to paint Brush [Colorado] red one day last week. One young man was shot through the foot and another beaten with a revolver. The citizens finally rallied and marched upon them in a body, disarming them, and arresting the leaders.[33]

A party of cowboys rode into the village of Stewart's Station, near [the] Kansas line last week and painted the town red. After a Wild West circus in the street they attacked the post office, rode inside and fired more than a hundred shots at everything in sight, making a pretty general wreck of the concern.[34]

A humorous cow puncher named Todd lassoed Mr. Bowring, a prominent citizen of Poncha, whom he imagined had insulted him, and dragged him several hundred yards as rapidly as his horse could run. The lariat was finally caught by friends of Bowring and cut, not, however, until the latter was badly bruised.[35]

Two cowboys made things interesting on Santa Fe avenue [Pueblo, Colorado,] for about half an hour this morning. They rode up and down the street, firing their revolvers, and also tried to ride into several saloons.
A policeman attempted to stop them in their wild career and fired a shot, thinking to intimidate them. Then they shot back at him.
Two officers got on horses and went after the wild riders, who were making their way toward the St. Charles river. About six miles from the city the cowboys separated, and the officers followed one of the men and captured him. They brought him to town and he gave the name of Charles Barnes, but it is said that his real name is C. A. Yates, and that he owns a ranch near the St. Charles river. The officers are now in pursuit of the other man, and say they will bring him in, but up to this hour he has not been heard from.[36]

PRIMROSE TRAIL

Naturally, the cowboys sought the comforts offered by the "soiled doves" of the towns. A mixture of desire, liquor, and competition inevitably led to the brandishing of weapons and a scuffle from which the cowboy often did not escape unscathed.

"Rum, cards, and women are the epitaphs in the cowboys' graveyard. Some bunches all three, and some cuts one out of the herd, and rides after it till he drops; but however they take 'em, those are the things that rounds up most of 'em. It's curious, but if they quit horseback, and go into business, those are the three businesses they choose from, or the two, I should say, for cards and liquor go together."[37]

A party of four Texas cowboys started out last evening for one of the larks peculiar to their fraternity. They first rounded up in a bagnio occupied by colored women on Wazee street, [Denver] where they displayed their cheerfulness by shooting at the lamps, putting out the lights and causing a general scattering of the inmates. Lamps were ignoble game, however, and having frightened all the women away, they next visited a Chinese residence, and one of the party put a bullet into the person of the first Chinaman that appeared. Having done this the party ran, pursued by the wounded man, who blew his whistle and drew to the spot officer Holland and Thos. Clarke, who, after a short chase, overtook the fellow and took him into custody. The others were also arrested and the quartette taken over to the cooler.[38]

Fred Kuhlman, ... was shot and killed at Hunnewell [Kansas] last Thursday morning by a man named Ed. Stokley, boss herder for Forsythe. The cause of the shooting was a woman, and a prostitute of course. The parties had some difficulty about the creature that night previous. On Thursday morning the two men met on the street, when Stokley pulled his revolver and fired at Kuhlman, shooting him in the right breast, the ball passing entirely through his body and coming out near the backbone.[39]

From all accounts they are having a genuine old rip-snortin' time of it in Pine Bluffs [Wyoming]. As the shipping season is at its height the neighborhood is filled with cowboys, while hangers-on of the most disreputable character flock about the place. A gentleman who returned from there last evening says that a degree of lawlessness prevails that is really astonishing. At all hours of the day or night men can be seen madly riding about wild with poor whisky and making the welkin ring with their shrieks and shouts. The promiscuous banging of revolvers is the only music ever heard, except when the lowing herd winds slowly o'er the lea and even then it is not quite so poetic as might be expected.

The other day a man, wild with drink, caught up a bronco and after tantalizing the brute to desperation deliberately shot and killed it. Shooting to see how close they can come to a person without actually hitting him is a favorite occupation. In some instances individuals have lost a portion of their pants' legs through eccentricity in aiming, but as yet no one has been seriously hurt in this recreation.

A few evenings since a couple of women of medium age arrived at Pine Bluffs. They were from Cheyenne. Both wore yellow hair and store complexions. The garments which they wore weren't very costly but they were rather variegated and colors bordering on to crimson predominated. Each had on a Leghorn hat, which was only less elevated than a steeple, and wore bangle bracelets and jewelry till you couldn't rest. The jewelry was of that character which is euphoniously termed "snide," but it shone like a tin pan on a milk house.

Why ladies so elaborately arrayed and apparently so wealthy should stop off at Pine Bluffs where the accommodations are so meager was not at first apparent. To add amazement to the wonder already existing, they camped on the depot platform. They seemed perfectly at home and allowed their feet to depend toward the track with considerable freedom. They didn't appear to be a very frivolous pair of girls, yet they were quite giddy. Without flattering them, neither could be said to possess classical beauty of face or form. A rich veneering of powder and paint rather completely cast into the shade the ordinary efforts of nature in the matter of complexion.

There were many cowboys in the vicinity, and finally one bolder than the rest, advanced toward the pair of females. He was received with ostentatious manifestations of kindness. One of the women addressed him as "Pete" and he called her "Maud." They seemed to be overjoyed to see each other. Other cowboys soon appeared, and, without the formality of an introduction, immediately became intimately friendly. Then followed beer. This was succeeded by more beer and in turn by beer. Then followed some beer, which was succeeded by quite a lot of beer. Then came beer.

From some standpoints the platform levee of the women might be considered a vivid and even a lurid success. For eight mortal hours the pale air was laden with disjointed chunks of revelry. It was a scene of the wildest and most extravagant carousal set down in the quiet midst of the bleak prairie, and one which would give life and reality to an early-day border romance.

At noon the next day not a man in the settlement could have worn less than a No. 12 hat.

It is said by the gentleman who gives this information that steps have already been taken looking to a repression of such exuberance in the future.[40]

In your paper of Saturday last I see an article headed "Cutting High Jinks. Some great capers of cowboys at Pine Bluffs, etc." It is an article reflecting severely on that class of people known as cowboys, and inasmuch as I have had considerable experience in dealing with men employed in the cattle interest in this part of Wyoming, I hope you will permit me just to say a few words.

Regarding the shooting of a horse, there was one shot here, and the man who shot the animal offered to pay for it. There were two females here of doubtful repute, and considering the limited accommodations of the station platform, they were treated as respectfully as women of their kind could be treated in Cheyenne, the boys buying several bottles of beer and taking it over to them.

The most surprising statement of all is telling a story of how the cowboys shoot, and that "in some instances individuals have been known to have a portion of their pants legs shot through by eccentricity in aiming." Now it is very strange this is the first I have heard of anything of the kind. I have a large amount of dealing with the boys, and certainly I ought to know something about them. There should be a large allowance made for the cowboys. For weeks and weeks they are camped on the wild prairies, looking after cattle most of the time. They are engaged in the most important industry of our Territory, and it is no more than natural that young men, as most of them are, should be expected to enjoy themselves when they come to a station like this.

In conclusion I will say that take the cowboys as a body of men, I have found as honorable and straightforward in their dealings as any body of men I ever met.

H. STURTH[41]

[Cheyenne, Wyoming, August, 1885.]

Last night at a house of prostitution on Eighteenth street a man named Hecket was badly hurt by a cowboy under the following circumstances. It seems that Hecket had a mistress at the house named Frankie, and he had been quarreling with her so much that the keeper of the house refused him admission when he went there last night, and when the girl appeared at the door he struck her in the face with his fist. A cowboy inside said something to Hecket about the meanness of such an act, when Hecket dealt him a blow in the face. The cowboy thereupon struck Hecket on the head with a six-shooter, and in doing so the gun was discharged, and the cowboy, who was partly undressed, ran away, thinking he had killed Hecket, and a rumor quickly spread about the town that a murder had been committed. Dr. Cook was called and found that the man had not been struck by the bullet and that the scalp wounds he had, three in number, were made by the barrel of the revolver. Officer Nolan was quickly on the spot and arrested the mistress of the house, Jessie Carter, and everybody there. The cowboy who struck Hecket was not found and probably never will be. Hecket's hurts were dressed by Dr. Cook, and though they are painful are not dangerous. They consist of two cuts on the left side of the head, which extend to the bone, and a big bruise on top of the head.[42]

A shooting scrape occurred last night about 12 o'clock in a house of prostitution in what was formerly Central Pueblo, kept by some colored women. A colored man named Dozier was shot three times by a cowboy from Walsenburg who was in town, but who escaped and whose name cannot be learned. Only one of the bullets struck the negro, and that passed through the left arm and tore away the left nipple. The man bled copiously, but he boarded a train and left town last night.

Dozier, it appears, is cook for Superintendent Robinson of the Midland road, who was in town in a special car yesterday. There was an exchange of blows between the cowboy and the negro before the shooting.[43]

[Denver, Colorado, September, 1892.]
A shooting scrape took place at 3 o'clock this morning between some twenty drunken soldiers and cowboys. Several soldiers were thrown out of a house of ill-repute by the cowboys.

The soldiers came up town, secured revolvers, and returned and riddled the building with bullets. The cowboys came out and an engagement took place, in which some 50 or 100 shots were exchanged. After the battle was over the only seriously injured found was one soldier with three bullets through him, and one cowboy with a bullet through his leg. The soldier will probably die.[44]

TAKEN FOR A RIDE

Pity the poor dude or tenderfoot who came west with preconceived ideas of what it took to be a cowboy! The most innocent visitor fell victim to the practical jokes of the cowboy, and the Western journalist filled many columns with hilarious stories about these unfortunates. The same newspapers also enumerated tales in which the tables are turned and the joksters become the victims of the "dudes" who were too sharp for them.

Yes, he could whip anything from a coyote to a well cultivated cow puncher, he could. Only give him half a chance and he'd shine Sixteenth street from end to end. Only just give him a little room and trot out somebody that wanted a pom[m]eling. "What! p'liceman take me, will he? Oh, just let him try once—only once." And the "cowboy" flared along the sidewalk held up by two friends.

"Whoop; Great God, won't somebody come and hit me! Just come and tap me and see me lay 'im out like dead all the same. What hev I got to live for, anyhow, show me a fist. Show——"

Just then a well-known citizen of Eddy street stepped up and offered to accom[m]odate the irrepressible "cowboy," just to obtain quiet. In fact he would take it right there, if necessary.

Then the "boy" got suddenly sick and speechless; he wanted to go home, and his friends led him off as docile as a starved cur.[45]

The Fort McLeod *Gazette* tells an amusing story of a high-toned tenderfoot who ventured on foot among some wild cattle in that region. The animals gazed upon him in dumb amazement for a few moments, but finally a ferocious old bull turned upon him and the verdant young man started to flee. The *Gazette* continuing the story says:

"The cowboys were watching the proceedings and at this time one of them rode up and roped the bull. Seeing a good opportunity for some sport he took a turn around the horn of his saddle, and shouting to the young man to run for his life, just held the bull in so that he could not quite reach him, and the race began in earnest. The cowboy pretended he could not hold the bull and the tenderfoot worked his legs and arms like a wind-mill in a hurricane; the bull was allowed to breathe all over him and occasionally just graze the setting-down part of his trousers. Urged on by the close proximity of the beast, and with all the horrors of being gored to death passing in a rapid panorama before his terrified vision, he fairly flew. Finally exhaustion brought about his collapse, and the cowboy, taking another turn around the horn of his saddle held the bull off a few paces, snorting and bellowing with rage. The cowboy informed the young man that he had a narrow escape, and that it was all he could do to manage the bull, advising him to go into training for the next race, as the pace which he struck would distance the best runner in the country in a mile."[46]

[Cheyenne, Wyoming, April, 1885.]
Two fantastically attired "cowboys" alighted from the eastern train last evening. They wore broad-brimmed white hats, worth, in the east, about six bits. Their "chaps" were of the regulation style, with fringe down the sides, but were brand new and seemed very uncomfortable. And their boots! That's where they "gave themselves away." They wore new boots, broad-soled, broad-heeled affairs, made for hunting purposes, or designed to see life in the humble sphere of the corn field. Their blankets were strapped in rolls and attached to the straps were bright new spurs of the most approved eastern pattern. Indeed, the entire outfit, boys and all, was very "new." The two tenderfeet promenaded the depot platform and seemed to expect some cattlemen would rush upon the scene, greet them with dime novel western cordiality, and employ them on the spot. The community may become excited to learn that they are here, but chilling doubts cloud the sanguine possiblity. In about two days these boys will be looking for a job to brand mavericks.[47]

A gentleman who arrived in Denver from the East a day or two ago, says that he met a Pennsylvania railroad conductor and wife on the train the other side of Chicago who were on their way to attend the Conductors' reunion. The lady expressed fears of a cowboy raid while crossing the plains and expressed a dread of the probabilities of having the train boarded by a crowd of reckless, long-haired pistol shooters. Upon being assured that she would be quite as safe from cowboys while crossing the plains as in riding through the state of Pennsylvania, the lady appeared equally surprised and relieved. She declared that her sources of information were the newspaper, but concluded that if the cowboys would let such abominable lies be told about them without shooting the heads off the newspaper writers, they were a very peaceable and loving set of men. Indeed she was emphatic in her declarations that evidently she devoutly wished the cowboys would go out on the war path against their traducers.[48]

True it is said that the cowboy was not always thus, but the day of the crop-eared coyote from Poison Creek is over in this latitude, his glory departed forever. The real article of cowboy knows this, and doesn't attempt any of the old-time pleasantries, but occasionally a cowboy of the tenderfoot variety, whose massive brain scored with tales of border life as found in nickel novels, attempts to revive the custom of the good old days—but he never repeats the experiment. Only the other day we had a case of this kind. A young Philadelphian, belonging to a good family and a gentleman when sober, probably, who was undergoing his first experience as a cowboy, came into town to show off his leather "chapps" and white hat. He held a glass under his nose a few times, and then started out to pave the street with human skulls. He soon found the contract was a big one. He made a "gun play" at a drummer for a St. Louis cigar house, who knocked him down and took the weapon away from him and spanked the bosom of his pantaloons with it. Then he braced up and tried to kill him with bare knuckles, but was knocked out and hung over the piazza banister like a wet towel inside of thirteen seconds. He revived after a while and started out after more skulls. He struck at a railroad man who laughed at him, and the twister of brake wheels uncorked his claret-jug and laid him senseless upon mother earth. Friends carried him off the bloody field, and the express train took him east that night.[49]

The boys at the depot yesterday had a picnic with an eastern cowboy, a passenger on the south-bound train. He was rigged out in accordance with the eastern idea of a thoroughbred cow puncher, and when the crowd got through with him the role he was playing had lost much of its romance.[50]

The next day the horses were rounded up from the adjacent pasture and the shoeing started. Part of a cowboy's education is to be able to shoe a horse; and this they can do to a certain extent, but the forge and anvil are sometimes very primitive; and I remember once on the round-up the tire of a wheel was the anvil and a bonfire the forge. At times it is very risky and needs a good deal of strength with patience. It was a big job, and as the horses had a long road before them back to New Mexico it had to be done carefully. I watched a while and then tried to get my hand in throwing the rope. The terms lasso and lariat are not used. I practiced on two dogs, on posts, and once on one of the boys. I missed him, however, and as he had his rope in hand asked for a lesson in the art. This he readily gave, and before I knew it a 5/8 in. rope encircled my neck, and as he playfully pulled me around the yard he said, "Do you catch on Tenderfoot?" I immediately "caught on," and I have always remembered how my neck hurt where he wore the skin off. As with everything else, practice is the only way to learn, and then even the old hands will often miss, which encourages beginners. To be able to catch any named foot of a steer in a dead run, while on horseback running behind, is no easy task I assure you, and only the best cowboys can do it.

That night we camped by a log cabin, in which we spent the evening watching five boys playing freeze-out poker for a steer, each one entering the game taking five dollars' worth of chips. The game was very exciting, and places near the board on which they played were at a premium. Not being able to get near enough to see I placed a board slanting against the wall and sat upon it, having a bird's-eye view. I was not let alone long, for one of the cowboys (Sketer) pulled the board from under me, so that I fell about four feet. This tickled "Sketer" but it hurt me a good deal.[51]

He sat opposite to an Evening *Star* man at the... table, and was an object of attention. He came into the dining room in an apologetic manner, as if he knew he was intruding, and looking around helplessly with an abashed air. He was arrayed in purple and fine linen, according to his idea of purple, which raiment consisted of first, a most wonderful hat. It was fawn-colored, wide brimmed, immaculately clean, and carefully dented in four places, making it peaked-shape. He had evidently come in with money, and discarding his primitive costume of blue shirt and overalls, purchased a dove-colored suit, three sizes too small. His pants were carefully thrust into a pair of boots very tight, also, and gorgeous, with a gold star on the top. Everybody smiled at him. The terror of the plains, who had galloped through many a town facing death and trouble, with both pistols popping, the cynosure of all eyes, fairly trembled at the quiet glances bestowed upon him by the inoffensive and civilized guests.

He stood embarrassed for a few moments trying to secrete his hat and hands under his clothes, until some charitable waiter pulled a seat out for him into which he fell with a sigh of relief. A bill of fare was handed him, and after gazing wild-eyed at the array of dishes therein set forth in bewildering French names, he asked plaintively for a "square meal." The square meal was brought and the primitive wanderer on the bounding plains made a dive for a piece of beefsteak with his fingers. It seemed to strike him that this, while eminently proper on the range, and considered just the "cheese," was not the proper thing at a hotel table and he dropped it. Then he picked up his knife and fork much as a stage villain holds a dagger. Then he began to sweat and grow red, and finally laying down his eating utensils, gazed at the Evening *Star* man, quietly observed his movements and proceeded to shovel in his food with a knife, eating very quickly and trembling for fear of cutting his mouth. The cowboy "caught on," and succeeded in stabbing himself on the third lap. Then his teacher substituted a tablespoon with which he ate roast lamb; the cowboy faithfully followed every motion. The Evening *Star* guyed him for a half hour and finished by eating ice cream with a fork. The cowboy did the same, and then arose with a sigh, and when the reporter passed him on his way out he observed that he looked more tired than if he had been on a round up for a month. Great is the cow boy.[52]

Sergeant Hardy, of Las Vegas, has been in New Mexico about four years, but for all that his appearance is of the eastern immigrant, and when he wishes he can adopt the unsophisticated look and manner of the tenderfoot from Maine or New York to a nicety. At Grant's the other day, having on this mask of innocence, by chance he was treated to a little exhibition by cowboys which did not pan out as the wild and woolly fellows thought it would.

Both full of tarantula juice, two of them rode up to the sergeant standing on the street in his city dress, plug hat, overcoat, gloves and neatly polished shoes, and began to go through the customary cowboy antics, which Hardy bore with equanimity. Becoming afraid that they were not making much of an impression, the sons of the plains inquired of the suppositious tenderfoot if he could ride, and receiving an answer in the negative, told him they would show him some fine equestrian feats. The saddles were taken off and recinched with drunken solemnity, one of the two resting his exactly on the hind quarters of the horse, and jumping astride the animals with brandished six-shooters, they started off with a yell. One of them, driving his long spurs into the bronco, went out of sight like a streak of lightning and didn't come back, his horse, probably running away with him. The horse of the other had made but a few jumps when his queerly cinched saddle turned under him, and the valiant cowboy went head-over-heels to the ground. Jumping up with a torrent of oaths he begun pumping lead into the trembling pony, which had stopped after he fell, firing four shots into the animal's body. Adjusting the saddle correctly then, he remounted and had gone about twenty yards when he was thrown again, this time by his horse falling dead under him.

Sergeant Hardy boarded the east bound train shortly afterwards, chuckling.[53]

It has, in the past, been too common a thing for some of the sporting fraternity to beat every cowboy they could get hold of out of his hard earned money, and apparently without any *det*[54] or hindrance on the part of the police force.[55]

A letter from Great Bend, Ks., May 28th, to the Kansas City *Times,* contains the following: Great Bend has its share of gamblers of every variety. Lately three, that we will name as tobacco-box confidence men, arrived here, and on last Monday they cleaned out one of the "cowboys" of his money. Late in the evening he induced them outside the business portion of the city and demanded that they return his money, the half of which they did return, but that was not satisfactory to the cowboy, and so he let go the contents of his six-shooter at them, wounding one in the stomach and the other in the leg. The men's reported names are Huntington, Thoad and Carlyle. The cowboy has not been arrested as yet.[56]

The cowboys at Coolidge, Kansas, one week ago yesterday morning made it decidedly interesting for C. S. Sullivan and J. H. Hamner, two monte men and confidence operators, who had been playing their nefarious games upon the unwary at that place for some time. It appears that these high handed thieves relieved a brother cowboy of several hundred, which fact he was not slow in reporting to his associates, who in return were as prompt in their action, securing a good strong lariat they proceeded to the Coolidge House where these gentry had taken lodging and going to their room they at once roped them and brought them up from their slumbers a standing, the same as they would a beef steer on the range, they assured them that their time on this terrestial sphere was limited and unless they would return this ill-gotten gain, they would swing. They pleaded for their lives and said money they had none, that their two companions who left the day before had committed the deed with which they were being charged, and had it not been for the untimely interference of the landlord of the hotel, a first class hanging might have been reported from the place. A fortunate interference for the robbers, the cowboys retired and hoped for a more opportune time when they might deal with them in their own peculiar way of meting out justice to that particular class. But in this they were foiled, as the confidence operators took the first train for this city, where they no doubt will continue to carry on their business, but we will first give these fellows a little bit of warning, that is, if they ever attempt it here and are caught at it, they will not fair [fare] so well as they did at Coolidge if our "minute men" ever get hold of them.[57]

Last Wednesday night, judging from the outcome of it, there was a nice muss out at the Heights, in North Denver. A cowboy named Evans, who owns quite a number of cattle on the Divide some twenty-five miles southwest of Denver, came into town to have a glorious good time. While here he met quite a number of his own kind, and of course spent his money freely among the boys. It did not take some of the hack drivers long to spot him as an easy victim for them and they treated him accordingly. About midnight he in company with a friend secured hack No. 40 and rode over to the Heights, and there they met this same gang who had "spotted" him during the day and it was then that he fell an easy victim. They used every endeavor to induce him to drink, but he informed a *Republican* reporter that he never drank a drop and was perfectly sober when he was robbed. During the evening he set up the drinks for the boys, and in paying for them he had a $50 bill changed, which was seen by the crowd of roughs, and without any provocation or warning they all at once dealt him a tremendous blow on the side of the head, which knocked him down. During the melee they robbed him of his money, some $30 in cash, and his hat and made good their escape. As soon as Evans learned of his loss he jumped into a hack and came over to the city. When seen by a *Republican* reporter about 5 o'clock yesterday morning he presented a pitiable sight. He was covered with blood and was hatless, but not discouraged, as he says he knows every one who was engaged in the fracas, and if it takes every steer on the hills which he owns, he will have them arrested and brought to justice. The driver of No. 40 told a *Republican* reporter that he knew all about it, but declined giving the names. Here is a good case for the police to look into, and if we have such hack-drivers in Denver they should be dealt with by the law.[58]

The Deming *Tribune* has the following: A confidence chap picked up a New Mexico cowboy on the depot platform a day or two since, and after a chat of a few seconds decided he had struck something soft, and proceeded to work the claim. In a few minutes the sum of ten dollars had been transferred from the cow puncher's pocket to that of the confidence chap. Just as the transfer was completed, the cowboy noticed the railway policeman approaching, drew his "45," and putting it uncomfortably close to the confidence chap's ear, yelled, "You d——d thief, hand back my twenty dollars." The officer seconded the motion, and although the confidence chap insisted that he only received ten dollars, the speaker decided the point against him, and he gave up the amount and disappeared as soon as the caucus adjourned. We don't think that sharp gentleman will care to tackle one of our prairie dudes again.[59]

Clem Aller, a young ranchman from Routt county, arrived in Denver yesterday morning. He had with him $20, a desire to have a good time, about 160 pounds of muscle, which he had acquired by hard work on a ranch, and a good opinion of his abilities as a fighter. Yesterday afternoon, not wishing to waste any of his time, Mr. Aller visited a saloon kept by Con Kelleher at No. 1856 Market street. Many ranchmen visit Mr. Kelleher's place. All of them do not escape as luckily as Mr. Aller.

He made several friends, a matter not at all difficult and to some of them he imparted the information that it was a great responsibility to have $20 to take care of. He displayed his wealth.

His friends immediately set to work to devise some plan whereby he might be relieved of his responsibility. Since he looked unusually vigorous, the friends thought that the favorite "strong arm" method would be ineffective.

Among the persons in the saloon was "Mike" Queenan,

who is looked upon with great respect because he is a prizefighter. In the course of the evening the ranchman modestly admitted that he "allowed he could fight a little himself."

Queenan immediately proposed that an impromptu prize fight be arranged for $20 a side. To this Aller consented. He would not place his wealth in the hands of a stakeholder, but said that if he was whipped he would pay. Queenan said that he would do the same "on his word of honor." The two men took off some of their clothes and went at each other, hammer and tongs.

It took a very few minutes for the ranchman to knock the feathers out of the prizefighter. He did a very complete job. When Queenan finally admitted that he was whipped, his face looked like a map of China. When Aller tried to collect his $20 he was hustled out of the saloon.

The conspirators told him that he had violated one of the rules of the saloon by fighting, and that he must never go within doors again. Then, Aller says, the bartender, Frank Plumer, armed with a billiard cue, followed him on the sidewalk. He struck Aller over the head, according to the ranchman's story, and cut a long gash in his scalp. Policemen Slack and Boughman declared the blow foul and sent Plumer to jail and Aller to the police surgeon's office.[60]

MURDER!

Almost daily the Western newspapers reported the bloody accounts of the "cowboys" terrorizing towns. Planned expeditions to overthrow the law and to establish rule by means of firearms were a common occurrence. Again, these accounts did not differentiate between the renegade and the regular range rider.

Still, the lone cowboy was not above using his firearms freely, and because of this he himself fell victim to his own impetuousness.

A fatal shooting affray occurred at Oneil City, Holt county, [Nebraska].... A party of ten cowboys, who were on a spree, tried to break up the sheriff's auction sale. The sheriff ordered them to stop their disturbance, and a lively passage of words followed. He then disarmed some of them and they withdrew for a short time. Upon returning they renewed the disturbance and one of them, Harry Dean, shot Sheriff Bernard Kearns, the ball striking his heart and killing him instantly. Shots were fired by two others and the deputy sheriff was wounded twice in the right leg, above and below the knee, and once in the shoulder, all the wounds being serious. The cowboys immediately left town on their horses before the citizens could capture them, and none of them have been arrested.

Upon reaching Neligh, in Antelope, they swore vengeance upon Oneil City, and threatened to return and make another raid on the town. Cowboys have greatly terrified the citizens of Holt and Antelope counties by their lawlessness and threats.[61]

Thomas Harper, a cowboy, was hanged at Tucson yesterday for the murder of John Talliday, last September. His demeanor on the scaffold was cool and jaunty. He made no confession, but left a letter to Curly Bill, a well known desperado, admonishing him to take warning from him and not be too handy with his pistol, and "to stand a heap from a man before you kill him."[62]

A terrible shooting affray occurred this afternoon. The fracas began in a dance house. After several shots three cowboys, Bill Mills, Allison Carter and Al. Chaplain came out, mounted their horses and rode up Main street, firing their pistols to the right and left. They rode down street again on the south sidewalk firing into doors and windows and when nearing the west end of the town Mayor A. T. Hughes opened fire upon them with a shotgun. Chaplain was shot in the face but rode until Mills' horse was killed and Mills seriously wounded in the back. Carter and Chaplain then turned back and continued shooting into the crowd. Miss Colder, who was passing by was shot in the forehead and instantly killed. Chaplain then took Mills on his horse and the trio left for the territory. Mills was so badly wounded that he was left on the prairie just across the line. A posse of citizens followed Chaplain and Carter and captured them several miles down in the territory after a stubborn resistance. Carter and Chaplain are in jail at this place. Mills is in a critical condition.[63]

Rice Brown and several fellow cowboys endeavored to run the town [Trinidad, Colorado,] on Friday. Marshal Kreeger attempted to stop them and they commenced to fire upon him. Kreeger killed Brown's horse and put three bullets into Brown's body. Brown's injuries were regarded as fatal from the first and he died during the night. The inquest was held this morning. The Coroner's jury returned a verdict that deceased came to his death at the hands of Marshal Kreeger, while in the performance of his duty, the killing being justifiable. Brown was buried this afternoon, the funeral being largely attended by cowboys. Threats have been made against Kreeger, but the citizens will stand by him.[64]

About 10 o'clock on Friday morning a report was circulated in town [Caldwell, Kansas,] that a cowboy had been shot near the stock yards. . . .
(Hugh) Calvert was a young man apparently about twenty-five years of age, about five feet seven or eight inches high, dark complexion, black hair, black eyes, smooth regular features. So far as we can learn he had a good reputation, at least those who were employed with him give him a most excellent character.[65]

A large number of cowboys, who had been working the beef roundup, came into town [Rock Creek, Wyoming,] yesterday afternoon and started in to paint the community a crimson color. A large number of them became fighting full of whisky and several scrimmages occurred. In the evening Leon Williams endeavored to take Harry Mason, who had got very quarrelsome, to bed. Mason started off quietly but soon turned and shot Williams through the right breast and shoulder, the ball passing out near the collarbone. Sheriff M. Doze was at once called, and when he attempted to arrest Mason the drunken cowboy emptied all the chambers of his six-shooter at him.

Fortunately they failed to take effect. Doze, nothing daunted, immediately knocked Mason down and placed him under arrest. Both Williams and Mason were taken to Laramie City, the former to the hospital and the latter to jail. Williams is thought to be badly hurt.[66]

A cowboy went into George Neiderouer's restaurant at Goshen [Indiana] and got his supper. Being unable to pay he left his hat for security. This morning at about 5 o'clock he went in and demanded his hat. Being refused, he drew a revolver and a scuffle ensued, the cowboy dropping his revolver and throwing Neiderouer down and choking him. He then started to run out of the building when Neiderouer picked up the revolver and shot the cowboy in the back, the ball coming out at the breast. He will probably die. Neiderouer was arrested and lodged in jail.[67]

Last Sunday morning a cowboy named Charles Miley, alias "Red Bill," was arrested for boasting while drunk that he was one of the gang of horse thieves. That night he was taken out of town [Lusk, Wyoming,] by Deputy Sheriff Trumble and a posse and whipped by Trumble until the posse interfered.

On Saturday night Miley was discharged and Trumble walked up to him and shot him through the heart. Trumble was arrested while trying to escape and bound over on the charge of murder in the first degree. Trumble was sent to Cheyenne today in charge of officers. The murdered man has been employed on a ranch during last summer and was well known to be quiet and peaceable.[68]

A special to the *Leader* from Hartville, Wyoming, gives details of a killing at that place at noon today. Sam Brown, a notorious desperado, was in Clark's saloon. Frank Williams, a cowboy, went into the saloon and asked Brown to step outside. Both went out and Williams shot Brown twice, once in the arm and once through the body. Brown died in about an hour. Williams mounted his horse and left town.

A warrant for his arrest was issued, but as he is well

mounted and acquainted with the country and has numerous friends among the cowboys, his capture is not probable.

Brown boasted of having killed four men. Trouble between him and Williams has been brewing for some days.[69]

Charles H. Harris, the Santa Fe railway agent at this place, [Coleman, Texas,] was shot and killed last night by Will Atley, a cowboy. Atley was drunk and entered the railway office, using abusive language. Harris ordered him out. Atley procured a gun and returning fired a shot through Harris' body. Atley mounted his horse and escaped. As he rode off Harris, who had fallen, drew his pistol and fired two shots at him. It is not known if Atley was hit. Officers are in pursuit. Harris only lived a few hours after being shot. He was one of the best agents in the Santa Fe employ....[70]

A shooting affray occurred this week at Rocky Ford, Bent county [Colorado]. A man named Wesley Mills, a ranchman, and Bill White, a cowboy, met in a saloon, and after exchanging hard names awhile, Mills proceeded to carve White with a jack-knife, whereupon the latter pulled a gun and shot his assailant in the face. Mills will die.[71]

NOTES TO CHAPTER FIVE

1. Cf. Clifford P. Westermeier, "Cowboy Capers," *Annals of Wyoming*, 22 (July, 1950), 13-14.
2. *Junction City Weekly Union* (Junction City, Kansas), October 29, 1870.
3. "Cattle Trade," *Baxter Springs Sentinel* (Baxter Springs, Kansas), June 8, 1872.
4. *Dodge City Times* (Dodge City, Kansas), April 28, 1877.
5. *Ibid.*, June 16, 1877.
6. "The Festive Cow Puncher," *Denver Tribune-Republican* (Denver, Colorado), October 31, 1886.
7. *Caldwell Post* (Caldwell, Kansas), September 2, 1880.
8. *Cheyenne Daily Leader* (Cheyenne, Wyoming), August 31, 1882.

9. Alfred M. Williams, "An Indian Cattle-Town," *Lippincott's Magazine*, XXXIII (February, 1884), 170.

10. *Ford County Globe* (Dodge City, Kansas), June 13, 1882.

11. Louis C. Bradford, "Among the Cow-boys," *Lippincott's Magazine*, XXVII (June, 1881), 569-70.

12. "Saturday Night in a Kansas Cattle Town," *Gunnison Review* (Gunnison, Colorado), August 14, 1880.

13. "A Battle with Cow-Boys," *Denver Tribune-Republican*, August 9, 1886.

14. "Cowboys on a Bender," *Denver Daily Times* (Denver, Colorado), July 19, 1877.

15. *Democratic Leader* (Cheyenne, Wyoming), July 2, 1884.

16. "He Preferred to Ride," *ibid.*, February 5, 1885.

17. *Democratic Leader*, April 15, 1884.

18. "Not Down in the Bills," *Denver Republican* (Denver, Colorado), March 27, 1883.

19. Julian Ralph, "A Talk with a Cowboy," *Harper's Weekly*, XXXVI (April 16, 1892), 376.

20. Ben C. Truman, "The Passing of the Cowboy," *Overland Monthly*, XL (November, 1902), 465.

21. Matthew J. Herron, "The Passing of the Cowman," *Overland Monthly*, LV (February, 1910), 199.

22. *Cheyenne Daily Leader*, July 24, 1878.

23. "Cowboy Killed," *ibid.*, July 11, 1879.

24. *Democratic Leader*, January 31, 1885.

25. "Telegraphic Brevities," *Fort Morgan Times* (Fort Morgan, Colorado), January 29, 1886.

26. *Democratic Leader*, February 27, 1886.

27. "A Cowboy's Fatal Mistake," *Cattlemen's Advertiser* (Trinidad, Colorado), December 15, 1887.

28. "A Drunken Cowboy's Exploit," *Denver Republican*, December 21, 1887.

29. "Rode Smash into a Cable Car," *ibid.*, August 1, 1896.

30. "Cowboys Try to Terrorize Denver," *ibid.*, October 24, 1900.

31. "Whites Practicing on Themselves," *Las Animas Leader* (Las Animas, Colorado), September 20, 1878.

32. "A Frontier Tragedy," *Caldwell Post*, July 8, 1880.

33. "Colorado Condensed," *Fort Morgan Times*, January 15, 1885.

34. "State News," *Boulder County Herald* (Boulder, Colorado), June 13, 1888.

35. "State News," *Trinidad Weekly News* (Trinidad, Colorado), March 15, 1889.

36. "Shooting Up the Town," *Denver Republican*, July 25, 1898.

37. Ralph, "Cowboy," p. 376.

38. "A Lark," *Denver Daily Times*, April 26, 1877.

39. *Caldwell Commerical* (Caldwell, Kansas), July 7, 1881.

40. "Cutting High Jinks," *Democratic Leader*, September 27, 1884.

41. *Democratic Leader,* October 1, 1884.
42. "A Brawl," *ibid.,* August 28, 1885.
43. "Three Shots at Him," *Denver Tribune-Republican,* November 16, 1886.
44. "Soldiers and Cowboys Fight," *Denver Republican,* September 11, 1892.
45. "He Wanted to Fight," *Cheyenne Daily Leader,* July 26, 1878.
46. *Democratic Leader,* April 15, 1884.
47. "We Are Here," *ibid.,* April 11, 1885.
48. "Afraid of the Cowboys," *El Anunciador de Trinidad* (Trinidad, Colorado), October 29, 1885.
49. "Tenderfoot Cowboy's Experience," *ibid.,* December 3, 1885.
50. "Local Brevities," *ibid.,* March 11, 1886.
51. "A Tenderfoot Among the Cowboys," *Texas Live Stock Journal* (Fort Worth, Texas), November 3, 1888, p. 4.
52. "The Cow Boy," *Trinidad Weekly News,* September 7, 1881.
53. "Teaching a Tenderfoot," *Albuquerque Evening Review* (Albuquerque, New Mexico), October 17, 1882.
54. Obsolete form and meaning of "debt"—bounden duty.
55. *Caldwell Commerical,* July 20, 1882.
56. "Shooting Affair at Great Bend," *Las Animas Leader,* June 5, 1874.
57. *Ford County Globe,* July 11, 1882.
58. "Slugged and Robbed," *Denver Republican,* November 10, 1882.
59. *Kansas Cowboy* (Dodge City, Kansas), August 23, 1884.
60. "A Prizefighter Purposing to Punch a Cowboy," *Denver Republican,* August 30, 1900.
61. "Double Tragedy," *Cheyenne Daily Leader,* March 31, 1881.
62. "Hanging a Cowboy," *ibid.,* July 10, 1881.
63. "A Kansas Shooting Affray," *ibid.,* September 29, 1881.
64. "A Dead Cow-Boy with Boots on," *Denver Republican,* January 1, 1882.
65. "A Cowboy Accidentally Killed with His Own Pistol," *Caldwell Commercial,* July 20, 1882.
66. *Democratic Leader,* August 30, 1884.
67. "A Cowboy Shot," *El Anunciador de Trinidad,* July 29, 1886.
68. "Deliberate Murder," *Denver Tribune-Republican,* October 11, 1886.
69. "Killed by a Cowboy," *Denver Republican,* September 14, 1886.
70. "A Drunken Cowboy," *ibid.,* September 18, 1888.
71. *Field and Farm* (Denver, Colorado), February 9, 1889, p. 9.

The "Sweet Bye and Bye"

SIX

    A careful scrutiny of the literature on the cowboy reveals a dearth of information concerning his moral, philosophic, and especially his religious interests. If one is to accept this lack of printed evidence as a positive sign of immorality, godlessness, and irreligiousness on the part of the cowboy, then the authors of the cowboy classics are correct in taking a negative attitude. They say little or nothing about this facet of the man. However, none of these writers says that the cowboy is immoral, godless, or irreligious. On the contrary, he is frequently pictured as a man with moral values and a simple philosophy in which religion has no place. He is too busily occupied with his daily tasks to consider religion as an important part of life.

His environment—the West—at most, during this time, was a frontier, a missionary field, as it still is in many areas at the present time. His work—on the range and later on the ranch—either took him away from centers of religious activity or occupied all of his time. His leisure—infrequent and unpredictable—afforded him so little time to accomplish so much while in town that he did not spend his freedom listening to "psalm-singin'."

It is obvious that the cowboy did not practice an orthodox religion. Although he was not a church-goin', prayer-meetin', Bible-readin' man, one must not conclude that he was an irreligious or godless individual.

Actually, the cowboy in the last three decades of the past century was a man with a strong moral code and a casual day-by-day philosophy which resulted from his closeness to nature. Yet, at the same time, he also showed a tendency toward religion, a trait which has been ignored by his biographers. They speak in general terms about his morality and philosophy, and in his daily actions these two aspects appear to dominate his life, but upon closer observation his way of life also reveals religious motivation.

He was aware of God, the Old Testament, the Gospels. He was conscious of the devil, hell, and sin; also of the soul, heaven, and prayer. Because of his environment his knowledge of right and wrong was crystal clear under his strict code—a code which might appear harsh in an older, conservative, and religious-bound society.

The cowboy's religious activity was manly, yet often colored by a deeply felt sentiment and an ostentatious display of generosity. Some cowboys displayed mockery, ridicule, vulgarity, and sometimes an outrageous conduct in regard to certain phases of religion, and yet they respected another man's religious beliefs and actions when convinced of his sincerity. The cowboy could understand the simple basic teachings of Christ and, when these were presented in all their simplicity, he recognized them as fundamental truths. Whether he followed these precepts or not is another question. He seemed to have complete confidence in God's understanding of his particular weaknesses and an unbounded hope in salvation.[1]

THE TEXT

In his interest in social justice on the range, the frontier journalist drew upon Biblical sources to support his reasoning and make it understandable to the cowboy.

The oldest historical book in the world tells us about Abram. His ancestors were cattlemen on the plains of Chaldea, from thence he went west to the land of Canaan. He is the great progenitor of pioneers. He was the first man, that we know much about, to go West and grow up with the country. He became great. He is a towering figure in the history of the race, and the most admirable thing about him is that he won all he got "on his merit."

Abram was very rich in cattle. A man builds up a business; we are quite familiar with the fact. We ought to be familiar with its correlative truth—the business builds the man. The saloon-keeper may be a considerable man to begin with, he is not likely to be much to end with. He makes a business, the business unmakes him....

In the days of Abram and Isaac, the greater part of the land was arid and the water supply was the great question. The range was unfenced, the cattle wandered far and wide. Cowboys heed the same jealousies, then as now.

Abram came from a long line of cattlemen, he was raised in that business. What kind of man was he? He was brave. That we could expect. The timid man stays at home, he is naturally conservative, and likes the protection of established institutions. He don't go West among strangers where enemies and all kinds of unknown difficulties may beset him.

Abram went West. He went in the year of one. The Indians were bad. "The Canaanite was then in the land."

He got rich, very rich. So did his nephew Lot, while he stuck to his business and remained with Abram. But their cowboys got to wrangling about the grass and water; the herds needed more room. . . .[2]

Away back yonder toward the dawn of creation when Abraham and Lot and the rest of them were engaged in the range cattle business it was settled at one of the round-up meetings that it was all right to work on Sunday if the cattle happened to fall into the ditch. This was liberally construed in after times, and it finally came to pass that the cowboys worked on Sunday even on ranches that had no ditches on them. The *Tascosa Pioneer,* however, says: It is announced that the XIT people have introduced its innovation in the ranch practices in the Panhandle. Last Sunday the foreman of the Capitol outfit announced to the boys that six days were enough in every seven for man or beast to work and that they would stop for twenty-four hours and observe Sunday. Nobody said nay, and accordingly the program is changed on the ranges of one cattle corporation.[3]

THE GOLDEN RULE

Sincerity, loyalty, generosity, and simplicity were the cornerstones on which rests much of the cowboy philosophy. A large measure of reckless courage supported it in an environment based on physical achievement.

Lest the impression be conveyed that these are irreligious and godless men, let the reader fancy a group of men, belted and spurred, seated in a rude arbor, listening reverently to a tall cowboy who has been selected by unanimous choice to read the Scriptures, and he can form an idea of the last Sunday I spent with the cowboys. With slow and deliberate utterance Phil Claiborne read out the words of the golden rule:

"As ye would that man should do to you, do ye also to them likewise." Then he proceeded, "These, my hearers, were the words of the Lord Jesus Christ, who spoke as no man ever spoke; and I pledge you my word, gentlemen, the Bible is a good egg." Profound attention greeted the speaker, and continuing he said, "Whatsoever is earthly can be soon replaced, but that which is on yon side of the grave is eternal. If you lose your property, you may acquire more; if you lose your wife, you may marry again; if you lose your children, you may have more; but if you lose your immortal soul then up the spout you go."[4]

"To accom[m]odate a man is what I live for." The man who uttered these words had just accom[m]odated a man who, to say the least, was not his personal friend. From time to time we have known many cowmen who branded to its proper owner, or drove, toward its proper home, all stock that came in their way—irrespective of like or dislike for the owner. Such men have always made the range and the world better.

Again, "given to hospitality," are words from the Bible. The round-up wagon feeds all who ride it. The ranch house lets every one who calls stay all night. There may not be blankets enough to go around, but the rule is "always room for one more." A more open-hearted hospitality is nowhere found on the range.

Then the absence of deceit. The average cowboy can tell whether he likes you or not, with about as cool a face as the next one. You may easily know where he stands. He practices sincerity rather than imitates it. The imitation article belongs to the accomplishments of polite society."[5]

Two old Texas ranchers, who had just helped bury a neighbor, were talking about religion, and one asked the other how pious he thought it was possible for a man to get in this world, if he was in real earnest. "Wal," said the other, reflectively, "I think if a man gets so't he can swop steers or trade horses without lyin' 'at he'd better pull out for the better land afore he has a relapse."[6]

MEETING ON THE HEAVENLY SHORE

As far as the cowboy was concerned, contacts with religion, rare as they might have been, produced various results—sometimes good and sometimes bad.

[Reverend W. H. Rankin] known as the "Colorado Cowboy Evangelist," ... has invaded the very haunts of the reckless cowboys of Colorado with his intrepid calls to Christ. Many times have his bold and fervid utterances, and calm and dauntless bearing in the cause of his Master quelled the fierce tumult of reckless, whisky fed passion, and won him the ear and respect of the wild rider of the cattle ranges.

As an instance of the power and intrepidity of this frontier evangelist, not long since he appeared at a certain isolated village in Colorado, calling sinners to repentance. He had no lack of field for his exertion, for the place was notorious as the chosen resort of as wild, dissipated and reckless cowboys as ever crazed themselves on bad whisky, or rode a bronco into a saloon. The evangelist of the border was in his element. Choosing the principal saloon in the place as his temple of worship, he entered it one evening when it was rife with whisky laden breaths, and alive with the voices of profanity.

Making his way in the place, he boldly mounted a chair, and launched upon the reeking air the pure precepts of the Divine Nazarene. At first his wild audience was too much taken by surprise to make any characteristic demonstration, but as they realized what was taking place the "wild and woolly" capabilities of the assembly suddenly developed themselves and a perfect pandemonium broke loose. The preacher was proffered brimming tumblers of whisky, from all quarters foul and loud epithets assailed his ears, while above all sounded the cheerful crack of the ready revolver, as the heavily armed cowboys strove to frighten the daring preacher by a general fusilade out of the windows and through the roof. Finally, several of the wild riders mounted their horses and rode them into the saloon, firing their pistols promiscuously as they came. But they had mistaken their man. The intrepid evangelist was of the stuff heroes and martyrs boast, and his voice rose loud and clear above the sound of oath and pistol shot, as he told them "that they were wasting their time and ammunition; that he had come to stay, and proposed to do it."

Struck with admiration at his pluck the cowboys suddenly grew quiet, and when three cheers were proposed for the "plucky parson," they were given with a will. The next thing was a proposition to hear him preach. This was also eagerly seconded, and the work of transforming the saloon into a church began at once. Beer kegs were ranged along the walls, and on these were placed planks. Here the cowboys ranged themselves, a most decorous and attentive assemblage. The sermon was preached, and today in that little frontier village beyond almost the outskirts of civilization, there is a Presbyterian church with forty members in regular standing. Such is the Rev. W. H. Rankin, the man who has gone to organize a church in Douglas.[7]

When [a traveling] writer first went to Las Vegas [New Mexico] in the early days of that town he went one night to a revival meeting, and everything passed off pleasantly until the preacher said: "All who intend to go to hell stand up." Only one man, a tough looking man, stood up. "O, my friend," wailed the preacher, "do you intend to go to hell?" "Yes, I do," replied the fellow, "and there are others in this house who'll go to hell d——d quick if they don't stand up and keep me company." Whereupon he whipped out a revolver and in two seconds every man in the audience was on his feet, the writer included. Singularly enough this belligerent revivalist died with his boots on before many months rolled around. He was run over by a swill wagon.[8]

A cowboy revivalist called "Lampas Jake" is stirring the boys up down in New Mexico and Arizona. He preaches in frontier saloons and dance houses, and enforces attention with a six-shooter. Although illiterate he is said to be sincere and in dead earnest. His illustrations and metaphors are drawn almost entirely from the range as the following peroration of a recently delivered sermon will show: "You're a nice lot of ruffians, ain't you? You'd look nice gallivanting around in Heaven, wouldn't you? Wouldn't Hell itself turn pale if it saw you coming? You can get yourself in condition. You can make your hides slick. There is the grass of salvation that is green all the year round. You can eat of it, and you'll make flesh from the word go. You can refuse it, and you'll grow poor and miserable till your old hides will flap on your bones like a bed-quilt on a ridgepole."[9]

[One week in December, 1884,] a man giving the name of H. S. Price arrived in Pine Bluffs [Wyoming]. He was very commonly clad, rather tall, wore a full red beard, and appeared to be about forty-five years of age.

Price claimed to be a clergyman of the Campbellite faith, and probably hailed from Missouri. He was destitute of money, and what food he obtained he received through charity.

He gave it out that he was willing to preach a sermon to those who wished to hear him on the following Sunday, and Mr. H. Sturth placed his grocery department of his establishment at the preacher's service.

As Price was the first preacher who had ever stopped in Pine Bluffs for any length of time, the novelty of the thing caused the news that a sermon was to be preached there to spread rapidly.

On Sunday morning cowboys from all the ranches for miles around began to pile into Pine Bluffs on horseback, and by 10 o'clock the three or four houses which comprise the town presented as animated appearance as is usual at the height of the cattle shipping season.

While everybody waited in expectancy for the ceremonies to open, whisky circulated quite freely, and the dominie himself was invited to indulge, so as to acquire the needed inspiration for a vigorous handling of his subject. It is said that he took only two drinks, but these were ladled out to him in large lemonade glasses, so that they represented a considerable quantity of raw spirits.

Price was finally placed on an improvised platform and

delivered a discourse that lasted about three-quarters of an hour. His remarks were not characterized by much brilliancy and at times they were marked by an incoherency that indicated too plainly his inebriated condition.

Meantime his auditory was approaching a dangerous condition of joviality, and six-shooters were being handled with careless grace and displayed with reckless prodigality.

The remarks of Price, such as they were, were applauded liberally and when he finally wound up he was vigorously encored, but quietly, yet firmly declined to respond.

Everybody in the audience crowded forward to congratulate the preacher.

"You're no duffer, parson, if you do wear a bald face shirt," said one, "and I do believe you could knock the speckled socks off'n half the preachers this side of New Jerusalem."

"Yer' from Arkansaw, pardner, I kin tell it by yer eye. Now come off, don't say you ain't, an' I'll bet my best cayuse you kin stampede more big words than any cuss this side of Cheyenne."

These remarks were supplemented by invitations to drink to which the parson graciously responded until the eighth lemonade glass was handed him.

This he declined.

He declined it for the very good reason that the limit of his capacity had been reached.

The parson wished to go to Antelope and as a wagon was bound that way he was loaded into it. He stood on his feet awhile endeavoring to make a parting speech, but it was only an unmeaning jumble of words. At length the team started and the parson after a few grotesque efforts to maintain his equilibrium toppled over and fell prone in the wagon.

The distance to Antelope is about twenty-two miles and during that time Price never stirred or spoke a word. The driver of the wagon paid little heed to this, however, thinking that the man was lying in a drunken stupor.

When Antelope was finally reached and an attempt

made to lift the parson from the wagon it was found that he was lying stark and stiff in death.

Coroner W. F. Moore, of Sidney, Neb., held an inquest over the remains and a verdict of death from unknown causes was rendered.

The body has been buried at the expense of the county.[10]

In the Omaha *Republican* ... appeared an article calling upon the public to rise and look into "the affair at Pine Bluffs," and see if Price was not murdered. A few facts regarding this man, and the correct facts in the case may be of interest to the general public. The appearance of Price in Pine Bluffs was that of a tramp and thief. He entered my dining room and having eaten his dinner, he said he had no money to pay for it. He also called for two drinks at the bar, each time filling his glass, and refused to pay for them, but he added, "I am going to preach Sunday and will take in a few chips and I will then settle up for the drinks." I then gave him his supper and told him to leave as I had no use for him any longer. He was, however, given permission to preach for the boys Sunday. His audience consisted of four cowboys and eight or nine gentlemen from Nebraska, who had large landed interests in this part of Wyoming and in Colorado. They were awaiting the eastbound train, and as there was nothing doing part of them gave their full attention to the remarks of the preacher. He had taken whisky freely during the morning preparatory to giving his sermon. The service was a mockery and would not have been allowed in my house had I known his intention. He was a first class tramp and this was his way of receiving a little money to spend for whisky. The article in the Omaha *Republican* referred to is a first class lie from beginning to end. All of the whisky drank by said Price was of his own free will and the man that made the statement that a revolver was drawn to force him to drink in my building during that day is a liar. A more peaceable lot of men never met together than did on that day at Pine Bluffs.

I call upon you who hear my statements to make contrary those I have here made. The ordinary idea of a "cowboy" is that of a monster; a more kind hearted, jolly set of men you seldom meet than the average cowboy.

H. STURTH[11]

[A saloonkeeper at Clayton, New Mexico, had been converted to the church and proposed to carry on his business in a proper manner. Shortly thereafter a crowd of cowboys gathered in his place and, after several rounds of drinks, became quite loud and unruly.]

"Hold on boys," said the saloonist, "this is no place for such riotous conduct. You know I have experienced a change of heart and am now an advocate of the peace."

"Oh, give us a slack on that chin music," howled the crowd. "We don't want no gospel grease spread onto our hair."

"But boys I don't want you to be so loud."

"Hi-yi," they shouted, "listen to the church organ playin' hymns; ain't it a whole meetin' house with a brass cupalow thrown in?"

"Listen to me, boys, I——"

"Hooray for a sermon! Let's have a hot one. Shovel the brimstone right in and make the fire sizz!"

Then he got mad and whipped out his revolver:

"Here [Hear] me out you rantankerous rioters of the Rockies. I am a man of peace; of meek and gentle humility; but this gun of mine is what she used to be, and the first d——d skunk of a cowboy that don't like my style will git it right where it will do the most good. I've started in to live a new life and I propose to act in accordance with it, and any white livered coyote that raises a howl will chaw dust in just five seconds and not be able to spit it out. I'll be d——d if I ain't going to run this shebang on strictly religious principles or shut her up. Now git out o' here quick; there's the church bell and I've got to conduct the service. You hear me! Skip!"[12]

I fear indeed, if [you] have ever heard of Farmington, [New Mexico] it has been as the rendezvous of the festive cowboy, a town to be avoided, not coveted, in fact, blacklisted from respectability and given over to the bullies of the cattle range.

One of these exploits really amused me and I will relate it.

A half drunken cowboy, one of the "tenors," happened to spy a minister who had lately come into the region, and with indifferent success was preaching at various points, walking down the street, and he concluded to have some of his style of fun. So he took out his revolver, and shot about six feet back of the reverend gentleman, following him in this way all the road home. He had no intention of hitting his target, and so unerring is the aim of these cowboys that he did not touch the clergyman once.

The latter, perhaps, knowing that the desperado did not mean to hit him, perhaps confiding his trust in Providence, walked quietly on without so much as turning his head, and thereby won the undisguised admiration of the cowboy.[13]

COWBOY DEVOTION

A bigger range, richer grass, more water, less dust, better horses, fatter cattle, a trusted companion—the cowboy's heaven!

My greatest trouble in making long trips west is that I am very often forced to spend the Sabbath in thinly settled portions of the country, where the opportunity of attending divine worship is denied me. Not so on this occasion, however, for we had preaching at a neighboring ranch.... A very good sermon indeed, and it seemed to sink deep in the hearts of those present. There would have been services in the afternoon, but most of the mourners had to attend a roundup a few miles off. The series of camp-meetings and other services which have been held out here this summer have had a marked effect on the boys and much good has been done. You should see how changed the boys are, and how careful they are to let their light so shine that they may show their faith by their work. Now for instance, last Sunday after attending church and the roundup with the boys I went home with Luther Clark to spend the night. Along about 10 o'clock Luther leaned back in his chair and said: "Well, boys, it's getting nearly bed-time; we'll play this jack pot and then engage in our evening devotions, as it's getting nigh on to bedtime and I don't believe in this way of bettin 'em so high and playing so late on the Lord's day." The jack pot was played and duly scooped in by Luther, after which he arose and asked some one to bring him the family Bible. One of the boys rustled among the old papers on a shelf in the corner a few minutes and then said: "That book ain't here—oh, yes, I remember now, Tom gave that book to Bruce Wheeler the other day, when he wanted some paper to make cigarettes of."

"Well, Tom, you shouldn't be so darned free with my property—'cause I thought a heap of that book here of late," said Luther, and then he hunted up his last *Stock Journal* and read a very pious article headed "Slade on His Rambles," after which he gave a short lecture about as follows:

"Fellers, this religious racket and family prayer business is kind of a new thing to me, and I know its kind of troublesome to take time every evening and stop the game and attend to this racket, and I believe in going the whole hog or none, and when I undertake to live religious, I'll do it, or bust a trace, and you can just bet your sweet life on that. Besides, it's a good thing to mortify the flesh a little now and then; all are apt to hold better hands afterwards. I believe in showing some faith by your works, and not acting the sneak in anything. Now, there's Bob Trice, who just set like a stolen bottle today when the preacher was passing the hat and never chipped in a cent. That kind of religion won't stand fire, I tell you——"

"Hold on a minute, pard," said Bob; "now see here, there ain't any man in this range that will chip into a little game quicker than me, but I didn't understand the game; I didn't know how much it took to play, nor what the limit was. I had my mind made up if the dealer would explain the game that I would raise the ante, stand pat and run a blazer over the entire mob, but I didn't know."

"Set down, don't interrupt the services again," said

Luther, and then he proceeded: "as I said before, I think it's right to mortify the flesh a little now and then, and I don't believe it's right to run a game too late on Sunday nights, and what's more, while we are all trying to lead a different life, I think you boys might quit holding out cards—especially on Sundays, for which let us pray."

And then all knelt down and kept quiet while Luther prayed: "Oh, Lord! we haven't got much to worry Thee about on this occasion, as things are running pretty smooth in this part of Thy moral range. The range is pretty good, water is not very scarce, the cattle are looking fine and the calf crop is panning out amazingly, and we are not the kind of boys to come begging to the throne of grace for little things we can rustle for ourselves. We might state, oh Lord! that it hasn't rained here for some time, and that we are soon going to need some moisture, but there is nobody hurt yet, and we suppose that the matter will be duly looked after. Lord, if an' according with Thy divine pleasure and opinions of how a decent game should be conducted, forgive Pitts Neal for stealing out that ace full which he wickedly played against my flush, but if it so be that Thou art on to his many sins and much iniquity as the rest of us are, and seest fit to give him a little sample of Thy divine wrath, Lord let it please Thee to place in his hands a diamond flush and cause him to buck against Thy servant, who shall be provided with a jack full. But, Lord, in this operation, it will be necessary to exercise a great deal of care lest he steal out four queens and scoop in the shekels of Thy servant, for verily he is mighty to pilfer, and in that case Lord, there would be an uproar thereabouts, and crushed and broken bones, and moreover a greal deal of faith would be shaken and lost, and Thy servant would perhaps backslide the length of many sabbath journeys. So mote it be —Amen."

After the devotional exercises were over Pitts Neal was heard to remark that he'd be darned if he played in the game with Luther again. He said he wasn't afraid that any one man could play dirt on him, but that he wasn't going to play against the entire kingdom of Heaven and all the boys too.[14]

The cowboys have coined a new bit of slang. They speak of attending church as "going to the Parson's round-up." A round-up with them is a gathering of animals, where brands are studied. Perhaps their new addition to the expressive slang of the time is felicitous, "for cannot brands be studied at church as well as on the range?" said a member of the cowboy fraternity to a *Tribune-Republican* reporter yesterday. "What matters it whether the gathering be one of quadrupeds or bipeds—of cows or human beings? Brands can be studied in both, for the mavericks that bear no marks are rare. In the human herd the red-hot iron has not burned into the skin a J B or a hash knife, but nature wrote on every part of the face another mark. Would it be fair to say that in the human herd, the most numerous brand is that of the great proprietors—the firm of the world, the flesh and the devil?

"If you go to church next Sunday," continued this soliloquizing cowboy, "and go early, while you are waiting for the preacher to come, study the brands. Perhaps you may see a lady or a woman somewhere in the audience whose silks and laces and flounces and feather and jewelry, whose dress and all her movements will be brands, speaking in the plainest possible way. They will be plainer than a three circle or a cut dewlap. The brand will be 'vain and vulgar.' It won't be hidden, no matter if it is woven in the superbest silks and the airiest lace, and jeweled in diamonds.

"Nature is a keeper, a herdsman who always brands. But her skill is subtle. Upon the persons of men she does not always put the brand in comeliness and strength. Often in the bowed frame and melancholy eyes she writes 'this is my worthiest.' And upon the figures of women it is not always with form and color, but with a beauty which is painted only by a pure mind and soul—on a plain face often—that the brand is read, 'this is my best.' "[15]

He was as fine a looking specimen of the western cowboy as ever cinched a bronco, or threw a rope, and as he rolled into the *Graphic* office, with his big sombrero on one side, Mexican spurs jingling, and persuader in his belt, we felt that nothing we could do would be too good for him. "Are you the religious boss of this ranch?" was the question with which he greeted us. We cheerfully answered in the affirmative, as he rolled a cigarette with one hand, toyed with the ivory handle of his gun with the other, closed one eye and scanned the Taylor cylinder with the other, he continued: "You see I ranged over your last Sunday's campin' place, and concluded I'd take your advice and get to the preach house. The last time I was in a herd of that kind, was back in the states, at an old fashioned Methodist roundup in the woods, where the sky pilot fired red-hot perdition among the boys, and knocked his desk out in three rounds, Marquis of Queensbury [Queensberry] rules, and made a grand stampede in the whole herd. Well, I was lookin' for some deal of that kind, and figured that I'd have a picnic with the boys. But I didn't. I got left on the first turn o' the wheel. I waltzed into the gospel factory with my sombrero over my eyes, but off it came at the first jump. I had on my sleds, and I hadn't gone more than half way up the chute till I tripped up on the skirts of a slick looking Jersey heifer who was goin' in ahead. I got myself together and squatted as quick as I could. I jest felt like a Texas maverick in a herd of short horns. Purty fine bunch of corn fed girls you've got on this range, ain't it? But, sir, when that feller got in his work on the cuttin' out and roundin' up of them words and speeches of his, I felt just like gettin' up and givin' him an old style three cheers and tiger. I only had to shut my eyes and I thought I was back in the old church at home with mother holdin' my hand, just as she used to do when I was a kid; and when I opened 'em, I'll be gol darned if there wasn't some drops of water on my face. First time such a thing happened since we planted my Texas chum out on the old Dodge Trail ten years ago. I thought I'd got over them feelings long ago, but they come onto me like long horns on a stampede. I don't believe much in this grand round-up business on the last day, and I don't just hitch onto the idea that all the stock found in the herd unbranded then will be left out to starve on the bare range. To my mind a half starved maverick, if he has rustled and made the best livin' he could when the range was short, will stand just as good a show to get in the blue grass paster as the slick Polled Angus who has been corn fed since he was a yearlin'. But be that as it may, bein' in that corral full last Sunday, and hearin' some things that had about escaped my memory, has done me more good than my feelin's will permit me to say. Only just say to the boys for me that takin' in that preach house and hearin' a few things they ought to, whether they believe them or not, is a darned sight better than loafin' around camp, ropin' long horns or breakin' broncos." And having finished his fifth cigarette he touched his hat and left us wondering if we wouldn't better tell the boys his experience, and ask them to take his advice.[16]

THE LAST ROUNDUP

It is only when sorrow and tragedy pierce the physical surface of the cowboy that his complex yearnings, dark moods, and starved affections are stirred. No one knows what struggle takes place in the heart and mind of a cowboy who rides away from the bleak and lonely grave of a fallen comrade.

A flash, a cry, a falling horse and man. Then all was over, no more night herding had Joe Bucket, his spirit was gone upward, caught by a stroke of lightning. Of all the dangers of the range this is the worst; and well the boys know it, but still they do their duty faithfully and hard though it may storm either day or night they stick to the herds they are holding and keep their stock from stampeding.

Joe Bucket was buried by Rev. Mr. Horsfall, the Episcopal minister. Joe's companion cowboys turned out in a body to attend the funeral. In all the regalia of the range they rode behind the coffin. The four line riders rode guard, two on each end of the remains. At Miles City cemetery the light colored, gold bedecked sombreros were held by the boys while they stood with bowed heads and tearful eyes listening to the touching words of the minister and noticing the dust to fall upon the handsome coffin of the dead. The clattering spurs jingled plaintively as they rode slowly toward the city and now on the broad range they again face many dangers that the noble cowboy is never afraid to meet when he is attending his duty.[17]

All the cowboys on the ranch liked Briggs because he was always so kind, so cool and brave, and had a nerve as strong as steel. He came to us one day when we needed hands and were getting ready to make a "spring drive." He asked for employment, and Bolly Jennings, the foreman, sized him up, liked his looks, and he became one of us.

His face was handsome, but grave, and his eyes were large and bright, and a peculiar pale blue color. When his blood was up not a muscle in his countenance moved, but his eyes would grow cold and gray and sharp, and his steady look appeared to pierce your brain, so intense was it. His form was tall, graceful and muscular, and as straight as an arrow. This will answer for a short description of Brigg's personal appearance. One night in the early part of December 1877, Briggs shot himself while cleaning his pistol, the bullet inflicting a fatal wound—a rather unromantic way for the hero of a story to be served, but it was so.

Poor Briggs' nerve was such that he did not believe he was going to die, but the doctor, who had been summoned a distance of forty miles, said there was no hope.

It was then the cowboys, rough and uncouth as they were, showed their affection for Briggs. They nursed him day and night as tenderly as a woman, and in his weakness he evidenced his appreciation of every little kindness by a smile that brought tears to the eye. There was no woman present—only a dying man among men—but those hardy fellows, who make the prairie their home, became gentle, almost womanly in their actions.

Briggs lingered until Christmas morning, and when he saw that he was sinking fast, Bolly Jennings, Jim Anderson, Ted Williams, Arkansas Bob, and the rest of the boys gathered about the bed.

"Is there any hope, Bolly?" he asked.

"I can't say, Briggs, but while there is life there is hope."

"Well there is darn little life left"; and he looked at us and smiled, "but I can stand what comes. God made me a man, and there is nothing else He has made that I cannot face."

We saw the life slowly fade out of his eyes—a strange chilly sight—and in death, with that smile of defiance and the cold fixed stare of his eyes, he looked as if he was face to face with an enemy. It was a touching sight to see how the boys stood around the dead form of Briggs, and endeavored to hide their emotion and failed.

The tears ran down the face of Arkansas Bob like rain off the gabled-end of a corn crib, and Ted Williams and Jim Henderson and several more bowed their heads, while their forms shook with the sobs they would not allow to escape.

The boys dug a grave on the banks of the Platte river, and that Christmas night as the clouds drifted away, and the moonlight fell upon the snow-covered ground and sparkled amid the ice-laden limbs of the tall trees, we laid poor Briggs down in his narrow resting place.

The only requiem that was sung was the roar of the turbid Platte, as it surged and tumbled along on its way to the sea—a mass sung by nature.

When the grave had been filled, Jim Henderson said: "I think we ought to have some kind of service. It ain't right by a darn sight to go away without sayin' somethin' over the grave—any you fellows got a bible?"

No one had a bible, nor had seen one in a number of years.

"Well, suppose some one says a sorter of a prayer."

The boys scratched their heads, glanced at one another for a moment and then looked away off into the woods.

Finally, some one whispered, "Sish! Arkansas Bob's going to pray," and he did.

"Oh, Lord!" he said, "I guess in your opinion I'm pretty tough, but I ain't askin' nuthin' for myself, it's for Briggs. He is dead now, but he was a white a man as ever walked. He never did no man a hurt, and he had a heart in him as big as a mule and no one, as I've heard, ever said a word agin him. I don't know as what I say will have much influence, but Briggs stood well with us down here, and although I don't know much about his career, or his history, or his family, he was a man as you could bank on every clatter. He gave a sick Mexican four dollars and fifty cents once for medicine, and then turned right around and nursed him through a fever, but the infernal rascal hadn't been well more'n two days before he stole Briggs' saddle-bags. Ah! Lord there ain't any preacher nowhere 'round here, or we'd had him to say something more pointed to you than I can say it. I never pattered any with the bible, and can't just now remember a hymn-song, but I'm a man of my word: I mean what I say, an' Briggs, if he gets a chance, will make as good a record in heaven as any one that ever got there. He had away down in his heart something that was square and as true as steel, an' oh! Lord you mustn't go back on that kind of man 'cause they are too skeerce in these parts. Amen."

The prayer was as rough as Bob, but no more sincere, as was evidenced by his tearful eye and trembling lip. After the prayer the boys ranged themselves on one side of the grave, and, drawing their six-shooters, fired a salute over their dead comrade, and while the sharp reports were still echoing through the vaults of the forest, they turned and slowly left the scene.

Who Briggs was, no one will ever know, but the solitary mound on the banks of the Platte, now matted over with rank grasses and creeping vines, rests one of the bravest men that ever faced eternity and his God.[18]

"The average cowboy," said a cattle dealer ... "does not bother himself about religion. The creeds and isms that worry civilization are a sealed book to the ranger, who is distinctively a fatalist. He believes that when the time comes for him to go over the range nothing can stand death off, and no matter what danger he faces previous to that time no deadly harm can come. The arch destroyer of the boys is lightning. More cowboys meet death from this source than from any other.

"One night when a party of us were driving a herd across the Staked Plains we had hardly made camp when a fierce storm, accompanied by terrific thunder and lightning, settled overhead. The crashes of thunder fairly shook the earth, and lightning seemed to dance from the tips of the cattle's horns. You see, when cattle become wet the steam arising from them forms a body of superheated air that rises upward two hundred or three hundred feet. In the absence of a tree, mountain or any better conductor, the lightning runs down this column of heated air. It is then almost sure to be attracted by the steel guns and trappings carried by the cowboys.

"Well, that wild night the whole gang were kept busy preventing a stampede. One of the party was Woods, as good a man as ever saddled a bronco. Jim had a premonition that his end was near at hand. All day he had been talking about his old mother back in the East, and the girl he used to go with. It was a sure sign that Jim had the blues. Well, when the storm broke, Jim went about his work with a white face and listless manner. In the gang, and stationed next to Jim was a young Texan, loud-mouthed and blasphemous. Every time a loud peal of thunder sounded and the lightning flashed unusually bright, the young bravado raised his clinched fist to the sky and muttered a volley of oaths.

" 'Go on, yer old pelter, ye can't hit us. We're thunder-proof, we air.'

"As quick as thought Jim rode up alongside the sacrilegious scamp, and pulling a six-shooter shoved it into the blasphemer's face. His face was white as chalk as he screeched: 'Get around on the other side, ye miserable skunk, or I'll shoot ye full of lead. Ye can't include me in none of your defies. My time's comin' soon enuf without spechully invitin' it. Now stampede.'

"The Texan fairly flew, and not a second too soon, for the flash of lightning and the thunder crash that followed took the soul of Jim Woods with it. One of the boys hurried to the spot and found Jim and his pony stiff and dead."[19]

" 'Last night as I lay on the prairie,
    And looked at the stars in the sky,
  I wondered if ever a cowboy
    Would drift to that sweet bye and bye.' "

Jack laid his pipe down and, turning to his pard, who was also star gazing, said: "Old man, what do you think of that proposition, anyhow?"

"What's that, old boy?"

"Well, this deal about the sweet bye and bye. Do you think a couple of toughs like us would stand any kind of show way up there among them angels, with their golden wings, the gold-paved streets, no end of harps, free music, everything coming your way, where everyone had his own private brand and the good Lord dead onto every angel in the herd? I've been sort of thinking this thing over, and it hits me bang in the short ribs that you and me had better sit in that kind of game, play close and see if we can't win, for——

  'The trail to that bright, mystic region
    Is narrow and dim, so they say;
  But the one that leads down to perdition
    Is staked and blazed all the way.'

"And that's dead right. It's no trouble to find the trail to hades; it's a cinch and you can't lose it, for the devil is the smoothest old boy in the deck. He sticks closer than that porous plaster I put on you that had been shot with bird shot. When the big round-up comes we want to be easy to find.

  'They say there will be a great round-up
    Where cowboys, like cattle, will stand—
  To be cut out by those riders from heaven,
    Who are posted and know every brand.'

"Now, old man, that verse is the apple dumpling of the whole lay out and shows that no monkeying goes for a minute. How are you going to get around it? You and me have been riding these ranges all our lives, and we ain't got a brand. We've got to croak some day. Look at pay-day; we get our dough and where is it? Booze—fairies and booze! A scrap or two and we go back to work. It's the same old game, and you can't beat it. Do you think a cow puncher could go to heaven, anyhow?

>'I wonder was there ever a cowboy
>   Prepared for that great judgment day,
> Who could say to the boss of the riders,
>   'I am ready to be driven away.'

"That last one is a hard crack. I don't see why a cowboy can't get there with both boots. I'm going to keep cases on them sky pilots and try to get onto their curves; but, old man, it's on the square and I know it. Listen to this:

>'They say He will never forsake you—
>   That He notes ev'ry action and look;
> But for safety you'd better get branded,
>   And have your name in the big tally book.'

"Now you've got the whole snap right in the neck. I'm going to get branded. You had better shake off your hobbles and cash in your chips with me. When we get up yonder and jingle our spurs at the gate of the big corral and St. Peter looks out, we'll just tell his royal highness that we are the two biggest thoroughbreds that ever came from Turkey Track range; that lately we've been on the dead square—no monkeying of any kind—and it's safe money that he'll say to some tenderfoot, 'Just fit these gentlemen out with wings.' Then we're in the game from that time on."[20]

NOTES TO CHAPTER SIX

1. Cf. Clifford P. Westermeier, "The Cowboy and Religion," *The Historical Bulletin*, XXVIII (January, 1950), 31.
2. "An Old-Time Cattle King," *Rocky Mountain News* (Denver, Colorado), February 1, 1886.
3. *Field and Farm* (Denver, Colorado), June 30, 1888, p. 9.

4. Louis C. Bradford, "Among the Cow-boys," *Lippincott's Magazine*, XXVII (June, 1881), 565.

5. "Ethics of the Range," *Cattlemen's Advertiser* (Trinidad, Colorado), April 29, 1886.

6. *Fort Collins Courier* (Fort Collins, Colorado), July 13, 1878.

7. "Saloon Preaching," *Democratic Leader* (Cheyenne, Wyoming), October 22, 1886.

8. *Field and Farm*, November 30, 1889, p. 6.

9. *Fort Morgan Times* (Fort Morgan, Colorado), April 9, 1886.

10. "His Last Sermon," *Democratic Leader*, December 11, 1884.

11. "The Preacher Price," *ibid.*, December 20, 1884.

12. *Field and Farm*, November 2, 1889, p. 6.

13. *Las Vegas Daily Optic* (Las Vegas, New Mexico), November 5, 1884.

14. "Cow Boy Devotion," *Cheyenne Weekly Leader and Stock Journal* (Cheyenne, Wyoming), October 11, 1883.

15. "The Parson's Round-Up," *Denver Tribune-Republican*, December 3, 1884.

16. "A Cowboy at Church," *Kansas Cowboy* (Dodge City, Kansas), March 14, 1885.

17. "A Cowboy's Funeral," *ibid.*, August 1, 1885.

18. "The Cowboy's Funeral," *Field and Farm*, March 6, 1886, p. 11.

19. "A Cowboy Felled by Lightning after Rebuking a Blasphemer," *Texas Live Stock Journal* (Fort Worth, Texas), January 21, 1888, p. 15.

20. "Frontier Sketches," *Field and Farm*, August 28, 1897, p. 6.

Buckaroo Rhymes

SEVEN

A figure so manly, vigorous, and coloful as that of the cowboy could not fail to rouse the most unimaginative journalist to poetic expression. As inspiration for Western journalism, the range rider stood as a bold, stark silhouette against a background of rolling, monotonous plains, turbulent, ever-changing skies, and restless, surging herds. The true spirit of the cowboy and his life is ever-present in the dangers of the occupation, the adven-

tures of trail and roundup, and the contacts with the fringes of civilization. The cowboy's horse, costume, and gear were also popular subjects for creative expression; his manners and habits, good and bad, challenged the writer to unleash rhythmic phrases. Actually, neither the man nor his traits escaped the discerning eye of the Western rhymsters, who, in their simple verse, preserved this elusive, romantic individual.

Not only did the frontier journalists create the mood of the period and the setting for their cowboy hero, but they also, in a descriptive and visual vocabulary, characterized him as a particular type of man. Their verses and jingles are filled with words and phrases of common usage in the cattle industry and in the daily conversation of the range rider. After exhausting that formidable array, they then approached their creations with a bucolic imagery which drew heavily upon surrounding nature. The occasional reference to characters or incidents—historical, Biblical, and allegorical—is more often a revelation of the rich classical education of the writers rather than a display of good taste in the rhymes. Attempts to simulate accent and dialect—the peculiarities of speech—are also evident in various degrees of success.

On the whole, verses and rhymes about the cowboy may be classified in three fairly distinct groups. First, and quite abundant, are those which laud the general character of the man, depicting him as a rider on the plains who bravely faces danger and hardship, who builds his hopes and dreams his dreams. The second group is the song type—of a rhythmical quality, not unlike the rollicking, chanty, lusty airs of the seaman. Those in the third group are narrative and relate particular incidents or situations in which the cowboy is the hero.

Obviously, the frontier journalist was neither poet nor ballader, and his rhymes and jingles were never heard around the campfire. This collection simply offers another form of interpretation of the cowboy as he was seen by contemporaries.

COWBOY LIFE

The Cow Boy[1]

Who rides his broncho through the street,
And shouts at each friend as they meet:
"Hello! Come in and I will treat"?
                  The Cow Boy.

Who "packs" a pair of Colt's Frontiers,
And sets the town upon its ears,
And man nor devil neither fears?
                  The Cow Boy.

Who plays "high ball" and "stud poker"
And drinks whisky like an old soaker,
And gambles like a stock broker?
                  The Cow Boy.

Who trips the light fantastic toe
To violin or old banjo,
And yells, more gin, *poco tiempo*?
                  The Cow Boy.

Who "runs" the town at dead of night,
And put the people in a fright,
Because he is a little tight?
                  The Cow Boy.

Who, when all is said and done,
Has only had a little fun,
And from the bake shop takes a bun?
                  The Cow Boy.
                      P. W. R.

The Cowboy[2]

What is it that has no fixed abode,
Who seeks adventures by the load—
An errant knight without a code?
   The cowboy.

Who finds pleasure, cows to punch,
When he would a whole herd "bunch"—
Who is ready for a fine grass lunch?
  The cowboy.

Who is it when the drive is done,
Will on a howling bender run,
And bring to town his little gun?
  The cowboy.

Who is it paints the town so red,
And in the morning has a head
Upon him like a feather-bed?
  The cowboy.

Who is it with unbounded skill
Will shoot big bullets with a will
That generally have the effect to kill?
  The cowboy.

Who is it, after all, who makes
Town trade good, and uniformly takes
For big hearts, what's called "the cake?"
  The cowboy.

The Cowboy[3]

We are sons of the prairie,
  Our hearts are light and gay,
We are up both late and early,
  And toil by night and day;
Our home is in the saddle,
  And our beds lie on the ground,
We're boys that are never idle
  When work is to be found.

The eastern press oft speaks of us
  With words of little praise,
And tells confiding readers
  Of our wild and reckless ways;

Their tales they are but stories—
    And they merit no belief,
For, were it not for cowboys,
    Where would you get your beef?

The lovely Sabbath morning
    The day our Savior blest—
For us it has no meaning,
    To us 'tis like the rest.
While others list' to preaching,
    Or worship God with praise,
The cowboy still is working
    Beneath the sun's hot rays.

                        M. S.

The Herder's Tale[4]

It's lonesome, eh?—a herdin' steers away out on Saline?
Well, stranger, no—when weather's fa'r, but roughish when it's mean.
You can't go fooling 'round and keep five hundred steers all right—
Jest try them broadhorns once yourself, some ugly stormy night.

Stampede, eh?—Well, I 'spect they do. You need seed it, eh?
It ain't what you've been usend to—for 'taint no nat'ral stray.
Che—hoop! they're off with tails sot straight, a-tearin' out o'sight!
It's bad in daylight, but it's jest infernal after night.

Ride around 'em, eh?—an' head 'em back?
Head back them Texas steers?
Stranger, when you was made, was stuff a-runnin' short for ears?
But then, you've had a show to l'arn, jest comin' out this fall:—
You're like them Yankee chaps that gets round here, and knows it all!

The storm you say? Well, Friday last we had a little
    muss:—
Jest rain, an' wind, an' sleet, an' snow—I reckon it
    couldn't be wuss.
Come dark, them critters went—"Old hoss," ses I—
    "jest let 'em rar!
Go humpin' to the Smoky now—I 'spect you'll find us
    thar!"

It wasn't mor'n forty miles, I guess, the way we run.
I foller'd, eh?—I went along; you'll allus count me one!
By daylight we was thar, you bet, in the valley by the
    bluff.
An' through the floating snow, I seed we had 'em sure
    enough.

Cold, stranger?—Well, it wasn't warm;—one o' them
    coldish days.
Five men all froze to death was found an' brought into
    Hays;—
Besides a dozen more, with feet, an' hands an' other
    parts
Used up—and only a little life a-creepin' round their
    hearts.

Exposure, eh?—You mean it's rough? I can't dispute
    your word.
But then I'm not the sort o' man to flunk an' lose my herd.
I hired out to tend them steers. The pay? It ain't so
    high;
But stranger, you can bet your life, I'd herd 'em till I'd die.

Their families?—Well it's like enough;—I reckon they
    had kin.
But we could only dig their graves and lay them softly in.
Us fellers—well, I s'pose we're rough, but still we're
    human men;
An' we'd be cryin' yet if 'twould bring back them boys
    again.

Their lot was?—Why bless your soul—there ain't no lot
    out thar—
Jest froze'd graves in the prairie, for it's prairie every
    whar!
You mean its hard to die that way? Well, stranger, so we
    thought;
Five men a-dyin' in their boots;—five men;—an' nary a
    shot.

R. S. Elliott

The Cowboy's Soliloquy[5]

All day over the prairies alone I ride,
Not even a dog to run by my side;
My fire I kindle with chips gathered round,
And boil my coffee without being ground.
Bread lacking leaven, I bake in a pot,
And sleep on the ground for want of a cot.
I wash in a puddle and wipe on a sack,
And carry my wardrobe all on my back.
My ceiling the sky, my carpet the grass,
My music the lowing herds as they pass.
My books are the brooks, my sermon the stones,
My parson a wolf on a pulpit of bones.
But then if my cooking ain't very complete,
Hygienists can't blame me for living to eat,
And where is the man who sleeps more profound,
Than the cowboy who stretches himself on the ground.
My books teach me constancy ever to prize,
My sermons that small things I should not despise,
And my parson remarks from his pulpit of bone,
That "the Lord favors them who look out for their own."
Between love and me lies a gulf very wide,
And a luckier fellow may call her his bride,
But cupid is always a friend to the bold,
And the best of his arrows are pointed with gold.
Friends gently hint I am going to grief,
But men must make money and women have beef.
Society bans me, a savage and dodge,
And Masons would ball me out of their lodge.

If I'd hair on my chin, I might pass for the goat
That bore all sin in ages remote.
But why this is thusly I don't understand,
For each of the Patriarchs owned a big brand.
Abraham emigrated in search of a range,
When water got scarce and he wanted a change.
Isaac had cattle in charge of Esau,
And Jacob "run cows" for his father-in-law;
He started in business clear down at bed rock,
And made quite a fortune by watering stock.
David went from night herding and using a sling,
To winning a battle and being a king.
And the shepherds when watching their flocks on the hill,
Heard the message from heaven, of peace and good will.

ALLEN McCANDLESS

The Herder[6]

An open range, far out and lone,
A cowboy sings in undertone,
As, resting idly on the grass,
He sees his herd, slow, feeding, pass.
He counts the steers, the heifers, cows,
Then counts the calves, an e'en allows
For such will prowl, what e'er his care.

His grateful pony crops the grass—
His feeding herd spread from the mass,
While flowers nod and wave and bend
As kissing winds caresses send.
The blue-joint gleams and flaunts its head
Above the modest floweret's bed,
And wild grouse and the timid quail
Fly up along the widening trail.

Some Texan steers that keep the lead
Now snort and start a mad stampede;
With tails aloft and bristling hair,
Distended eyes with frenzied glare,
Loud, frantic clash and bellowing roar,

Each seeks to lead or rush before.
Transformed, each one looks at least
Like some new, strange ferocious beast,
With bounding bellowing, break-neck speed,
All blindly join the wild stampede.

The herder mounts and springs away
Nor will he lose one single stray;
With cracking lash like pistol shot,
He soon will gather—bunch the lot;
His well-trained pony seems to know
Just how to turn and where to go.
With ruthless lash and racing speed
He does not try to gain the lead,
But lash and whoop and cowboy yell
Will turn one side and bunch them well.

The Cattle Man's Prayer[7]

Now, O Lord, please lend Thine ear,
The prayer of the cattle man to hear;
No doubt many prayers to Thee seem strange
But won't you bless our cattle range?

Bless the round-up, year by year,
And don't forget the growing steer;
Water the land with brooks and rills,
For my cattle that roam on a thousand hills.

Now, O Lord won't you be good,
And give our stock plenty of food;
And to avert a winter's woe,
Give Italian skies and little snow.

Prairie fires won't you please stop?
Let thunder roll and water drop;
It frightens me to see the smoke—
Unless it's stopped I'll go dead broke.

As you, O Lord, my herds behold—
Which represents a sack of gold—
I think at least five cents per pound
Should be the price of beef th' year 'round.

One thing more and then I'm through—
Instead of one calf, give my cows two,
I may pray different than other men,
Still I've had my say, and now, Amen!

The Paean of the Cowboy[8]

Oh! I am the cowboy of legend and story,
    Whom the back-eastern youngsters so greatly admire;
The slaughter of pilgrims is ever my glory,
    And few have escaped when they drew out my fire.

Astride of my broncho I speed o'er the prairie,
    A terror to all who my daring behold;
I deny any civilized constabulary
    And all vigilantes the country can hold.

As free as the proud soaring bird of the ocean
    I skim on my way over mountain and plain;
And no man dare make the least treacherous motion
    That he lives for a minute to do it again.

The joys of existence I don't claim forever—
    Some day I must mizzle like other galoots;
But the "Old Boy" will be most devilish clever
    If he gets me laid out while I stand in my boots.

When I'm roped at the round-up of judgment eternal,
    And corraled in a furnace forever to dwell,
I'll be able to show them some capers infernal—
    I won't be a tenderfoot rooster in h—l.

In the Woolly West[9]

There's health and vigor in the air
   Out in the woolly West.
The breezes clip the wings of care,
   And that's no idle jest.
The sun-rays dance upon the hills,
And sparkle in the mountain rills,
And life and inspiration fills
   With gladness every breast.

The people are in love with life,
   Out in the woolly West.
Their days are free from every strife,
   Their nights are nights of rest.
They're full of jollity and fun,
Start in just when the day's begun,
And keep it up from sun to sun,
   A sort of frolicfest.

There are no men of "terror" grade
   Left in the woolly West.
With boots on they have all been laid
   To their eternal rest.
We all are high-graded Christians now;
To Satan we no longer bow,
No sins now corrugate the brow,
   No troubles weight the breast.

The pistol of the early day
   Is missing from the West.
Men never meet in deadly fray
   With anger-swollen breast.
If we have wrongs that need redress
We seize the pen with eagerness,
And battle through the daily press
   Till passion is at rest.

Our loyalty is out of sight
   Here in the woolly West.
We whoops for country day and night
   With patriotic zest.

Just turn a flag loose in the air,
Our yells raise old Oom Satan's hair[10]
And start the echoes on a tear
   In jangled-up unrest.

O, ye, who for contentment yearn,
   Come to the woolly West.
We've joy and happiness to burn,
   And warrant it the best.
Here you can sip from pleasure's bowl,
Find manna for the troubled soul,
And now a wave of care will roll
   Across a peaceful breast.

The Poet Lariat of the Ranches[11]

My broncho is no Pegasus
   To reach Olympian heights,
But still up Rocky Mountain slopes
   He takes me in his flights.
'Tis here that thoughts come "rounding up,"
   To nature near akin,
So I throw my mental lariat,
   And strive to "rope them in."

HARRY ELLARD

The Cowboys[12]

Out in our grand and western land,
There lives the happy cowboy band.
'Tis here they ride their bronchos strong,
'Tis here they throw their lariats long.

They lead a life so free from care
In Colorado's sunshine fair,
And on the Rocky Mountain slope
They chase the deer and antelope.

And as they hunt the game so rare,
They breathe the pure and healthful air.
They climb the steep, they cross the plain,
A fresher vigor yet to gain.

To rope the steers in rapid flight
In round up is their keen delight.
With burning irons and steady hand,
On every calf they place a brand.

And when at night their work is o'er,
They enter in the ranch house door,
To tell their tales of chasing steers,
Then sleep the sleep that knows no fears.

HARRY ELLARD

The Rough Rider[13]

Where the long horns feed on the sun-cured grass, in the blaze of a cloudless sky;
Where the cactus crawls and the sage brush spreads on a plain of alkali;
Where the gray wolf prowls and makes his feast on the range calf gone astray;
Where the coward coyote yelps by night but slinks from the face of day;
Where the mountains frame the pictured plain with a border line of snow;
Where the chill of death from the blizzard's breath falls with a sting and blow,
There rides a man of the wild, wide West, blest of the sun and air,
A simple man, with a face of tan, and a heart to do and dare.

From "rope" and "quirt" and ripping "gaff" and the strangling "hackamore,"
The untamed broncho learned his will and a master burden bore
Over the sloughs and the gophered ground, and in time of his greatest need

When he rides in the peril of hoof and horn at the head
   of the night stampede.
He is slow of speech, but quick of hand, and keen and
   true of eye,
He is wise in the learning of nature's school—the open
   earth and sky;
His strength is the strength of an honest heart, he is
   free as the mountain's breath;
He takes no fear of a living thing and makes a jest of
   death.

RICHARD LINTHICUM

ROLLICKING RHYMES

The Captain of the Cow-Boys[14]

I'm Captain Jack of Kurber Creek,
I wear good clothes and keep 'em sleek.
On what I buy I ask no "tick,"
For I'm captain of the cow-boys.
I do that work which I think to be,
   think to be, think to be,
Consistent with the dignity
Of a captain among the cow-boys.

Twice a year I corral my cattle,
And if one turns to give me battle,
The way I make the fence poles rattle,
Would draw a smile from a preacher.
And when I try to rope a calf, rope a
   calf, rope a calf,
My perseverance would make you laugh,
But I mostly catch the creature.

If a visit to Blackjack ranch you pay,
By way of advice just let me say,
You'd better not come on branding day,
If beauty is your portion;
For what with dust and what with blows,
   what with blows, what with blows,
A dirty face and a broken nose,
Will likely change your notion.

The Jolly Vaquero[15]

The jolly vaquero is up with the sun,
And quick in the saddle, you see,
He swings his quirt and jingles his spurs—
    A dashing vaquero is he.
He "Hangs and rattles" and "Hits the high places,"
    That bound the lone prairie;
And woe to the steer, when he draws near,
    For a bold bad roper is he.

Chorus: Whoop-la! "Set 'em afire!"
        Shouts the rider free,
        "Give 'em the spurs" and "Burn the earth!"
        A cowboy's life for me.

Over the cow-trail, leaping the sage,
    His pony can't be beat.
He'll "Git That Eli," "Sure's you're born,"
    See how he "Handles his feet!"
The rider "Stays with him," and "Don't you forget it,"
    True knight of the saddle is he—
And he "Hits the breeze," and rides at ease,
    And swings the lariat free.

"You can bet your life" "He's got the sand,"
    Whenever there's work to be done,
He "Rounds 'em up" and "Cuts 'em out,"
    And "mavericks" just for fun;
In rain or shine, or sleet or hail,
    He rides the wild prairie—
Oh! who wouldn't envy a life like this
    Of the cowboy, wild and free!

Though often "Dead broke"—his saddle "in soak"—
    He never loses his pluck;
He'll share his "Stake" with his partner, too,
    If he meets him "Out of luck";
He'll "wack up" his blankets, or share his "grub,"
    No need of "Calling him down,"
He'll "Spend his wealth" in drinking your health,
    Whenever he comes to town.

With the Cowboys[16]

I am cook of the cowboy's camp,
A dancing, roving, musical tramp.
I can fry a slice of bacon to the acme
    of perfection.
And my latest batch of duff will bear
    the closest inspection.
I can boil a pot of 'taters 'till they
    are in the right condition,
And can handle the harmonica just like
    an old musician.
A break-down, clog or hornpipe I can
    dance with great agility,
And dish you out a plate of beans with
    even facility.
I grind a mess of coffee every morning
    with dexterity.
And get the breakfast ready with unusual
    celerity.

A Cowboy's Sweetheart[17]

Little bunch o' lightnin' snap,
    Full o' girlish animation,
Sort that makes a youngish chap
    Love the whole female creation.
Eyes a flashin' full o' mirth,
    Laugh that rips the air in tatters,
An' a smile that beats the earth
    In the sunshine that it scatters.
Angels hain't got much the best
O' this wild flower o' the West.

Doesn't wa'r no toney clothes,
    Ain't no jewels on her flashin',
Sort o' up'ards hurls her nose
    When you hint at fuss an' fashion.
Ruther crude an' rough in speech
    When her thoughts she is expressin',

But I reckon she could teach
    City gals a modest lesson.
Figure! You jest bet yer spurs
Juniper'd envy hers.

When she sings I've of'n thought,
    With the music 'round me ringin',
That the heaven angels ought
    To adopt her style o' singin',
Seems to hit agin yer heart
    There to sort o' break an' scatter
Through yer soul, each note a dart,
    Tipped with song enough to shatter
Every nerve with sweet delight!
Honest Injun, pard, that's right!

Ought to see her ride an' rope!
    Pardner, she's a ten-times winner!
Ain't no cowboy on the slope
    That kin hold his own agin her!
Ropes the toughest bronk, an' fights
    Him while cinchin' on the saddle,
Makes a suddent jump, an' lights
    On the crazy cuss astraddle!
Let him buck! She's there to stay
If he bucks till jedgment day!

Got a hope staked out in me
    'F I'd corral her on the quiet
An' let go the rope, that she
    Wouldn't make no run to shy it.
Got an idee she would stand,
    Sort o' glad that I had nipped her,
Till the preacher put the brand
    On us, 'cordin' to the scriptur',
But I ain't dead sure, an' I'll
Let her run fur yit a while.

FUN AND FROLIC

The Wichita "Poker Craze"[18]

Which I says for a heathen Injun,
    Who hasn't civilized ways,
That Yellow Dog of the Wichitas,
    Was a regular draw-poker "craze,"
When we camped on the Canadian,
    Down low on the Southern fork,
"Missouri Dan" had a greasey deck,
    And we settled down to the work.

Dave dealt the papers to "Baltimore,"
    (Which Hal was also his name);
Hal "antied," Yellow Dog "staid in,"
    As likewise I did the same.
Then Dan "passed out," Hal "raised the blind"
    And "Throwed to the center" to draw,
And Yellow Dog stood to the raise of Hal,
    Which the same I also saw.

I drawed two cards and Hal drawed one,
    And Yellow Dog he drawed three,
And I knowed that Hal had "filed his haul"
    By the wink he wunk at me.
Then the fun began, and the Injun "bucked,"
    And I saw "Missouri" laugh,
He knowed whoever won the "pot,"
    That we was all "half and half."

When all the "rocks" which the party had
    Had been put on the board,
And all the fixin's about the camp,
    And even the stock we rode,
I called for a "sight," throwed down my hand,
    When, as sure as I'm alive,
"Baltimore Hal" he hilt *four ones*
    Whilst the Yellow Dog *he hilt five*!

Stranger, of course, we was surprised,
    But the rules of the game declare
That "whenever the redskin cheats the white
    He must 'climb the golden stair.' "
And there he was a wicked Injun,
    For he tried to "raise a gale"
By "roping" us innocent cowboys;
    So we "tuck him off the trail."

Way down on the South Canadian,
    Where the waters wildly sweep.
Where the osier sighs to the sage bush,
    The Wichita Yellow Dog sleeps,
Which is why I says of the Injun,
    Who hasn't civilized ways,
For to tackle a cowboy at poker,
    He must have a "poker craze."

A Memory of the Trail[19]

The cowboy sat on his old gray horse
    And afar off viewed the town,
And softly sighed as he noticed that
    Its color was mostly brown.
"Oh for a glimpse of the good old days,"
    The sad-eyed puncher said,
"When me with a gang of bullies brave
    Used ter paint the old place bright red."

"We'd spur like mad up ther busy streets,
    Make the sheriff hunt his hole,
Shoot glasses and hats and ther damage pay
    From a big fat greenback roll.
The store man he would lock his door,
    The tenderfoot run like h—l,
And the barkeeper buckle on his gun
    When he heard our Texas yell."

"Ther perleece would suddenly disappear,
    Ther dance-hall man would grin,
And the monte bank would open up
    To swallow in our tin.
The girls would holler 'hello old punch,'
    And we'd shoot out the lights;
The resterant man would take in his sign,
    Fur he knew our appetites."

And the cowboy felt in his pockets deep,
    In search of vanished wealth,
And said, as he turned his back to the town,
    "I guess the ranch is best fur my health.
No, I won't go to town for a couple of years,
    I'll stay out at ther old ranch instead,
And besides that two dollars is might few paint
    Fur to color a whole town red."

"Ther cowboy he hain't got no show eny more,
    Ther country's a settlin' too fast,
He'll go where ther Buf'lo and Injun hev gone,
    But he'll be bully boy to ther last."

A Cowboy in Wall Street[20]

I was riz on a ranch in old Texas, yer know,
    Whar they growed the wild steers and all sich,
But the bizness plum played—so I thought I'd jest go
    Tew the city on aim ter get rich;
I hed heer'd uv New York and the stock men up thar,
    An' them brokers that range on Wall street,
I wuz posted on bulls, I hed carved up a bar,
    An' I 'lowed ez I couldn't be beat.

I got shet uv my cattle at ole Abilene,
    An' the keers ter Old Gotham I took;
Je whiz! wot a teown! them sights wot I seen
    Would fill up a powerful book!

Well I moized around, an' I loafed awhile
    Fer I soon struck a boss campin' spot,
But at last I concluded I'd add to my pile,
    Fer the money iz thar—tew be got!

Then I went tu a feller wot hed a big name
    Fer keepin' uv thoroughbred stock,
An' when I hed studied hiz neat little game,
    I anteed fer quite a pert block;
The brand thet I got wuz "The C. B. & Q."
    They said that the outfit might pay,
An' bein' a tenderfoot thar, an' green, too,
    I sorta believed wot they'd say.

Well, thet market hit riz at the big stock exchange,
    An' I seen I wuz playin' to luck!
Then didn't I swell! huh! I owned the hull range,
    Fer a fortune I reckoned I'd struck.
So I kept on playin' till I staked my hull lump,
    All my money an' cash from them steers,
But all in a sudden there came a big slump,
    An' I lost my hull savings uv yeers!

Then I ciphered an' figured, an' ciphered around,
    'Till I giv the hull bizness a d—n!
Fer my scads wuz all gone! an' I pretty soon found
    That I wuz a Texas sheared lamb!
Yes, that's wot they called me, a peert kind of name,
    Fer I seen I wuz green an' wuz fooled,
I hed staked my hull wad on some other chap's game,
    Some feller, perhaps, like Jay Gould.

So I gathered my ole paper grip-sack again,
    Thar wuz nuthin' else fer me to do,
An' I pulled my old freight to an out-goin' train,
    An I "vamoosed" the town, P.D.Q.!

My Lord and the Broncho[21]

He was a fair young Briton, he bore a titled name,
It took two lines of minion, we're told, to print the same;
Clamped in his starboard optic he wore a circle glass,
And used the other looker to see things as they'd pass.
He'd read about the cowboys and Indians and things,
The buffalo that watered at Colorado Springs,
And came out to this country to see the bloomin' show,
And brought his title with him as ballast, don't ye know.

He drifted to a rancho where cattle roam the plains,
He carried ten umbrellas and quite a bale of canes,
His "man" marched close behind him, stepped as if built on springs,
And carried two port-man-choos stuffed full of lots of things.
The cowboys gazed upon him in wonder most supreme,
And sharply spurred each other to see if 'twere a dream,
And grinned when he addressed them in words drawled beastly slow:
"I'm Lord Alphonso Paget De Lawncey, don't ye know."

He said that as a rider at 'ome he set the pace,
Be'ind the 'ounds he'd ridden in many a frightful chase,
And if 'is 'unter bolted he'd teach 'im with the crop
'Twas Lord Alphonso Paget De Lawncey who was up,
He eyed the raw-boned bronchos bunched up in the corral,
And said they were but palfreys, were anything but swell,
And when a bawth he'd taken he'd hawlf a mind to go
And back a beastly creature for a canter, don't ye know.

The Christian cowboys told him it gave them pain to say
Their thoroughbreds were feeding on ranges far away,
But if with condescension he'd back a bronk, they'd choose
A pet that wasn't stylish, but great on the amuse.
They roped a flea-bit cowhorse that seemed 'bout half asleep,
That stood while being saddled as quiet as a sheep,
And when Milord was mounted he said: "Now let 'im go!
'E'd never make a 'unter; too stupid, don't ye know."

That broncho stood a moment, as mapping out its job,
Then every muscle in it begin to jerk and throb,
An o'er the plain it bounded with wild, excited vaults,
And turned a lot of single and double somersaults!
With tender hands the cowboys bore that astonished lord
From where his titled body had battered up the sward,
And when his wond'ring sense returned he muttered low:
"Such bloody blawsted conduct was beastly, don't ye know!"

The Cowboys' Christmas Ball[22]

The boys had left the ranches and cum to town in piles;
The ladies, kinder scatterin', hed gethered in fer miles,
An' yet the place was crowded, ez I remember well—
'Twus got fur the occashun at the Morning Star Hotel.
The music wuz a fiddle an' a lively tambourine,
An' a viol cum imported, by stage from Abilene.
The room was togged out gorgeous with mistletoe and shawls,
An' candles flickered frescoes around the airy walls.
The wimmin folks looked lovely, the boys looked kinder treed,
Till the leader commenced yellin': "Whoa fellers! Let's all stampede!"
An' the music started sighin' and a-wailin' through the hall,
Ez kind uv introduction to the cowboys' Christmas ball.

The leader wuz a feller thet cum from the Milliron ranch—
They called him Windy Billy, from little Dead Man's Branch.
His rig wuz kinder keerless—big spurs and high-heeled boots,
He hed the reputation thet comes when fellers shoots.
His voice wuz like a bugle upon the mountain's heights,
His feet were animated and a mighty movin' sight.
Then he commenced to holler: "Neow, fellers, stake your pen!
Lock horns to all them heifers an' russle 'em like men!

Salute yer luvly critters! Neow swing and let 'em go!
Climb the grapevine round 'em—all hands docedo!
Ye mavericks jine the round-up—jest skip her waterfall!"
Huh, hit wuz gittin' active—the cowboys' Christmas ball.

The boys were tolerable skittish, the ladies powerful neat,
That old bass viol's music jest got there with both feet!
And Windy kept a singin', I think I hear him yet—
"O yes, chase your squirrels, an' cut 'em to one side,
Spur Treadwell to the center, with Cross P Charley's bride,
Doc Hollis down the center, an' twine the ladies' chain,
Varn Andrews pen the fillies, in Big T Diamond's train,
All pull yer freight together, neow swallow for an' change,
Big Foster lead the trail herd, through little Pitchfork's range.
Purr 'round yer gentle pussies, neow rope 'em! balance all!"
Huh! hit was mighty happy. The cowboys' Christmas ball.

The dust riz fast an' furious, we all just galloped 'round,
Till the scenery got so giddy that Z bar Dick was downed.
We buckled to our partners, and told 'em to hold on,
Then shook our hoofs like lightning, until the early dawn.
Don't tell me of cotillions or germans, No sir'ee!
That whirl at Anson City just takes the cake with me,
I'm sick of lazy shufflin's, of them I've had my fill.
Give me a frontier breakdown, backed up by Windy Bill.
Dancin' masters ain't no whar! when Windy leads the show,
I've seen 'em both in harness, and so I sorter know—
Oh Bill, I shan't forget yer, and I'll often-times recall
That lively gaited sworry, The cowboys' Christmas ball.

NOTES TO CHAPTER SEVEN

1. *Trinidad Weekly News* (Trinidad, Colorado), September 28, 1882.

2. *Las Vegas Daily Optic* (Las Vegas, New Mexico), November 12, 1884.

3. *Trinidad Daily Advertiser* (Trinidad, Colorado), May 23,

1884. This poem appears again in the *Rocky Mountain News*, September 24, 1897, "Dedicated to Frontier Day" and over the name of F. William Stuart, U. S. Mail Service, formerly a cowboy.

4. *Trinidad Daily Advertiser*, March 11, 1885.
5. *Ibid.*, April 9, 1885.
6. *Socorro Bullion* (Socorro, New Mexico), November 21, 1885.
7. *Ibid.*, October 30, 1886.
8. *Denver Tribune-Republican* (Denver, Colorado), December 19, 1886.
9. *Denver Evening Post* (Denver, Colorado), May 30, 1898.
10. *Oom*—South African Dutch for "uncle."
11. *Facts* (Colorado Springs, Colorado), IV (July 22, 1899), 23.
12. *Ibid.*, August 19, 1899, p. 21.
13. *Denver Republican* (Denver, Colorado), August 7, 1900.
14. *Out West*, I (New Series) (September, 1873), 68.
15. *Cheyenne Weekly Leader and Stock Journal* (Cheyenne, Wyoming), August 23, 1883.
16. *Kansas Cowboy* (Dodge City, Kansas), August 1, 1885.
17. *Denver Evening Post*, September 23, 1898.
18. *Denver Republican*, May 6, 1883.
19. *Field and Farm* (Denver, Colorado), August 6, 1887, p. 10.
20. *Stock Grower and Farmer* (Las Vegas, New Mexico), October 10, 1891.
21. *Denver Evening Post*, July 19, 1899.
22. *Field and Farm*, December 25, 1897, p. 6.

Tales--Tall and Tangy

EIGHT

The cowboy was a natural storyteller. In relating tales he was no longer the silent sentinel of the range. His voice was not hesistant or were his words curt and brief; in a colorful and enthusiastic vocabulary the tales flowed from his loosened tongue and were, consequently, his best medium for self-expression.

The outstanding traits of the cowboy—his courage and bravery, faithfulness and sincerity, daring spirit, sense of justice, kindness and generosity—usually supply the themes for the countless tales, legendary or factual, which are associated with his life and work.

Danger threatened the cowboy in many forms and from every side. Some of the stories reveal such danger as constantly surrounded him in his daily occupation; in others, his reckless and daring nature lured him to seek danger beyond his scope of work. Not only were the cattle and horses in his charge a source of danger, but also the predatory animals that stalked both men and herds. These adventures afforded an exciting source for stories, and the range rider, who did not have in his collection an experience with a "varmit" or "critter" of some kind, was not worthy of the name "cowboy."

There were, of course, stories which any cowboy, if he considered himself a storyteller, had at his finger tips— secondhand tales, related by the original participant or by "a friend of a friend." Such stories verged on the improbable and always caused a bit of speculation and wonder on the part of his comrades.

His tall tales—spectacular and wonderful, and sometimes weird and frightening—were told with such utmost sincerity that oftentimes the listener accepted them at face value. Only the complete acceptance of such a yarn by the cowboy audience would arouse suspicion in the outsider.

The cowboy was a practical joker, and a rough one, too! Many of his stories relate with boisterous enthusiasm the disastrous outcome of pranks played on the tenderfoot, the dude, or fellow riders. But none of these planned incidents is any more ridiculous or harder on the victims than some of the situations in which the cowboy finds himself when removed from familiar surroundings. His encounters with the hazards of the city, with the "modern" conveniences of that day, and with the city dweller who turned tables on him are as humorous and mirth provoking as any stunt which he devised to "tickle the tenderfoot."

Groups of men, gathered around the flickering campfire, some wearied into silence by the arduous activity of the day, were appreciative listeners. Thus, through the years, and night after night under the cold, gleaming starlight, in a silence broken only by the voice of the narrator and the far-off mournful cry of the coyote, the cowboy tales were told.

THE GOOD HEART

How a Cattle Man Saved His Life[1]

One hot day in July, 1860, a herdsman was moving his cattle to a new ranche further north, near Helena, Texas, and passing down the banks of a stream, his herd became mixed with other cattle that were grazing in the valley, and some of them failed to be separated. The next day about noon a band of a dozen mounted Texan rangers overtook the herdsman and demanded their cattle, which they said were stolen.

It was before the days of law and courthouses in Texas, and one had better kill five men than to steal a mule worth five dollars, and the herdsman knew it. He tried to explain, but they told him to cut it short. He offered to turn over all the cattle not his own, but they laughed at his proposition, and hinted that they usually confiscated the whole herd, and left the thief hanging on a tree as a warning to others in like cases.

The poor fellow was completely overcome. They consulted apart a few moments and then told him if he had any explanation to make or business to do they would allow him ten minutes to do so, and defend himself.

He turned to the rough faces and commenced: "How many of you have wives?" Two or three nodded. "How many of you have children?" They nodded again.

"Then I know who I am talking to and you'll hear me," and he continued:

"I never stole any cattle; I have lived in these parts over three years. I came from New Hampshire; I failed there in the fall of '57 during the panic; I have been saving; lived on hard fare; I have slept out on the ground; I have no home here; my family remain east; I go from place to place; these clothes I wear are rough and I am a hard-looking customer; but this is a hard country; days seem like months to me, and months like years; married men, you know that but for the letters from home—(Here he pulled out a handful of well-worn envelopes and letters from his wife)—I should get discouraged. I have paid part of my debts. Here are the receipts," and he unfolded the letters of acknowledgement. "I expected to sell out and go home in November. Here is the testament my good old mother gave me; here is my little girl's picture," and he kissed it tenderly and continued: "Now, men, if you have decided to kill me for what I am innocent of, send these home, and as much as you can from these cattle when I'm dead. Can't you send half the value? My family will need it."

"Hold on, now, stop right thar!" said a rough ranger. "Now, I say, boys," he continued, "I say, let him go. Give us your hand, old boy; that picture and them letters did the business. You can go free; but you're lucky, mind ye."

"We'll do more than that," said a man with a big heart, in Texan garb, and carrying the customary brace of pistols in his belt, "let's buy his cattle here and let him go."

They did, and when the money was paid over, and the man about to start, he was too weak to stand. The long strain of hopes and fears, being away from home under such trying circumstances, the sudden deliverance from death, all combined to render him helpless as a child. He sank to the ground completely overcome. An hour later, however, he left on horseback for the nearest stage-route, and as they shook hands and bade him good-by, they looked the happiest band of men I ever saw.

Bound to a Horse's Back[2]

When Mr. Boussaud reached his ranch about the middle of June, he found the cowboys nursing a young man whom they had rescued from the back of a broncho. When discovered, the modern Mazeppa was lashed to the horse, entirely naked and unconscious. The animal was about broken down, as if from long running, and was easily lassoed by the cowboys, who cut the thongs and released the strange captive.

This happened about two weeks before Mr. Boussaud's arrival and during all the time the stranger had lain in a stupor. A few days before Boussaud left on his return journey to Omaha, having a little smattering of medical knowledge, he succeeded in restoring the patient to consciousness and his recovery was rapid. When able to talk he said his name was Henry Burbank, that he was an Englishman, and 34 years of age. About three years ago at Falmouth, England, he formed a partnership with a friend named Thomas Wilson, some years his senior, and with him came to America to embark in the cattle business. They cast around for a while and finally settled in northwestern Nebraska, where the range was unlimited and herders few and far apart. They built a comfortable ranch on a little stream, where Wilson's young wife reigned as housekeeper, attended by two or three female domestics.

Burbank was a handsome young gallant, and while Wilson was absent riding about the range found it agreeable to make love to the latter's wife. This went on for some months, until in the latter part of May one of the cowboys who had a grievance against Burbank surprised him and Mrs. Wilson in a compromising situation and informed the woman's husband, whose jealously had already been aroused. That night Burbank was captured, while asleep in bed, by Wilson and three of his men, and bound before he had a chance to resist. Wilson had him stripped of every bit of clothing and bound on the back of a wild broncho, which was started off by a vigorous lashing.

Before morning Burbank became unconscious, and is therefore unable to tell any thing about his terrible trip. He thinks that the outrage was committed on the night of May 27 and he was rescued on the morning of June 3, which would make seven days that he had been traveling about the plains on the horse's back without food or drink and exposed to the sun and wind. Wilson's ranch is about two hundred miles from the spot where Burbank was found, but it is hardly probable that the broncho took a direct course and therefore must have covered many more miles in his wild journey. When fully restored to health Burbank proposes to make a visit of retaliation on Wilson and will be backed by Boussaud's men and also a squad from the Ogalalla [Ogallala] Land & Cattle Company whose range is near Boussaud's.

Days Gone By[3]

A hot Arizona day had burnt itself out and lay in lazy blue smokewreaths under the cool shadows of the San Francisco peaks. The air was heavy with dust too lazy to descend to earth, and the great sugar pines had perspired until their aromatic scent seemed the most pungent life then existing. The cattle and horses came poking slowly up to the big corrals, and the cowboys jogging sullenly behind, too listless to even swear at their charges. Just as the last animal was crowded into the corrals, one of the boys called the attention of the rest to a brown speck away off on the plains to the east, coming as though some mighty terror was pursuing. As the speck drew near it shaped itself into a horse and the horse was recognized as one ridden by Bert Halleck two days before, to warn the settlers on the Coloranita at Sunset crossing of a band of Apaches. No one was riding the horse, but as he came up at a long, swift gallop to the corrals the boys noticed a small bundle, and when old Pete had stopped at the bars they noticed a long cactus limb tied to his tail that explained his haste and sundry wicked kicks. Jack Emmonds loosened the bundle, and as he did so unrolled it, and showed the face of a baby with a slip of paper pinned to its frock underneath. The slip had been torn from an old newspaper, and on it was scrawled, with a lead end of a cartridge:

"Picked this up at the crossing. Patches is here and Pete's playful. Am going to stay and fight.

B. H."

"The baby had been jolted till there wasn't a cry left in it," as Tom Eldridge remarked, and one of the boys hastened with it to the house, while the rest began catching up fresh horses. Just as fast as nervous hands could fasten cinches, the horses were made ready, and in less than fifteen minutes from "old Pete's" appearance six cowboys were racing back over the track he'd come. Silently they rode, but five miles away they drew rein and dismounted, for their errand was accomplished, and there lay their former comrade, with his body bristling with arrows, the crown of his head bare and white in the twilight, and a grim smile on his face as though even death could not conquer his resolute spirit. Afterwards the wagon and its dead owners, from which Bert had taken the baby after the Apaches had murdered its parents and rode away to leave it to die, were found near the Sunset crossing, and so the boys adopted the little waif and named it Sunset. She only lived a year and a half though, and now the boys are scattered, the Apaches corraled, the whole barren country settled and blooming with the fruits of man's labor, and the old past is like a dream.

The Cowboy's Pet Colt[4]

Early in the fall we had orders to drive southward into what is now a part of Oklahoma. There was a dun pony only a week old then and hardly fit to travel. We had to go, however, and as for this colt (or any number of colts for that matter), why, if he could not travel he must die.

The first two or three days he kept up very well, but it was hard work. Afterward he began to weaken. I was tender then and it made my heart ache to see him try to keep up, with his little legs bending under him in a manner which made them appear all out of joint. His mother a spirited animal, would lag behind with him and her pitiful endeavors to obtain a little rest for her colt would often cause me to lag far behind with my charge, for which I would be sure to get a "round-up" from Stevenson.

One of the last days on the drive it began to blow from the north and soon it was bitterly cold. Toward evening I had fallen behind again, this time farther than usual, and the first thing I knew Stevenson came riding back. He was furious, but without saying a word, he roped this colt's mother and in a few minutes had transferred his saddle to her. He then rode up to me. The poor colt tried to follow him as he galloped along, but could not, and finally stood still and sent up a pitiful neigh after its mother. All Stevenson said to me was, "Now you can either help me hustle these horses along or you can get off your horse and stay here with that good-for-nothing colt."

I was angry at once with his imperative way and the cruelty to this colt and its mother.

I jumped off without saying a word. This was not what Stevenson expected, for he looked considerably put out. His anger rose again, however, and he cried, "Well, hoof it to camp, then, you——fool," and away he went driving my riding pony along with the rest.

Well, there we were, the poor, weak colt and myself. It was cold and getting colder, but I knew that the outfit would camp not far ahead, so I set myself to the task and by 9 o'clock that night I had succeeded in driving that colt within half a mile of camp. Here I was met by Stevenson and one of the men. The former told me to get up behind him, and then they drove the colt to camp.

The next morning by Stevenson's orders the colt was placed in one of the wagons and its mother tied behind. You bet I kept up then. Of course I was guyed by the rest, and the colt was known afterwards as Dick's baby, but then I could stand that. Two years passed and I was still with the same outfit. I had made a pet of "Baby," as I called the colt, and he would follow me about like a dog. I could even send him back to camp from any point by simply telling it to go.

The Cowboy's Start in Life[5]

"And now he's one of them millionaires," mused the grizzly frontiersman whose relatives had induced him to come back for a brief visit in a center of civilization. "I see it right here in the paper. He owns railroad stock, minin' stock and lots of other stock. I knowed that there same Henry H. Holdem when he did nuthin' but punch stock for other people out on the plains. He was a genuine cowboy and as fast a feller in a roundup as ever I see."

"You must be mistaken, uncle."

"Nothin' of the kind. When I talk about people you can bet I'm allus dead certain of my fac's. We called him Hank them days, and he was jest as handsome a youngster as ever throwed his leg over a saddle. Jest by puttin' things together as they kim out, I l'arned as how he was a college gradyate and was goin' so fast a clip and scatterin' the ole man's money that they sent him out there fer to git a schoolin' in economy and built up ag'in. He was soon the fav'rite on all the ranches 'bout here, fur he was squar' as a dye and not afeard o' nothin'.

"Well, this here girl what he married kim out to stay fer a while on her dad's cattle range, that j'ined our's. Some of the swell people up to Leadtown, 20 miles away, what knowed her people gave a ball fur her. Her and her dad went over in the cool of the forenoon, and after takin' dinner was in a lawyer's office talkin'. It seems Hank got some money from the same law office once a month, and was there too. He heerd the old man laughing and telling how they kim away from the range with the wrong valise, leavin' her ball dress ahind, and her almost crazy about it. Hank never says a word, but jumps on his horse, goes that 20 miles as though Injuns was after him, gits the dress, changes critters, and throws the girl into a fit o' happiness when he delivers the goods on time. A year's courtin' wouldn't have made him solid. The very next winter they was married. Hank was as steady as a deacon, both ole men boosted him, and now you see where he is."

PLAYING WITH DANGER

The Demon Steer[6]

George Wilson, a well known cowboy, tells the following story:

There has roamed on the ranges adjacent to the Platte and Laramie rivers, for these many years, a mastodon wild steer whose aggressiveness and power makes him the dread of every round up outfit. This combative beef bears not a brand, but no "rustler" dares appropriate him.

The "Demon steer" as the pugnacious brute is called, knows no fear, and with lowered head, glistening eyes and sonorous bellow will charge upon anything in his course. Time upon time he has been rounded up with his comparative docile companions, but he invariably rushes past the line riders as if no such obstruction to his flight existed. Once a C Y outfit determined to effect the capture of the big fellow, but after he had gored two horses and scared the wits from a half dozen riders, the undertaking was abandoned.

This prairie terror only last season, in a fit of rage at those who dared to intrude on the peaceful solitude of the range, charged at midday into a camp, creating a panic, to which was ideal quietness the clatter incident to the stampede of the fabled bull in the china shop. There was a scattering of equipage and a disordered flight of the diners. One of these latter was so incensed that, contrary to orders, he sent a six-shooter ball after the massive steer, but the missive flew wide its mark.

Wilson asserts that he will undertake to prove that the demon steer killed a large bear in a fair fight on the Sybile three years ago, and the cowboys will bet all their earthly belongings that the demon steer can conquer any bull in the territory. The combat with the bear was a terrific affair. Bruin was forced to the defensive from the first, and for a time pluckily met the fearful onslaughts of the fighting steer, jarring the great form with blows from his paws. The activity of the steer was marvelous. He played around his antagonist as the sparrer annoys his foe, and at nearly every charge ran his long, sharp horns into the bleeding sides of the bear with the wicked "swish" which accompanies an effective sword thrust.

Wilson thinks the demon steer will die of old age. The man who attempts his capture takes his life in his hands.

Roping Wolves[7]

While riding a bronco Perry Stiff, one of Baxter's cowboys, saw a pack of wolves chasing a bunch of horses in the rear of which was an old mare and a colt, the object of the chase being fresh colt meat. Stiff got behind a hill, and as the frightened horses flew by, put spurs to his bronco and singling out the largest wolf in the pack made the chase.

As the cowboy's horse was fresh and the wolf already pretty tired, it was not long until the noose was dropped over the head of the big gray. The animal's fore feet went through the loop, however, and the rope tightened around his body in such a way that he was able to make a strong pull. Finding himself at the end of the rope the brute, after failing to cut it with his sharp teeth, made a dash for liberty in another direction. The movement drew the rope about the broncho's hind legs and tail and the natural result was some very hard bucking.

Between the bucking horse and the wolf, Stiff had his attention pretty well taken up. He held to the bucking strap and finally got straight with the wolf at the end of the rope and square in front of the horse. By this time the wolf refused to run but sat up, and showing his long, sharp teeth, was ready for a fight. This was just what the cowboy wanted. Riding up close to his wolfship to get as much slack as possible, he turned quickly and applied the spurs. When the rope tightened the wolf turned a couple of sommersaults and was almost broken in two, but the rope held firm to the saddle horn.

By a series of such maneuvering the wolf was finally worn out and dragged to the ranch.

Capturing a Bear[8]

There are any number of bears up in the North Park country and cowboys often have a roundup with them.

After an hour's weary traveling down the winding way we came out on the plain, and found a small cow outfit and under a tree lay a dead silver tip, while a half dozen punchers squatted about it. It appeared that three of them had been working in the foothills, when they heard the dogs, and shortly discovered the bear. Having no guns, and being on fairly good ground, they coiled their riatas and prepared to do battle. The silver tip was badly blown, and the three dogs which had stayed with it were so tired that they sat up at a respectful distance and panted and lolled.

The first rope went over bruin's head and one paw. There lies the danger. But instantly number two flew straight to the mark, and the ponies surged, while bruin stretched out with a roar. A third rope got his other hind leg, and the puncher dismounted and tied it to a tree. The roaring, biting, clawing mass of hair was practically helpless, but to kill him was an undertaking. "Why didn't you brand him and turn him loose?" I asked the cowboy. "Well," said the puncher in his native drawl, "we could have branded him all right, but we might have needed some help in turning him loose." They pelted him with stones and finally stuck a knife into a vital part, and then, loading him on a pony, they brought him in. It was a daring performance, but was regarded by the punchers as a great joke.

THE TALLEST TALES

A Real Wild Man[9]

Two cowboys who just came in from Camas prairie relate an experience which will probably go a great way toward re-establishing the popular faith in the wild man's tradition. On the first day of this month two cowboys searching for cattle lost in the storm, passed over some lava crags and were startled by seeing before them the form so often described to them. They were so terrified that they sat upon their horses looking at it in dread. Mustering courage and drawing their revolvers they dismounted and gave chase, but the strange being skipped from crag to crag as nimbly as a mountain goat. After an hour's pursuit both young men were so completely worn out that they laid down, seeing which the wild man gradually approached them and stopped on the opposite side of a gorge of lava, from which point he regarded the cowboys intently. The wild man was considerable over six feet in height, with great muscular arms which reached to his knees.

The muscles stood out in great knots and his chest was as broad as that of a bear. Skins were twisted about his feet and ankles and a wolf skin about his waist. All parts of his body to be seen were covered by long, black hair, while from his head the hair flowed over his shoulders in coarse tangled rolls and mixed with a heavy beard. His face was dark and swarthy and his eyes shone brightly, while two tusks protruded from his mouth. His fingers were the shape of claws, with long, sharp nails, and he acted very much as a wild animal which is unaccustomed to seeing a man. The boys made all kinds of noises, at the sound of which he twisted his head from side to side and moaned—apparently he could not give them any "back talk," so, wearying of eyeing him the two boys fired their revolvers, whereupon the wild man turned a double somersault and jumped fifteen feet to a low bench and growling terribly as he went.

It is supposed that this is the same apparition that has so often been seen before. The man, no doubt does as the Indians did for subsistence and lives on camas roots, which grow wild by acres, and he, no doubt kills young stock, as many yearlings and calves disappear mysteriously and nothing but skeletons of them are ever found.

A "Cowboy" Dog[10]

A cowboy just returned from the roundup was heard in a Butte resort ... explaining how intelligent was the dog which lay at his feet:

"Last week," said he, "while we was cutting out my boss' spring beeves from the roundup herd, I seed that 'ere dog around among the animals examining 'em very close. I wondered what the dickens he was at, an' kep' my eye on him. Purty soon he waltzed up close to a steer an' after lookin' at it a minute, he run around it an' drove it out of the herd into our bunch. Then he went back an' purty soon he chased another'n out. After he'd did it several times, I dropped to it. He was jest a-watchin' for the boss' brand and whenever he'd see a critter with it on he'd drive him right slap out into our bunch. Here! Zip!" and he scooped a handful of crackers from the bowl on the bar and tossed them one by one to the clever dog, who caught them neatly on the fly, while the admiring crowd stood by watching.

Horsemanship![11]

It is related of a prominent citizen of Arizona that he once met a prominent citizen of Montana on the neutral ground of Colorado. The subject of bucking horses coming up, the prominent citizen of Arizona said: "We have some very skillful riders down in my country. This of course shows out particularly when they are breaking wild bronchos to ride. When an infuriated mustang, saddled for the first time, and rearing and bucking with all the terrific energy of its savage nature, looks up out of the tail of its eye and watches its rider calmly roll and light a cigarette, it has an excellent effect on it, and usually cools down, realizing the hopelessness of its task."

Then spoke the prominent citizen of Montana: "That will do very well, I dare say, for the comparatively mild and inoffensive horses of your southern latitude, but it has been found to have no influence whatever on our fierce and vicious beasts. But when one of our cowboys mounts a broncho for the first time it helps greatly to subdue the creature when, after it has leaped and pitched for fifteen minutes, it happens to glance back and find its rider quietly shaving, holding a small mirror in one hand and the razor in the other, with the mug, hot water, and bay rum in a little basket on his arm. Ah, it's all in knowing how, this subjugating a Montana broncho!" Then the meeting of prominent citizens adjourned.

The Petrified Broncho[12]

H. Clay Emmet, a young cowboy from Belton, Texas, reports a singular find made by him during a cattle hunting roundup in the panhandle country recently. The find was nothing more or less than a petrified pony, standing erect and complete in all its parts. Emmet says that he and his partner, B. C. Woodville, were riding across the prairie late one afternoon, when their tired ponies neighed and whinnied as if they were aware of the presence of another animal. Looking around, they discovered what they thought was a broncho tethered to a mesquite which crowned the summit of a little knoll to the northward.

They rode up to the spot and found that the horse was fastened by a chain, but stood so rigidly still and seemed altogether so mysterious that their own horses reared and plunged as if in fright. Finally they dismounted and found that the pony was petrified, not a hair or hoof amiss. Emmet says that some ranchman years ago must have chained the poor horse there, leaving it to starve on the plains. As the ribs of the animal were plainly visible in the petrifaction and it seemed to have been otherwise much emaciated, this is most probably the case. Emmet will arrange to have the strange find exhibited in some museum. It frequently happens that horses fall into the habit of going to sleep while standing and it must have been under these circumstances that the panhandle broncho departed this life to join the great majority.

A Wild West Tale[13]

"Speaking of the dare-devil characteristics of Western cowboys," said an old plainsman, "I recall an adventure that might have proved fatal to myself and a man named Henry but for the great presence of mind displayed in an emergency by my cool-headed companion. The incident happened in Montana.... We were traveling along a narrow trail on the border of the Grande Ronde river [Oregon?] when we suddenly came to a landslide that was about 25 feet across and left no trail in the smooth precipitous rock. The trail was so narrow that our horses could not turn back, and, realizing that it would be folly to expect the animals to jump the chasm, it looked as though we were trapped. But directly above the 25-foot break in the trail there was a huge rock which was split in the center. Henry saw the crack in the rock, and having a strong riata 70 feet long on his saddle, he coiled it up, steadied himself in his saddle, swung the rope over his head and then hurled it high in the air. Being an expert in the use of the riata, it went true to the mark, and was soon firmly fixed in the crevice of the rock.

"While I was wondering what he was going to do with the rope, he took in the slack and wound it around the horn of his saddle, which was very strong and supplied with double cinches. Then he urged his horse to the edge of the precipice.

"The faithful beast stood firm. He would not step over, but Henry again drew up the slack and pulled with all his might. Inch by inch he drew the straining horse forward till his feet slipped and he swung over the yawning chasm. For a moment I held my breath and shut my eyes, and expected to hear the slender rope snap and its burden disappear into the raging river below.

"When I did open my eyes he had swung across the gap, and, demounting, he backed up the trail and tugged at the reins to aid the horse in gaining his feet. He pulled hard and the animal lunged up into the trail, with the chasm far behind.

"Safe on the other side, Henry urged me to make the perilous trip in the same way as he had done. For some time I couldn't muster up the necessary courage, but at last, when I realized that there was no other way of continuing the journey, I consented to swing myself across the chasm. After landing on the other side Henry returned for my horse and having swung the beast safely across the gap, we rode away and left the rope dangling for the use of the next wayfarer who chanced to come that way."

THE JOKESTER

A Cowboy Joke[14]

It seems a young Englishman with more money than brains has been "doing" the blarsted country for the past few months, and thought that his tour would not be complete without visiting Arizona. Hither, accordingly, he came, full of the spirit of adventure and anxious to learn all about us in a few hours. At Deming he made his first stop, but was not favorably impressed with the place, in consequence of receiving a rather odd introduction at the start. Some gentlemen with broad brimmed hats, jingling spurs and a general air of abandon, were disporting themselves on the platform when he alighted. He wore a plug hat and regulation style eye-glasses. He had hardly set foot on the platform when one of the gentlemen described above as wearing broad-brimmed hats stepped forward and in the friendliest manner possible, lifted the glasses from the stranger's nose and placed them on his own. He then likewise took off the plug hat and placed it over his shaggy locks. Then he stepped aside and allowed his companions to contemplate him. Presently one of them pulled his gun and standing in front of the bedecked cowboy, deliberately fired a bullet through his nobby Pall Mall headgear. The wearer of the tile for the time being took no notice of such peccadillos, and a regular fusilade was kept up at the unlucky hat, the fellow retaining it on his head all the time with a firm hold on the brim. When the hat was completely perforated he took off the eye glasses, and holding them out at arm's length, with his fingers clutching the extreme end, offered to bet any one in the crowd that they could not send a bullet through the glass at ten feet without hurting the gold rim. The bets were instantly taken up, and ere three shots were fired, both glasses were shattered into a thousand fragments on the platform. The gold frame was then given to the owner with much ceremony, and he retired instantly, hatless to the security of his palace car and did not show his nose outside again until the train had proceeded some miles from Deming.

The episode was the cause of much amusement to the passengers, as the stranger had regaled them with the feats of personal daring and adventure all the way from Kansas City. He was made the butt of considerable joking and feeling restive under the continual torrent of wit, resolved to get off at Wilcox, and "lay over" for a train in order to avoid the jokes made at his expense.

Fun with the Tenderfoot[15]

"Did yer ever hear Jake Wallace tell of the time on the San Simon when he bit off more nor he could chaw?" queried the cowboy. A universal "no" was the response.

"Well, a lot of the boys had just come into San Simon well heeled. They had run off a bunch of cattle belonging to the Corralitos company, in Old Mexico, an' had got the cash for it, and they started in to have a high old time an' whoop her up. They took possession of a large canvas tent near the Silver Palace saloon, an' there bein' no women, inaugurated a stag baile. While they were dancing a train pulled in an' some of the passengers who didn't care to invest a dollar in frijoles and bacon, attracted by the music, entered the tent. Among the crowd was a regular dude of a chap who, looked as though he was just walkin' around to save funeral expenses. Jake 'lowed as how he'd have some fun with him.

"Walkin' up to him he covered him with his gun, an' ordered him out to dance. The tenderfoot looked at the gun, looked at Jake an' 'lowed as he had to do it. When Jake got tired of the fun he asked the young fellow to take some whisky straight an' out of a tin cup, and they went to the Palace saloon. Jake had one of those handsome ivory-handled, silver-plated Colt's, an' the young chap asked him what it cost. Jake told him $35, an' the fellow commenced to laugh. He says to Jake, says he, 'I'm in that line myself, a drummer, an' I could sell you as good a gun for $20.' Jake he pulls her out, an' says, 'Not much you don't, just look at her,' an' hands her over. The moment the drummer got the gun in his hands he pulls right down on Jake. 'Now,' says he, 'd—n you, you've had your fun, an' now I'll have mine. Dance, d—n ye, or I'll make a lead mine out of ye.' "

"Did Jake dance?"

"You bet yer sweet life he did. After he got through the drummer asked him out to have a drink, an' says Jake to him: 'Young man, where did ye come from?' 'I've just come from California,' said he. 'H—l,' said Jake, 'I thought as how you'd come from New York.' "

The Tail of a Cow[16]

There is much excitement in Tampas over the disappearance of a prominent young society man. The story runs about as follows: Having become struck on the free, untrammeled life of the cow-puncher, he came to Trinidad, and after convincing one of our leading cattlemen of his eminent fitness for the position, he was engaged. Investing in an outfit which included a lariat, he made a break for home, to practice up a little before tackling the untamed bovines of the plains. He first roped an old cow that stood perfectly still, being a good-natured old animal. Highly elated with his success, he next made a break on a highbred Cherokee cow, just to show the boys how nicely he could flop her. The lariat was hurled at the unsuspecting bovine, immediately followed by a commotion. When the cloud of dust lifted, the embryo cowboy was seen holding on to the rope and following that cow at a rate of speed that would make a Santa Fe engine green with envy. They finally disappeared over a hill and the young man has not been seen since. The next day a dead bovine of the Cherokee breed was found about five miles from town, with a rope firmly fixed on her tail. On examination it was found that a rain of the night before had swelled the rope and choked the critter to death. The young man's outfit cost $70, and has been attached by the owner of the cow.

Making Milord Drink[17]

A nobby and snobbish milord of British extraction traveled from Big Horn with us and Abe Idehman on the stage coach.... Milord was excessively exclusive. He wouldn't be social and spoke to no one except the two

"John Henry" servants he had with him, and was altogether as unpleasant as his snobbishness could make him. At a dinner station there were a lot of jolly cowboys on a lark, and one of them, "treating" everybody, asked the Englishman to drink. Of course, milord haughtily refused. The cowboy displayed a dangerous-looking six-shooter and very impressively insisted on his drinking. "But I cawn't, you know; I don't drink, you know," was milord's reply. Mr. Cowboy brought the muzzle in dangerous proximity to the knot in which milord's brains were supposed to lie hidden somewhere, and then he said he'd drink—he'd take soda water, you know.

"Soda water nuthin," said Mr. Cowboy. "You'll take straight whisky."

"But, aw, this American whisky, I cawn't swallow it, you know."

"Well," said the cowboy, "I'll make a hole in the side of your head so that we can pur it in," and he began to draw on milord, and milord said, "Aw, that'll do, I'll drink it."

Then the cowboy invited milord's servants to drink, which horrified him. "They don't drink, you know," he said. "Well, we'll see whether they do or not," said Mr. Cowboy. "The chances are you don't give 'em a' hopportunity. Come up here, you fellows, and guzzle some," and the two John Henrys, with a little show of reluctance, but really glad to get a drink, came up and the cowboy passed a tumblerful of torchlight procession whisky for milord, and the servants poured for themselves. Then the cowboy made the John Henrys clink glasses with milord and all drank, and there was great fun. Milord tried after that to be jolly, and the stimulant assisted him decidedly. But in the coach he fell back into his exclusiveness and retained it throughout, and has probably got it yet.

Cowboy and Limburger[18]

They were genuine cowboys and in for a day's recreation in the city, and they looked upon the liquor when it was red. Yea, they gazed often, but finally that the inner man needed something besides liquid filling, they repaired to Prof. Bach's Park street hash foundry and great lager beer and Switzer case emporium and called for beef steak. While the meal was being prepared, c. b. No. 1 fell asleep in chair, No. 2 obtained a piece of limburger cheese and gave the well-grown mustache of No. 1 a good coat of that odiferous product of the dairy. The professor, with that princely mien of his, approached the table in graceful curves and placed the steaming juicy steak before his guests and gently aroused the one who was sleeping. The cowboy yawned, looked about in a dazed sort of way, picked up his fork and speared the beef steak. Then he began to sniff the air. He raised the beef steak to his nose and smelt of it, and dropped it into the plate with disgust, he called out, "Here, you-bald-headed-son-of-a-coyote, come here."

"Did you make a remark to me?" asked the urbane professor, with a Chesterfieldan bow.

"Did I?" yelled the c. b. "Well, I should say I did. Here, you take this piece of dead cow out of the town and bury it—it's rotten—and then you waltz up here with a piece of cow that didn't die a natural death and is well cooked—do you hear me warble?"

The professor bowed, examined the steak carefully, smiled in his gracious way, wiped his hands on the after part of his pants and said, "Mine friend, this is the very nicest of steak and you shall have it only and no more."

"I tell you it stinks," yelled the cowboy; "it's rotten."

"Dot proposition is not correct and you must pay me, and eat it or not, just as it pleases you."

The cowboy became weak from the stench, kicked over his chair, advanced to the counter to pay, willing to submit to anything in order to get away from his steak. He went as far from the table as possible and dug up his money.

The professor approached with outstretched hands saying, "Mine friend, that was just as nice a steak as the market affords."

"It's rotten," yelled the cowboy, "it stinks; go away from me; you stink; the house stinks; let me have fresh air," and, throwing some money on the floor, he fled into the street and drew one long breath of outside air. But it was no use. Turning to his companion, with a look of dismay, he exclaimed, "Jim, this whole gosh darned town is spoilt; it stinks. You can cut the stink with a knife; let's pull for the ranch, Jim, 'fore we smother," and the boys mounted and rode off.

ESCAPADES

A Cowboy Prize Fighter[19]

Alex. Thebold is a cowboy who has obtained quite a reputation among the bold buccaneers of the plains as a hard hitter. In fact, he knocked out every man who had the hardihood to stand up before him. During the leisure hours passed at the cowboy's camp, indulging in the "manly sport" became the chief pastime, and it was here that Thebold acquired a reputation for pugilistic propensities. Quite recently he was located at Fort Fetterman, and here he continued "walloping" every cowboy, freighter or other personage who contested strength with him. A few days ago he had several rounders at a cowboys' camp in Colorado, and man after man fell down before him.

"Why don't you go to Denver, Alex," his cowboy friends insisted, "and show them what you can do there. You are the best man in the state, from a pugilistic point of view, and you should have the credit."

Fired by the eulogism lavished upon him by his friends, Thebold decided to come to Denver and challenge the man who boasted of being the champion of the state.

He arrived here, accompanied by several of his friends, on Saturday afternoon, and at once began looking about for a foe worthy of his steel. Clow was found and negotiations were soon entered into, Clow announcing himself willing, although a total stranger to Thebold, to contest at any time or place the right he claimed to holding the State championship. The stakes were placed at $50 a side, although this fact was not openly announced, owing to the existence of the law making it a penitentiary offense to fight for stakes of any amount. Seconds were named for each side, and the numerous other minor details arranged. Where to hold the fight so that the police and deputy sheriff would not interfere, was the only unsolved question. Finally the grounds of the Athletic Base Ball club were agreed upon, and the time at midnight. Although the greatest secrecy was observed, the rumor of a prize-fight soon spread, and the sporting fraternity were soon on the anxious seat. They knew that some sporting event of note was about to take place, but just what it was they did not know. Before midnight had approached several hack-loads of men were driving slowly about the central portion of the city ready to follow at great speed the movements of any party leaving the city.

Promptly at midnight several hacks containing the principals and those intimately associated with each left the city. They drove up Larimer street, and were followed by a string of hacks, the occupants of which knew that they were following on a hot trail. The destination was then unknown. The hacks pulled up to the Athletic Grounds, and the men disembarked. It was a motley crew, and their movements were cautious enough to lead an observer to believe that a worse crime than prize fighting was about to be committed.

By the aid of dark lanterns a temporary ring was soon built, and in fifteen minutes after the park was entered both the principals were in the ring and prepared for the combat. There was the best of good humor. As the two men faced each other, there was such a marked disparity in size that betting on Clow suddenly stopped. Heretofore the money had all been put on Clow's superiority. The cowboy loomed up in the semi-darkness like a Sullivan. He was about six feet high and would weigh over 165, and looked one-third lighter than his opponent.

When time was called, the cowboy at once assumed the aggressive, and it was seen at once that his intentions were to knock the champion out in a very short time. Several passes were made, when the cowboy, with a tiger-like leap, landed his right on Clow's nose, bringing the blood. Before the cowboy got back on his feet again, Clow hit him a tap with his left under the left ear. The cowboy's head went over to the right and in a jiffy Clow struck him a right-hander on the side of the neck, knocking Thebold to the ground with a kink in his neck. He did not get up for a minute, and when he did he said he guessed he had had enough. He refused to re-enter the fight, and the victory was given to Clow amid much laughter. The cowboy was dazed for awhile, but soon recovered and good-naturedly admitted that he could probably meet with better success in punching cows than punching the face of an adversary in the prize ring.

A Cowboy in a Sleeping Car[20]

"Where do I camp?" he inquired, and was shown the lower berth next to me.

"That's my pigeon hole is it? All right, old son; just watch my motion while I file myself away."

At this juncture he was desired to turn over his revolver to the porter, which he declined to do in a most prompt and spirited manner.

"Old Dad—his revolver—and me always sleep together, and we don't want no divorce," he explained.

The conductor remonstrated, but was advised not to try "to braid this mule's tail."

"This here's a sleepin' car, ain't it?" he at length indignantly inquired.

"Yes."

"Well, why in —— don't you let people sleep then, when they've paid and gone into your game? If your aiming to keep people awake and want company, just dance into the next car, there's lots of folks there that don't want to sleep no how, an 'll be glad to see you."

The conductor withdrew and my friend pulled off his boots and stretched himself, with many comments in an undertone, on the poverty of the surroundings.

In about ten minutes this erratic person had his head out in the aisle.

"Say! you boy"—to the porter.

"Well, sah."

"Come a runnin'."

The porter drew near and was handed a pillow about as big as a pin cushion.

"Take that gooseha'r thing away," commanded the cowboy.

"Don't you want a pillow, sah?"

"That ain't no pillow, and I don't want it, no how. I'm afraid it 'll git into my ear."

After this, silence, and for a short time I slept. I roused up however, at an exclamation on the part of my neighbor.

"Hold on there, son, jest drop them boots."

"I was jest gwine to black 'em boss."

"Drop 'em." They dropped.

"Just gwine to pull them spurs, I reckon. Now don't monkey 'round my camp taking things no more. If you want anything speak fer it. If you can't speak make signs, and if you can't make signs shake a bush. You hyar me."

"Yes, sah."

After this more silence. The wheels and rails again sang together, the car again kept approving time and presently I slept without interruption.

A New Mexico Cowboy in London[21]

Red Pugh, a cowboy who was in the employ of Jack Fleming . . . some years ago, but who is now with Buffalo Bill's Wild West Show, created a terrific hubbub in London recently. Red went into a restaurant and ordered a rare beefsteak. The waiter brought him one so rare that it jerked around on the plate. Red drew his gun and fired three or four shots through the steak "to kill it," as he explained, when everyone in the establishment joined in a general stampede. After killing the steak Red sat down to eat his meat, but was interrupted in a few minutes by the arrival of about fifty police, who told him that it was against the laws of Her Majesty Queen Vic to make such John Branch plays in Hengland. He was arrested and fined. The particulars were cabled over to the American papers. Grant county boys can always be relied upon for an item when away from home.

The Cowboy and the Folding Bed[22]

The crowded condition of the Denver hotels this week brought out a number of amusing incidents, one of which occurring at the Brown Palace reminded the writer of a case that occurred at the Windsor during the international range convention in 1886. A cowboy up from the Texan panhandle was a guest at the house and as the clerk who attended to him is still in Denver we will allow him to tell the story in his own way: "He had on store clothes and a red necktie, and what he didn't know wasn't worth knowing. When he started up to his room at night, I told him there was a folding bed in it, and, if he wished, the bellboy would show him how it worked. But not much; he didn't want to be shown any thing. He knew a thing or two about the city, he did, even if he did live down on the range.

"So I let him go, and next morning he paid his bill without a word and went away. About noon I happened to be on that floor, and a chambermaid called me to take a look in his room. And what a sight met my eyes! The bottom drawer of the bureau was pulled out as far as it would come, and in it were all the rugs in the room, with a towel spread over one end for a pillow. Evidently he had tried to sleep there, for pinned up on the glass was a sarcastic little legend reading: 'Gol dern yore folding beds. Why don't you make 'em longer and put more kivers onto um? Mebbe you expect a man to stand up and sleep in your durned old cubberd.' The durned old cubberd was one of our best folding beds."

Frontier Dentistry[23]

Many years ago a group of cowboys rode into Pueblo and, while cantering down Santa Fe avenue, came to a sign—"Painless Dentistry." They emptied their guns into it, and then one of the company dismounted and went in to get a sore tooth attended to. The dentist was a quiet looking young man. "See here!" shouted the cowboy, as he advanced toward the chair, "I want a tooth fixed, and I don't want any hightoned prices charged either." He threw himself into the chair laid his gun across his lap, and told the dentist that if he hurt him he would shoot the top of his head off.

"Very well," replied the dentist with a slight laugh; "then you must take gas for this is a bad tooth and will give trouble." The cowboy swore, but finally yielded and presently was insensible. The man of the forceps pulled the tooth and then before his customer regained consciousness, he securely tied him hand and foot to the chair. Then taking the bully's gun the dentist took up his position where the patient could see him when he came to. As the cowboy struggled back to consciousness, the first thing of which he was sensible was the dentist pointing the revolver at him, and saying, in quiet tones: "Now, then, don't move.

"Just open your mouth as wide as possible, and I will shoot the bad tooth off. This is the painless process. No danger, sir, unless you happen to swallow the bullet. Are you ready? Then here goes! One, two, three!" Bang went the gun, knocking a hole in the wall behind the chair, and the dentist rushed forward, holding out the tooth in his hand to show to the bully, who roared for mercy. The dentist cut his bonds on condition that he should restore the sign outside the office. After paying five dollars for the tooth, the cowboy departed convinced that even a tenderfoot may have nerve.

Soothing Syrup for Cowboys[24]

The Northern Pacific train from the West came ... with twenty-five or thirty cowboys, bound for Fort Worth. The festive cow punchers had taken possession of the emigrant sleeper. Every one of them had a huge revolver slung to his belt, all of them were full of bug juice, each man sporting a bottle of forty-rod whisky. When the Dakota division conductor came into the car for their tickets they refused to produce the pasteboards, drawing instead their bottles of chain lightning, and insisting on the ticket puncher drinking with them. A quiet old German passenger who had been much annoyed by the hilariousness of the wild riders of the Western plains, took the conductor to one side and said:

"If I were the conductor of this train I would expend a half dollar at some convenient drug store for opium and slip it into their bottles."

On reaching Bismarck the conductor acted on this happy suggestion, and sent his brakeman to a drug store for 50 cents' worth of the quieting drug. The brakeman went into the car and accepted their generous offer to imbibe, and, while pretending to drink, quietly slipped a small quantity of the soothing drug in each bottle. Quiet soon reigned where before all had been pandemonium. These denizens of the wild, rowdy West were soon sleeping sounder than the Cardiff giant. The exultant conductor rolled them over like logs, went through their pockets, punched their tickets and rolled them back in their berths. A more peaceful car of passengers never traveled over the Northern Pacific—in fact, the train load of deaf mute excursionists of the past summer were hilarious compared with the quiet Texas cowboys. They were turned over to the conductor of the Minnesota division at Fargo, with the remainder of the unexpended drug to use if any emergency should arise before reaching St. Paul.

NOTES TO CHAPTER EIGHT

1. *Cheyenne Daily Leader* (Cheyenne, Wyoming), September 9, 1879.
2. *Democratic Leader* (Cheyenne, Wyoming), July 18, 1884.
3. *Raton Weekly Independent* (Raton, New Mexico), January 28, 1888.
4. *Field and Farm* (Denver, Colorado), November 29, 1890, p. 6.
5. *Denver Republican* (Denver, Colorado), December 12, 1897.
6. *Deming Headlight* (Deming, New Mexico), December 7, 1889; *Field and Farm*, September 5, 1891, p. 3.
7. *Field and Farm*, April 2, 1892, p. 6.
8. *Ibid.*, August 17, 1895, p. 6.
9. *Ford County Globe* (Dodge City, Kansas), November 28, 1882.
10. *Trinidad Daily Advertiser* (Trinidad, Colorado), July 2, 1885.
11. *Field and Farm*, April 18, 1896, p. 6.
12. *Ibid.*, September 5, 1896, p. 6.
13. *Denver Republican*, December 11, 1898.

14. *Albuquerque Evening Review* (Albuquerque, New Mexico), September 30, 1882.
15. *Las Vegas Daily Optic* (Las Vegas, New Mexico), October 8, 1884.
16. *Trinidad Daily Advertiser*, April 23, 1885.
17. *Denver Tribune-Republican* (Denver, Colorado), November 22, 1885.
18. *Black Range* (Chloride, New Mexico), October 22, 1886.
19. *Denver Tribune-Republican*, September 1, 1884.
20. *Rio Grande Republican* (Las Cruces, New Mexico), January 24, 1885.
21. *Raton Weekly Independent*, January 28, 1888.
22. *Field and Farm*, June 30, 1894, p. 6.
23. *Ibid.*, February 9, 1895, p. 6.
24. *Texas Live Stock Journal* (Fort Worth, Texas), April, 1887 [monthly ed.], p. 23.

It's a Great Life

NINE

One of the most pleasant contacts between the cowboy and the society of the cow country was the cowboy dance. This was usually an annual event, known as the Cowboys' Reunion or Cowboy Ball—an elaborate social function of dancing and feasting for the elite of the ranches. These affairs, which were generally arranged by large cattle companies, offered the cowboy an opportunity to meet other members of the profession and, more important, members of the fair sex.

Cowboy romance was never a fertile subject in Western journalism. The few recorded accounts are usually humorous and leave one with mixed feelings concerning the range rider's affairs of the heart. Probably more interesting than the cowboy's romance is the role of the courageous women who invaded the cattle industry and undertook the management of cattle ranches or, on some occasions, actually worked in the saddle as range riders. These women were not especially welcome; however, if success favored them, cowboy admiration was unbounded.

The cowboy, during his heyday, was the subject of numerous periodical and newspaper articles. With eloquent pen the journalists made him a romantic figure; their glowing accounts of his daring, adventuresome life and work, his reckless, high-spirited freedom, his wild and woolly environment, were avidly read by both young and old. Yearning welled up in the breast of every young, red-blooded, apple-pie-eating American boy; the bait was attractive and irresistible; the outcome was only natural —the young man "went west."

Throughout the United States, and also in England and other parts of Europe, the stories about the American cowboy created in the hearts of youth an overwhelming affection and admiration for the glamorous, undaunted, and fearless man of the saddle. This hero worship, which persists even today, mounted like wildfire in the world of restless, receptive youth and lured all eager lads westward.

BOOTS AND BELLES

Social activities in the cow country were rare events, and consequently the Western press described them in every detail. For weeks in advance the preparations were carefully recorded and then followed up by a complete account. The annual cowboy dance was considered a highlight of range social activities.

We have heard considerable chat in the city for the past few days in reference to the cowboys' ball, some stating that they would "get on a h—l of a drunk and somebody would get shot." This kind of talk is all nonsense—perfect balderdash. The local of the *News* has been more or less familiar with the Texas cowboys for the last thirty years, has been quite familiar with them; and has never got hurt yet. As we have said before, the avocation of a cowboy, forever on the trail, makes him a little rough, but he is a gentleman in his instincts and youthful training, and knows as well as anybody how to behave himself when placed in society where it is necessary for him to do so. We may truthfully say that our cowboys are an exception to the general rule, and no one needs be afraid of them, if they offer no insults to them. Depend on it, there will be no fights in Trinidad while the cowboys are here unless they are courted, and then there might be some fun, as their mode of life makes them brave and rash rather than cowardly and timid. But rest easy, things will go on peaceably on this reunion.[1]

The ball at Mitchell's hall . . . for the cowboys of the XL ranch was a great success. The hall was comfortably filled early in the evening, and after the close of the entertainment at the opera house, there was a regular jam. Mr. Grubb, the general manager for the Prairie Cattle company, was everywhere, seeing that everything was done to promote the pleasure of the guests, and everyone appeared to be happy as a clam in high water. The hall was handsomely decorated, the music was splendid and in nothing was anything lacking to make it one of the pleasantest entertainments ever given in the city.[2]

"Is that you, cap?"
"Aye! Aye!"
"Did you bring that band?"
"You bet yer life."
And amid a tremendous chorus of "Yip! Yip!" and a salute of revolver shots we rode up to the door of the big white house on the Crosselle ranch on the bank of the Dry Cimarron . . . just at dark. The ride had been a tedious

one, and two good teams had been fagged in making the sixty-four miles, but our welcome from the big hearted, jolly people was warm enough to drive away the cramps from tired limbs.

But we started in to write about the Cowboys' Third Annual Reunion, ball and banquet, given by the Prairie, Muscatine and Western Cattle Companies, but the remembrance of what we had to eat in the house switched us off. To the east of the house, about eighty feet way, was constructed a fine tent, forty by seventy-five feet in size, connected with the verandah by a covered walk. The floor was laid with two-inch matched plank, dressed, and was superior to the majority of floors in halls. The interior was heated with big stoves, and was brilliantly lighted, and, you may be sure, handsomely decorated with evergreens, mottoes, etc., and comfortably seated around all sides. Opposite the entrance were two mottoes, "Merry Christmas," and "Welcome All," and extending clear across the north the couplet, worked in red and white,

> Despite of distance, time or weather,
> Let Christmas find our hearts together.

All around the walls were hung the various brands of the companies worked in white on a large red ground—the Prairie Company's Cross L, JJ and LIT, the Muscatine's ZH, the Western's 101, and many others. As near as we could get an estimate, from 225 to 240 people were present. Of course the boys were in the majority, but there were ladies enough to fill the big floor full every quadrille. As the music prepared to open the grand march, Mr. R. G. Head, the general superintendent of the Prairie Company, stepped into the center of the room, and said:

"Friends and fellow cowboys: We have met tonight to commemorate one of the institutions of our business which occurs annually. I am sorry I cannot trip the light fantastic toe with you, but, my friends, in behalf of the Prairie Cattle Company, the Muscatine Company, and the Western Company, I bid you a hearty welcome to our third reunion. On with the dance; let joy be unconfined."

And the dance went on. We only wish some of the smart-alec newspaper writers who have been bleating about the employes of some of these very companies, could have been present and witnessed this party of elegantly-dressed, fine looking young men and women, and observed how quiet, courteous and considerate they all were. There are hundreds of dances given in our towns where no such good order and civility prevail. The programme embraced the Prairie Boys' waltz, the Western quadrille, etc., besides all the round dances we can remember hearing of.

From 11 o'clock the supper was served. The large diningroom in the house accom[m]odated from 50 to 60 people at a time. The bill of fare included oysters in every style, roast beef, boiled ham, roast turkey and chicken, biscuit and bread, tea, coffee, cakes, nuts, candy, fruit and other things too numerous to speak of. We have heard some phenomenal stories about appetites, but we never thought they could be true until that night. Here again was shown Mr. and Mrs. Grubb's kind thoughtfulness and good management. Every one's wants were supplied promptly and completely. The dance went on until 5 o'clock in the morning, when, in charge of the same faithful driver who took us out we all bade the folks good-bye, and just as the sun was lighting the hills and crags with his first red rays, we started up the beautiful valley of the Dry Cimarron, all tired but good natured.[3]

The cowboys of northern New Mexico are studying the refining arts that humanized mankind. The latest illustration of this fact was the recent ball and reunion at Raton. The knights of the leather breeches and rattling spurs gathered from all parts and Raton entertained them right royally. The large hall was decorated in keeping with the occasion. The feast is reported to have been a real banquet. All rudeness was laid aside, and these cavaliers of the broad prairies, in their new costly clothes, would have passed muster in the most refined circles of the East. The Raton papers gave full details of the reunion, and we hesitate not to accept these flattering reports as simply a correct statement of a splendid occasion.[4]

The Grand Union was the scene of one of the pleasantest gatherings last night that has ever before taken place in Trinidad, the occasion being a complimentary ball and supper tendered by the cowboys of the neighboring ranges to their friends. About sixty couples were in attendance....[5]

There is considerable sociability wrapped up in the hide of the average cowboy and he likes to show it once in a while with genuine spirit. The cowboys of Colfax county and northern New Mexico are preparing to give a grand dance and banquet at Raton,... and elaborate preparations are being made by the committees having the matter in charge to excel the efforts of the cowboys last year, which resulted in one of the most enjoyable affairs ever held in that section.[6]

The cowboy's ball at Raton on last Friday night is reported to have been an elegant affair and largely attended. The managers spared neither pains nor expense to make it a big success, and are to be congratulated.[7]

There is talk of having a cowboys' reunion at this place July 5th, [1886] Medicine Lodge, Kansas, and if the proper interest can be awakened, it will be the event of the season. In and around this place are some of the original cow-punchers—men who followed the calling when the southwest was the home of buffaloes and Texas cattle, and some of these men have ridden broncos in every state and territory west of the Missouri river. They are engaged in various pursuits now—banking, merchandizing, farming, etc.,... What a sight it would be to have all the old-timers in this county, and the hundreds of others in adjoining counties, meet here, rigged up with their slickers, leggings, broad-brimmed hats, colored shirts, high-heeled boots and other paraphernalia of the cowboys, and have a regular old roundup on some convenient flat. Have them go into camp with a "chuck wagon," hobble out their horses, sleep on their saddle blankets and slickers and indulge in telling lies incident to camp-life. We have heard several persons speak of this proposed reunion, and all favor it. So send the news along the line. . . .[8]

LADIES' CHOICE

A range romance was always considered a choice morsel, and the journalist never was reticent about exposing a cowboy's success or failure in love. Fortunately for the lovers, information of this nature did not, too often, reach an editorial desk.

A Kansas paper says a party of roundup cowboys were invited to dinner at Maulding's ranch, and the unexpected appearance of a young lady had the following effect upon the dudes of the prairie. After filling up their hungry tanks, they were invited by the hostess to enter the sitting room for a quiet chat. Everything went on well till a fair maiden of 16 summers put in her graceful appearance. The sight of the young lady—a sight rarely seen by the wild and reckless cowboy—caused a disastrous stampede, and the leaders turning, running over and dragging caused slight injuries to some of the herd. A great deal of the sidewalk was slightly damaged, and the wire fence which encircled the yard was badly used up, the cowboys in their mad flight knocking down about 20 yards of it. After careful handling, they were rounded up; mounting their steeds and left for their camp.[9]

Florence Chester is a sister of Mrs. Millie Price Dows, who married the millionaire's son here. James Everrett is a cowboy who lives near Cheyenne, Wyo. He met Florence Chester and she gave him a ring like a hoop on a molasses barrel. She was to have been married Friday night, but "Reddy" Gallagher, of pugilistic fame, took the girl and disappeared. Everrett was heartbroken and swears that he will remain in Denver a month, recapture the girl and make her his wife. Gallagher brought the Chester woman with him from San Francisco, and hated to be outdone by a cowboy.[10]

Wyoming has developed a Lochinvar whose courageous daring obscures the bravery of the medieval hero and crude Davey Crockett. He is James Kidd, an Omaha drummer, who incidentally killed a man before fleeing with his lady love.

Three months ago the Widow McCool, whose natural beauty and grace is heightened by her somber attire, became agent for the stage company at Dry Cheyenne, an important station between Douglas and Buffalo. She was a heart breaker from the old house, and every cowboy and ranchman in the region became a victim of her fascinations. While few travelers left the place heart whole, Mrs. McCool finally selected Frank Meade, son of a wealthy rancher, and they were to have been wedded this month.

Last week Kidd, who is a handsome and lively fellow, passed the place. He became enamored of the widow and soon returned to press his suit with great fervor. The glib tongue, stylish dress and polished manners of the traveler captured the widow and she surrendered.

The jilted lover sulked in jealousy and awaited a favorable opportunity for revenge or redress. Tuesday night a large crowd attended a dance at Dry Cheyenne. When the festivities were most hilarious, Meade, overtaking Kidd in the center of the ballroom, slapped his face and gave him a frightful tongue lashing.

The widow, with snapping eyes, twitted her new lover of cowardice. Thus encouraged, he drew a revolver and commenced firing recklessly, being too frightened to use the weapon effectively.

In an instant a dozen six-shooters were in action. No one heeded the wounded, but when Ed Cook, Meade's partner, fell with a bullet from the drummer's gun through his brain, there was a cessation of artillery music.

There were cries of "lynch the tenderfoot," but the drummer had become a Westerner in a remarkably short time. He backed to the door with the widow as a shield and the pair mounted one horse and dashed away.

They soon reached a railway, proceeded to Chadron, Nebraska, where they were united in marriage.

Sheriff Williams of Converse county is in pursuit of Kidd and his bride.[11]

A wedding which took place in this city [New York] last evening is the culmination of a story so romantic in its details that it might well serve as the plot of a play or novel. The bride and groom are both persons of wealth and good standing, the former being Miss Helen Dodd, daughter of Sir Thomas Dodd, of England, and the latter, George W. Campbell, son of Jas. H. Campbell, who is a Chicago millionaire cattle dealer and head of the James H. Campbell Company of Chicago, St. Louis, Kansas City, and Omaha.

Young Mr. Campbell's career has been a checkered one. He is now 25 years old with a physique thoroughly trained by the exposure to outdoor exercise of a life on the plains. At 15 he ran away from home and went to Texas, where he lived on ranches and among cattlemen for several years. Later his relatives discovered his whereabouts and tried to induce him to return home. Five years elapsed before he did so, however, then he entered the employ of his father's firm, which was largely interested in the buying of cattle.

Three years ago the firm sent him to England to take charge of a number of cattle which were being sent there, and it was while on this mission that the interesting events, which led up to the wedding yesterday, took place. After transacting the business of the firm, he found himself in Liverpool with nothing to do. At that time Mexican Joe's Wild West show was in camp near Liverpool, and for amusement Campbell went out to see it. He found among the cowboy employes several of his former companions on the plains. By their invitation, he spent a week in the Wild West company and in a spirit of fun took part in the daily exhibitions of riding, lassoing, and shooting. An expert rider, possessing a face and figure that would attract attention anywhere, he was an object of interest to all who attended the show. One day, after completing his favorite performance of picking up a silver dollar from the mud while riding his horse at full gallop, young Campbell received, as usual, tremendous applause.

None applauded so vigorously, however, as a young girl, who, with her father, occupied one of the private boxes. While waving her handkerchief to the gallant rider a gust of wind snatched it from her hand and carried it out to the center of the track, where it fell in the dust. Campbell was coming down the course on full run and saw the bit of lace fall. Without checking his horse he bent low in the saddle, and as he swept by, picked it up. He was cheered to the echo as he turned his pony and riding up to the box, returned the handkerchief to its fair owner. The occupants of the box proved to be Sir Thomas Dodd, of West Derby, near Liverpool, and his 18-year-old daughter, Helen.[12]

Requisition papers were made out ... from the governor's office for the purpose of bringing John Terwilliger from Benkleman, Neb., to Elbert county, Colorado, where he is wanted on the charge of kidnapping Nellie Cook.

Terwilliger is a cowboy. He has ridden the range in Elbert county for a number of years. He is about 26 years old. He has frequently worked for Joseph Cook, Nellie's father, who is a wealthy cattleman.

On July last he persuaded her to leave her father's house. They came to Denver and were married. The girl's parents started in pursuit of the couple. They induced her to return with them, and tried to make her forget her cowboy husband.

Mrs. Terwilliger went home with her parents. Her love for her husband, however, still continued. When he appeared in the vicinity of her home, last August, she readily consented to go with him.

They went to Kansas City, and thence to Benkleman, Neb., where Terwilliger's parents live. There they began preparations to start their married life. Terwilliger secured employment on a ranch in the vicinity and placed his young wife in the care of friends. Their dream of happiness received a rude awakening yesterday, when an officer of Dundy county, Nebraska, arrested Terwilliger on information received from Sheriff Adin G. Putnam of Elbert county, charging him with kidnapping Nellie Cook on July 31.

Extradition papers were given to Sheriff Putnam, and he left for Benkleman ... to bring back Terwilliger and his wife.[13]

PETTICOATS ON PONIES

A member of the fair sex—wearing pants!—engaged in a man's work in a predominately male environment is a subject of much discussion, even in modern newspapers. A rumor, a story, or the truth of such an incident on the Western ranges in Victorian America was a sensation to be repeated and reprinted from coast to coast.

Yesterday afternoon there came in on the Kansas Pacific train a festive appearing cowboy. His face was smooth and features quite the reverse of masculine. His complexion was fair and eyes were blue. But for his shape and the fair neck which was exposed by the open collar of the red woolen shirt he wore, he would have been taken for an overgrown youth, whose voice was just changing, and passed for a sure enough boy. He wasn't a boy, however, but a well proportioned woman of twenty two summers, who wore the inevitable high-heeled boots characteristic of the cowboy. Her tightly fitting pants were stuffed in the boot tops, and an old much worn white felt hat, pulled far down on the head, hid in part the straight light-brown hair, which had been cut short to deceive.

This woman is a native of Nebraska, having been raised in the vicinity of Omaha. Three years ago she was courted by a young man who won her affections, and who had promised to marry her. The day for the nuptials had been set, and every preparation made for the happy event. A day or two before the marriage was to have taken place, the young man suddenly disappeared, no one knew how or when. A few months after he had so cruelly deserted her, she learned from an acquaintance of his that he had gone down toward Texas, on the cattle range, where he was herding stock. Learning this much about him, she started out to find him, not that she desired to become his bride, as her love had turned to hate, but she desired to confront him, tell him of his infamy, and then return to her home. With this view she adopted the costume of a man—or, in other words, donned pantaloons—and started on his trail. Through the wild country she passed, often hearing of but never seeing him. For months and months she has stood upon the prairie, herding cattle, watching and waiting for him. Latterly she has been at work near Clay Center, in the capacity of cowboy, riding horse back as reckless and fast as any of the boys. She has sat by the camp-fires with them, and heard recounted the wild scenes in the life of the cowboy, and never once was suspected of being a woman. A few weeks ago she came up with her faithless lover in the vicinity of Clay Center. Under some pretext she induced him to ride with her away from the others who were herding, and when out of sight and out of hearing of all others, she drew her revolver and made herself known to him. What she did she refused to tell, more than this. She remarked: "I'll bet he won't trifle with another girl's affections. I am satisfied, and am going home."[14]

Reports come from the range that a woman is doing that country in male attire. She represents herself to be the nephew of August Belmont, and the son of one of the largest cattle dealers in Texas. She is said to be a good talker. A few days ago she made a contract to deliver three thousand head of cattle to a dealer, well-known in this city, on Soldier creek. She made a raise of six hundred dollars at Russell, Kansas, in a way best known to herself, and from there went to Larned where she expected to make a big haul in some kind of speculation, but failed, and went south on the range. We learn from a gentleman where she stayed all night, that she admitted herself to be a fraud, but denied that she was a woman. She has a traveling companion, a young man, who says that this great cattle dealer is a woman, and he knows it. California and Missouri have been giving their reports of females doing their state in male attire, and we are glad to see Kansas toe the mark while such things are all the go.[15]

In the Fourth District Court . . . Mrs. Helen T. Loveless, of Paradise Valley, who was found guilty on two separate indictments of killing cattle belonging to stockmen in the valley, was sentenced to three years in the State Prison. The defendant owns a ranch and some cattle and horses in the valley. She employed several hands in the summer season, and supplied them with beef from the cattle running at large. Although of uncertain age herself, probably forty-five years, she married a youth of nineteen recently who lived with her a few months and then decamped with a lot of her best horses (Smart boy). The conviction of a woman for any offense is unusual in this part of the country, and if the evidence of her guilt had not been very positive the jury would not have found her guilty. No, nor would the jury have found her guilty had she been young and lovable instead of Loveless.[16]

Miss Maude Reed has been located for five years on the Little Dolores.... Coming from Sweden a poor girl, Maude launched out into the far West, and started with a few head of cattle, and by strict attention, economy and braving all the hardships of a frontier life, she is today one of the shrewdest and ablest cattle owners in Mesa county. Many is the gallant cowboy that has doffed his sombrero and bestowed his most devoted attentions upon fair Maude, but up to the present writing she is yet heart-whole....[17]

"There's the best subject for an interview in the house," said a clerk at the Galt House ... as a tall, lank, slim man with high cheek bones, piercing black eyes and dark bushy mustache was noticed pacing the corridors. "Here's his name." The scribe glanced at the register and noticed in scrawling letters the chirography. "Professor W. Zursna, Austin, Texas."

"Take a seat, sir. Glad to give any information I can," answered the lank stranger, as the interviewer sank into a chair and told his mission. "I am here for only a few hours. My home is between Austin and Marcos, in the hills that stretch along the valley to San Antonio. Aside from the stories of the growth of that portion of the country, I suppose there's nothing that would interest you so much as the facts I can give you about the cattle girls of our region."

The reporter smiled, and the Texan continued.

"I know that there is an air of seeming improbability about this, but it is nevertheless a fact; there exist in the hills ranging along from San Marcos to San Antonio from forty to fifty cattle girls. Some of them belong to the best families in that part of the state; some to the worst. They are, however, the finest riders in the west, and can whoop up a herd of ponies better than a Mexican. They have a leader, a brunette, with long black hair, that cracks like a whip when she is riding. They own four or five hundred head of steers. They have only been there two seasons. The leader came from Oklahoma Territory, and was said to be a fast friend of the Oklahoma outlaw, Payne. Cody attempted to get the girls to join the Wild West show, but it was no go. They can often be seen on the streets of Austin, though they are never known to stay in town over night. They have a number of frame cottages built for them about ten miles from San Marcos by Scotch settlers. Of course they afford our part of the Lone Star state a good deal of romantic talk."[18]

[Cheyenne, Wyoming, April, 1885.]
The Cattle Queen of the Pacific slope . . . passed through the city on her way to Chicago, where she will have a train load of cattle which will sell for about $10,000. She is Miss Mary Meagher, a tall, majestic woman not long past thirty years of age, and she hails from Walla Walla, where she owns the biggest ranch in Washington Territory.

Miss Meagher, notwithstanding her calling, is not at all masculine, neither in appearance nor in manners. She will travel 2,500 miles in a cattle train caboose, which carries ten drovers, and she is on pleasant, but not familiar terms with her neighbors. As she does not mind tobacco smoke, and is slightly partial to a friendly game of poker, the drovers were not much put out by her company.

"How do you keep the cowboys within bounds?" was asked by a reporter during a short conversation.

"Oh, I suppose it's because they admire pluck. If a man talked to some of them as I have he would have been killed long ago. I never had but one unruly cowboy. He would not go to the Sunday school I established. He delighted in teasing the calves. I reasoned with him, but to no purpose, and at last I was obliged to hand him over to his brother cowboys. They had begged me all along to let them fix him, but I held out as long as possible. Then I said:

"Take him, boys; but don't treat him too tough."

"That was all that saved his life. They took that cowboy to the edge of the ranch and thought up a just punishment. They took off his sombrero, the badge of manhood, and put a plug hat on his head and turned him adrift. Besides the indignity of the thing the change in headgear probably cost him his life, as an Indian was seen inside the hat about a week later."

There was a merry twinkle in the lady's eyes which rather belied her words and somehow it occurred to the reporter, whose plug hat rested on his knee, that Miss Meagher was "playing him for a tenderfoot."[19]

GO WEST!

Probably no occupation of the post Civil War West had greater appeal and fascination for the young man of America than that of the life and work of the cowboy. Encouraged to "go west" by statesmen, press, and economic opportunity, he expected life in the cow country to fulfill his adventuresome yearnings.

"Yes, sir, that's perfectly correct. As the advertisement says, $100 pays for three months' instruction in rearing, tending and caring for horses, and cattle and sheep with board and the use of a good saddle horse on a stock ranch in west Texas, and a young man after learning the business can get immediate employment in it at $50 a month or more."

The speaker was the local agent of the Texas farm association, who went on to explain:

"This association has nothing to do with the matter except to receive applicants for this practical tuition. The man who makes the offer is Col. Byron Von Raub, owner of the Don Carlos ranch, which is twenty-two miles north of San Antonio. But we know the offer to be made in good faith, and that the colonel is a perfectly square, trustworthy man. He is an old Prussian officer, who has ideas about training young men, and does this thing more because it does good and amuses him than for any profit from it. He has 8,000 acres of land stocked with some 400 ponies, a lot of horses—I don't know how many—and 4,000 head of cattle and sheep. His plan is to teach young men to be stockmen by making their daily life for a time a steady accumulation of knowledge of results indelibly fixed by experience. Each branch of this intricate and profitable business will be taught by experienced men, including feeding, herding, branding, lassoing, marketing, riding, and a thousand things about camp life that can only be taught by experience. The pupils will not only be taught by the work of his own ranch, but will be taken to visit the other great ranches in the vicinity, some of which have on them 1,000 to 2,000 horses, 10,000 to 50,000 head of cattle and 10,000 to 60,000 sheep and goats. There are now on Col. Von Raub's ranch forty-four young men, between the ages of 15 and 35 years, going through the course of instruction. A number of them are Englishmen, and there are also some from Nova Scotia, and several from Boston and other parts of New England. None have yet gone from New York, but it is probable that the offer will not fail to attract a good many here. This is the best season for them to go out to learn the winter work. Practically, one month in December and January, covers all the bad part of the Texas winter. For eleven months in the year one can camp out there in the open air without danger or discomfort. The fare from New York to San Antonio is $56.50 by boat and rail, $57.25 by all rail, first class limited.

"No, the elements of draw poker and seven-up and the use of the revolver are not included in Col. Von Raub's course of instruction, nor even permitted on his ranch. It is a popular error to suppose that the Texan goes about constantly with a howitzer on his hip and in normal condition of inebrity. The country is settling up rapidly with good, law-abiding citizens, who respect rights of person and property just the same as people do elsewhere. Our association has sent out there within 6 years some 1,600 settlers, the best class of emigrants, many of them from other states, and thousands go without our direction or knowledge."[20]

One seldom or ever meets an Englishman on a ranch who does not enjoy his life; but, after all, the life is not such a one as to recommend itself to parents as desirable to young men. There is a certain amount of excitement connected with it which makes it enjoyable for a young man, while, if he has brains and has got a fair start with cattle, his capital rapidly increases. There are, however, many things connected with the life which ought to influence parents to consider well before encouraging their young sons to take to cowboy's life.

On every side one hears of an over-supply of young men wishing to get employment as cowboys, and young men from this country every year find it more difficult to get a start even, although they are willing to work for a considerable time for their food without any pay. It is quite evident that ranching is every year being put more and more on a business footing, and owners of cattle herds cannot, or will not, afford horses for idlers to ride upon, but make a point of keeping as few hands as possible, and having those thoroughly efficient.[21]

My intention, however, in approaching the great cow industry, which, by the way, is anything but an industry, being in fact more like the seductive manner whereby a promissory note acquires two per cent per month without ever stopping to spit on its hands, was to refer incidentally to the proposition of an English friend of mine. This friend, seeing at once the great magnitude of the cow industry and the necessity for more and more cowboys has suggested the idea of establishing a cowboy's college or training school for self-made young men who desire to become accomplished. The average Englishman will most always think of something that nobody else would naturally think of. Now, our cattlemen would have gone on for years with his great steer emporium without thinking of establishing an institution where a poor boy might go and learn to rope a 4-year-old in such a way as throw him on his stomach with a sickening thud.

But now that the idea has been turned loose I shall look forward to the time when wealthy men who have been in the habit of dying and leaving their money to other institutions will meet with a change of heart and begin to endow the cowboy's college and the Maverick hotbed of bronco sciences.

We live in an age of rapid advancement in all branches of learning, and people who do not rise early in the morning will not retain their position in the procession. I look forward with confidence to the day when no cowboy will undertake to ride the range without a diploma. Educated labor is what we need — cowboys who can tell you in scientific terms why it is always the biggest steer that eats "pizen weed" in the spring and why he should swell up and bust on a rising Chicago market.

I hope the day is not far distant when in the holster of the cowboy we will find the Iliad instead of the killiad, the unabridged dictionary instead of Mr. Remington's great work on homicide. As it is now on the ranges, you might ride till your Mexican saddle ached before you would find a cowboy who carries a dictionary with him. For that reason the language used on the general round up is at times grammatically incorrect, and many of our leading cowboys spell "cavvy-yard" with a "k."

A college for riding, roping, branding, cutting out, corraling, loading and unloading, and handling cattle generally, would be a great boon to our young men who are at present groping in the dark and pitiable ignorance of the habits of the untutored cow. Let the young man first learn to sit up three nights in succession, through a bad March snowstorm, and "hold" herd of restless cattle. Let him then ride through the hot sun and alkali dust a week or two, subsisting on a chunk of disagreeable side pork just large enough to bait a trap. Then let his horse fall on him and injure his constitution and preamble. All these things would give the cow student an idea of how to ride the range. The amateur who has never tried to ride a skittish and sulky range horse has still a great deal to learn.

The young Maverick savant could take a kindergarten

course in the study of cow-brands. Here a wild field opens up to the scholar. The adult steer in the great realm of beef is now a walking Chinese washbill, a Hindoo poem in the original junk-shop alphabet, a four legged Greek inscription punctuated with jimjams, a stenographer's notes of a riot, a bird's-eye view of a premature explosion in a hardware store.

The cowboy who can at once grapple with the great problem of where to put the steer with "B bar B" on left shoulder, "Key circle G" on left side, "Heart D. Heart" on right hip, left ear crop, wattle to wattle, and seven hands round, with "Dash B Dash" on right shoulder, "vented," wattle on dew lap vented, and "P.D.Q.," "C.O.D.," and "N.G." vented on right side, keeping track of transfers, range, and postoffice of last owner has certainly got a future which lies mostly ahead of him.

Perhaps I have said too much on this subject, but when I get thoroughly awakened on this great porter-house steak problem I am apt to carry the matter too far.[22]

To anyone who contemplates trying a season's riding, I would say this: You will build up your constitution for life; you will meet rough fellows, hear hard swearing and see some fighting, but you will hear fewer indecent stories on the range than in the average club room. Your "outfit," or your bed, clothing and equipments, will cost you half your earnings and if you smoke freely and do not try to save money, the end of the season will leave you neither richer or poorer. You will often have a wet bed and thank Heaven for getting to it wet as it is; you will eat coarse food, everything fried in lard; you will be in saddle from 12 to 18 hours a day; you will often suffer for the want of food and water during a long day's work in the hot sun; you will expose yourself to some peril of life and more of limb; you will be for much of the time as absolutely cut off from civilization as if you were on a vessel in mid-ocean; you will vow three times a day that when you strike the ranch again you will quit; you will be sore and bruised, cold at night scorched by day; wet to the skin one hour and parched with thirst the next; and for the rest of your life you will look back to your life on the range with longing thoughts of its charms. Very few men are rich enough to indulge their taste for riding by keeping more than two saddle horses. A "puncher" often rides a dozen and does much of his work on a full run. He breathes the finest air on earth, eats beef as freely as an ordinary workingman eats cabbage and potatoes, and fancies that the class to which he belongs are the aristocracy of labor. He is generous, always quick to appreciate pluck and kindliness in others, chivalrous to the few women he ever sees, ever ready to help hang a horse thief and undergoes more hardship and danger than a dozen soldiers.[23]

I contend that a year spent on the hurricane deck of a cow pony is one of the most useful and valuable pieces of experience a young man can possibly have in fitting himself for business of almost any kind; and if I were educating a boy to fight the battle of life, I would secure him a cowboy's situation as soon as he was through with his studies at school. A term of service on a frontier cattle ranch will take the conceit out of any boy; it will at the same time teach him self-reliance; it will teach him to endure hardships and suffering; it will give him nerve and pluck; it will develop the latent energy in him to a degree that could not be accomplished by any other apprenticeship or experience I know of. Many of the most successful business men in the Western towns of today served their first years on the frontier as "cow punchers," and to that school they owe the firmness of character and the ability to surmount great obstacles that have made their success in life possible.

I contend that the constant communion with nature, the study of her broad, pure domains, the days and nights of lonely cruising and camping on the prairie, the uninterrupted communion with and study of self which this occupation affords, tend to make young men honest and noble, much more so than the same men would be if deprived of these opportunities, confined to the limits of our boasted "civilization," and compelled to constantly breathe the air of adroitness, of strategy, of competition, of suspicion and crime. If every young man reared in town or city could have the advantages of a year or two of constant study of nature, we should have more honest men.[24]

The cable news from London would seem to indicate that the coming year will witness a large hegira of armed goslins from England who intend to prosecute the cow-gentlemen and stage robbing business on our frontier. It is perhaps unnecessary to state that Buffalo William, the graceful and courteous hirsute wonder from Nebraska, is largely responsible for this. Wherever he has gone with his eccentric, dark-eyed, self-made Indians and his speckled broncos he has sown the seeds of discontent in the grammar schools and bred open rebellion and mutiny in the primary department.

Look along the red-hot trails of B. William and you find the American and foreign youth alike turning with undisguised loathing from educational pursuits to immerse his legs in a pair of chaperajos [chaparajos] to wield the brief but stinging quirt, to whoop-up the red-eyed, haughty and high-tailed Texan maverick, or shoot large, irregular holes into the otherwise poorly ventilated savage.

And what is the result of all this? I do not ask it in a light or flippant manner, but in a tone of deepest solicitude.

Buffalo Bill is encircling the earth with his Wild West show. Everywhere the fever follows his performance. Wherever he goes his high-heeled boots, lariats, tarantula juice and hair rise to a fictitious value. Boys leave the farm to follow the show away. Picnics lose their flavor and seem flat. Climbing a shag-bark tree to fasten a swing does not seem so daring a feat as it used to. The custard pie vainly beckons to the young man who is near-sighted and who wears lavendar pantaloons to come and set on it. In the rural districts the watermelon ripens and goes to decay, and petty larceny everywhere seems tame, dull and flabby. No one wants to steal wealth unless it has gore and hair on it. Dollars or watermelons that can be taken without walking over a corduroy road of dead bodies seem hardly worth taking.

Already the tide of young and fuzzy cowboys has set in from the mother country and an extra detective and police force haunt the wharf at Liverpool to prevent the exodus of leggy and pimply young patriots who desire to roll up their trousers and wade in the hot, fresh blood of our rapidly disappearing red men. Already every steamer that plows the wide waste of blooming moisture which separates us from the home of the patient yacht-builder brings us one to several aspiring young gentlemen in flannel shirts who pant to imbue their hands in the blood of Old Git-Up and Sit-Down.

And so it is likely to continue while Mr. Bill is on his wild, whooping, shrieking, and coliseum storming career. After a while it will not be the British Isles alone that will contribute to our languishing frontier cemeteries, but saturated with a wild desire to snort across the American plains and provide themselves with Indian Pocahantases, the youth of all lands and all climes will buy wide, white soft hats, fur pantaloons with lambrequins down the side; the low, gruff-voiced American revolver, with the dry, hacking cough; the noisy and voluminous Mexican spur and the foundering mustang, with one white eye and the gift of appearing to look like a cyclone, while really making mighty poor time. Then they will invade our Western borders and there will not be an Indian apiece for them by next spring.

I do not wish to be considered an alarmist, but unless we bring our Indians in at night, the cowboys of Great Britain and of France will sweep our Great West, and together with road agents from Rome, the pilgrim from Palestine and the tenderfoot from Turkey, they will wipe out our pigeon-toed Piutes and the cute little Crows, our urbane and genial Utes and our low-browed Digger Indians before snow flies next year.

I can see that in a dramatic way Buffalo Bill has opened up a new route, besides starting towards America a perfect swarm of amateur cowboys who desire to cross the plains and rescue a beautiful young lady who is walking from Julesburg to Walla Walla wearing a pearl *francaise, en bouffant*, lined with oyster velvet and edged with heavy elephant's breath silk cord, while in the v-shaped corsage nestles a large bunch of Marshal O'Neil roses.[25]

If young men who have the cowboy fever had any idea of the apprenticeship they are likely to serve before becoming fullfledged cowboys, most of them would be cured without the expense of trip a thousand miles west, ... It is nearly twenty years since I had the fever and went out to be cured. My first work was watching the line between Wyoming and Dakota. Line or fence watching is an assignment frequently given to a newcomer and the duties consist in riding up and down the line and preventing the cattle from straying over it. Several men have lost their reason in this work and I came very near doing so myself. All the glory and adventure we read of in books is absent, and solitude is terrible. I could cover my distance in about two days, and did nothing else but ride up and down the lines watching for the stray cattle, which never strayed my way. Sheep herding is said to be the most terribly monotonous work a man can be put to, but there are few cowboys in the west who have not an acute recollection of the sufferings they endured when doing such work as I describe. There are hundreds of men doing it today, but each of them is looking forward to obtaining a new job with almost the eagerness of a convict who knows that his sentence has nearly expired.[26]

I WANNA BE A COWBOY!

The youthful "Roy Rogers" and "Hoppys" of the eighties and nineties presented the same problems to parents, police, and press as do the young "cowboys" of this second half of the twentieth century. Give a boy boots, a big hat, blue jeans, and a brace of cap pistols and you have the spirit of the American cowboy, regardless of the time or age.

[Denver, Colorado, March, 1882.]
A couple of young men, in imitation of the wild and uncivilized cowboy, thought it fine sport riding their borrowed livery horses around a couple of blocks, bounded by Fourteenth and Fifteenth streets, at break-neck speed, to the danger of pedestrians at crossings. This was just

at dusk, and was repeated again and again, and no police were about to stop the performance.[27]

[Cheyenne, Wyoming, February, 1885.]

Two detectives arrived from the East last evening in search of a boy named Shephard, who ran away from New York several weeks ago. Mr. Shephard is a New York banker and has offered a reward of $10,000 for the safe return of his son. The detectives will separate here, one going to Texas among the cowboys, and the other, after traveling through Wyoming, will go to Arizona. The officers were interviewed by a reporter of *The Leader* last night and the following particulars of the boy's escapade were learned.

It is the old story of dime novel reading. Fred, the missing boy, accumulated a choice library of all sensational literature extant. The last novel he read was found on his desk at school, open at the place where a young cowboy detective unmasks his father's murderer and carves him into mincemeat to quick music and while holding the minor villains in subjection with two revolvers held in one hand.

Scrawled at the bottom of the page was the line: "I'm goin' West to be a cowboy detective."

Fred's tin savings bank, which must have contained $20 in dimes and quarters, was found broken open and entirely despoiled of its contents. Nobody saw him make his departure, but it was made in the old romantic way of going to rest early on the plea of a headache, and then climbing out of the window on an L, and then down the spout.

His mother is greatly distressed over Fred's rash act, and she has baked cookies and made preserves enough to keep him at home a year after he is brought back. She regrets deeply her refusal to give him a quince tart only the day before he ran away, and she remembers that he hinted that she wouldn't be troubled with him very long.

Mr. Shephard takes the matter more coolly and says it will be a good lesson for the boy. Nobody would hurt the youngster who is a pert youth of eleven birthday anniversaries.

The detectives are urged to activity by the large reward and will make a thorough search of the West for the child who wanted to be a "cowboy detective."[28]

Bert Fairchild, the cowboy of Garfield county, who is obtaining a wide reputation as a desperado, was formerly a resident of Boulder [Colorado]. His parents lived at the mouth of Left Hand Canon, and Bert was largely raised there. They moved to Ashley Valley, Utah, ten years ago, Bert then being about 17 years old. He was always a great admirer of the dime novel style of hero, and imitated him in his dress. His parents were among the most honorable and respected citizens of Boulder county.[29]

Two boys, Louis Spindle, aged 14, and Charles Oberrither, aged 15, excited the suspicion, by their appearance and actions, of Police Officer Wallace at the union depot [St. Louis, Missouri,] and he arrested them. On being searched at police headquarters there were found on them three railroad tickets to San Antonio, Tex., two new rifles, two revolvers, a cartridge belt, a large knife and belt and some dice. In a valise they had two sombreros, a bottle of whisky, a broad waist-belt, a black-snake whip and other requisites for the cowboy life. The third ticket was for another companion, Frank Simon, about the same age, who managed to elude the policemen. All the money they had was $4.20, but having attended a dime museum in town they had become fired with a desire to become cowboys, and notwithstanding the low state of their finances had determined to start out and makes themselves terrors of the country.

The boys were detained at the police station until their parents could be notified and it could be ascertained where they had obtained the money to buy outfits and tickets.[30]

The following has been received by *The Stock Grower*, and is published with the hope that some of the numerous boys now in the ring, who have come west with the same ideas which possess the writer will recount him their experience and ideas, and give him advice.

BRIDGEWATER, MASS., June 23, 1891.

TO THE STOCK GROWER

DEAR SIR:—I am a young man 22 years old and having a great desire for a cowboy's life thought I would write you for information concerning a cowboy's life. First, what wages are paid a green hand, and is there work the year round. Is there likely to be plenty of herding for years to come or not. I am used to roughing it; I have been brought up on a farm. Are cowboys as a rule a good class of men? When would be the best time to come and what would I need to bring with me? Can you buy as cheap out there as you can here. I like your paper very much.

Respectfully,

W. A. CASS[31]

NOTES TO CHAPTER NINE

1. *Trinidad Weekly News* (Trinidad, Colorado), December 28, 1882.
2. *Ibid.*
3. *Texas Live Stock Journal* (Fort Worth, Texas), January 12, 1884, p. 8.
4. "Doing Well," *Trinidad Daily Advertiser* (Trinidad, Colorado), February 5, 1884.
5. "Cowboys' Ball," *El Anunciador de Trinidad* (Trinidad, Colorado), January 14, 1884.
6. *Field and Farm* (Denver, Colorado), January 16, 1886, p. 4.
7. "Local Brevities," *Cattlemen's Advertiser* (Trinidad, Colorado), February 18, 1886.
8. "Cowboy Reunion," *Medicine Lodge Index* (Medicine Lodge, Kansas), May 21, 1886.
9. "Stampeded Cowboys," *Arizona Mining Index* (Tucson, Arizona), November 29, 1884.
10. *Stock Grower and Farmer* (Las Vegas, New Mexico), February 20, 1897.
11. "Bloody Fight for a Bride," *Denver Republican* (Denver, Colorado), March 8, 1889.
12. "A True Love Story," *Texas Live Stock Journal*, September 20, 1890, p. 24.
13. "Is Charged with Stealing Wife," *Denver Republican*, September 2, 1900.
14. "A Romantic Young Woman in the Role of a Drover," *Cherokee County Republican* (Columbus, Kansas), January 26, 1877.

15. "A Female Cattle Dealer in Male Attire," *Caldwell Post* (Caldwell, Kansas), February 13, 1879.

16. "A Female Cow Boy," *Texas Live Stock Journal*, April 21, 1883, p. 8.

17. *Great West* (Denver, Colorado), July 12, 1884.

18. "Texas Cattle Girls," *Kansas Cowboy* (Dodge City, Kansas), February 28, 1885.

19. "A Cattle Queen," *Democratic Leader* (Cheyenne, Wyoming), April 23, 1885.

20. "Taught to be Cowboys," *Cheyenne Daily Sun* (Cheyenne, Wyoming), November 14, 1882.

21. "American Cattle Ranching," *Breeder's Gazette* (Chicago, Illinois), February 5, 1885, p. 194.

22. "A Cowboy's College," *Field and Farm*, January 16, 1886, p. 11.

23. "Facts for Would-Be-Cowboys," *Trinidad Weekly News*, March 12, 1886.

24. "The Festive Cow Puncher," *Denver Tribune-Republican* (Denver, Colorado), October 31, 1886.

25. "Nye and the Cowboys," *Texas Live Stock Journal*, December 3, 1887, p. 13

26. *Field and Farm*, November 10, 1894, p. 9.

27. *Rocky Mountain News* (Denver, Colorado), March 20, 1882.

28. "A Western Hero," *Democratic Leader*, February 1, 1885.

29. "Ranch and Range," *Denver Tribune-Republican*, September 13, 1886.

30. "Eager to Be Cowboys," *Cattlemen's Advertiser*, January 13, 1887.

31. "He Wants to Be a Cowboy," *Stock Grower and Farmer*, July 4, 1891.

Sports of the Range

TEN

A bright, but somewhat neglected, thread runs through the variegated fabric of the rich tapestry woven around the American cowboy, and through the years it has gained in vitality and brilliance. This is the great cowboy sport known today as rodeo. The contests of modern rodeo are far removed from a depiction of the actual range work of the cowboy; however, disregarding concessions made to entertainment techniques, they are not so far removed from the early pastime and sport of the man, as practiced and enjoyed by him in his regular work.

Very little is recorded of these early typical cowboy sports, and at times the thread is difficult to follow. Now, sufficient evidence has been found, and a clearly defined pattern appears, typical throughout the cowboy's domain. Early exhibitions of cowboy skill were simultaneous in the West, for the cowboys depended upon their daily activities to provide what little sport and relaxation they had. This was carried on within the individual outfits; eventually, certain men proved themselves superior in riding and roping, and were then pitted against the best men of rival outfits. Out of these simple competitions grew the beginning of modern rodeo, the cowboy tournaments and contests of the last quarter of the nineteenth century.

The Great Plains area was the cattleman's range and lay in the path of the herds being driven to the northern feeding grounds. The foregoing chapters show that many aspects of the life of the cowboy were of interest to the pioneers and were treated in the newspapers, but his sport was rarely mentioned. Unfortunately, the early chroniclers were not often in a position to witness this activity, or perhaps they did not consider it worthy of note. Not until the late eighties, when the range cattle industry made way for the ranch cattle industry, did the cowboy sport attract the attention of newspaper reporters, and then it was simply recorded as the passing sport of the rapidly disappearing cowboy.

Few records remain of the early inter-camp or rival-outfit cowboy competitions. These contests usually took place on the trails, far from the towns and cities whose newspapers might have recorded the incidents. If and when they did take place at the edge of a cow town, too many events took precedence in print. These demonstrations of skill could be witnessed daily on the main streets of these termini, as hundreds of thousands of cattle with their cowboy guardians coverged upon them.

However, in the late eighties we find an increased interest in cowboy sports. By this time the cattle industry had settled down. The losses sustained on the open range because of overstocking, drought and hard winters, speculation and price declivity, the incoming granger and the wire fence, brought about a collapse of the range cattle industry—what had been an exciting, stimulating adventure was now converted into a hardheaded systematic business. As the industry underwent a change, the cattleman, the cattle, and the cowboy likewise changed. The nomadic life which spread over thousands of miles was ended; the cowboy was confined to a few thousand acres, he was closer to civilization, to the towns and cities, and, if he remained in the business, he became a member of the community.

In the community, and particularly from the community spirit, the second phase of cowboy sports developed—the cowboy tournament. The agricultural fairs, which best expressed this spirit, provided for exhibits of fine cattle, stock, and horses from the surrounding ranches; also the various grains, fruits, and vegetables of neighboring farms were displayed. The races, of which the cowboy race was one of the main attractions, were a part of every county fair, but the tournaments of cowboy skill in bronco busting and steer roping were the dramatic highlights of the community enterprise. The desire on the part of the pioneers to preserve the memories of a passing age led them to revive, through celebrations, some of the earlier activities of the plains, among them the exhibitions of the one-time daily work and sport of the cowboy.[1]

EARLY COWBOY SPORTS

It is only natural that the sport of the cowboy should grow from his daily work. The environment in which he lived offered all the requirements necessary for sport and games; his strength, daring, and skill provided the spark to stir the spirit of competition, so strong among outdoor men.

One of the earliest accounts of cowboy sports is recorded in a letter dated June 10, 1847. It was written by Captain Mayne Reid in Santa Fe, New Mexico, to Samuel Arnold of Drumnakelly, Seaforde, county Down, Ireland. In part it says:

The town from which I write is quaint; of the Spanish style of building and reposes in a great land kissed by the southern sun. You have cows in old Ireland, but you never saw cows. Yes, millions of them here, I am sure, browsing on the sweet long grass of the ranges that roll from horizon to horizon. At this time of year the cowmen have what is called the round-up, when the calves are branded and the fat beasts selected to be driven to a fair hundreds of miles away.

This round-up is a great time for the cowhands, a Donneybrook fair it is, indeed. They contest with each other for the best roping and throwing, and there are horse races and whisky and wines. At night in the clear moonlight there is much dancing on the streets.[2]

[Deer Trail, Colorado, July 4, 1869.]

... They were the best horsemen in the state, and they were out to do one another up in the contests or die. The old cattlemen grinned as they watched the younger ones fooling around and wondered, as they looked at the kicking and bucking nags in the pen, just how many of the boys were going to be laid up before the day was over. The prize was a suit of clothes, and the conditions were that the horses should be ridden with a slick saddle, which means that the saddle must be free from the roll usually tied across the horse, that the stirrups must not be tied under the horse, and that the rider must not wear spurs.

Those in charge made no secret of the fact that all the horses they had were outlawed horses, which it had been impossible to break, and the conditions made it dangerous riding. Many of the boys shook their heads, but Will Goff, a slim, young cow puncher from the Bijou jumped out and said he'd ride anything with hair on it. A quiet looking bay pony was cautiously led out. "I'll ride," said Goff, and amid great applause, he pulled off his coat, threw his suspenders aside, took a reef in his belt, and with one bound, landed on the bay's back. Swish! and his felt hat whistled through the air and caught the broncho across the side of the head. The pony hitched violently for fifty yards, making about 300 revolutions to the minute. Then he started to run, and the crowd howled. "Give me my spurs and I'll make him pitch," yelled Goff, and they did give him his spurs, and he cut the pony to bits, but the exhibition was not satisfactory. The rider had too easy a time.

Drury Grogan, the pride of the Arickaree, tackled a little sorrel of the Camp Stool brand next. The animal was a notorious outlaw and had never been ridden. As soon as Drury was on its back it began to pitch with saddle cinched. This was a direct violation of the rules, but the sorrel, evidently, had no respect for the conditions of the contest. It plunged and kicked, jumped into the air, and made a seesaw, but Drury held on and was marked down as a successful rider, amid cheering. Emilnie Gardenshire, of the Milliron ranch, was the next rider. Gardenshire let it be known that he wanted the worst animal in the pen, and he got it in the shape of a bay, from the Hashknife ranch, known throughout the section as the Montana Blizzard.

Gardenshire, rawhide whip in hand, crawled aboard cautiously, and, once firm in his seat, began to larrup the bay unmercifully. A sight followed which tickled the spectators hugely. The Englishman rode with hands free and kept plying his whip constantly. There was a frightful mixup of cowboy and horse, but Gardenshire refused to be unseated. For fifteen minutes the bay bucked, pawed, and jumped from side to side, then, amid cheers, the mighty Blizzard succumbed, and Gardenshire rode him around the circle at a gentle gallop. It was a magnificent piece of horsemanship, and the suit of clothes, together with the title "Champion Bronco Buster of the Plains," went to the lad from the Milliron ranch.[3]

Fourth of July is a great day among the cowboys and the following tale by one of them is a fair recitation of the "doings" that take place out on the range: "I remember the time we had one Fourth of July in Wyoming. The boys were all tired that day, and to go to town as they usually did on the Fourth meant a big time, and they decided to have some fun on the ranch. We were about fourteen miles north of Cheyenne then, and the regular thing was for everyone around to bring in the meanest horses they could get hold of and have some fun. The worst one is picked out and some one goes around and takes up a collection. The next is the riding.

"A good man tops the horse and stays with him until he gets the dirt out of him. The man busts the horse or the horse busts the man. That horse will be mean until he discovers he has a master. That will be sometimes ten minutes and sometimes half or three-quarters of an hour, and sometimes until the horse is played out. The rider who succeeds in staying with the horse takes the money. If he is thrown they try other riders until one succeeds. They take a collection for each horse and keep up the fun until they have used up the horses or are tired of it, and try roping, racing and fancy riding, and the day winds up with a dance and everyone feeling pretty lively."[4]

The most exciting and laughable part of the programme races was the riding of a wild steer by "Witcomb's Sam," the most accomplished horse jockey in the Territory. He retained his seat with great skill and dexterity, and accomplished the mile 1:16¼.[5]

[Cheyenne, Wyoming, September, 1873.]
It is a very interesting sight to see a bull-whacker seated astride of a broncho horse, that has but a limited acquaintance with his rider, or the roughness, that he is to be put to; and with Spanish spurs roweling the life out of the poor brute nearly, and making him rear his ends in the air, alternately while an idle crowd gather to witness and curse the exhibition made by both horse and rider.

We are induced to speak thus, in consequence of having witnessed a display of such a horse and such a rider ... near the corner of Seventeenth and Ferguson streets. There was quite a crowd and some quiet swearing. But would not such exhibitions be in better taste out on the prairie? Suppose one of these bronchos should run up the side of a brick building to the roof, or up a telegraph pole to the cross-bars and insulators, would the rider keep his seat? These bronchos are liable to do these things; we have known them to do worse things.[6]

There has been considerable chaffing variegated with especially lurid illustrations of the possibilities of profanity, on the merits of two bulls, and for several nights the smoke hung low over the campfires, as if listening, too awe-stricken to rise, to the various stories of their prowess in former struggles. Murcheson's men were to the westward of the trail, but they came over to Zingman's roundup, two miles to the east, every evening to talk over their bull, and speculate on the chances if Zingman's men felt the spirit of ownership in anything they wanted to pit against him. . . .[7]

A Texas correspondent to the Pittsburgh *(Pennsylvania)* Dispatch *was much impressed by the reckless daredevil type of man he encountered in the cowboy.*

There were no old men among them. A man of forty was looked upon as a patriarch, one who was entitled to be a candidate for admission to the home of the aged and infirm. These young men rode up and down the Texas cattle trail from Trinity River to the Republican. When in Texas, to gather their herds, they rode furiously; they hunted panthers; they coursed after wolves; they ate mavericks almost without number, and on the round-up they were the most reckless of all the hard-riding men that gathered on the southern ranges. When they returned to Kansas with their cattle they had many stories about the skill of the Texas cowboys to relate. A young acquaintance of mine told me of the Texas cowboys tailing steers—that is, riding alongside a running steer and grasping his elevated tail, and by giving it a powerful lifting jerk, throwing it heels over head, much to his discomfiture and subsequent rage. I smiled incredulously. The young man offered to perform the trick. We got into a wagon and drove to where my herd was grazing. The cattle were just off the trail and were not strong. My friend contemtuously said there was no need of his mounting one of the herder's ponies to "tail" those steers; he could do it on foot. The herders gathered round to see the spectacle. The young man jumped from the wagon and ran swiftly to a steer which he grasped firmly by the tail. Then, looking confidently at us, he gave the tail a savage jerk. There was some hitch in the performance. The steer did not turn a somersault. He looked around, and seeing a man fastened to his tail, bellowed with intense rage, and turned to impale him on his polished horns. My acquaintance, still grasping the steer's tail tightly, ran round and round. The steer kicked and bellowed, and turned faster and faster after him. The entire herd gathered and stood in a vast circle, looking at the gruesome spectacle. Soon the tail-pulling young man called for help. We could not have helped him if his life depended on it. The herders had laughed until they could hardly sit in their saddles. I held to the sides of the wagon box to keep from falling out. Bare-headed, with his long hair streaming behind him and incessant calls for aid pouring out of his mouth, and an occasional howl at the contracting circle of cattle that were being excited, to give variety to the furious uproar, my friend sped round and round. And the steer, with many bellows and intense rage, chased his tail and the two-legged animal that had presumptuously fastened on to it. Finally I recovered my strength, and drove the wagon close to the revolving pair. My friend loosened his grasp on the tail and the circular motion being stopped, steer and man went in a promiscuous heap to the ground. The steer bellowed in an agony of rage and my friend again shrieked a plaintiff wail for help, as in a dazed and shattered condition he struggled to get away from the four legs of the animal, that were making sixty revolutions a minute in every possible direction. Five of the herders quickly roped the steer, and one of the funniest scenes I ever saw on the range was at an end. Afterward my friend mounted a pony and neatly "tailed" that steer, with great satisfaction to himself and damage to the animal.[8]

The rodeo of the upper division of the lower Sulphur Valley roundup association is at present at B. Rigg's ranch. There are about forty-five men in the outfit, with two cooks and two night horse-herders.

All of the "professional cowboys" have one or more bronchos in their mounts. The crowd expects to see bucking at every fresh mount, and they are not often disappointed. When the untamed steed is mounted such expressions as these will be heard: "Stay with him!" "Build to his crooks!" "He is sure getting there in great shape!"[9]

EXHIBITIONS

The widespread and sustained interest in the cowboy which had persisted for two decades was spurred by a growing public admiration for his sports and thrilling competitions. Enterprising showmen soon recognized the popularity of this type of natural entertainment and brought cowboys and spectators together.

About a month ago, A. B. Grady, residing at Lockhart, Caldwell county, [Texas] organized a company of cowboys for the purpose of giving exhibitions in the principal cities of the country of the scenes and incidents that attend the life of the Texas cowboy, embracing the roping and tying down of wild stock, horsemanship, etc. The company as organized consists of Virgil Carter, Tom Hale, Joe Lovelady, Pad Nixon, Will Roach, Will Cardwell, James C. Witter, Webster Witter and John Riddles. All are young men, Texas boys, raised principally on the ranches of Caldwell county. They are sober, steady, intelligent young men. On the first and second two days of May they give exhibition[s] at San Pedro park, this city, going hence to Galveston, where they appear on the 4th and 5th, and go thence North. The young men will be uniformed in large Mexican silver hats, purchased at Laredo, leather jackets finely fringed, Angora leggins and large Mexican spurs. The ponies they will ride are all paints, specially selected; and the saddles are of the regular Mexican make and trim, with long toe fenders. Their exhibition here will consist simply of riding and roping and tying down wild beeves. One of the young men, Will Cardwell, can rope and tie down a wild steer in one minute and five seconds; Will Roach, in one minute and twenty-five seconds and J. C. Witter, third best, in two and a quarter minutes. The organization will take all necessary stock with them on their northern tour. This is the first company of the kind that ever was put on the amusement list, and will undoubtedly draw large crowds, especially in the distant North where the very name of a cowboy has carried terror with it. It will give people in the cities a very fair idea of cowboy life and adventures and experiences.[10]

At San Pedro park in this city [San Antonio, Texas,] last week were given two exhibitions by Grady's Cowboy Company.... About 600 persons assembled the first day to witness the exhibition, which was announced to consist of riding, using the lariat, lassoing and tying down wild cattle. And the programme was carried out, though the cattle proved to be not very wild—were rather thin and weak, and not in condition to give the boys much work.

At 3 o'clock p.m. the boys appeared in full rig on the track, a half mile, which they rode around in double file, and then retired to the southwest part of the grounds to "cut out" the cattle....

... There was little variation on the second day other than furnished by a party of San Antonio boys who entered as competitors and took the shine off of some of the "professionals" by getting in the quickest and best work.

While Mr. Grady has with him an excellent set of young men, and who will no doubt greatly interest the people of the large cities, there are many boys today about our streets who are far more expert in handling the lariat, and who, as riders, can not be excelled.[11]

Rox Hardy will give an initial exhibition of cowboy life at the Albuquerque Fair. If the thing looks as though it would pan out pretty rich, he will write some glowing articles about his marvelous adventures among the wild cowboys, and then start out with a show *a la* Buffalo Bill. He is cultivating his hair and mustache under the direction of a scientific Las Vegas barber.[12]

"Buck" Taylor, who was recently with the Buffalo Bill troupe and who was billed as the "King of the Cowboys," has returned to Cheyenne and will probably be here some days. The troupe that was here has disbanded for the season, and Buffalo Bill is now preparing to go forth with his "Wild West" troupe, and in so doing is to be accompanied by Taylor. The mission of Buck Taylor to Cheyenne is to procure a lot of horses which will have to be taken along with the show. Taylor is, therefore, looking around and is investing in old and superannuated horses, but all right for the business Buffalo Bill will have with them.[13]

Jay Gould and party, who have been making quite a tour through Mexico, returned via Eagle Pass, arriving in San Antonio on Saturday, April 5 [1890]. After riding about the old city and noting the extensive changes in progress, it was his intention to have left on Sunday, but those live and enterprising horse dealers, J. E. Price and Thos. H. Gilroy, with blandishments so well used on horse buyers, induced the party to lay over another day in order to witness an impromptu Wild West show at the Traders' National Stock Yards. Accordingly, on Monday morning the party, including Miss Gould, took seats on the gallery of the second story of the office of the stock yards, where some of the most expert cowboys and breakneck riders, including Dave Allen, the pockmarked negro who rides without saddle or bridle anything with hair on, rode wild mules and horses, and threw the rope in every conceivable manner, to the great edification of the distinguished party and the especial delight of Miss Gould, who seemed to enter heartily into the spirit of the exciting scenes. All expressed themselves greatly pleased and well paid for the delay of 24 hours, which means much to a man whose time is as valuable as that of Jay Gould. Although these scenes are common enough, if it had been known in the city that the great railroad magnate was attending such an exhibition, thousands of people would have been there also; as it was, the little show attracted no outside attention. Now, if the Prince of Wales wants something first-class when he makes his contemplated visit, laying into the shade the tame affairs of Buffalo Bill, all he has to do is to give Price or Gilroy half an hour's notice, and it will be furnished.[14]

[Denver, Colorado, December, 1892.]

Frank Hammitt, chief of cowboys of the Wild West show is in town. He intends to spend some time in the Rocky Mountain country engaging riders and expert lasso-throwers for the Wild West show during the World's Fair. The intention is to have 400 rough riders of all nationalities at the show. There will be Tartars, Cossacks, Mexicans, Indians and cowboys all clad in their peculiar costumes.[15]

ROPING vs. TIME

During the last decade of the nineteenth century the riding and roping feats of the cowboy were fast becoming legendary. Records of their speed and dexterity were preserved and compared by the alert journalist who witnessed the beginning of a typical American sport.

In these days, cheapness seems to be taking the lead. It is not now the question of "where did you get," but rather, "how much did you give?" The cheaper worker is gradually crowding the old-timer to the wall, and band spur is growing more frequent, and the sea-grass has long ago usurped the time-honored rawhide. More cattle are handled every year which calls for more hands, more roping done, consequently, everybody cannot afford to buy rawhide plaits. But though the rawhide has gone it is not forgotten, and whenever called upon to rope, in a breeze, anybody that has ever used one sighs for the old time lasso. The later mescales are not long enough for range work, and the ordinary sea-grass is too light. With the new era of ropes, comes a new era of hands. Good ropers seem to be scarce and phenomenal lassoers have departed altogether. At El Paso, New Mexico [Texas], in '77, I saw a Mexican cast a one hundred and twenty feet rope its length, and catch a steer while at full speed. In Utah and southern California it is not uncommon to find range ropers that use sixty to eighty feet ropes entirely in their work. Chris Hunter, of Utah, would bet $10 any time that he could catch any two feet of a horse at the end of a forty feet lasso. But these men all used rawhides, and declared a sea grass roper must depend upon guess work to help him out. A well made rawhide, properly cared for, will last two to five years. I broke one last summer that I bought in Nevada in '79. They are contestably easier on the hands, more accurate on a cast, less affected by the wind, less wearing on the saddle horn, stronger and more durable than any other rope I know of. I'm speaking of the California style rope; one that the maker puts his conscience into; one that the best hide has been selected, and utmost pains used in the cutting, trimming, rubbing and braiding. Such a rope is flexible, elastic and immensely strong, and contains that nice weight to every foot that makes what is called a "perfectly balanced rope." I've made a long talk about the kind of rope, because the more perfect the tools, the more perfect the workman should be. A good roper seldom has accidents happen. His horses don't throw themselves against the fences, and drive stakes between their ribs, nor fall so as to break legs, nor set back so hard that they pull their neck down, nor his roped cows have sprung knees, dislocated hips, knocked off horns, and muscles stretched so as to be painfully useless. All this and much more, however, happens to the man with the wooden head that knows it all and imagines the art of stock-handling to consist of overcoming his victims by bull force. Such a man when holding the broncho to the snubbing post, understands naught of drawing slack and stopping a bolt gradually, but will set his weight back and let his victim "yank his head off" at the end of a thirty feet rope on slack. If, therefore, rawhides will make better stock hands out of some of the poor range timber, I will advance an equal share with anybody to be invested in the needful.[16]

In the matter of authentic records for roping with the lariat none probably exist. One hundred and sixteen feet has been claimed for a California man now traveling with Buffalo Bill's show, while ninety-four feet has been published for a Billings (Mon.) man, but both of those records are preposterous. The average cow puncher from Texas to Montana uses a rope which barely reaches fifty feet, and from twelve to fifteen feet must be deducted from this measure for the circumference of noose. Sometimes a so called "California loop" exceeds this by nearly five feet. In catching a wild horse or steer, after the noose is over the animal's neck or legs, the end of the rope is swiftly tied around the horn of the saddle, the horse being braced back to resist the shock, which in most cases either snaps the rope or sends the captured animal all in a heap.

What the possibilities of roping to catch are is hard to say. No doubt with a horse at full gallop down hill, the wind favorable and a good long rope, an expert may reach 100 feet, but such cases are few and far between, and most good ropers feel extremely pleased when they can reach out the full length of their forty-five foot rope and catch.

If roping was conducted under the conditions to which most athletic competitions are subjected, as regards level ground and standing at a scratch, a fifty foot throw would be a good record, while a seventy-five foot one would be an extraordinary one and, in fact, considered by many to be well nigh impossible. Of course, in throwing a rope, accuracy must be essential. The accomplishment would be a most useful one to the mounted police of large cities, though the full benefit of roping can only be had with the use of the cow saddle.[17]

An exhibition of skill with the lariat at Austin, Texas, at the ... state fair, drew a crowd of 10,000 persons. Ten cowboys contested for a silver-trimmed saddle worth $300, to be given to him who roped, threw and tied down a steer in the shortest space of time. The winner accomplished the feat in 1 minute and 45 seconds.[18]

A colored cowboy at Mobeetie roped, secured and tied down a steer in one minute and thirteen seconds. This is said to be the best time on record.[19]

The cowboys' tournament at the Denver exposition ... will bring ropers here from Texas, New Mexico, Montana,

Wyoming and a whole raft from Colorado. The best record, by the way, in hog-tying a steer at 300 feet run is fifty-eight seconds which was made by a Laramie City boy two years ago. The best time this year was made at Albuquerque fair last week in 1:19, which will probably be discounted at the exposition here this month.[20]

In a cowboy's tournament at Agua Fria, A.T., John Lane roped and tied three steers in 4:49 minutes this being the best time ever made in Arizona. John Merrill beat the record also by roping and tying a single steer in a little over a half a minute.[21]

THE RACE

It was as natural for the cowboy to race as it was for him to ride. This was a superb test of endurance and skill for both man and beast; here the cowboy could, before the eyes of his comrades, vindicate his knowledge and judgment of horseflesh. The cowboy race has been a part of the Western scene since first a man on his pony rode off to greet the rising sun.

The speed-ring attractions closed with a "chicken pulling," in which there were five contestants, mostly cowboys.[22]

The most interesting of all was the cowboy race of five miles, riders to change horses at the end of each mile. There were four entries and the race was run amidst the greatest excitement and some of the changes were made in remarkably quick time and with great expertness. The race was won by the Parker Stable of Canon City. The time was not taken. When the winning rider returned to the stand hundreds of people surrounded him. He won on the last mile by fully 60 feet.[23]

The old-time cowboys of northern Nebraska met at Chadron, Nebraska, October 31, 1892, and organized a company to run a race from that city to the Nebraska building at the World's Fair. The race will be on ponies, and a purse of $1,000 and a gold medal will be given to the winner. It will begin May 15, and nearly 300 riders will take part. In addition to the prizes named the contestants will contribute an entrance fee, which will aggregate several thousand dollars, to be divided among the winners.[24]

Two bicyclists propose to match the relative speed and endurance of the tandem wheeled vehicle and the western broncho during the cowboy race to Chicago. They will cover the distance on their bicycles, with the promise of a large premium if they arrive at the goal before the first horseman. This race between man and beast will be watched with much interest.[25]

A suspicious telegram from Cheyenne, Wyoming, reports that the cowboy race from Chadron, Nebraska, to the world's fair has been declared off. The reason assigned is that the persons entering have failed to put up the stipulated fee. Nothing definite regarding the matter is known, but it is probable that the race will take place just as planned.[26]

The great Chadron cowboy race is on. Just before six o'clock last Tuesday afternoon the shot was fired which was the signal inaugurating what promises to be the greatest race ever seen. There were only ten starters, a great many who entered having been deterred by the threats of the humane society from making the run. One Colorado man, Joe Campbell of Watkins, a few miles east of Denver, is among the contestants. Mrs. Emma Hutchinson went from Denver to Chadron for the purpose of entering the race, but backed out at the last minute. "Doc" Middleton, the outlaw from Chadron, riding the famous Geronimo, is a hot favorite. The start was made at jog trot, which is the gait that is predicted as the winning one. The best judges say that the winning rate of speed will be a uniform one of about sixty miles a day. The winners must have their horses in fairly good condition at the conclusion of the race in order to get the prizes.

A rider cannot have his horse drop dead at the finish and get any money.[27]

Favorites do not seem to be "in it" this year. In fully two-thirds of the big races of the season, outsiders have run away with the money. Not to be out of the style, the cowboy race is offering a repetition of the common occurrence. Doc Middleton, the favorite dropped out at Sioux City with only two-fifths of the distance covered, both of his horses having practically given out. Joe Gillespie and Emmet Albright stand the best chance of winning now, with all the others except Dave Douglass, who dropped out at O'Neil and Middleton who dropped out at Sioux City. still in the race. Most of the horses are in fine condition, and bear no evidence of abuse. The humane official who is accompanying the riders has had no occasion as yet to offer any interference, and probably will not have unless the finish is a close one. Most of the riders used but one horse each during the first half of the race and are now finishing on the before unused animals. They are increasing their speed as they progress, and the leaders expect to finish next Wednesday.[28]

The cowboy race which has stirred up so much discussion has been run and won. Last Tuesday morning at 9:25, just a few hours less than fourteen days from the start, John Berry, riding a little brown broncho stallion, appeared at Buffalo Bill's wild west show in Chicago, the first one in from the 1,000-mile jaunt. A few hours later Emmet Albright, then Joe Gillespie, and still later C. W. Smith appeared. The other riders straggled in the next day. Although Berry, who is an engineer and surveyor for the Elkhorn Valley road, was the first to arrive, it is not likely he will be awarded the cowboy $1,000 prize offered by citizens of Chadron, Nebraska, as he rode under protest, having made the map of the route. Besides this it is claimed that he violated the agreement in riding a half-thoroughbred instead of a broncho. The horses of all the riders as they arrived were inspected by the humane officials and all found to be in good condition, although Berry's stallion had made 150 miles in the previous twenty-four hours, Albright's broncho, 146 miles in the same time, and several of the other horses but a trifle less. The outcome of the race demonstrates the fact, not only that western bronchos are possessed of remarkable endurance, but also that cowboys know how to handle them humanely while still working them to the limit of their powers. The people who have been harping on the inevitable brutality of the race have nothing left to say. There has been no brutality, although better time than was expected has been made.[29]

Paul Fontaine, the judge of the recent cowboy race, awarded the prizes today. It was agreed that he should settle the controversy and his decision satisfied all. These are the amounts each received in the distribution of "Buffalo Bill's Wild West Purse of $500": John Berry $175; Joe B. Gillespie, James H. Stevens, $50 each; C. W. Smith, George A. Jones, $75 each; Doc Middleton, J. E. Albright, Joe Campbell, $25 each.

The Chadron, Nebraska, purse of $1000 was divided as follows: Joe B. Gillespie, C. W. Smith, $200 each; George A. Jones, James H. Stevens, $187.50 each; Doc Middleton, J. E. Albright, Joe Campbell, $75 each.

Winner of saddle offered by Montgomery, Ward & Co., John Berry. Winner of Colt's revolver, Joe Gillespie.[30]

Four cowboys will start from the '49 mining camp in a race to Atlanta, Georgia.... Friendly rivalry is the cause of the race of 906 miles. The contest is for a purse of $2,000 and is between H. G. Payne and Harvey Campbell, representing the stock yards, and Henrico Schultieg, a Spaniard, and Arthur Bingham, alias, "Billy, the Kid," a Chileno is [are] representing the '49 mining camp....[31]

The five-mile cowboy relay race was the event of the week. Each rider was required to ride his horse one mile, change saddles without assistance and remount. Three strings of five horses each were entered, one by Buzzard, of Hotchkiss, Delta county; one by Ben Lowe of Delta, and one by Alex Calhoun of Telluride. Some lightning saddling was done, the changes of the winning rider averaging

12 seconds. Ben Lowe's rider captured first money, Calhoun second, and Buzzard third. Time 12:15, purse $150, of which $100 went to winner of first, $50 to second.[32]

CONTESTS AND TOURNAMENTS

The first cowboy tournaments which attracted spectators in great numbers also drew the attention of the Western journalist. Lively, full-blooded, and detailed descriptions of the events appeared in the newspapers for the benefit of readers who had not attended, and to lure them when next such an opportunity was presented.

The following are the conditions of a match, which, according to the *Stock Growers' Journal*, Miles City, Montana Territory, concluded a recent roundup at the Capital X ranch, to determine the merits of different cutting horses: Each contestant was to cut out ten steers from the roundup, and a man was put into the herd to show the contestants the particular steer to cut, and in all cases the steer should be at least 20 feet from the edge of the roundup. The prizes were to be awarded to the men who should cut the required number of steers in the smoothest and easiest manner with the least amount of running. The time in which it was done not being the deciding point, but simply one of the points to be considered in deciding the match. The fastest time was 4 minutes 30 seconds, and the slowest 10 minutes. The time made by the cowboy to whom the first prize was awarded was 5 minutes 10 seconds; he of the fastest time receiving the second prize. A roping match was held at the same place a few days earlier to decide who could throw and tie a steer in the shortest time after the animal was cut out of the roundup. The best time was 2 minutes 10 seconds; the next best 2 minutes 40 seconds, but in this case the cowboy had to rope the animal twice; his first rope breaking he had to untie a second from his saddle.[33]

At the ... fair at Albuquerque, New Mexico, the cowboy tournament was the main feature. This new feature in Western sports is thus described by the special of the New York *Herald*:

The tournament was to take place at 2 o'clock, and when the hour arrived the display of fine stock and the various products in the main hall were ignored and every one crowded to the race track. In a pen at one end of the enclosure were a dozen wild Texas steers, just driven in from the range, chafing and bellowing over their confinement in such close quarters. These wild creatures were to be released from the pen one at a time, and as each dashed from the enclosure out into the open field a chosen cowboy was to mount his horse, rope in hand, fly forward in pursuit, rope the animal, throw it down and dismount and tie its feet together in one bunch, or, as the boys term it, "hog tie" it. It seems an incredible feat, and yet the experienced cowboy can accomplish it in a few seconds. The boy who roped and tied his steer in the shortest space of time was to receive the first prize, an elegant saddle, valued at $75.

The first animal released was a noble black fellow. For a moment he stood gazing upon the great crowd outside of the fence, his eyes distended, his flanks quivering, and then, with a defiant toss of the head, he flew away like a deer. In a moment a cowboy was in pursuit, swinging his riata over his head in graceful circles and with voice and spur urging his horse to greater speed. Closer and closer he drew to the fleeing steer until the opportune moment arrived, when the rope left his hand and flew through the air. A shout of derision went up from the other cowboys when it was seen that he had failed to catch the animal, and when he rode back to the waiting group his ears were assailed by such cries as "Was your rope too short, Johnny?" "Go and get it stretched," "Go off and corral yourself," etc. It was afterward learned that he was an amateur, who had been on the range but a few months, and the boys forgave him and told him he did very well for a "tenderfoot."

A moment later the signal was given, and a beautiful red steer, with flashing eyes, came forth, and, without pausing an instant was off like a flash. "Whoop, la!" shouted Dick Greer, as he sprang upon his wiry little animal and dashed in pursuit. It seemed but a moment ere his rope was seen to leave his hands and fly through the air, dropping over the horns of the affrighted steer. Like a flash his well-trained horse wheeled and started on the back track, bracing him for the coming shock. A second later a rope, which was secured to the horn of the saddle, became taut, and the steer rolled over on the ground. He was on his feet again instantly, leaping, tugging at the rope and bellowing with rage and fear, but the horse, which had turned about and was facing the animal, braced his feet forward and held the struggling animal securely until he ceased his mad antics and stood looking defiantly at his captor. With an easy, swinging gallop Greer now started his pony around the animal until he had described a circle, which brought the rope around the steer's legs, and then starting his horse off at a right angle, the rope suddenly tightened, the animal's legs were drawn together and he again rolled to the ground. "Now hold him!" shouted the rider, as he sprang to the ground, and the noble little animal braced himself and held the fallen creature so securely that he could not release his legs from the rope. As Greer ran toward the struggling beast, he drew a short piece of rope from his belt, sprang upon the prostrate steer, and in less time than it requires for me to write it stood erect and held up his hat as a sign that the feat was accomplished. The three judges galloped forward to see that the work was done according to the rules, and announced the time as one minute and fifty-eight seconds. The announcement was greeted with loud cheers from the assembled multitude and Dick was highly complimented by his fellow knights of the rope and saddle.

There were several trials of skill of a similar nature, the time of the winner, I believe, being one minute and forty-two seconds from the time the steer left the pen until he lay on the ground securely tied.

The pen was then filled with unbroken bronchos whose backs had never felt the pressure of the saddle. The cowboy ever prides himself upon his horsemanship, and a lively interest was manifested in this contest of skill and expertness. According to the rules each horse was to be roped in the corral, who was to ride it must succeed in bridling it, then the rope was removed and the task begun.

The first horse brought out showed an unusually vicious spirit, leaping and pitching, and striking wickedly with his forefeet. It was found necessary to throw him to the ground before he could be bridled, and this was accomplished by roping his hind feet and suddenly pulling them from under him, at the same time pulling him over with the rope, which encircled his neck. After being thrown he was bridled and blindfolded, and then allowed to regain his feet. Being unable to see he stood trembling in every limb, but made no attempt to escape. He was quickly saddled, and, with a quick, easy motion, the cowboy sprang to his back and fixed himself firmly in the saddle, and then, reaching over the animal's head he snatched away the blind and the fun began. For a moment the air seemed to be filled with whooping cowboy, broncho legs and dust, and then, with terrific leaps, the animal bounded away. Its every effort to dislodge its rival proved futile, the daring equestrian sitting as unconcernedly as if the animal were standing still. After exhausting itself, it walked about sullenly at the guidance of the rider, and was soon released and sent scampering back to the herd.

This "bucking" horse tournament ended the sports of the day, and wilder or more exciting sport was never seen at a state fair in America.[34]

[Montrose, Colorado, September, 1887.]

The cowboys' tournament in which roping from the ground, from the saddle, heading and heeling, riding bucking bronchos, etc., afforded much sport, but well nigh terminated fatally. One of the cowboys was riding a bucking broncho when the animal made a dash towards where the ladies were seated and could not be checked before he struck Mrs. James A. Ladd, who was thrown violently to the ground beneath the animal's hoofs. The horse struck the lady with its front feet on her chest and pinioned her to the earth for a second or two, but he was quickly grasped by one or two gentlemen who stood near the lady and prevented from trampling her to death. Every lady on the grounds screamed and one or two fainted.[35]

[Denver, Colorado, October, 1887.]
The cowboy tournament was a success both as to attendance and exhibition. More than 8,000 spectators crowded the grandstand and grounds. They were packed in like sardines on the unroofed amphitheater and massed twenty deep around the big corral. Nearly all of them could see. All of them could yell and they all did.

It was both a novel and a great show. There wasn't much hippodrome about it. Every cowboy who entered the arena did his best, and the untamed broncos and long horned steers did their best to get away. It was hard work for all of them and yet everybody enjoyed it.

The cowboys were real, the broncos were real and the steers were to the manor [manner] born. The horses and the steers struck and kicked and squealed and bellowed, while gentlemen in silk hats pounded with their canes and ladies clapped their gloved hands together in excited delight, and the cowboy yell mingled with the cheers from everywhere.

The crowd of itself was a sight worth going to see. Long before 2 o'clock a line of people a half block long were extended from the ticket window up the street. Tickets couldn't be sold fast enough. Carriages in a long line passed through the big gates for a solid hour and yet they were still coming. The small boy and big boy hoodlum dispensed with the formality of buying admission pasteboards and jumped the fence. Small boys, more than a score, crawled under the grand stand, dug holes for their heads through the dirt and looked out upon the show. When a dashing horse or a wildly plunging steer threw the dirt in their eyes the whole row of heads disappeared, only to bob back in a twinkling.

So eager were the crowd around the high fence to see that they stood on anything. Twelve men mounted one horse and when the animal fell under them with the strain they all tumbled together. Every now and then a board would become too heavily loaded with men and boys who persisted in climbing on it and down would come the whole row with a crash. From one of these falls Walter Conger sustained a broken arm and dislocated a shoulder. He was taken to the Eagle Hotel and given surgical attendance.

All in all it was a big day for the Exposition and the people. The feats of horsemanship and cowman's exploits were performed with a great deal of vim and some skill. The time made by William Cook in roping and tying a steer so that the animal could not move was remarkable and only a few seconds greater than the best on record....

Bill Smith was the first man in the ring. He rode out on a clean-limbed pony and waved his hat in response to the greeting of admiring friends. Then the bunch of broncos that had never known a rope were turned in. A sorrel was pointed out to Smith and after him he went. A throw from the pony was unsuccessful and the bronco dashed away with his head up and tail streaming. Smith dismounted and tried it on foot. His rope whirled through the air and when the loop came down it was over the now thoroughly frightened animal's head. Then came the tug of war. Around the corral the horse dragged the man, the rope all the time drawing tighter and tighter and choking the captive. The battle was short and sharp. The bronco plunged and kicked and pulled, but every tug cost him a foot of liberty, for the iron-muscled man was gradually crawling upon him. At last, trembling in every nerve, the brute stood still. Then came the delicate work of putting on the blinds. Once, twice it was essayed, but the horse didn't understand that little cap, and with a snort and plunge he shook it off. At last it was fastened and before the astonished animal knew what was up the blanket and saddle were deftly thrown on his back. How he did buck and kick and squeal! But the nervy hands were fast at work and the cinch was drawn and straps buckled in a twinkling, while all the time the rope was choking tighter and tighter. Then into the saddle vaulted the victor.

Buck!

Buck isn't a name for it. Up in the air and down with all four legs bunched stiff as an antelope's, and back arched like a hostile wildcat's, went the animal. But the rider was there, and deep into the bowels he sank the spurs, while he lashed shoulders and neck with the keen stinging quirt. It was brute force against human nerve. Nerve won. A few more jumps and the horse submitted and carried the man around the corral on a swinging lope. It had all been done in seven and a half minutes. The crowd cheered, and an admirer dropped a box of cigars into the hands of the perspiring but plucky victor.

Frank Wells of Living Springs appeared and a small dark bay was pointed out to him. The rope circled a few times and settled over the animal's head. The next instant Wells was rolling in the dust. Around and around the corral he chased the horse, and three times he caught the rope with determined grip. But the cunning brute was as quick as lightning and would dash into the midst of the bunch of unfastened animals and drag the man rolling and tumbling until the rope tore the skin from his hands and he had to let go. Wells would corner him and almost get a firm hold on the lasso, when with a spring one way and then a dash in another the wild bronco would get away. The contest lasted fifteen minutes, and at length the judges called time.

Pinto Jim was the name of the next cowman. He was a rawboned colored man. A sorrel was pointed out to him. He made several failures in getting the rope in the right place and then had a battle that was fierce. At last, when the horse was well nigh worn out with constant plunging, Jim caught a jacquima [jaquima] on him, had a saddle in place and was on his back in a minute more. Thirteen minutes were consumed, but the crowd cheered the perspiring man, nevertheless, and he deserved it.

A gamier animal than the sorrel that Bronco Jim Davis, another colored man, fought with for nearly half an hour never wore hair. He wouldn't give up. The rope was around his neck and drawn so tight that twice he fell down, but the man could go no farther. Every attempt to put the blinds over his eyes would be met with fiercest resistance. Up on his hind legs the animal would rear and strike with a viciousness that knew no taming. Davis had him down time and again and tied him as often. It became evident that a prolongation of the fight meant death to the horse or injury to the man. Davis's blood was up, and he practiced the cruelest tactics. But nothing would subdue the wild creature. The judges at last ordered the contest stopped, and the crowd were glad to witness it no farther.

None knew who the next man was who rode out on a white pony. They called him Dull Knife and he was from Meeker. That was all the information obtainable. But Dull Knife was a daisy. With new white sombrero, Mexican saddle, leather-fringed chaparejos, flaming red 'kerchief, belt and ivory-handled revolver and knife, he was all that the Eastern imagination of the typical cowboy could picture. As a bronco-breaker, however, he wasn't a brilliant success. A bay was pointed out to him and away they flew. It didn't take that cunning bay bronco more than a second to determine that he would fool somebody. Dashing here and there, with flashing eyes and streaming mane and tail, the animal was a pretty picture. The white pony was too cunning for him, though, and soon put his rider in a position where the rope could be thrown and the arched neck caught in the running loop. The captive was thrown by twining the rope around his limbs and then Dull Knife made a skillful move. He cut the rope loose and held the struggling animal by the nose. But while he was subduing the horse the man had gotten too far away from his saddle and couldn't get back to it. The judges at length called time and the pretty bay was free.

F. Maxwell was a tall, well-formed athletic man, and he went for a sorrel animal with a rush. His work was expeditious and skillful and not three minutes had elapsed before the saddle was on. Maxwell took a Mexican hitch around his horse's nose and had the brute under perfect control—until he mounted. Then there was a whole circus and sacred concert to wind up with. Up and down went the fractious animal. And finally with a sudden spring and wild plunge he unseated Maxwell, who fell against the side of the corral ingloriously on his back. As he struck the dust the vicious heels of the bronco smashed against the boards, missing Maxwell's head by a hair. The rider was on his animal again in a twinking, but the fall had ruined his chance of winning.

Another great feature of sport was in readiness when the horsebreaking was over. A bunch of wild steers which had never known handling since they were branded, were let into the corral. The initiatory contest was to rope and "hog-tie" a steer. Dull Knife was the opening candidate for honors. He chased a steer around several times and made several ineffectual efforts at catching the animal's leg. At last he put the rope over the horns and then ensued a doughty tussle. Twice he was down and twice he was on his feet before the rider could get to him. The judges at last called time as it was evident the steer was hurt and ugly and the horse too tired to continue the contest. When the animal was released it showed one hind foot broken. The time was 6 minutes. Troy Franklin rode out bare headed and looked generally tough; but Franklin was a singed cat. He captured his steer on the first throw and tangled the struggling animal up so that it didn't know whether it was on its horns or its tail. Franklin made a neat "hog-tie" and when he held up his hand the watch showed a time of 3 minutes and 15 seconds.

William Cook of Platteville appeared again and made a marvelous catch and tie. Cook was attired in typical costume. He worked like a flash. The first throw caught the animal and a sudden skillful turn of his horse brought the steer down. Cook was off and on the surprised animal's back and endeavored to force it over by main strength. The big fellow shook him off and made another dash. This time Cook caught him sure and make a quick and solid tie. One horn of the steer was broken by a fall when it went tumbling on its head. The time was close to the best on record and was announced, amid cheers, to be 1 minute and 55 seconds.

The actual count of those present yesterday is as follows: Tickets sold 7,700; free admissions, 800; exhibitors and employes, 300; total, 8,800.[36]

A roping contest has been arranged for the [San Antonio] State Fair to be participated in by the cowboys. Thirty-five head of wild cattle, mostly young steers, are to be brought from the coast jungles, longhorn fellows, to be used for the purpose. $300 have been set aside by the association to be given as premiums, $100 for the first prize, $50 for the second and $25 for the third. The three best ropers will thus capture $175 of the money appropriated for the purpose. The remaining $125 will be given to a second contest, the participants to consist of the three poorest ropers in the first contest.

The limit of entries in the contest is to be 25 men, the entry fee to be $10 each.

The judges are to be selected from known experts in the roping and handling of cattle. The Fairgoers will thus have a splendid opportunity to note the difference between skilled and unskilled ropers.

There will be five judges; two to supervise the tying and two the time occupied in throwing and tying; the fifth to preside.

Rules to govern the contest are substantially as follows: The ropers are to draw their numbers from a hat or box, and rope in order of their number. Steer to have 40 feet the start from the mouth of the chute before word is given to "go." Roper to be near the chute with rope done up to horn of saddle, with right hand raised above his head so that all can see he is not holding the rope instead of the horn string on the saddle.

When the animal has been roped and tied down, the roper must hold both hands up in the air that the time keepers may get the exact time occupied in throwing and tying. The tying must consist of no less than three legs—two fore and one hind leg. The judges are to be mounted, that the animal may be reached as soon as possible after tying.

This is a splendid opportunity for some of our active cowboys to establish a reputation and the *Stock Journal* will be there to write the name of the happy ones in the foreground.[37]

[The roping contest is] a feature peculiar to the range stock industry, and as this section of the country is the cradle of this industry, it is here [San Antonio, Texas,] that is supposed to be where the crack ropers are to be found. Much interest has been manifested in this feature of the fair, but owing to several postponements the crowd to witness the contest that took place last Saturday was not nearly as great as it would have been had the weather permitted the carrying out of the programme according to the first intention. As it was, the attendance was one of the largest of the fair. Also, several contestants who originally intended to compete were absent. The cattle consisted of heifers which are considered by many as more difficult to catch than steers.

The cowboys who entered the contest were J. B. Moore, S. E. Lewis, James Cueller, Green Hollen, Jesse Barton, A. B. Horton, J. A. Bennett, W. P. Brown, Dick Johnson and Simms Guerrera.

Moore roped, threw and tied his cow in 59½ seconds and won first prize of $100; Lewis in 1:17¼ secured the second prize; Cueller in 1:18½ secured the third, and $50 prize, and Hollen got the $25 fourth prize in 1:26¼. Horton's time was 1:39 1/5 and he threw his cow five times before he could tie her. Barton failed to get his cow before he was ordered out, and his animal broke down the fence and had to be led back by a bystander who roped her. Guerrera failed utterly also to get his cow, and it took Johnson two minutes and eight and a-half seconds to capture and tie his steer. Moore belongs to Live Oak county, and the boys from there were hilarious over the victory of their favorite. Dick Johnson formerly belonged to Buffalo Bill's outfit, and it was he who had the fight with the London police, and was sent to prison for six months, but was pardoned through the intercession of the Prince of Wales.[38]

In connection with the mid-summer fair [Calgary, Canada,] there will be a series of interesting cowboy sports. Mr. Geo. Lane, of High River, is making all the necessary arrangements. The first event will be a roping contest by the crack ropers of the Northwest. Wild steers will be driven in from the ranges and each competitor will have an animal selected for him by the judges. A watch will be held on him from the start, until the steer is tied down with three feet. The man who performs this feat in the shortest time is the winner. The first prize will be a $75 saddle presented by Messrs. Carson & Shore; second prize a silver mounted bridle and spurs from the society. Another event will be a cowboy race—600 yards with three turns around the post. The first prize will be a $75 saddle presented by Messrs. Hutchings & Riley; second prize same as in the roping contest. This is the first thing of the kind ever attempted in Calgary and should prove one of the most attractive features of the fair.[39]

The [above mentioned] exhibition was entirely new to probably a majority of those present and they watched the sport with the keenest enjoyment. The horses bestrode by the cowboys were important factors in the contest. The hardy little brutes seemed to be possessed of human intelligence and the manner in which they performed their allotted parts was a revelation.[40]

... Cheyenne has announced a "Frontier Day" for Thursday, September 23, 1897. It is to be devoted to the games and sports and exhibitions which have made the range and the border famous throughout the land. There will be wild horse races and broncho riding, and lassoing, and an Indian attack on a stage coach, and other incidents peculiar to the early days on the frontier. Such an exhibition can be made one of especial interest, and there is no point in the West where it can better be presented than at Cheyenne.

It is a strange assertion to make, but it is true, nevertheless, that very many people both in Colorado and Wyoming have but a very faint idea of the frontier scenes which it is proposed to reproduce at Cheyenne, and that until the first Mountain and Plain Festival in this city, perhaps a majority of the people of Denver had never seen an Indian. Hence the interest which can be given to a frontier day, and the opportunity of enjoying it should not be neglected. Railroad rates from Denver and all Northern Colorado points over the Gulf and Union Pacific lines have been made so low, and the trains run at such convenient hours, that a large attendance should be assured at this event. If we remember correctly, it is the first thing in the line of a festival that Cheyenne has ever attempted, and as her people are annual patrons of our Mountain and Plain Festival it is hoped that this city will send a train load of people to witness her Frontier Day exhibition, and partake of the hospitality of Cheyenne people.[41]

No single event of the autumn festival season has aroused a larger degree of interest than Frontier Day at Cheyenne. Old timers are familiar with the pastimes of the cowboys, and with their famous feats of riding and roping, with the pony express and the stage coach and the prairie schooner, and Indian raids, not to mention an occasional organization known as a vigilance committee. It has been many years, however, since they have seen or had any practical experience with these things which used to be every day events back in the 60's. During these intervening years, however, Colorado and Wyoming have filled up with people from the East, and children or grandchildren have grown up who know nothing about them, and who listen to the stories of grey-headed plainsmen and pioneers very much as they do to fairy tales. ...[42]

[Arkansas Valley Fair, Rocky Ford, Colorado, September, 1900.]
... the largest third day crowd in its history thronged the steer throwing exhibition. It was not an inspiring spectacle, but there was nothing revolting in it. There was no blood drawn and not so much suffering as is commonly inflicted in the process of branding.

A company of cowboys rounded up the herd in the center of the speed ring and lassoed one of the steers. Then the three Pickett brothers came forward and seized the animal by the horns. While the lasso ropes were still on him, two of them fastened a rope with hand loops around the steer's body. One of them mounted, the creature was turned loose and bounded down the race course. The crowd, safe upon the grand stands, yelled and the crowds lining the ring fences scattered indiscriminately, but he was not a very wild steer, and soon submitted to being ridden without ado. He was turned back in to the herd and another selected.

He was a fine Texan, and gave his tormentors more trouble. The lasso ropes chanced to get around the animal's neck and his tongue lolled out. The crowd protested, and many of the women left the stand. One was heard to remark, "I've seen all I want to." Another woman exclaimed, "Pshaw, I've seen worse than that on the range." The chief of the three performers, having got the bull finally by the horns, simply twisted his neck till he succumbed and rolled over on the ground, while the crowd applauded. Then, with the aid of the two brothers, he climbed upon the back of the beast and rode across the grounds. He had not ridden far when the animal lay down on him and refused to be further entertaining.

He was therefore abandoned and a third steer loosed from the corrals on the grounds. This one was of better mettle and at once made a spirited break for liberty, going through the first fence and gracefully over the second, out in the open country. After him rode half a dozen cowboys and he was soon brought back. The ropers held him fast until the three negroes approached him carefully from the rear. As they did so he gave one of them a ferocious kick, but did not disable him. William Pickett grasped the creature by the horns to twist, but with a ferocious rush he broke away and had to be run down again by the horses. Again the negro took him by the horns and was tossed overhead, but held his grip upon the horns. Then the mad beast rushed him to the fence, got him down and pinned him to the earth. It was one more round for the steer, but the two brothers came to the rescue again and the pinioned negro, being released, again got the animal by the horns and, securing his twist upon the steer's neck, brought him to the ground and held him there. The crowd cheered and the negro let the steer up and mounted his back. The fagged brute staggered three times in his attempt to rise with the negro upon him, but the fourth time he succeeded and made one more bold dash down the track. The crowd on the railing fell back as the beast threatened to take the fence again, but the cowboys closed in and rounded him up, the negro slid off his back, waved his adieus to the applauding crowd and the show was out.[43]

PRAISE AND PROTEST

The widespread publicity given to the cowboy tournament by the press was bound to bring forth differences of opinion as to the true worth of such entertainment. Public opinion in favor of cowboy contests finally prevailed. In succeeding years they were to grow in size and number until the riding and roping techniques of the range became recognized as the nationally known cowboy competition and sport—rodeo!

The cowboy tournament attracted nearly ten thousand persons to the Exposition grounds yesterday afternoon. The entertainment which the cowboys furnished was decidedly novel and well worth witnessing. Wild horses were lassoed, saddled and ridden, and steers were lassoed from the herd, thrown and tied. As a whole it was unique and characteristic, and it was so well received by the vast audience that there can be no question that such an exhibition could be made successful annually.

We believe that if the right kind of men would take the management of an enterprise of this character a week's tournament could be given in Denver every fall that would attract thousands of visitors from all parts of the United States. Cowboys from all over the West would come here to compete for the prizes which would be offered.

It is much more desirable, and decidedly more profitable to get up a show that is peculiarly Western in its characteristics than to imitate the methods of the East. The tournament of yesterday was as exciting as a bull fight, without the latter's barbarous features. It was thoroughly enjoyed by the large audience. It is the kind of sport nine men in ten like, and if Denver is wide awake she will give similar exhibitions every year and advertise them thoroughly all over the country.[44]

The Humane Society threatens to arrest the Chamber of Commerce if it repeats the cowboy exhibition of yesterday. The prospects of a conflict between two institutions of such prominence is interesting. But it will be wise for both to act with judgment. The Chamber of Commerce Committee which is running the Exposition should not permit any amateur cow-punchers to take part in the contests, and the Humane Society should keep cool even if a steer should bark his shins or break off a horn. We believe that the gentlemen of the Chamber of Commerce may be trusted to keep the exhibition within bounds, and we therefore suggest that the Humane Society employ its time today in hunting up the poor humans who, though lame and sick, are compelled to labor while in constant pain and the little children who are half-fed and badly clothed. We offer this simply as a suggestion.[45]

To The Republican:

Numerous complaints have come to the Humane Society as to the way the exhibition at the Exposition was conducted yesterday. The society is informed that out of a dozen or fifteen steers roped, one had a horn broken and one a leg, and that one horse had his neck "kinked" in being roped. It is unnecessary to say to anyone at all familiar with the cattle business that such is not an exhibition of scientific cattle-roping, but of botch work, which all cattlemen must in self-defense condemn. No cattleman would employ a man for fifteen minutes who would cripple one steer out of every dozen he roped. An expert would not have been guilty of brutality and awkwardness such as must have occurred yesterday in order to maim and disable so large a number out of so few roped. When Buffalo Bill was exhibiting in the Wild West show in New York three years ago, the first horn broken killed that feature of his show completely. The same thing happened in London.

The people who went to the Exposition grounds yesterday paid their money to see how cattle are handled on the plains, not to see horns and legs broken and horses maimed for life by inexperienced men on green horses. The spectacle of dumb animals like cattle and horses maimed and bleeding in the view of gazing thousands is one not calculated to please humane people or to raise the managers of the exhibition much in their esteem. Such inhuman scenes are well calculated to prejudice the public against the cattle business on account of its brutality and barbarity.

The Agent of the Humane Society was present on the grounds but was unable to get near enough to see what occurred. The Humane Society gives notice that if today's exhibition is characterized by the same bad management and witnesses a repetition of the disgraceful scene of yesterday the proceeding will be stopped.

E. K. WHITEHEAD
Secretary Colorado Humane Society[46]

When the cowboy fell from his horse at the tournament yesterday it was thought at first the fall had killed him. The audience fully expected to see the Humane Society step in and stop the show. But the H.S. had its eye on the steer. It did not see the cowboy.[47]

This afternoon and evening the cowboy tournament will be continued and persons who have never seen the cowboy in his element should not miss this rare treat. The sport is exhilerating and the excitement it creates is something wonderful. It consists of roping or lassoing, and saddling and riding of wild bronchos who do not know the touch of man.... The performance will conclude with an exhibition by Professor Blake of his new method of breaking and training vicious and spoiled horses by kindness, showing the effect of five lessons on a bunch of eight bronchos that had never been handled up to ten days ago.[48]

[Denver, Colorado, September, 1890.]
The alleged cowboy tournament given at Broadway Athletic Park yesterday afternoon and evening was a howling farce, both from a point of merit and attendance. While the fact remains undisputed that each contestant is possessed of marked ability in his particular line of

work, yet the rough handling of dumb brutes for the public's amusement received a back-set yesterday that will long be remembered by those interested in its management.

The seating capacity of the park yesterday was not overtaxed by the 200 people in attendance for many left before the performance was over.[49]

The hide-bound editor of the *Texas Live Stock Journal* grows cynical when he says: "A humane society at Denver prevented a steer-roping contest by interfering with the program. Humane societies, while they embrace a great many good people, are largely made up of cranks, who neglect their families while running around over the country to put a plaster on the raw end of a stump-tail pig."[50]

NOTES TO CHAPTER TEN

1. Cf. Clifford P. Westermeier, *Man, Beast, Dust: The Story of Rodeo* (Denver, 1947); Westermeier, "Seventy-Five Years of Rodeo in Colorado," *Colorado Magazine*, XXVIII (January, 1951), 13-14.
2. A letter written by Captain Mayne Reid to Samuel Arnold of Drumnakelly, Seaforde, county Down, Ireland. Now in the manuscript collection of Colin Johnston Robb, Drumharriff Lodge, Loughgall, county Armagh, Ireland.
3. *Field and Farm* (Denver, Colorado), July 8, 1899, p. 6.
4. *Ibid.*, July 4, 1896, p. 6.
5. *Cheyenne Daily Leader* (Cheyenne, Wyoming), July 6, 1872.
6. *Ibid.*, September 11, 1873.
7. "A Genuine Bull Fight," *Caldwell Standard* (Caldwell, Kansas), July 3, 1884.
8. "'Tailing' a Steer," *Denver Tribune-Republican* (Denver, Colorado), November 22, 1885.
9. "Arizona Rodeo Notes," *Stock Grower and Farmer* (Las Vegas, New Mexico), October 11, 1890.
10. "A Company of Cowboys," *Texas Live Stock Journal* (Fort Worth, Texas), May 5, 1883, p. 1.
11. "The Cowboys' Exhibition," *ibid.*, May 12, 1883, p. 1.
12. "Northern New Mexico," *Cattlemen's Advertiser* (Trinidad, Colorado), August 13, 1885.
13. *Democratic Leader* (Cheyenne, Wyoming), April 11, 1886.
14. "Gould's Private Wild West Show," *Texas Live Stock Journal*, April 12, 1890, p. 6.

15. "A Cowboy Herder," *Denver Republican* (Denver, Colorado), December 5, 1892.
16. "Ropes and Roping," *Cattlemen's Advertiser*, December 2, 1886.
17. "Roping with the Lariat," *Deming Headlight* (Deming, New Mexico), January 11, 1890.
18. "Stock Notes," *Las Animas Leader* (Las Animas, Colorado), December 15, 1882.
19. "Live Stock Notes," *Fort Morgan Times* (Fort Morgan, Colorado), November 13, 1884.
20. *Field and Farm*, October 1, 1887, p. 9.
21. *Ibid.*, September 14, 1889, p. 9.
22. "The Gunnison Fair," *Denver Republican*, September 30, 1888.
23. *Denver Republican*, October 5, 1888.
24. "A Novel Race," *Stock Grower and Farmer*, November 26, 1892.
25. *Field and Farm*, May 20, 1893, p. 9.
26. *Ibid.*, May 27, 1893, p. 9.
27. *Ibid.*, June 17, 1893, p. 9.
28. *Ibid.*, June 24, 1893, p. 9.
29. *Ibid.*, July 1, 1893, p. 9.
30. "Cowboys Awarded Prizes," *Denver Republican*, July 2, 1893.
31. "Another Cowboy Race," *ibid.*, August 15, 1895.
32. "Races at Montrose Fair," *ibid.*, September 26, 1897.
33. "Cowboy Dexterity," *Texas Live Stock Journal*, November 14, 1885, p. 2.
34. "A Cow-Boy Contest," *Rocky Mountain News* (Denver, Colorado), January 4, 1886.
35. "The Montrose Fair," *Denver Republican*, September 30, 1887.
36. "Cowboys and Wild Horses," *ibid.*, October 15, 1887. (This contest was held ten years before the inauguration of the world-famous Cheyenne Frontier Days.)
37. "A Roping Contest," *Texas Live Stock Journal*, June 30, 1888, p. 10.
38. "The Roping Contest," *ibid.*, December 1, 1888, p. 14.
39. *Calgary Weekly Herald* (Calgary, Alberta, Canada), May 16, 1893.
40. *Ibid.*, June 25, 1893.
41. "Cheyenne's Frontier Day," *Rocky Mountain News*, September 15, 1897.
42. "Sports of the Plains," *ibid.*, September 20, 1897.
43. "Struggles of Man and Beast," *Denver Republican*, September 8, 1900. This is one of the earliest accounts of the cowboy event—bulldogging or steer wrestling. Cf. "Bull Fight Plan Is Thrown Over." *Denver Republican*, November 26, 1898; "Says Texas Holds Steer Roping Record," *ibid.*, August 28, 1903. Both accounts mention a Texas Negro who used the tactics of a thoroughbred bulldog to hold the steer after it had been thrown by hand.

44. "The Cowboy Tournament," *Denver Republican*, October 15, 1887.

45. *Denver Republican*, October 15, 1887. Cf. Westermeier, "Cowboy Sports and the Humane Society," *Colorado Magazine*, XXVI (October, 1949), 241-44.

46. "The Humane Society," *Denver Republican*, October 15, 1887.

47. *Denver Republican*, October 16, 1887.

48. "Cowboy Tournament Today," *Rocky Mountain News*, September 9, 1890.

49. "It Was a Fizzle," *Denver Republican*, September 10, 1890.

50. *Field and Farm*, October 4, 1890, p. 9.

Sunset Trail

ELEVEN

    The phenomenal rise of the cowboy in the short span of two decades to a position where he, as the most important and notorious figure, dominated the cattle industry, was in part due to exploitation by the journalist. There is no denying that, in himself, the cowboy presented a romantic, colorful, glamorous figure, but this is true only in the light of the more adventuresome aspects of his life and his infrequent contacts with civilization. The roundup, trail drives, riding herd, the breaking of wild horses, the roping and branding of cattle, the stampede, the storms of dust and wind, and the blizzards gave birth to exciting, stimulating, and fascinating stories, when bound between the covers of a magazine or when used as a "filler" in a newspaper column. However, to the cowboy these cruel elements of nature and work were the crude, harsh, dangerous realities of his hard life.

Long winter evenings sped by rapidly and bowls of apples and popcorn disappeared as avid readers about the wild West appeased greedy, insatiable appetites. Every phase of the cowboy's life and his work, his traits and adventures, were elaborated in detail in these tales of the Great Plains; and a special pleasure rose out of the exaggerated lawlessness, recklessness, and immorality of the man. As this information concerning the cowboy spread through periodicals and newspapers, the readers demanded more; the journalist continued to supply it, but at this time a new note appeared in his tone of writing.

Changes were taking place in the cow country; the westward-reaching railroads brought the farmer; with him came the breaking up of the range, the rise of towns, and, finally, the collapse of the range cattle industry. Law, order, improvement, politics, system, and capital came to the West. The free, raw, wild and woolly frontier was being leveled and smoothed by the inevitable pressure of civilization. The men who opened the West now stood by it and became its first citizens, for, having made it a reality, they now wished to maintain it as such. Among these citizens of the new West there was none more staunch than the cowboy. He was steadier and quieter now, but still hard working and loyal. He continued in the trade he knew and loved and was willing to practice it under the changed conditions of his environment.

The Western journalist witnessed this momentous change and anticipated the result—the passing of the cowboy—but his fluent pen had, by this time, already made the cowboy known to the nation and to the world. The cowboy was the last of the West's children and its most beloved; his passing was dramatized at the beginning of the end of his brief, short hour, for he was the most chivalrous of modern heroes.

FAREWELL COWBOY!

Professor E. H. Moore, of Colorado, read a paper at the National Stock Growers Association, St. Louis, Missouri, 1885, upon "The Cattle Industry of the United States" in which he presented many statistics and favored national quarantine laws. Concerning the practice of illegal fencing of the public lands, he said:

"This is as much condemned by the range men as it would be by Connecticut farmers; we only want what the law gives us, the right to occupy these lands until settlers come; and now that we can come from our ranches in palace cars, it is plain to see that the days of the range are numbered; as the Indian gave way to the pioneer, so must the cowboy go before the settler, and the rancher take the place of the ranger, until eight million acres of land now roamed by cattle shall teem with villages and model farms for the cultivation of refined cattle cared for —not by cowboys with revolvers—but by cowboys with brains."[1]

The festive cowboy has been quite numerous around the bulyvards this week, but like the baron, his glory has departed. The heels of his boots are as high as of yore, but when he sits "straddle-legged" on the corner of a monte table now he "blows in" a quarter when formerly he staked a note, and though he still damns a sheepman, he no longer rolls his profanity under his tongue like a sweet morsel, but wears the look which indicates but too plainly that the barbed-wire fence and "the man with the hoe," have done him up. Farewell, festive cuss, and as you "pull your freight" towards the setting sun, you may find in the land of the Montezumas long-eared mavericks and dark-eyed senoritas to console you for your enforced expatriation, and may you never be forced to herd sheep, edit a newspaper, or rob stages, as some of the rest of us have to do to make an honest living. What though in your palmy days you were a trifle "handy with your pop," and had a deep aversion to eating your own beef, you were ever gentle with children and women with a chivalrous courtesy worthy a knight of the middle ages; quickly lured by the song of the siren and an easy prey to the wiles of the sport, you never "roared" when they "tapped your game," or proposed to a newspaper man to "shake" as long as you had a quarter. Festive cuss, farewell.[2]

The cowboy has at the present day become a personage; nay, more, he is rapidly becoming a mythical one. Distance is doing for him what lapse of time did for the heroes of antiquity. His admirers are investing him with all manner of romantic qualities; they descant upon his manifold virtues and his pardonable weaknesses as if he were a demi-god, and I have no doubt that before long there will be ample material for any philosophic inquirer who may wish to enlighten the world as to the cause and meaning of the cowboy myth. Meanwhile the true character of the cowboy has become obscured, his genuine qualities are lost in fantastic tales of impossible daring and skill, of dare-devil equitation and unexampled endurance. Every member of his class is pictured as a kind of Buffalo Bill, as a long-haired ruffian who, decked out in gaudy colors and tawdry ornaments, booted like a cavalier, and chivalrous as a Paladin, his belt stuck full of knives and pistols, make the world to resound with bluster and braggadocio. From this character the cowboy of fact is entirely distinct. It is true he is brave and independent; he is reckless of his own life, and pays small heed to the lives of others; but he is not of those who seek the bubble reputation by meaningless folly and overbearing swagger. He is in the main a loyal, longenduring, hardworking fellow, grit to the backbone, and tough as whipcord; performing his arduous and often dangerous duties, and living his comfortless life, without a word of complaint about the many privations he has to undergo.[3]

One of the most picturesque characters to be found in the story of American frontier life, the cowboy, will soon be seen no more. There will be great farms devoted to stock raising for many years to come, but the cowboy of the unfenced range has lost his occupation. The range has been covered first on one side and then on another by the flood-tide of homesteaders, until there is no place left in the southwest, save on the waste lands of the Indian territory and a part of western Texas, where cattle can be raised and kept on the range, subsisting on the grass and water that nature supplied spontaneously the year round. No Man's Land, which from its not being subject to entry would, one would think, have been the last stronghold of the cowman, as the cattle-owner is called, and his assistant, the cowboy, has been cut up into homesteads, and but one cattle range worth mentioning, that of Ludwig Kramer, on Clear Creek, remains, and he has but hundreds of cattle where once there were tens of thousands.

The cowboy resisted the grangers, as they call the settlers, desperately. They drove their herds across the settlers' fields, they rounded up and drove the settlers' little bunches of cattle and horses off. They shot his sheep and hogs. They shot the settler himself. One case is on record where two settlers were bound in chains, saturated with kerosene, set on fire and burned to death. But the advance of the settler was not even checked by the efforts of the cowboy. The settler could and did shoot as well as the cowboy, and for every stalk of corn and for every sheep and hog that fell before the advancing herds of cattle and their attendants it is likely that ten steers paid the cost with their lives, and quite as many cowboys as settlers died violent deaths. With the cowman it was a question of profit. As he got hemmed in by the settlers he found not only the feed for his cattle circumscribed, but he found the increase in his herds seriously cut off by the Winchesters of the settlers in spite of the vigilance of his cowboys. There was nothing for it but to sell out and go into some other business.

People all over western Kansas and No Man's Land are full of stories and reminiscenses of cowboy life. In fact, a plenty of the citizens of these western villages served as cowboys at one time and another before they became merchants, mechanics, professional men, etc., in some favorite location for a town site. One hears on every hand expressions that were technical in the cowboys' camp.

When anything is tied it is said to be roped, from the term which the cowboy applied to the use of the lasso. A man's household goods are termed an outfit. So is his kit of tools, if a mechanic, his library and appliances, if a surgeon or lawyer; his safe, desks, etc., if a banker. So too, is the clique he associates with socially. He belongs to a poker outfit if he plays cards with regularity, or to a pious outfit if he goes to church....[4]

Much glamor and romance have been thrown around the figure of the cowboy. He was not the dashing and chivalric hero of the burlesque stage, in gorgeous sombrero and sash, nor was he the drunken, fighting terror of the dime novel. He was a very average Westerner, dressed for comfort, and with the traits of character that his business induced. The cowboy lived a hard life. For months he never saw a bed, nor slept beneath a roof. He seldom had access to a newspaper or book, and had none of society's advantages to lift him to higher things. The roughest of the West's immigrants, as well as many Mexicans, drifted into the business because of its excitement and good wages, and this class by its excesses gave the world its standard for all. With the influences of actual contact with bucking bronco ponies and ferocious Texas steers, themselves by no means elevating, added to the temptations of the cattle towns, all the worst in the herder's nature was sure to be brought out. But hundreds of cowboys were sons of Christian parents, and when they had made a start in life settled down at last as good citizens of the great West they had helped to develop.

The cowboy with his white, wide-brimmed hat, his long leathern cattle whip, his lariat, and his clanking spurs is a thing of the past. The great Texas ranches are enclosed with barbed wire fences, and a genuine Texas steer would attract almost as much attention in the old cattle towns as a llama.[5]

The cowboy, like the buffalo, the prairie wolf, the painted redskin, and the highway robber of the plains, is rapidly becoming extinct in the West. Civilization is as hard on cowboys as it is on the other animals enumerated above. The cowboy, however, has been largely a myth. He has been existing in the imagination of Eastern writers, just as several very fine Indians were turned out of Cooper's mind. There are many herders of cattle and sheep in the mountains and valleys of the West. But the herder is the reality out of which the mythical cowboy came.

I saw the cowboy element just as it was, never totally depraved, but always wild and often dangerous. There were Pawnee Indian women around the camps and equally barbaric white women in the village. The herders all drank and gambled. They would run accounts between pay days, and a fair percentage of the debts were paid. At times a herd of herders would take possession of the village; that is, they would fire up on forty-rod whisky, mount their ponies, and with pistols cracking and lariats flying they would ride and run over the town like wild, yelling Comanches. Then it was dangerous to be out and about. Then doors were locked and such windows as had shutters were closed. Now and then a man would be hurt, but the law was afraid and nothing was done. When the whisky worked off, the boys would tell yarns on each other and laugh over their frolic. If they had been a murderous lot I would not now be writing.[6]

Time and fashion pass away and manners and customs change in western Texas just as everywhere else. The old time cowboy is no more. He passed in his checks with the free grass custom. The big pasture has introduced a new order of cowboy, who sleeps in a house and obeys orders or quits. The old cowboy was the companion of his boss and shared his pleasures and hardship. No manager in his big headquarter rock house reminded him of his inferior rank in society, nor did any modern ranch accessories mar the common dangers, the pleasures and the freedom and the tranquility of the whilom cowboy and cowman. But the ranch in the olden time was a cottonwood log house to cook in, and for roof and protection from the weather the slicker was used and mother earth supplied their beds. The broad range and the overhanging sky answered for house and home.

Such was the old way. The boys were courteous and kind, they were generous and brave, industrious and honest, but they would not stand any hightoned nonsense. A new era has set in. Which is best we cannot say, but one thing is sure, with all his faults, and they were many, the old time cowboy was a man to be trusted in peace or war, and the very soul of honor. May his best parts ever be present among his successors in western Texas.[7]

The cowboy, like the buffalo, is fast becoming extinct. In the dawn of the new century now approaching he will be regarded as a curiosity. Ten years hence he will almost have attained the dignity of tradition. History which embalms the man in armor and exalts the pioneer, holds a place for him. The niche may be a modest one; but he has had his part in conquering a new country, and no impartial record of Western evolution can omit his picturesque figure. Before civilization devours his identity let us try to detain it a moment in its real likeness and garb.... Yet this man has been a factor of civilization. He is among those who led the way through the iron age of a new country to the threshold of its golden era.... Now that his occupation is gone, the distinctive traits are disappearing. Dismounted, and deficient in any knowledge apart from cow and pony, he has turned to freighting and bar-keeping,—occasionally to "grangering." Ever since Achilles "punched" cows for King Admetus, the cowboy in all climes has claimed kinship with things classical. But the pastoral life in its large sense is nearing the end. As a final word, may not there yet arise another Maurice de Guérin to write an obituary for the last of the Centaurs?[8]

"A picturesque figure in American life is rapidly passing away," said L. Hatfield of Texas.... "I refer to the cowboy of fiction, the man with the big sombrero, the bucking broncho and the shooting irons that he used to operate with reckless disregard for consequences as he rode at breakneck speed through some frontier town, yelling the while at his loudest. Such was the cowboy of dime novel lore, and though the assertion has often been denied, he has existed and does exist yet in limited numbers. It is this class of the cowboy that is rapidly disappearing. The cowboy of practical existence, or 'cowpuncher,' as he is known in the vernacular of the plains, is an important factor in western life. He wears a sombrero and can set a bucking broncho with all the grace of his more romantic brother, but his shooting irons are for use in guarding his herd from cattle thieves rather than the terrorization of peaceful citizens and he is as hard worked and industrious a citizen as you will meet within a day's travel. Instead of leading the wild life of a nomad, he is more likely to have a wife and several young hopefuls at the ranch house. He works hard, because he has to, and if his guns are ever taken from his holsters, it is for the same reason. We have a great many more undesirable citizens in this country than the Texas cowpuncher."[9]

The idea suggested ... some time ago for a reunion of cowboys is beginning to attract the attention and interest of many old "throwers of the rope." Apart from the social side of such a gathering there are other things that would make it both interesting and profitable, particularly to such as have continued in the business and are still either cowboys, foremen, managers, or it may be bosses of their own herds,—in the company of note, discussing methods and new ideas of conducting the business to meet the changed conditions which time and circumstances have brought about. New conditions demand new ideas, new ways and methods, and a full and free discussion and interchange of ideas are always found of benefit. To all such who have passed the stage of frolic and fun and have entered in and settled down to the stern realities of life as proprietors of herds, this would be an occasion for intercourse and practical talk. To those who long since dropped out of the ranks, disposed of their saddle and have hanged up their spurs as memento of former employment can thus meet in social converse and for the time being live over again one evening of festivity and re-enact the merry good times of yore. A jolly roundup of all in a merry dance would make them feel glad to be there and cause them to feel for the moment that they were all cowboys again.

The cowboy of former times is not the cowboy of today. The former is a memory, the latter a sort of day-herder, with but little knowledge experimentally or practically of the days of long hunts and extended drives, of night watches and stampedes, of hastily eaten meals at the tail end of a grub wagon or squatted upon the ground Turkish fashion drinking their black coffee from a tin cup. The true cowboy like the Indian is passing; his duties as in former days performed are fast becoming a lost occupation. The cow puncher in the days when cattle outnumbered by a thousand per cent those of today, were a battalion of fearless riders, equal to the Indian and surpassing the cavalry of the army; a picturesque body of happy-go-lucky boys who could get more fun to the square yard out of life than could be found in the bacchanalian festivities of the ancients.

Age, time and circumstances have changed all this, and though their ranks are decimated and their mode of life changed yet there are remaining a goodly number scattered here and there in the various walks of life to whom a reunion would be a happy event.[10]

NOTES TO CHAPTER ELEVEN

1. *Democratic Leader* (Cheyenne, Wyoming), November 24, 1885.
2. "The Decayed Cowboy," *Cattlemen's Advertiser* (Trinidad, Colorado), July 22, 1886.
3. John Baumann, "On a Western Ranche," *Fortnightly Review*, XLI (April 1, 1887), 516.
4. "A Fading Race," *Topeka Capital-Commonwealth* (Topeka, Kansas), April 19, 1889.
5. Charles M. Harger, "Cattle-Trails of the Prairies," *Scribner's Magazine*, XI (January, 1892), 741-42.
6. "The Passing of the Cowboy," *Colorado Sun* (Denver, Colorado), November 12, 1892.
7. "Old Time Cowboy," *Stock Grower and Farmer* (Las Vegas, New Mexico), November 4, 1893.
8. William T. Larned, "The Passing of the Cow-Puncher," *Lippincott's Magazine*, LV (August, 1895), 267, 270.
9. "Good-bye to the American Cowboy," *Denver Republican* (Denver, Colorado), July 28, 1900.
10. "The Cowboy of Former and Later Days," *Range Ledger* (Hugo, Colorado), August 1, 1900.

Epilogue

Thus at the peak of his career, and also that of the range cattle industry, the cowboy was summarily dismissed by the frontier journalist, one of the most significant of his chroniclers. For two decades this journalist had treated every phase of cowboy life. A good portion of his writing was actual on-the-scene observation—he had trailed his subject on the roundup, on the long drives, and into the cow towns; he had appeased his healthy appetite with the simple chuck-wagon fare and had slept on the hard earth under the open sky. At times, he defended the cowboy loyally, praised his work and his virtues; again, he deplored the reckless attitude, the flagrant use of the six-shooter, and the defiance of the law. Then, when the range gave way to the ranch, when order was established, and when the cowboy stepped out of his role as the dominant figure in the industry, the man with the pen turned his thoughts to gentler happenings.

Though the journalist had now laid aside his prolific pen in relation to this important man of the range, he had, nevertheless, unconsciously perhaps, in his diversified accounts produced a new American hero, a magnetic attraction for a great number of admirers who were irresistibly drawn through the pages of the glamorous, exaggerated, and even sensational fiction of the time. But this was no lengendary hero to be consigned with his faithful horse to the realm of folklore; actually, the cowboy per se did exist, he was a real man who lived, worked, and played in the days of the range cattle industry; consequently, the bond between hero and hero worshipper which resulted from the vivid and colorful tales only grew stronger and tighter, and, in the minds of his admirers, the man on horseback did not ride into the sunset.

At this time of fond farewells to the passing cowboy, there appeared in print *A Texas Cowboy*, an autobiography by Charles A. Siringo. This tangy tale, subtitled *Fifteen Years on the Hurricane Deck of a Spanish Pony*, heightened the interest in, and the admiration for, the hero of the West. Also, this was the era of the famous Wild West shows of Buffalo Bill, Pawnee Bill, and Charlie Meadows, all of which attained national, and some, international prominence. In the nineties, when agriculture was steadily gaining ground, the numerous county fairs and exhibits featured cowboy tournaments as a part of the entertainment. And these lusty sports, depicting the work and skills of the men on the range, continued in popularity at fairs, festivals, and pioneer celebrations, even after such passing fads as balloon ascensions, horse races, and other fanfare died a natural death. These cowboy events were "grass roots," so to speak; witnessing them, old-timers fondly recalled their own experiences on the range, and the young proudly acclaimed the feats that grandfather used to do.

At the turn of the century the works of W. S. James, Emerson Hough, and Andy Adams again strengthened the hold of the cowboy on his admiring readers. Although Owen Wister said, in *The Virginian* (1902), "...the cowboy will never come again. He rides in his historic yesterday...," the book still enjoys wide circulation, and its immortalized hero still gallops over stage and screen. A decade or so later, *The Cowboy*, a monumental volume by Philip A. Rollins, joined the classics of Adams and Hough. Perhaps too recent, as yet, to be included among these as a classic is *Shane* by Jack Schaefer, but in scope and true delineation of the brutal yet beautiful forces of the Old West it is unexcelled.

As long as there is a cattle industry in the United States, there will be cowboys to do the work that it entails. True, the lone-riding, six-shooter, town-painting cowboy has disappeared, just as have the long trail drives, the stampedes, the endless months of isolation, and the open range. Progress and the inventions of a highly technical age have, fortunately, alleviated the conditions of living and working in the cow country. The present-day cowboy goes to town whenever he pleases, in a fast speeding car over superhighways; with the cattle securely corralled for the night, he may sit in an up-to-date ranch house and listen to the radio. Science, too, regulates the drives that do take place. New Mexico's Magdalena Driveway for stock operates by very modern methods, including a speed limit and government traffic police; and a not unfamiliar sight is the jeep or truck, used to drive cattle a great distance.

As for the man himself, basically, a cowboy is a cowboy. Changes in the way of life, the methods of work, and in the cattle industry as a whole, do not permit a just comparison; nevertheless, the cowboy of today has inherited many of the qualities of his predecessor. He is daring, frank, generous and fun loving; due to the nature of his work, his language, to a certain extent, still bears traces of the old range lingo; he is wary of outsiders; also, as do some members of other professions, he drinks whiskey and plays poker.

But the old-time cowboy did come again out of "his historic yesterday." With all his gear and chivalry he came galloping out of the wild and woolly West, as the daring hero, into the films, to the radio and television. At the beginning of the present century "Bronco Billy" Anderson appeared on the silent screen to lure the admirers of the glamorous knights of the saddle; then came William S. Hart, the Farnum brothers, and the star of stars, Tom Mix, who, with his famous horse Tony and his colorful custom-built attire, swelled the box-office receipts for a quarter of a century. Sound films, once the technique for shooting outdoor scenes was developed, became a natural for Western films. Early in this period came Ken Maynard and Hoot Gibson, and the present popularity of such stars as Gene Autry and Roy Rogers indicates that the trend is not waning.

Radio and television are perpetuating this old-time Western hero even more. With undue emphasis on the gun-play motif, and with a wide variety of programs, these two media make every effort to satisfy that craving for "adventure, thrilling stories, and excitement," which educators concede is a necessity of modern youth. Yet, although the method of approach is new and more embracing, the substance is not new—the same theme of the fearless man with the six-shooter and his faithful horse filled the same need for the youth of the past who read dime novels and was lured westward.

Architecture, fashions, and furnishings have also capitalized on the Western craze. Ranch houses are designed for convenience and comfortable living; pottery, glassware, and other household accessories display famous brands, sombreros, spurs, and bucking horses. Inspired by the colorful costumes and gear of the Western hero of the screen, fashion has created glamorous attire for the "dude," adapted shirts and Levis for vacationer, coed, and housewife; and every year poor Santa Claus is buried in letters requesting cowboy outfits.

Meanwhile, a truer portrayal of the old-time cowboy, his life and his work, was, and still is, in process. The early cowboy tournaments and exhibitions have increased, both in scope and popularity, in the great Western sport—rodeo. Under the name of Stampede, Round-up, Frontier Days, and various other appellations, it has taken a strong hold on the American public; it has become a year-round, nationwide affair, and has also attracted considerable attention abroad. Many present-day cowboys, amateur and professional, are engaged in this sport. For some, it is strictly a full-time profession; others, engaged in ranch work, compete whenever time and conditions permit. The work of the dude wrangler, the cowboy who is employed on a dude ranch to entertain vacationing guests, is, like that of the man in rodeo, a means of livelihood.

The literary classics mentioned earlier became the impetus for scholarly research concerning, not the already overemphasized picturesque cowboy, but, rather, his contributions in the building of the empire in the West. As a result, an accurate record of this once-neglected phase of the man on the range now exists. In addition, other valuable works are contained in the literary files on cowboy life and lore—diaries, historical novels, reminiscences, ballads, lyrics, and tall tales. Juvenile literature, especially, has made rapid strides. It is paradoxical that, in an age of atom bombs, rocket ships, and men from space, the most popular type of juvenile tale is the action-filled story of the rider—and his horse—for in the child mind, as with the French, the two are inseparable—*sans cheval, pas de cowboy*. However, it seems only natural that for a child, who has heard hobbyhorse rhymes and ridden a broomstick pony from the time of infancy, the bold, daring rider on a charging steed should hold first place in the world of make-believe.

All this is the outcome of those first day-by-day accounts of the frontier journalist. If his pen was prolific in recording the story of the cowboy, the results of its fluency are even more prolific, for now actually a dual cowboy exists—the one, an almost legendary character, fast becoming immortal through commerical glamor and adventure-packed fiction; the other, an authentic man of the frontier who forged the way for a great industry and whose exploits are recorded in the history of the West. The former never faded in the minds of his admirers and still he rides into the heart of restless youth as he did some sixty or seventy years ago. The latter, for a time sunk in oblivion while his attractive and picturesque counterpart galloped to the fore, also exists as the prototype of those who followed in his footsteps and, frank and fearless, hospitable and independent, go their way in the western homeland where prairies still stretch endless and mountains stand eternal.

Bibliography

NEWSPAPERS:

Albuquerque Evening Review (Albuquerque, New Mexico), 1882-1900.
Albuquerque Morning Journal (Albuquerque, New Mexico), 1881-1886.
Arizona Mining Index (Tucson, Arizona), 1883-1886.
Baxter Springs Republican (Baxter Springs, Kansas), 1876-1877.
Baxter Springs Sentinel (Baxter Springs, Kansas), 1872.
Beef and Bullion (Tucson, Arizona), 1885.
Black Range (Chloride, New Mexico), 1882-1895.
Boulder County Herald (Boulder, Colorado), 1880-1888.
Breeder's Gazette (Chicago, Illinois), 1882-1885.
Caldwell Commercial (Caldwell, Kansas), 1881-1883.
Caldwell Post (Caldwell, Kansas), 1879-1883.
Caldwell Standard (Caldwell, Kansas), 1884.
Calgary Weekly Herald (Calgary, Alberta, Canada), 1883-1895.
Cattlemen's Advertiser (Trinidad, Colorado), 1883-1887.
Cerrillos Rustler (Cerrillos, New Mexico), 1891.
Cherokee County Republican (Columbus, Kansas), 1876-1877.
Cheyenne Daily Leader (Cheyenne, Wyoming), 1867-1884.
Cheyenne Daily Sun (Cheyenne, Wyoming), 1877-1890.
Cheyenne Weekly Leader and Stock Journal (Cheyenne, Wyoming), 1879-1883.
Colorado Chieftain (Pueblo, Colorado), 1868-1890.
Colorado Sun (Denver, Colorado), 1891-1894.
Columbus Journal (Columbus, Kansas), 1874-1875.
Daily Colorado Miner (Georgetown, Colorado), 1869-1888.
Daily Express (Fort Collins, Colorado), 1873, 1881-1884.
Daily Missouri Democrat (St. Louis, Missouri), 1858-1872.
Deming Headlight (Deming, New Mexico), 1882-1890.
Democratic Leader (Cheyenne, Wyoming), 1884-1887.
Denver Daily Times (Denver, Colorado), 1872-1886.
Denver Evening Post (Denver, Colorado), 1892-1900.
Denver Republican (Denver, Colorado), 1881-1887, 1887-1900.
Denver Tribune-Republican (Denver, Colorado), 1884-1886.
Dodge City Times (Dodge City, Kansas), 1876-1893.
El Anunciador de Trinidad (Trinidad, Cololado), 1882, 1887.
Ellsworth Reporter (Ellsworth, Kansas), 1871-1900.
Field and Farm (Denver, Colorado), 1886-1899.
Ford County Globe (Dodge City, Kansas), 1878-1884.
Fort Collins Courier (Fort Collins, Colorado), 1878-1900.
Fort Morgan Times (Fort Morgan, Colorado), 1884-1900.
Georgetown Courier (Georgetown, Colorado), 1879-1900.
Great West (Denver, Colorado), 1880-1884.

Gunnison Review (Gunnison, Colorado), 1880-1882.
Junction City Weekly Union (Junction City, Kansas), 1865-1900.
Kansas City Journal of Commerce (Kansas City, Kansas), 1873.
Kansas Cowboy (Dodge City, Kansas), 1884-1885.
Laramie Weekly Sentinel (Laramie, Wyoming), 1877-1895.
Las Animas Leader (Las Animas, Colorado), 1874-1883.
Las Vegas Daily Optic (Las Vegas, New Mexico), 1879-1900.
Leadville Daily Herald (Leadville, Colorado), 1880-1886.
Medicine Lodge Index (Medicine Lodge, Kansas), 1880-1890.
New York Daily Tribune (New York, New York), 1866-1900.
Range Ledger (Hugo, Colorado), 1889-1900.
Raton Weekly Independent (Raton, New Mexico), 1883-1898.
Republic (St. Louis, Missouri), 1887-1900.
Rio Grande Republican (Las Cruces, New Mexico), 1881-1900.
Rocky Mountain News (Denver, Colorado), 1869-1900.
San Marcial Reporter (San Marcial, New Mexico), 1886-1893.
San Miguel County Republican (Las Vegas, New Mexico), 1886.
Santa Fe New Mexican [title varies] (Santa Fe, New Mexico), 1865-1900.
Santa Fe New Mexican Review [title varies] (Santa Fe, New Mexico), 1883-1885.
Socorro Bullion (Socorro, New Mexico), 1883-1888.
Socorro Chieftain (Socorro, New Mexico), 1882-1886.
Southwest Sentinel (Silver City, New Mexico), 1875-1890.
Stock Grower and Farmer (Las Vegas, New Mexico), 1890-1897.
Sunshine and Silver (Tucson, Arizona), 1884-1885.
Texas Live Stock Journal (Fort Worth, Texas), 1882-1890.
Times (Baxter Springs, Kansas), 1878-1880.
Topeka Capital Commonwealth (Topeka, Kansas), 1874-1889.
Trinidad Daily Advertiser (Trinidad, Colorado), 1882-1900.
Trinidad Weekly Advertiser (Trinidad, Colorado), 1882-1900.
Trinidad Weekly News (Trinidad, Colorado), 1878-1889.
Weekly New Mexican Review (Santa Fe, New Mexico), 1864-1883.
White Oaks Golden Era (White Oaks, New Mexico), 1884.

DOCUMENTS:

A letter—"Santa Fe, 10th June, 1847." Written by Captain Mayne Reid to Samuel Arnold of Drumnakelly, Seaforde, county Down, Ireland. Now in the manuscript collection of Colin Johnston Robb, Drumharriff Lodge, Loughgall, county Armagh, Ireland.

United States Congress, 48th Congress, 2nd session, *House Executive Document*, Nimmo, Joseph, "Range and Cattle Traffic," v. XXIX, no. 267 (ser. no. 2304).

ARTICLES:

Bacon, Alfred T. "A Colorado 'Round-Up'," *Lippincott's Magazine*, XXVIII (December, 1881), 618-22.
Baillie-Grohman, William A. "Cattle Ranches in the Far West," *Fortnightly Review*, XXXIV (October, 1880), 438-57.

BIBLIOGRAPHY 401

Baumann, John. "Experiences of a Cow-Boy," *Lippincott's Magazine*, XXXVIII (September, 1886), 308-20.
―――. "On a Western Ranche," *Fortnightly Review*, XLI (April 1, 1887), 516-33.
Bechdolt, Frederick. "The Field Agent of Settlement—The Cowboy's Contribution to American Civilization," *Collier's Weekly*, XLIII (September 18, 1909), 19, 34.
Bradford, Louis C. "Among the Cow-Boys," *Lippincott's Magazine*, XXVII (June, 1881), 565-71.
"Cattle-Herding in the Great West," *Littell's Living Age*, XVIII (April 14, 1877), 126-28.
Ellard, Harry. "The Cowboys," *Facts* (Colorado Springs, Colorado), IV (August 19, 1899), 21.
―――. "The Poet Lariat of the Ranches," *ibid*. (July 22, 1899), p. 23.
Harger, Charles M. "Cattle-Trails of the Prairies," *Scribner's Magazine*, XI (January, 1892), 732-42.
Herron, Matthew J. "The Passing of the Cowman," *Overland Monthly*, LV (February, 1910), 195-99.
Holmes, Thomas. "A Cowboy's Life," *Chautauquan*, XIX (September, 1894), 730-32.
Hyacinth, Socrates. "On the Texas Prairies," *Overland Monthly*, II (April, 1869), 369-74.
Larned, William T. "The Passing of the Cow-Puncher," *Lippincott's Magazine*, LV (August, 1895), 267-70.
Michelson, Charles. "The War for the Range," *Munsey's Magazine*, XXVIII (December, 1902), 380-82.
Nimmo, Joseph, Jr. "The American Cow-Boy," *Harper's New Monthly Magazine*, LXXIII (November, 1886), 880-84.
Osbourne, F. M. "Sargent's Rodeo," *Lippincott's Magazine*, XXV (January, 1880), 9-20.
Ralph, Julian. "A Talk with a Cowboy," *Harper's Weekly*, XXXVI (April 16, 1892), 375-76.
Remington, Frederic. "A Rodeo at Los Ojos," *Harper's New Monthly Magazine*, LXXXVIII (March, 1894), 515-28.
Reynolds, M. J. "The Texas Trail," *Munsey's Magazine*, XXIX (June, 1903), 576-81.
"The Captain of the Cow-Boys," *Out West*, I (New Series) (September, 1873), 68.
"The Cowboy's Stratagem," *Facts* (Colorado Springs, Colorado), IV (July 8, 1899), 11.
Truman, Ben C. "The Passing of the Cowboy," *Overland Monthly*, XL (November, 1902), 464-67.
Westermeier, Clifford P. "Cowboy Capers," *Annals of Wyoming*, 22 (July, 1950), 13-25.
―――. "Cowboy Sports and the Humane Society," *Colorado Magazine*, XXVI (October, 1949), 241-52.
―――. "Seventy-Five Years of Rodeo in Colorado," *Colorado Magazine*, XXVIII (January, April, and July, 1951), 13-27, 127-45, 219-32.
―――. "The Cowboy and Religion," *The Historical Bulletin*, XXVIII (January, 1950), 31-37.
―――. "The Cowboy—Sinner or Saint!" *New Mexico Historical Review*, XXV (April, 1950), 89-108.
―――. "The Legal Status of the Colorado Cattleman, 1867-1887," *Colorado Magazine*, XXV (May and July, 1948), 109-18, 157-66.

White, Stewart E. "The Mountain, XIX—On Cowboys," *Outlook*, LXXVIII (September 3, 1904), 82-88.
Williams, Alfred M. "An Indian Cattle-Town," *Lippincott's Magazine*, XXXIII (February, 1884), 167-75.
Wingate, General George. "My Trip to the Yellowstone," *American Agriculturist*, XLV (April, 1886), 152.
Zogbaum, Rufus S. "A Day's 'Drive' with Montana Cowboys," *Harper's New Monthly Magazine*, LXXI (July, 1885), 188-93.

BOOKS:

Abbott, E. C., and Smith, Helen Huntington. *We Pointed Them North; Recollections of a Cowpuncher*. New York: Farrar & Rinehart, Inc., 1939.
Adams, Andy. *The Log of a Cowboy; A Narrative of the Old Trail Days*. Boston: Houghton Mifflin Company, 1936.
Adams, Ramon. *Cowboy Lingo*. Boston: Houghton Mifflin Company, 1936.
———. *Western Words; A Dictionary of the Range, Cow Camp and Trail*. Norman, Oklahoma: University of Oklahoma Press, 1944.
———. *Come an' Get It; The Story of the Old Cowboy Cook*. Norman, Oklahoma: University of Oklahoma Press, 1952.
Arnold, Oren and Hale, John P. *Hot Irons; Heraldry of the Range*. New York: The Macmillan Company, 1944.
Bechdolt, Frederick R. *Tales of Old-Timers*, New York: The Century Company, 1924.
Branch, E. Douglas. *The Cowboy and His Interpreters*. New York: D. Appleton and Company, 1926.
Bratt, John. *Trails of Yesterday*. Lincoln, Nebraska: privately printed, 1921.
Clay, John. *My Life on the Range*. Chicago: privately printed, 1924.
Collins, Hubert E. *Warpath & Cattle Trail*. New York: William Morrow & Company, 1933.
Cook, James H. *Longhorn Cowboy*. New York: G. P. Putnam's Sons, 1942.
Coolidge, Dane. *Texas Cowboys*. New York: E. P. Dutton & Company, Inc., 1937.
———. *Arizona Cowboys*. New York: E. P. Dutton & Company, Inc., 1938.
Dale, Edward Everett. *Cow Country*. Norman, Oklahoma: University of Oklahoma Press, 1945.
Dobie, J. Frank. *A Vaquero of the Brush Country*. Boston: Little, Brown and Company, 1946.
Haley, J. Evetts. *Charles Goodnight; Cowman & Plainsman*. Norman, Oklahoma: University of Oklahoma Press, 1949.
Henry, Stuart. *Conquering Our Great American Plains; A Historical Development*. New York: E. P. Dutton & Company, Inc., 1930.
Historical and Biographical Record of the Cattle Industry and Cattlemen of Texas and Adjacent Territory. [By James Cox.] St. Louis: Woodward & Tiernan Printing Company, 1895.

BIBLIOGRAPHY

Hough, Emerson. *The Story of the Cowboy.* New York: Grosset & Dunlap, 1897.
Hunter, J. Marvin, comp. and ed. *The Trail Drivers of Texas; Interesting Sketches of Early Cowboys and their Experiences on the Range and on the Trail during the Days that Tried Men's Souls—True Narratives Related by Real Cow-Punchers and Men who Fathered the Cattle Industry in Texas.* Nashville, Tennessee: Cokesbury Press, 1925.
James, W. S. *Cow-Boy Life in Texas or 27 Years a Maverick.* Chicago: Donohue Brothers, 1893.
King, Frank M. *Wranglin' the Past; The Reminiscences of Frank M. King.* Pasadena, California: Trail's End Publishing Company, Inc., 1946.
Lake, Stuart N. *Wyatt Earp; Frontier Marshal.* Boston: Houghton Mifflin Company, 1931.
McCoy, Joseph G. *Historic Sketches of the Cattle Trade of the West and Southwest.* Kansas City, Missouri: Ramsey, Millett & Hudson, 1874.
Osgood, Ernest S. *The Day of the Cattleman.* Minneapolis, Minnesota: University of Minnesota Press, 1929.
Peake, Ora Brooks. *The Colorado Range Cattle Industry.* Glendale, California: The Arthur H. Clark Company, 1937.
Pelzer, Louis. *The Cattlemen's Frontier.* Glendale, California: The Arthur H. Clark Company, 1936.
Ridings, Sam P. *The Chisholm Trail; A History of the World's Greatest Cattle Trail.* Guthrie, Oklahoma: Co-Operative Publishing Company, 1936.
Rollins, Philip Ashton. *The Cowboy; An Unconventional History of Civilization on the Old-Time Cattle Range.* New York: Charles Scribner's Sons, 1936.
Rollinson, John K. *Pony Trails in Wyoming.* Caldwell, Idaho: The Caxton Printers, Ltd., 1944.
———. *Wyoming Cattle Trails.* Caldwell, Idaho: The Caxton Printers, Ltd., 1948.
Rush, Oscar. *The Open Range and Bunk House Philosophy.* Caldwell, Idaho: The Caxton Printers, Ltd., 1936.
Schaefer, Jack. *Shane.* Boston: Houghton Mifflin Company, 1949.
Shaw, James C. *North from Texas; Incidents in the Early Life of A Range Cowman in Texas, Dakota and Wyoming, 1852-1883.* Evanston, Illinois: The Branding Iron Press, 1952.
Siringo, Charles A. *A Texas Cowboy or Fifteen Years on the Hurricane Deck of a Spanish Pony.* New York: William Sloane Associates, Inc., 1950.
Stuart, Granville. *Forty Years on the Frontier; the Reminiscences and Journals of a Gold Miner, Trader, Merchant, Rancher, and Politician.* Cleveland, Ohio: The Arthur H. Clark Company, 1925.
Taylor, Bayard. *Colorado; A Summer Trip.* New York: G. P. Putnam's Sons, 1867.
Thorp, N. Howard (Jack). *Pardner of the Wind.* Caldwell, Idaho: The Caxton Printers, Ltd., 1945.
Vestal, Stanley. *Queen of Cowtowns; Dodge City.* New York: Harper & Brothers, 1952.
Webb, Walter P. *The Great Plains.* Boston: Houghton Mifflin Company, 1936.

Westermeier, Clifford P. *Man, Beast, Dust: The Story of Rodeo.* Denver: The World Press, 1947.

Wright, Robert M. *Dodge City, The Cowboy Capital and The Great Southwest in The Days of the Wild Indian, the Buffalo, the Cowboy, Dance Halls, Gambling Halls and Bad Men.* [Wichita, Kan.: Wichita Eagle Press, ca. 1913].

Index

Abilene, Kans., 191, 279
Adams, Andy, 8, 395
Agua Fria, A. T., 355
Albough, Kid, 174
Albright, Emmet, 357, 358
Albuquerque, N. Mex., 172, 350, 355, 359
Alleghenies, 77
Allen, Dave, 351
Aller, Clem, 222
America, 24, 54, 287, 327, 334, 362
American(s), 180, 185
Amusements, *see also* escapades, gambling, jokes; 28, 47, 53, 70, 82, 192, 197-223, 259
Anderson, "Bronco Billy," 396
Anderson, Jim, 248
Anglo-Saxon, 23
Animals, wild, 29, 31, 33, 36, 40, 71, 269, 347, 386, 388
Antelope, Wyo., 239
Antelope County, Nebr., 224
Apaches, 142, 174, 184, 185, 288, 289
Arapahoe County, Colo., 176
Arapahoe Reservation, 140
Arickaree Ranch, 345
Arizona, 18, 48, 53, 81, 84, 87, 136, 141, 142, 156, 168, 182, 237, 288, 296, 299, 336, 355; *see also* individual cities
Arkansas, 239; *see also* individual cities
Arkansas River, 99, 130
Arkansas Valley Fair, 371
Arnold, Samuel, 343
Arthur, President (Chester A.), 51, 354
Ashland, Kans., 159
Ashley Valley, Utah, 337
Askew, policeman, 207
Associations, Humane, the, 148; Lincoln County Livestock, 149; National Stockgrowers, 383; National Tanners, Hide and Leather Dealers, 147; Sulphur Valley Roundup, 348; Texas Farm, 327
Assoten, Wash. T., 159
Atkins, commissioner, 168, 169
Atlanta, Ga., 358
Atley, Will, 227
Augur, General (C. C.), 168
Austin, Tex., 51, 325, 354
Autry, Gene, 396
Axelbee, outlaw, 137

Bach, Prof., restaurant proprietor, 303
Badlands, the, 139, 140
Badmen, 8, 110, 112
Baker, cowboy, 104
Ballads, *see also* rhymes; 10
Bannock Butte, Idaho, 97
Barnes, Charles (alias C. A. Yates), 208

Barnhauser, policeman, 207
Barton, Jesse, 369
Baxter Springs, Kans., 111, 192, 293
Bear, *see also* "Capturing a Bear"; 33
Beck, Charlie, 102
Bed, 63, 69, 70, 78, 81, 260, 331
Belmont, August, 324
Belton, Tex., 297
Benkleman, Nebr., 322
Bennett, J. A., 369
Bent County, Colo., 227
Bernalillo, N. Mex., 180
Berry, John, 357, 358
Bible, the, 10; references to, 232, 243
Big Horn, Wyo., 301
Bill, "Curly," desperado, 224
Billings, Mont., 353
Bingham, Arthur, 358
Bisbee, Ariz., 165
Bismarck, N. Dak., 310
Blackjack Ranch, 270
Blake, Prof., horse trainer, 375
Blanket, 38, 61, 65, 67, 72, 78, 271
Blinn, Dr., physician, 158, 159
Blizzards, 63, 94, 100, 269, 382
Blocker, J. R., 176
Bob, Arkansas, cowboy, 248
Bonheur (Marie Rosa), 86
Boots, 8, 23, 27, 31, 32, 64, 69, 75, 79, 80
Boston, Mass., 328
Boughman, policeman, 223
Boulder, Colo., 337
Boulder County, Colo., 337
"Bound to a Horse's Back," 286-88
Boussaud, rancher, 286, 287, 288
Bowie knife, 29, 47, 72
Bowring, citizen of Poncha, 208
Bozeman, Mont., 104
Branding, 63, 64, 66, 67, 70, 74, 147, 382; iron, 23, 62, 65
Brands, 64, 103
Brazos River, 70, 94
Breaking broncos, 84, 85-94, 382
Bridgewater, Mass., 338
Bridle, 23, 30, 73, 75, 91, 92, 94
Briggs, cowboy, 248-50
British Isles, 334
Briton, 274
Brock gang, cattle thieves, 139
Bronco(s), 9, 30, 62, 63, 75, 84, 86, 89, 92, 104, 119, 193, 259, 266, 268, 388; names of, "Colorado Cloudburst," 86; "Dakota Demon," 86; "Montana Man-Killer," 86; "Montana Blizzard," 345
Bronco buster, 19, 45, 87, 345
Brown, Duchy, 184
Brown, Rice, 225
Brown, Sam, 226
Brown, W. P., 369

406 INDEX

Brush, Colo., 207
Brutality, 145-49
Bucket, Joe, 247
Buffalo, Wyo., 320
Buffalo Bill, 307, 333, 334, 350, 351, 353, 357, 358, 369, 374, 384, 394
Bulls, 66, 80, 179, 214; bull riding, 347
Burbank, Henry, 287
Burke & Murphy's, saloon in Denver, Colo., 206
Burlington, Tex., 204
Burner, Harry, 155
Burnett, policeman, 205
Buzzard, horseman, 358, 359

Caldwell, Kans., 112, 115, 193, 225
Caldwell County, Tex., 349
Calgary, Canada, 369, 370
Calhoun, Alex, 358
California, 18, 21, 36, 87, 301, 324, 352, 353, 354
Call, Senator, 142
Callison, John, 116
Calter, farmer, 115
Calvert, Hugh, 117
Calves, 62, 65, 67, 93, 97, 264
Camas Prairie, 294
Camp(s), 10, 33, 42, 74
Campbell, George W., 321, 322
Campbell, Harvey, 358
Campbell, Jack, 137
Campbell, Jas. H., 321
Campbell, Joe, 356, 358
Camp Robinson, Wyo., 165
Canada, 26
Canadian River, 127, 173, 274
Canaditas Cattle Ranch, 157
Cannon Ball River, 140
Canom, S. Dak., 156
Canon City, Colo., 355
Capital X Ranch, 359
"Captain of the Cow-Boys, The," 270
"Capturing a Bear," 293-94
Card playing, see gambling, monte, poker
Cardwell, Will, 349
Carlisle, cattleman, 169, 171, 181
Carlyle, confidence man, 220
Carson, Hank, 83
Carson & Shore, donor of prize, 370
Carter, Allison, 224
Carter, cowboy, 113
Carter, George, 161, 162
Carter, Jessie, 212
Carter, Virgil, 349
Cartright, W. B., 184
Cass, George, 161, 162
Cattle, 35, 38, 41, 53, 63, 66, 67, 70, 71, 72, 76, 77, 80, 82, 95, 98, 99, 100, 102; Texas, 176
Cattle Companies, Ceralitos, 300; Diamond A, 174; Dubuque, 181; Erie, 165; Gila, 158; Graham and White, 158; Home Land and, 178; Illinois, 157; James H. Campbell, 321; Johnson and Son, 163; Muscatine, 316; Ogallala Land and, 288; Old and New Mexico Ranch and, 174; Prairie, 121, 145, 155, 161, 180, 181, 315, 316; Red River, 163; Western, 316
Cattle drives, 73
Cattle industry, 7, 8, 9, 17-18, 34, 36
Cattle kings, 24, 42

Cattleman, 77, 80, 81, 122; old-time, 9; Texas, 18; Western, 18
"Cattle Man's Prayer, The," 265-66
Cattle ranches, Arickaree, 345; Blackjack, 270; Canaditas, 157; Capital X, 359; Corrigan's, 101; Crosselle, 315; Dalglish, 158; Dead Man's, 279; Don Carlos, 327; Fisk's, 138; Hardman's, 82; Hashknife, 345; Head, 100; Juan de Dios, 160; Lake, 157; Leustrom, 159; Maulding's, 319; Milliron, 279, 345; Morrison's, 207; O—O, 177; Prairie Cattle, 155; Rigg's, 348; San Bernadino, 184; Watt's, 136; XL, 315
Cavitt, Dick, 159
Cayuse, 45, 87, 93
Ceralitos Cattle Co., 300
Chadron, Nebr., 182, 320, 355, 356, 357, 358
Chamber of Commerce (Denver), 374
Chaplain, Al, 224
Chaps and chaparejos, 19, 32, 69, 80, 102
Chastain, cowboy, 113
Chaves, Jesus Maria, 182
Cherokee Strip, 64, 67, 115, 179
Cherry, judge of city court, 205
Cherry Creek, 197
Chester, Florence, 319
Cheyenne, Wyo., 197, 198, 199, 202, 211, 212, 215, 226, 319, 326, 336, 345, 351, 356, 370, 371
Cheyenne, Wyo. T., 55, 141, 156, 192, 210
Cheyenne "Frontier Day," 370, 371
Cheyenne Indian Reservation, 143
Cheyenne (Indians), 166, 171
Cheyenne River, 156
Chicago, Ill., 55, 127, 215, 321, 326, 330, 356, 357
Chickasaw Nation 159, 162, 175
Chinese, 209
Chiricahua (Indians), 52
Chloride, N. Mex., 158
Chronicle, Red River, N. Mex., 114
Chuck-a-luck, 71
Chuck wagon, 63, 64, 65, 66, 394
Church attendance, 245
Cimarron, N. Mex., 207
Civil War, 79, 327
Claiborne, Phil, 234
Clark, Thos., 208
Clarke, Luther, 243
Clay Center, Kans., 324
Clayton, N. Mex., 139, 241
Clothing, see cowboy, attire
Clow, pugilist, 304-6
Coffee, 24, 31, 70, 72, 73, 78, 80, 81, 180, 263
Colder, Miss, pedestrian, 224
Coleman, Tex., 227
Colfax County, N. Mex., 132, 318
Colorado, 18, 20, 39, 40, 70, 99, 100, 114, 120, 122, 123, 130, 132, 166, 167, 171, 177, 181, 183, 205, 206, 213, 236, 241, 268, 296, 304, 322, 335, 355, 356, 362, 370, 371, 375, 383; see also individual cities
Colorado Springs, Colo., 278
Colt revolver, 200, 201, 259, 358
Comanche Indians, 37, 53, 119, 387
Conger, Walter, 364
Connecticut, 383

INDEX 407

Contests, 344, 359-73
Conventions, 51, 94, 112
Cook, cowboy and ranch, 41, 65, 66, 67, 70, 72, 73, 78, 82, 272
Cook, Dr., physician, 212
Cook, Ed, 320
Cook, Joseph, 322
Cook, Nellie, 322
Cook, William, 264, 367
Coole, sheriff, 204
Coolidge (Dane), 8
Coolidge, Kans., 220, 221
Coolidge, N. Mex., 174
Cooper (James Fenimore), 387
Corrigan's Ranch, 101
Cossacks, 352
Cowboy, appearance, 23, 27, 32, 34,; attire, *see also* individual items; 10, 74, 195, 331; character and traits, 18, 20, 21, 25, 26, 27, 28, 29, 30, 31, 35, 38, 42, 44, 46, 48, 50, 52, 54, 62, 283, 284, 386, 394; criticism of, 373-76; decline and passing of, 381-90; education, 24, 25, 53, 54; equipment or gear, *see* individual items; hero, 26, 386, 395, 396; home, *see also* tents; 25, 72, 260; influence, *see* cowboy influence on; juvenile, 334, 335-38; modern, 390, 395; myth, 384, 387; nicknames, 34; old-time, 81, 355, 371, 387, 388-90, 396; origin, 18, 25, 34, 37, 55; radio and television 396; recreation, *see* amusements, escapades, gambling, sports; speech, *see also* profanity; 18, 29, 36, 43, 44, 45; training and schools for, 327-31; types, *see* cowboy types; work, *see* cowboy work
Cowboy, The, 395
"Cowboy, The," 259-63
"Cowboy and Limburger," 302-4
"Cowboy and the Folding Bed," 308
Cowboy Ball, 313
"'Cowboy' Dog, A," 295-96
"Cowboy in a Sleeping Car, A," 306-7
Cowboy influence on, clothing, 396; decoration, 396; films, 396; literature, 394-95, 397; speech, 385, 386; youth, 266, 333-38, 397
"Cowboy in Wall Street, A," 276-77
"Cowboy Joke, A," 299
"Cowboy Prizefighter, A," 304-5
Cowboy types, American, 314, 325, 341; Arizona, 142; Colorado, 39, 53; Missouri, 37, 75; Montana, 40; Nebraska, 53; Negro, 157, 178, 203, 213, 354, 365, 371-73; New Mexico, 222, 307; Northern, 38; Oregon, 37; South Dakota, 36; Southwestern, 171; Texas, 36, 37, 38, 39, 40, 41, 55, 125, 127, 209, 310, 315, 347; Wyoming, 53
Cowboy wages, 41, 42, 100, 125-30, 134-35
Cowboy work, *see also* roundup; 61, 62, 63, 335, 394
"Cowboys, The," 268-69
Cowboy's Cattle Company, 131, 132
"Cowboys' Christmas Ball, The," 279-80
"Cowboy's Pet Colt, The," 289-90
Cowboys' Reunion, 313, 316
"Cowboys' Soliloquy, The," 263-64
"Cowboy's Start in Life, The," 290-91
"Cowboy's Sweetheart, The," 272-73

Cowgirls, 323-27
Cowman, *see also* cattleman; 22, 23, 25, 33, 46, 118
Cow pony, 31, 41, 49, 63, 70, 71, 79, 84, 87, 89, 92, 94, 96, 264
Cowpuncher, 25, 41, 42, 45, 46, 49, 53, 78, 80, 85, 87, 99, 101, 177, 202, 216, 260
Cow town(s), 8, 9, 191, 393
Coyote, 77, 213, 269
Crockett, Davey, 320
Crosselle Ranch, 315
Crow (Indians), 334
Cueller, James, 369
Culture, American, 8
Cunningham, cowboy, 137
Custer, S. Dak., 156
Cutting out, 92, 359

Dakota(s), 17 38, 39, 104, 335; *see also* individual cities
Dale (E. E.), 8
Dalglish, Jack, 158
Dalglish Ranch, 158
Dancing, 279-80, 313-19
Dangers, 94-104, 153-85, 284
Davis, Bronco Jim, 365
Davis, W. J., 103
Davis, William, 177
Dawes, Senator, 142
"Days Gone By," 288-89
Dead Man's Ranch, 279
Deadwood, S. Dak., 137, 156
Dean, Harry, 224
Death, 97-98, 247-51
Deer Trail, Colo., 131, 344
De Graftenreid, Dick, 160, 161
De Guérin, Maurice, 388
Delta, Colo., 358
Deming, N. Mex., 177, 299
Deming *Tribune*, 222
Democratic Leader, the, 336
"Demon Steer, The," 291-92
Dentistry, 308-9
Denver, Colo., 94, 95, 100, 156, 163, 171, 176, 192, 197, 205, 206, 209, 213, 215, 221, 222, 804, 308, 319, 322, 335, 352, 354, 356, 363, 370, 373, 375
Denver *Republican*, 221
Denver *Tribune*, 156
Denver *Tribune-Republican*, 90, 167, 184, 245
Desperadoes, 8, 40, 55, 126, 224
Detaille (Jean B. E.), 86
Diamond A Ranch, 174
Dickinson, N. Dak., 139
Disarming of cowboys, 109-23
Dobie (J. Frank), 8
Dodd, Helen, 321, 322
Dodd, Sir Thomas, 321, 322
Dodge City, Kans., 191, 192, 207
Dodge Trail, the, 246
Dog, *see* "'Cowboy' Dog, A"
Dolores River, 170
Domeo, Myer, 182
Don Carlos Ranch, 327
Dorsey Station, N. Mex., 132, 133
Douglas, Dave, 357
Douglas, Wyo., 237, 320
Down County (Ireland), 343
Dows, Millie Price, 319
Doze, M., 225
Dozier, colored cook, 213

INDEX

Drinking, *see also* whiskey; 82, 110, 161, 179, 192, 201-7, 271, 301-2
Driskell, cattleman, 193
Drives, 8, 73, 260; Texas, 177
Drover(s), 23, 194; Texas, 194
Drumnakelly (Ireland), 343
Dry Cheyenne Station, Wyo., 320
Dry Cimarron River, 315, 317
Dubuque Cattle Co., 181
Dudes, 32, 213-23
Dundy County, Nebr., 322

Eagle River, 101
Eagles Pass, Tex., 351
Ear marking, 64
Easterner(s), 46, 193
Eastern people, 33, 193
Eastern press, 33, 45, 46, 55, 260
Eaton, Governor (B. H.), 170
Eckman, John, 182
Eddy, Pres. (Lincoln County Live Stock Assoc.), 149
Edmunds, Senator, 142
Edwards, sheep raiser, 182
Eggleston, editor, 179
Elbert County, Colo., 196, 322
Eldridge, Tom, 289
Elias, J. N., 184
Ellard, Harry, 268, 269
Ellenmeyer, Will, 138
Elliott, R. S., 263
El Paso, Tex., 352
Emmett, H. Clay, 297
England, 24, 314, 321, 333
Englishmen, 39, 93, 287, 299, 302, 328, 329, 345
Equipment, *see* cowboy equipment or gear
Erie Cattle Co., 165
Ernest, cowboy, 156
Escapades, 82-83, 189-223
Estes, George L., 156
Europe, 24, 39, 314
Evans, cowboy, 221
Everrett, James, 319
Exhibitions, 84, 346, 349-52

Fairchild, Bert, 337
Fair Oakes, Va., 23
Falmouth, England, 287
Fargo, N. Dak., 310
Farmer, 26, 71, 72, 177, 382, 383
Farmington, N. Mex., 241
Farnum Brothers, the, 396
Far West, the, 21
Fetterman, Wyo., 100
Fifteen Years on the Hurricane Deck of a Spanish Pony, 394
Fisk's Ranch, 138
Fitzgerald, traveler, 171
Fleming, Jack, 307
Foes, frontier, 153-85
"Fogg's Ferry," 199
Follis, Jim, 181
Follis, William, 181
Folsom, N. Mex., 100
Food, 23, 31, 45, 65, 67, 68, 70, 73, 75, 78, 80, 81, 180
Fort Collins *Express*, 130
Fort Custer, Mont., 171
Fort Fetterman, Wyo., 304
Fort Keogh, Mont., 171

Fort Lewis, Colo., 170
Fort McLeod *Gazette*, 214
Fort Reno, Wyo., 143
Fort Smith, Ark., 175
Fort Union, N. Mex., 136
Fort Wingate, N. Mex., 172, 174
Fort Worth, Tex., 38, 125, 309
Foster, Coon, 96
Fourth of July, 345
France, 334
Franklin, Benjamin, 82
Franklin, Troy, 367
Frenchmen, 39, 180
Fretwell, Lawson, 178
Frintares, Chicuahua, Mex. T., 184
"Frontier Dentistry," 308-9
Fruita, Colo., 164
Fun, *see* amusements
Funeral(s), 225, 247-50
"Fun with the Tenderfoot," 300-1

Gallagher, "Reddy," 319
Galveston, Tex., 51, 343
Gambling, 19, 116, 143-45, 149, 193, 195, 220, 259
Garcia, Francisco, 161
Garden City, Kans., 130, 131
Gardenshire, Emilnie, 345
Garfield County, Colo., 337
Garland, Senator, 142
Garrett, Pat, 122
Gatling gun, 119
Gayhart, John, 160
Gear, *see* cowboy equipment or gear
Genteur, farmer, 170
Genthner family, the, 168
Georgia, 117
Germans, 39
Gettysburg, Pa., 23
Gibson, Hoot, 396
Gila Cattle Co., 158
Gillenstein, Frank, 205
Gillespie, Joe, 357, 358
Gilroy, Thos. H., 351
Goff, Will, 344
Goodnight (Charles), 24
Goshen, Ind., 226
Gosper, Governor (John L.), 140, 141
Gould, Jay, 351
Grady, A. B., 349, 350
Grady's Cowboy Co., 350
Graham and White Cattle Co., 158
Graham, Ed, 156
Grand Junction, Colo., 177
Grande Ronde River [Oregon?], 297
Granger, 123, 154, 176, 177, 192, 385
Grants Station, Ariz., 181
Grass, 63, 64, 81, 192, 264, 269
"Greaser," 183-85
Great Bend, Kans., 220
Great Britain, 334
Great Plains, the, 342, 382
Green, Billy, 160, 161
Greer, Dick, 360, 361
Grogan, Drury, 345
Grubb, manager, Prairie Cattle Co., 315, 317
Guerrera, Simms, 369
Guiteau (Charles J.), 83
Guns, *see also* Colt revolver, pistol, revolver, rifle, six-shooter, Winchester; 30, 40, 109

INDEX 409

Hale, Tom, 349
Hallbeck, Bert, 288
Hamilton, James, 113
Hammer, J. H., 220
Hammitt, Frank, 352
Hancock, Daniel, 98
Handkerchief, 32, 64, 79
Hardman's Ranch, 82
Hardy, policeman, 219
Hardy, Rox, 350
Harper, T. S., 196, 197
Harper, Thomas, 224
Harris, Charles H., 227
Harris, T. B., 125, 126, 127
Hart, William S., 396
Hartley, cowboy, 204
Harvard (University), 53
Hashknife Ranch, 345
Hat, 8, 19, 23, 27, 31, 32, 36, 37, 38, 45, 63, 64, 75, 80, 102, 119, 245, 386, 388
Hatch, Rufus, 64
Hat Creek, Wyo., 166
Hatfield, L., 388
Hays, Kans., 262
Hays (Rutherford B.), 37
Hawley, Senator, 142
Head, R. G., 100, 121, 145, 316
Head Ranch, 100
Hecket, citizen of Cheyenne, 212
Heidelberg (University, Germany), 54
Helena, Mont., 137, 138
Helena, Tex., 285
Henderson, Jim, 249
Herd(s), 8, 24, 25, 29, 47, 49, 63, 64, 65, 66, 67, 68, 73, 79, 84, 95, 98, 122, 156, 176, 192, 194, 260
Herder(s), 25, 27, 47, 71, 72, 76, 77, 100, 102, 103, 175, 180, 182, 192, 264, 387
"Herder, The," 264-65
"Herder's Tale, The," 261-63
Herding, 28, 71, 261; night, 68, 77
Hewens, E. M., 113
Hoffer, Lieut. John, 127, 129
Holdem, H. H. (Hank), 291
Holland, policeman, 209
Hollen, Green, 369
Holt County, Nebr., 223, 224
Home, see cowboy home
Home Land and Cattle Co., 178
Hommel, Louis, 120
Horse(s), 9, 10, 27, 28, 35, 63, 65, 73, 75, 76, 78, 84, 85, 87, 100, 101, 103, 156, 275, 382
"Horsemanship!" 296
Horse thieves, see also rustling; 170, 171, 226
Horsfall, Rev., 247
Horton, A. B., 369
Hotchkiss, Colo., 358
Hot Springs, S. Dak., 182
Hough, Emerson, 8, 395
"How a Cattleman Saved His Life," 285-86
Howard County, Ark., 166
Howard, George, 156
Howard, W. H., 160
Huerfano County, Colo., 138
Hughes, Mayor A. T., 224
Hughes, sheriff, 203
Hugo, Colo., 196
Humane Associations, the, 148
Humane Societies, 376

Humane Society (Colorado), 374, 375, 376
Hunnewell, Kans., 209
Hunter, Chris, 352
Huntington, confidence man, 270
Huntsville, Tex., 52
Hutchings & Riley, business firm, 370
Hutchinson, Emma, 356

Idaho, 18, 38, 95, 97, 159
Illinois Cattle Co., 157
Indian pony, 85, 87
Indians, Apache, 142, 174, 184, 185, 288, 289; Cherokee (nation), 175; Cheyenne, 143, 166, 171; Chickasaw (nation), 159, 162; Chiricahua, 52; Comanche, 53, 119, 387; Crow, 334; Lipan, 37; Navajo, 172, 174; Pawnee, 386, 387; Pidgeon, 171; Piute, 334; San Carlos, 130, 168; Ute, 167, 169, 170, 171, 334; Yaqui, 174
Ingalls, Senator, 142
Ingersoll, detective, 206
"In the Woolly West," 267-68
Iowa, 178
Ireland, 343, 344

Jackson, Captain, 171
Jackson, Lieut., 175
Jackson, Luke, 204
Jake, Lampas, revivalist, 237
James, W. S., 395
James, Will, 8
James H. Campbell Co., 321
Jennings, Bolly, 248
Jerky, 24, 73-74
Jim, Pinto, 365
Johnson, Dick, 369
Johnson, Murray, 157, 158
Johnson, Thomas, 157, 158
Johnson and Son Cattle Co., 163
Jokes, 24, 73-74
Jolly, Charlie, 100
"Jolly Vaquero, The," 271
Jones, Albert, 102
Jones, captain of cowboy strike breakers, 130
Jones, David, 138
Jones, Dick, 159
Jones, George, 157
Jones, George A., 358
Jones, sheriff, 139
Juan de Dios Ranch, 160
Julesberg, Colo., 334

Kansas, 17, 39, 99, 194, 220, 319, 324; see also individual cities
Kansas City, Mo., 156, 300, 321, 322
Kansas City Times, 220
Kearney Junction, Nebr., 175
Kearns, Bernard, 224
Kelleher, Con, 222
Kelly, John, 156, 157
Ketchum, cowboy, 136
Kidd, James, 320
Kimball, "Budd," 102-3
King, Chas., 156
King, Frank, 8
Kiowa, Colo., 196
Kiowa, Okla., 173
Kiowa Springs, Colo., 176
Kirkwood, Secretary, 140, 141

INDEX

Kit Carson, Colo., 176, 177
Kramer, Ludwig, 385
Kreeger, sheriff, 225
Kuhlman, Fred, 209

Ladd, Mrs. James A., 362
Lahr, Charlie, 102
La Junta, Colo., 136
Lake Ranch, 157
Land, S. E., 134
Landow, W. J., 205
Lane, Geo., 369
Lane, Hon. Mr., the, 51
Lane, John, 355
Langston, Okla., 178, 179
Language, *see* cowboy speech
Lapham, O. K., 147
La Plata County, Colo., 167
Laramie City, Wyo., 226, 355
Laramie River, 292
Lariat, lasso, 30, 32, 38, 42, 46, 73, 90, 102, 193, 271, 386, 387
Larned, Kans., 324
Las Vegas, N. Mex., 219, 237, 250
Law(s), 21, 37, 42, 394
Lawlessness, 21, 35, 47, 48, 49, 51, 140-43
Lawson, Charley, 192
Left Hand Canon (Colo.), 337
Leustrom Ranch, 159
Lewis, S. E., 369
Lewiston, Idaho, 136
Lightning, fear of, 96, 247, 251
Lincoln County Live Stock Assoc., 149
Linthicum, Richard, 270
Lipan (Indian), 37
Little Dolores River, 325
Little Rock, Ark., 166
Liverpool, England, 321, 322, 334
Lochinvar, 320
Lockhardt, Frank, 206
Lockhart, Tex., 349
Lomax (John A. and Alan), 8
London, England, 307, 333, 369, 374
Lone Star State, 36
Love affairs, 272-73, 319-24
Lovelady, Joe, 349
Loveland, Colo., 138
Loveless, Helen T., 324
Lowe, Ben, 358, 359
Lund, Sam, 182
Lure of the West, 22, 24, 329, 332-44
Lusk, Wyo., 226
Lynch, court judge, 157
Lyon, railroad official, 130

Madden, Minnie, 199-200
Madison, N. Mex., 155
Magdelena Driveway (N. Mex.), 395
Maine, 219
"Making Milord Drink," 301-2
Mansico, Wm., 136
"Marrow-guts," 74, 78
Martin, Joe, 100
Martin, policeman, 202
Martyn, police captain, 206
Mason, Harry, 225
Masons, 263
Materson & Springer, saloon, 192
Maurice, Charley, 204
Maus, Arthur, 206, 207
Maxwell, F., 365
Maynard, Ken, 396

Mazeppa, 260
McAuliffe, Tim, 178
McCandless, Allen, 264
McCarthy, citizen, 204
McCarthy, James, 169
McCool, Widow, the, 320
McCulloch, Col. (H.), 37
McKeon, Billy, 160
Meade, Frank, 320
Meadows, Charlie, 394
Meagher, Mary, 326, 327
Meals, *see* food
Medicine Lodge, Kans., 318
Meeker, Colo., 366
"Memory of the Trail, A," 275-76
Mendonez, Michael, 185
Merk, gardner, 177
Merrell, John, 355
Mesa County, Colo., 139, 325
Mesquite, 31, 73, 297
Mexican(s), 24, 74, 100, 101, 112, 136, 180, 181, 184, 185, 352, 386; hat, 349; herder, 163; saddle, 330; spurs, 245, 334, 349
Mexican Joe's Wild West Show, 321
Mexico, 26, 37, 174, 184, 300
Middle Park, Colo., 205, 206
Middleton, Doc, 204, 356, 357, 358
Miles, General (N. A.), 143
Miles City, Mont., 137, 247, 359
Miley, Charles (alias "Red Bill"), 226
Military action, 143, 168-70, 175
Miller, Henry, 100
Milliron Ranch, 279, 345
Mills, Bill, 224
Mills, cowboy, 113
Mills, Wesley, 227
Minneapolis, Minn., 130
Mississippi River, 21, 25
Missouri, 37, 201, 238, 324, 383; *see also* individual cities
Missouri River, 39, 63, 139, 143, 318
Mitchell, cowboy, 136
Mix, Tom, 396
Mobeetie, Tex., 123, 127, 354
Montana, 297, 353, 354; *see also* individual cities
Montana cattle drives, 177
Monte, 27, 71, 144, 220, 383
Montgomery Ward and Co., 366
Montrose, Colo., 134, 362
Moore, Captain, 175
Moore, J. B., 369
Moore, Prof. E. H., 383
Moore, W. F., 240
Mora (Jo), 8
Morris, Henry, 206
Mountain and Plain Festival (Denver, Colo.), 370, 371
Murchinson, cattleman, 347
Murder, 223-27
Murphy, M. D., 177
Murphy, W. A., 177
Murray, cattleman, 159
Muscatine Cattle Co., 370, 371
Mustang, 85, 87, 92, 98, 192
"My Lord and the Broncho," 278-79

National Stock Growers Assoc., 383
National Stockman, 55
National Tanners, Hide and Leather Dealers Assoc., 147
Navajo (Indians), 172, 174

INDEX

411

Neal, Pitts, 244
Nebraska, 202, 240; see also individual cities
Nebraska cowboy, see cowboy types
Negro cowboy, see cowboy types
Negroes, 178-79
Neiderouer, George, 226
Neleigh, Nebr., 224
Nevada, 18, 21, 45, 93, 353; see also individual cities
Newcastle, Wyo., 103
New England, 328
New Hampshire, 285
New Haven (Conn.), 31
New Mexican Review, 157
New Mexico, 100, 114, 120, 125, 138, 141, 149, 157, 163, 176; see also individual cities
"New Mexico Cowboy in London, A," 307
New York (State), 20, 54, 219, 328, 336
New York City, 104, 276, 321, 374
New York *Herald*, 360
New York *Hour*, 52
New York *World*, 54
Nixon, Pat, 349
Nolan, policeman, 198, 212
North Dakota, see individual cities
Northern New Mexico Small Cattlemen and Cowboys' Union, 132
Northern New Mexico Stock Growers Organization, 133
North Park (Colo.), 293
Northwest, the, 19, 180
Northwestern Livestock Journal, 45, 143, 144
Nova Scotia, 328
Nye, Bill, 84

O—O Ranch, 177
Oberrither, Charles, 337
O'Donald, Mary, 202
Oelrichs, Harry, 104
Ogallala, Nebr., 104, 191, 202
Ogallala Land and Cattle Co., 288
O'Hara, member of sheriff's posse, 137
Oklahoma, 175, 289, 326; see also individual cities
Old and New Mexico Ranch and Cattle Co., 174
Old Testament, the, 232
Old West, the, 8, 395
Omaha, Nebr., 104, 287, 320, 321, 323
Omaha *Republican*, 240
O'Neil City, Nebr., 203, 224, 357
Oregon, 18, 37
Organizations, 131-35
Osgood (Ernest S.), 8
Ouray, ex-delegate of Arizona, 168
Outlaws, *see also* desperadoes; 40
Owens, N., 172
Owens, Wallace, 172
Oyee River, 95

"Paean of the Cowboy, The," 266
Painting the town, 30, 207-8
Palo Pinto County *News* (Palo Pinto County, Tex.), 50
Panhandle, the, 49, 82, 100, 123, 124, 125, 127, 129, 207, 234, 308
Paradise Valley, Tex., 324, 325

Parker, Henry, 203
Pawnee, Bill, 394
Pawnee Indians, 387
Payne, Capt. D. R., 175
Payne, H. G., 358
Pecos River, 29
Pelasco, Juan, 185
Pennsylvania, 55, 215, 347; see also individual cities
Perea, J. M., 180, 181
"Petrified Broncho, The," 297
Pickett, William, 372
Pickett brothers, 371
Pidgeon (Indians), 171
Pierre, S. Dak., 140
Pine Bluffs, Wyo., 209, 210, 211, 238, 240
Pistol, 27, 31, 47, 113, 122, 157, 200, 236, 267, 387
Pittsburgh, Pa., 55, 347
Piute (Indians), 334
Plains, 25, 26, 32, 34, 38, 40, 50, 61, 62, 72, 100, 119, 194, 389
Platte River, 99, 175, 249, 250, 292
Platteville, Colo., 367
Player, H. H., 156
Plumer, Frank, 223
Poems, "Captain of the Cow-Boys, The," 270; "Cattle Man's Prayer, The," 265-66; "Cowboy, The," 259-60; "Cowboy, The," 262-63; "Cow Boy, The," 259; "Cowboy in Wall Street, A," 276-77; "Cowboys, The," 268-69; "Cowboys' Christmas Ball, The," 279-80; "Cowboy's Soliloquy, The," 263-64; "Herder, The," 264-65; "Herder's Tale, The," 261-63; "In the Woolly West," 267-68; "Jolly Vaquero, The," 271; "Memory of the Trail, A," 275-76; "My Lord and the Broncho," 278-79; "Paean of the Cowboy, The," 266; "Poet Lariat of the Ranches, The," 268; "Rough Rider, The," 269-70; "Wichita 'Poker Craze,' The," 274-75; "With the Cowboys," 272
"Poet Lariat of the Ranches, The," 268
Poker, 27, 217, 259, 274-75
Polk, Col. Alexander, 166
Pony, see cow pony
Porter, Jack, 138, 139
Poudre River, 138
Prairie Cattle Co., 121, 145, 155, 161, 180, 181, 315, 316
Prayers, 50, 242-44, 250, 265-66
Preacher(s), 236, 237, 238-42; priest, 23; revivalist, 237
Presidio, Tex., 186
Press, see Eastern press
Price, H. S., 238
Price, J. E., 351
Prince of Wales, 351, 369
Prize fighting, 222-23, 304-6
Profanity, 19, 27, 30, 38, 43, 44, 45, 46, 50, 79, 196, 383
Prostitution, 38, 208-13
Pruden, Jesse, 137
Pueblo, Colo., 102, 208, 213, 308
Pueblo *Chieftain*, 146
Pugh, Red, 307
Purgatoire River, 181
Putnam, Odin G., 322

412 INDEX

Quadrille, see also dancing; 196, 317
Queenan, Mike, 232
Queensberry, Marquis of, 246

Races, 100, 346, 355-59, 370
Ranch(es), see also cattle ranches; 18, 28, 29, 30, 31, 56, 80, 82
Rancher(s), 18, 23, 50, 55, 77, 80, 81, 87, 115, 118, 383
Randall, Ed, 100, 101
Range, 7, 10, 17, 32, 33, 38, 49, 66, 72, 82, 95, 99
Rankin, Rev. W. H., 236
Raton, N. Mex., 178, 317, 318
"Real Wild Man, A," 294-95
Red River, 127
Red River Cattle Co., 193
Reed, Maude, 325
Reid, Capt. Mayne, 343
Religion, 30, 35, 231-53, 263, 265, 266
Remington (Philo), 330
Republican River, 347
Reunion, see also Cowboys' Reunion; 389-90
Revolver, see also Colt revolver; 37, 38, 45, 47, 48, 54, 109, 111, 114, 115, 116, 117, 120, 160, 177, 193, 334
Rhymes, see poems
Riddles, John, 349
Riding, 63, 75, 91-94; bronco, 344-47; bull, 347
Rifle, 28, 70, 72, 112, 114
Rigg's Ranch, 348
Rio Grande River, 66, 185
Roach, Will, 349
Robinson, superintendent, 213
Rock Creek, Wyo., 225
Rockies, see Rocky Mountains
Rocky Ford, Colo., 227, 371
Rocky Mountain News, 168, 169, 171
Rocky Mountains, 26, 85, 241, 268, 352
Rodeo, 341, 348
Rogers, Roy, 335, 396
Roller skating, 198-99
Rollins, Philip A., 8, 395
Rollinson (John K.), 8
Rope, 23, 36, 352-53
Roping, 9, 63, 270, 344, 346, 349-51, 359, 360 73; records of, 352-55, 359, 360, 367, 369
"Roping Wolves," 293
Rosebud River, 171
"Rough Rider, The," 269-70
Roundup, 29, 45, 63-83, 95, 100, 102, 103, 122, 123, 127, 148, 197, 225, 265, 344, 347, 381, 389, 393
Routt County, Colo., 222
Ruff, Rufus (Windy), 157
Russell, Kans., 324
Rustlers and Rustling, 8, 38, 135-40

Saddle, 19, 23, 24, 28, 30, 32, 38, 63, 73, 75, 78, 87, 102, 271; Mexican, 330
Sagebrush, 77, 90, 95, 269, 275
St. Charles River, 208
St. Louis, Mo., 216, 321, 337, 383
St. Louis Republican, 129
St. Paul, Minn., 310
Saline, Kans., 261
Saloons, 30, 31, 38, 43, 116, 155, 192, 195, 196, 202, 237

San Antonio, Tex., 51, 325, 328, 337, 350, 351, 367, 368
San Bernadino Ranch, 184
San Carlos Indians, 130, 168
Sandoval, Nestor, 161
Sandy Creek, Wyo., 163
San Francisco, Calif., 319
San Hilano, N. Mex., 120
San Marcial, N. Mex., 164
San Marcos, Tex., 325, 336
San Miguel County, N. Mex., 138, 157
San Pedro River, 184
San Simon, Ariz., 171
Santa Cruz, N. Mex., 183, 184
Santa Fe, N. Mex., 157, 343
Santa Fe Trail, 156
Santee, Ross, 8
Saratoga (N.Y.), 31
Schaefer, Jack, 395
Scherer, Jacob, 176
School, see cowboy training and schools
Schreyer (Adolf), 86
Schultig, Henrico, 358
Scotchmen, 39
Seaforde (Ireland), 343
Senate Judiciary Committee, 142
Shane, 395
Sheep, 181, 183; men, 154, 163, 179, 180, 181
Sheldon, Gov. L. A., 120
Shephard, Fred, 336
Sheriffs, 8, 136, 138, 159, 162, 178, 196, 203, 224, 275, 320, 322
Sherman, Gen. (W. T.), 166
Shirt, 27, 31, 32, 75
Shook, Wm., 203
Shooting, 46, 47, 48, 157, 158, 159-85, 194, 203, 204, 207, 208, 223-27, 260
Shoshone Falls, Idaho, 95
Shows, see Wild West Shows
Shroyer, Louis, 136
Shugnue, Mike, 159
Sidney, Nebr., 240
Sidney Texas Independent, 81
Simon, Frank, 339
Singing to herd, 69, 75, 77, 97
Sioux City, Iowa, 357
Siringo, Charles, 8
Six-shooter, see also guns, pistol, revolvers, weapons; 19, 28, 29, 38, 42, 52, 54, 64, 70, 72, 102, 110, 111-23, 189, 220, 394
Sketer, cowboy, 217
Slack, policeman, 223
Slaughter, W. B., 182
Slocum, James, 173, 174
Smith, Bill, 197, 364
Smith, C. W., 357, 358
Smoking, 63, 80, 99
Socorro, N. Mex., 132
Socorro Bullion, 132
Sodbuster, 175, 179
Sombrero, see hat
Sonoro, Mex., 184
"Soothing Syrup for Cowboys," 309-10
Sorrows of Werther, 27
South Dakota, 140, 182; see also individual cities
Southerner(s), 20
Southwest, the, 112, 130
Southwestern cowboys, 171
Southwesterner, the, 19
Spaniards, 180

INDEX

413

Speare, M. H., 158, 159
Spearfish, S. Dak., 137
Speech, *see* cowboy, speech
Sports, 10, 28, 342, 343-49, 394
Spotts, Henry, 138
Springer, N. Mex., 157, 163, 181
Spurs, 19, 23, 31, 32, 35, 64, 79, 80, 119, 245, 271, 386; Mexican, 334, 349
Staked Plains, the, 251
Stampede(s), 25, 63, 68, 79, 80, 94, 97, 98, 99, 251, 264, 270, 382
Stanley, cowboy, 177
Steer(s), 9, 27, 30, 35, 38, 42, 46, 53, 66, 77, 95, 96, 103, 119, 261, 264, 265, 269, 291-92; tailing, 347, 348
Stein's Pass, N. Mex., 171
Stevens, George W., 101
Stevenson, rancher, 289, 290
Stewart, Frank, 138
Stiff, Perry, 293
Stock Grower and Farmer, 337
Stock Growers' Convention, 94
Stock Growers' Journal, 359, 368
Stokley, Ed., 209
Stollsteimer, Indian Agent, 169, 170, 171
Stone, Peleg Q. C., 128, 129
Storms, *see also* blizzards; 66, 68, 75, 80, 94, 96, 251, 262, 271, 272, 382
Strike(s), 121-31; breakers, 130
Stuart, Granville, 137
Sturgis, S. Dak., 193
Sturth, H., 212, 238, 241
Sullivan, C. S., 220
Sulphur Valley Roundup Assoc., 348
Sweden, 325
Sybile River, 292

Tabor Grand Opera House (Denver, Colo.), 199
Tacoma, Nevada, 45
"Tail of a Cow, The," 301
Tales, *see also* tall tales; old-timer, 9
Talliday, John, 224
Tall Tales, "Bound to a Horse's Back," 286-88; "Capturing a Bear," 293-94; "Cowboy and Limburger," 302-4; "Cowboy and the Folding Bed, The," 308; "'Cowboy' Dog, A," 295-96; "Cowboy in a Sleeping Car, A," 306-7; "Cowboy Joke, A," 299; "Cowboy Prizefighter, A," 304-5; "Cowboy's Pet Colt, The," 289-90; "Cowboy's Start in Life, The," 290-91; "Days Gone By," 288-89; "Demon Steer, The," 291-92; "Frontier Dentistry," 308-9; "Fun with the Tenderfoot," 300-1; "Horsemanship!" 296; "How a Cattleman Saved His Life," 285-86; "Making Milord Drink," 301-2; "New Mexico Cowboy in London, A," 307; "Petrified Broncho, The," 297; "Real Wild Man, A," 294-95; "Roping Wolves," 293; "Soothing Syrup for Cowboys," 309-10; "Tail of a Cow, The," 301; "Wild West Tale, A," 297-98
Tampas, N. Mex., 301
Tartars, 358
Tascosa, Tex., 123, 125, 126
Tascosa Pioneer, the, 234
Taylor, Bayard, 20
Taylor, Buck, 350, 351
Taylor, cowboy, 204-5

Taylor, detective, 206
Taylor, sheriff, 162
Tenderfoot, the, 29, 45, 46, 47, 78, 84, 130, 155, 213-23, 266, 275
Tents, 25, 26, 38, 75, 79, 81
Terwilliger, John, 322
Terry & Hunter's, livery stable, 202
Tesquiquile, N. Mex., 181
Texan(s), 37, 103, 175, 176, 196, 197, 207, 251, 372
Texas, 18, 24, 29, 31, 33, 37, 39, 41, 42, 43, 51, 53, 56, 70, 81, 84, 85, 100, 112, 114, 118, 122, 124, 130, 138, 144, 146, 157, 176, 184, 201, 202, 207, 246, 275, 276, 277, 285, 286, 321, 323, 324, 327, 328, 336, 347, 349, 354, 385, 387, 388; cattle, 125, 177, 192, 318; cowboy(s), 37, 38, 40, 41, 55, 127, 156, 209, 310, 315, 347; steer(s), 77, 103
Texas Cowboy, A, 394
Texas Farm Assoc., 327
Texas Live Stock Journal, the, 112, 114, 115, 118, 119, 125, 126, 129, 376
Texas Rangers, the, 37, 127, 129
Texas Stockman, the, 48
Theater, cowboy at the, 199-201
Thebold, Alex, 304
Thoad, confidence man, 220
Thomas, Carlos, 185
Thomas, Rufe, 116
"Thrillers," Western, 9
Tobacco, use of, *see* smoking
Todd, cowboy, 208
Tombstone, Ariz., 143
Tombstone Record, the, 121
Tournaments, 10, 343, 359-73, 394
Trail(s), 8, 18, 156, 166, 246; Dodge, the, 246; drives, 177, 382, 393; Montana, the, 177; Santa Fe, the, 156; Texas, the, 347
Tremble, Ed, 204
Tricks on the cowboy, 308-10
Trinidad, Colo., 156, 178, 184, 207, 225, 301, 315, 318
Trinity River, 347
Trousers, corduroy, 31; jeans, 194, 195; pants, 218
Trumble, sheriff, 226
Tucson, Ariz., 48, 183, 184, 224
Tucson Star, the, 142
Tuttle, cowboy, 137
Twain, Mark, 84

Union, Northern New Mexico Small Cowmen and Cowboys, 132
United Kingdom, 18
United States, 23, 39, 46, 140, 143, 184, 185, 314, 373
Utah, 18, 171, 337, 352
Ute Indians, 167, 169, 170, 171, 334

Vandervert, Buck, 199
Vaquero, 36, 74, 271
Victoria, Queen, 307
Virginia, 20
Virginian, The, 395
Von Raub, Col. Byron, 327, 328

Waco, Tex., 51
Wages, *see* cowboy wages
Wales, Prince of, 351, 369
Wallace, Jake, 300
Wallace, policeman, 337

414 INDEX

Walker, Andrew, 103
Walla Walla, Wash. T., 326, 334
Waller, Henry, 177, 178
War, the Civil, 7, 9, 327
Washington (state), 18
Washington, Sam, 178
Wasson, Jerome, 98
Watt's Ranch, 136
Wayland, R. L., 132
Weapons, *see also* guns, pistols, revolvers, six-shooters, Winchester; 32, 37, 38, 48, 110, 155, 223, 259, 388, 389
Weather, *see also* blizzards, lightning, fear of; 36, 62, 72, 79, 99, 261, 269, 331
Weaver, painter, 192
Weld County, Colo., 123
Wells, Frank, 365
West, Bill, 159
West, the, 19, 32, 46, 62, 180, 232, 325, 337, 342, 373, 382, 386, 387, 397, 398; far, 21, 45; lure of, 327-38; new, 8; old, 8, 395
West Derby, England, 322
Western films, 396; sports, 360; towns, 332
Western Cattle Co., 316
Westerner(s), 19-22, 46, 386
Wheeler, Bruce, 243
White, Bill, 227
Whitehead, E. W., 375
Whiskey, 25, 26, 27, 35, 45, 53, 63, 115, 172, 201-7, 225, 259, 344, 387
"Wichita 'Poker Craze', The," 274-75
Wilcox, Ariz., 184, 300
Wild West, the, 149; exhibitions, 83, 350
Wild West Show(s), 86, 208, 352; Buffalo Bill's, 307, 333, 334, 351, 374, 394; Charlie Meadows', 394; Mexican Joe's, 321; Pawnee Bill's, 394
"Wild West Tale, A," 297-98
Wilde, Oscar, 25
Willard, Fred, 137
Williams, cattleman, 159

Williams, Frank, 226
Williams, Leon, 225
Williams, sheriff, 320
Williams, Ted, 248
Wilson, cattleman, 95
Wilson, George, 291, 292
Wilson, Thomas, 287
Wimms, Bill, 204
Winchester (rifle), 70, 110, 160, 168, 181, 182, 185
Winslow, Ariz., 204
"With the Cowboys," 272
Witter, James C., 349
Witter, Webster, 349
Wister, Owen, 395
Wolf, *see* "Roping Wolves," 293
Wolfe Creek district, Tex., 127
Women, *see* cowgirls, love affairs, prostitution; cowboy respect for, 18, 29, 42, 48, 52
Woods, Bill, 161, 162
Woods, Jim, 251
Woods, ranch manager, 157
Woodville, B. C., 297
Woodward, 206, 207
Work, *see* cowboy work
World's Fair, the, 356
Wrangler, 45, 75, 76
Wyoming, 18, 36, 38, 39, 141, 145, 176, 215, 240, 326, 335, 336, 345, 346, 355, 370, 371; *see also* individual cities

XL Ranch, 315

Yale (University), 53
Yankee, 20, 261
Yaple, Charley, 158, 159
Yaqui (Indians), 174
Yellowstone River, 66, 171
Young, C. J., 132

Zingman, cattleman, 347
Zursna, Prof. W., 325